John E. Bryan

on

Bulbs

BURPEE EXPERT
GARDENER SERIES

John E. Bryan

on

Bulbs

MACMILLAN · USA

Macmillan
A Prentice Hall Macmillan Company
15 Columbus Circle
New York, New York 10023

Library of Congress Cataloging-in-Publication Data

Bryan, John E., 1931–
    John Bryan on bulbs.
        p.   cm.—(Burpee expert gardener series)
    Includes index.
    ISBN 0-671-87049-1
    1. Bulbs.   2. Bulbs—United States.—I. Title.—II. Title: Bulbs.
    III. Series: Burpee expert gardener.
    SB425.B75   1994
    635.9'44—dc20   93-17915
                                                         CIP

Designed by Levavi & Levavi, Inc.

All photographs by John E. Bryan, unless otherwise noted.

Line drawings on pages 7–9 by Elayne Sears.

Manufactured in the United States of America

10   9   8   7   6   5   4   3   2   1

First Edition

Cover & Preceding pages: Bulb lovers from all over the world make pilgrimages to the Keukenhof. Located in the heart of the bulb-growing area in the Netherlands, this garden is devoted to spring-flowering bulbs.

For "my girls," Daphne and Jasmine,
and the next generation, Davina Yasmine
and Sophia Anapalina Bryan-Ajana.
My love of bulbs cannot compare with my love
for you. God bless you, and thank you
for so many happy times.

CONTENTS

In parts of the world with Mediterranean climates, *Zantedeschia aethiopica* has escaped from gardens and established itself in the countryside, thriving with no care.

Photographed at the Cape of Good Hope. Frequently this species' name is given to the common Agapanthus, correctly called *Agapanthus praecox* ssp. *orientalis*. It is a much larger plant. Agapanthus are popular in California, being easy to grow, drought resistant and trouble free.

INTRODUCTION

One thing particularly stands out after many years of working with and appreciating plants: Everything about them is logical. We may be far from understanding exactly what takes place inside them, but I can tell you that what I have observed appears to occur logically and in sequence. Books such as this are seldom read from cover to cover as one would read a novel. It is hoped readers will find straightforward answers to their questions about bulbous plants here. I have tried to follow a logical sequence in putting this book together, and questions that may arise as a result of reading one section are answered in the next. If a reader thinks an answer is illogical, I would think that answer incorrect; I hope that would never be the case here!

One might ask, "Why another book on bulbs?" There are indeed many good books on these fascinating plants. In my own two-volume work, I address bulbs in an academic rather than scientific way, providing information I think essential to the understanding of these plants, and covering the wide range of genera that comprise "bulbs," in the broad sense of the word. However, I would be the first to admit that the two-volume work omitted many personal observations, comments and opinions. I have been connected with the profession of horticulture since the 1940s, and there was much I was not able to set forth in such a work. *John E. Bryan on Bulbs* approaches the subject in a personal way. Gardening should reflect what one likes, rather than another person's taste.

Bulbs have nearly always been a part of my life. I distinctly recollect the "onion men," as we called them, walking through the streets of my hometown of Plymouth, England. Hanging from the ends of stout sticks balanced on their shoulders were plaited strings of onions. Housewives purchased the onions, and the strings would grow shorter as the onion sellers progressed. My mother would remark that a certain man's onions surely were good because his strings were shorter. For the most part these men came from France, and wore colorful red scarves around their necks. The onions glistened in the sun with shiny, light brown coats, and all of them, I seem to remember, were of equal size.

Other recollections of bulbs (I must admit I did not know them as bulbs) were of the leeks certain Welsh regiments stuck in their hats on particular days; this remains a tradition today.

The next bulb I remember is the English bluebell. In spring the woods are filled with them. We would pick them for our mothers, but what a waste of time—they just do not make good cut flowers. I remember being told it harms the bulb if the flowers are pulled. You were supposed to cut the stems; a length of 24 or more inches, about half of which is white because it grows underground, indicates just how deep these bulbs had grown into the soil. I knew nothing about contractile roots when I was picking bluebells, and I never gave a thought as to how the bulbs reached that depth when they started out as seed on the surface.

I became an indentured apprentice to a

Hyacinthoides non-scripta is a long name for the lovely English bluebell that carpets many woodland areas in springtime. These plants multiply quickly, but such beauty can never be a pest.

nurseryman in South Devon by the name of R. T. May, and for the princely sum of 10 shillings, I worked 48 hours a week. In those days we started work on time, and we worked hard, and I regard such practical experience as an essential ingredient of a sound career in horticulture. There is no good substitute for "hands-on" experience.

Forcing bulbs for the market is an operation that takes quite a lot of time. Wooden crates would arrive for the R. T. May nursery from Holland, and inside we would find paper sacks filled with the bulbs, with wood shavings used as packing material. Just after the war, bulbs were in short supply, and we handled them with great care.

At Somerset Agricultural College, the use of bulbs in the garden—simple elements of design— was just one aspect of bulb culture that occupied my time. Just how large an industry bulb culture is started to become apparent to me then. *Anemone pulsatilla, A. coronaria, A. nemorosa*, various ornamental onions such as *Allium moly* and *A. karataviense, Cyclamen* species, dahlias, gladiolas, lilies, freesias and crown imperials were to be found in the collections grown. Bulbs' lovely forms and colors, the different shapes and textures, gave me much food for thought and, I think, formed a solid foundation of interest in these miracles of nature. To hold in your hand the dry tubers of anemones and then plant them and see, in a comparatively short space of time, the appearance of fernlike foliage, then flowers of wonderful color, is still a miracle to me.

I worked with bulbs at the Parks Department of the city of Bournemouth; as a student at the Royal Botanic Garden, Edinburgh; and during my graduate studies at the Royal Horticultural Society's Garden at Wisley. I can remember, while at Wisley, seeing lilies produced at the Oregon Bulb Farms planted among rhododendrons and azaleas, and noting how well they were suited for such areas. No matter how well known and busy my mentors and teachers were, they took time to talk with me, something I have never forgotten. So, even when I am feeling rather rushed and have much to do, I try to find time for those to whom I may be of some help, remembering how generous others were in sharing their experience with me.

When I was awarded the Gardeners Scholarship in 1955, I chose to study in Holland, even though I wasn't considering a career in the bulb industry. I wanted to see more of this country so intimately connected with bulbs and with other sectors of the nursery business. During my last year of studies, I had the good fortune to work in Paris. (For the education of any person, a sojourn in Paris is recommended! Even on a student's stipend it is a fun city.) I was very fortunate to have an introduction to that great landscape architect Russell Page, and indeed had the pleasure of working with him during my entire stay in France. Many an instructive hour was spent with him, and he heightened my interest in bulbs.

After my years in France, I left Europe to settle in the United States. Jan de Graaff offered me a position in his prestigious firm, the Oregon Bulb Farms. Now, occupied with bulbs every day, I found myself truly "hooked."

Jan de Graaff pioneered the cultivation of lilies. With Earl Hornback, Harold Comber and later Ed McRae, de Graaff brought one hybrid lily after another into the gardening world. His Mid Century Hybrids opened the floodgates, and today the modern hybrids available in many colors in the many forms of the Asiatic Hybrids are entirely due to the original work he accomplished in Gresham, Oregon. From those days I especially recall the thrill of examining new hybrids flowering for the first time, and the ticklish work of naming new introductions. After I left the farms of de Graaff, I spent several years at the Strybing Arboretum as director. As the arboretum was part of the Parks Department of the City and County of San Francisco (and thus short of funds) I made use of my contacts to obtain many thousands of bulbs. We conducted experiments seemingly without end, and sent information back to Holland, where it was used to prepare booklets for gardeners growing bulbs in warmer climates.

In the late seventies I had the opportunity to visit South Africa. If I had loved bulbs before, I was enraptured after seeing such genera as

Jan de Graaff and the author. One of my great memories is working with Jan de Graaff. In summer we would select, from thousands of seedlings, plants we considered worthy of being named. (Photo courtesy of Herman V. Wall.)

Freesia, Agapanthus, Dierama, Dietes, Ornithogalum, Anapalina, Babiana, Bulbine, Clivia, Crinum, Drimia, Gloriosa, Haemanthus, Ixia, Lachenalia, Nerine and *Tritonia*, to name but a few, growing in their native habitats. There is undoubted beauty in the selections and hybrids of genera we grow in our gardens. But the purity of form and subtle colors of plants in the wild, when growing well, cannot be surpassed. Even after many trips to this part of the world, I am still thrilled by bulbs growing in the wild. One of my granddaughters has, as her middle name, Anapalina.

I am so pleased that I am encouraged by the publishers to make this book a personal one, to share with readers thoughts long held but not recorded elsewhere. As you read this book, do remember that the opinions expressed are mine, and that the selections of genera, species and cultivars are a reflection of my interests. After such a rich and pleasant life with these, my favorite plants, I hoped I might have a few helpful points to pass on to the reader. If I accomplish this, I will be glad. If I do not, I am nonetheless happy to again set pen to paper to write about bulbs!

This yellow Crown Imperial (*Fritillaria imperialis* 'Lutea') is magnificent in springtime, bold and clean looking, long lasting and a good companion for other spring-flowering bulbs.

ONE

The Basic Botany of Bulbs

We tend to think of vegetables as things to eat. For this reason I prefer the classification Plant Kingdom, as is used in Great Britain, rather than Vegetable Kingdom. But where in the order of things do plants fit? The Roman writer Pliny devised a classification, not scientifically accepted today, that I am sure is used by gardeners the world over, the majority of them knowing nothing about Pliny, and possibly caring even less! Pliny's criteria are size and form, and he divides the plant kingdom into trees, shrubs and herbs—a very sensible arrangement. In the Middle Ages another classification, also quite sensible, divided plants into medicinal, edible and poisonous varieties. However, this tells us nothing about the actual plant; a tree, for example, can be considered all three. Still, this was, when combined with the earlier classification, a useful tool. We could have a medicinal tree, an edible herb and a poisonous shrub. Man was getting there.

Looking closely at plants, the great Swedish botanist Carolus Linnaeus devised a classification based on the number of stamens in the flowers of plants. Although this classification was discarded, Linnaeus introduced a system of naming plants still used today. The scientific, or botanical, name of a plant is the same the world over, and each plant has only one correct name. Our Easter lily is *Lilium longiflorum* to someone from China, England or France. Locally used common names vary widely, but scientific names are recognized by all. Linnaeus devised the scientific, two-name method of identification, the genus (plural, genera) being the first, followed by the species name, the second.

The plant kingdom is divided into two subkingdoms: Thallophyta (plants that do not form embryos), such as bacteria, slime molds, various algae and true fungi, and Embryophyta (plants that form embryos), the subkingdom into which bulbs fall. Embryophyta is broken into Bryophyta (mosses and liverworts), obviously not bulbs—and Tracheophyta, plants with vascular systems. Tracheophyta includes the subphyllum Pteropsida, which is divided into three classes: Angiospermae, the true flowering plants; Filicineae, the ferns; and Gymnospermae, the cone-bearing plants and their relatives, such as the conifers.

With bulbs as our topic, we are concerned with only one of these classes, the Angiospermae. But there are many flowering plants, and this class is divided into two subclasses: Dicotyledoneae and Monocotyledoneae. In everyday speech these plants are referred to as "monocots" and "dicots." Monocots produce one leaflike structure after the seed germinates; dicots, two.

After germination, as plants develop, they produce true leaves. Monocots have leaves that are generally alternate, with parallel veins and simple form. The flowers are constructed of four alternating whorls of parts—sepals, petals, stamens and carpels—with each part being trimerous (in threes or multiples of three). This is worth knowing, as it helps in the identification of flowers.

Dicots have leaves veined in a netlike pattern, and usually the leaves are narrow at the base and have a petiole. In dicots the parts of the flowers are usually in multiples of five and are called pentamerous (5-merous), or in fours and called tetramerous (4-merous), and they have a distinct calyx and corolla. (Some of these terms might be foreign to the reader. Turn to page 6 for a discussion of flower parts and their functions.)

These classes and subclasses are again divided into orders, each order containing one or more families. If this sounds complicated, don't worry; now we are getting to the more relevant information on the orderly classification of our bulbous plants.

Order

It is perhaps easier to understand what comprises an order if we examine one in particular. Lilies are my favorite flowers, so let's look at the order in which these lovely plants belong, together with the iris and the amaryllis. Similarities join these families—Liliaceae, Iridaceae and Amaryllidaceae—in the broadest way. This trio of families make up the order Liliales.

All these families have flowers made up of three petals and three sepals; ovaries that are in three parts; and six stamens in two rows of three each (Iridaceae have one row of three). It is certain an iris is different from a lily, yet if you picture the single flower of a gladiolus, a lily or an amaryllis, you can begin to appreciate that they have quite a lot in common.

Family

The ovary is located in the center of the flower. The petals and sepals are attached to the flower below the ovary in the case of the lilies; because the ovary is above that attachment point, it is called "superior." Tulips and lilies are in Liliaceae. In Amaryllidaceae the flowers have the same parts as they do in Liliaceae, but the ovary is located below the point where the petals and sepals are attached, and thus it has an "inferior" ovary. The amaryllis and the daffodil have inferior ovaries, and are classified in Amaryllidaceae.

When we take a look at the iris, gladiolus and crocus, we find that, like the plants in Amaryllidaceae, the flowers have inferior ovaries but only three stamens. There is another significant difference in these members of the Iridaceae; the outside petals are broad and recurved (they curl back), and the inner ones are narrow and erect. At first glance there are many similarities among these three families (remember, they are classified in the same order: Liliales). Upon closer examination, however, differences are evident, and so they merit being classified into three different families.

The juxtaposition of petals and sepals, the number and placement of several parts of the flowers, is similar, yet the differences are sufficient to merit three different families. It's rather exciting to realize that if you do not know the name of a flower but note that it has three sepals, three petals, an inferior ovary and three stamens, you know it belongs to Iridaceae. You can then check the genera (singular form: genus) in this family, and so arrive at the identification of the plant.

GENUS

But we have now introduced another word, *genera*. Every family has one or more genera. All daffodils and narcissus, for example, belong to the genus *Narcissus*. The flowers of plants that are structurally the same are classified in the same genus. While the tulip seems, in number and placement of flower parts, the same as the true lily, there is an obvious difference, one that can be seen just by looking at the plants; apart from the flowers, the foliage is different. The tulip has no foliage on the stem, but the lily does. The lily has several flowers on each stem, but the tulip seldom more than one, and the form of the flower head is different. Thus, while related (both in the order Liliales and in the family Liliacea), the tulip and the lily are different. The tulip is placed in the genus *Tulipa*, and the lily, in Lilium. Now we have an understanding of the meaning of the word *genus*. This brings us to the next step of classification.

SPECIES

There is a difference between an Easter lily and a tiger lily. The plants are classified in different species. The Easter lily is *Lilium longiflorum*, the tiger lily is *Lilium lancifolium*. How is the species name determined? It can describe the flower— "*grandiflorum*" means "large flower," "*rubrum*" means "red," "*album*" means "white." It can honor the person who discovered it, as in the case of *Lilium davidii*, named after Armand David, who discovered it in western China in 1904. A specific name can provide information about the geographical area where the plant grows, as in the case of *Lilium canadense*, a lily that grows wild in eastern Canada. Frequently a plant of one species may look very much like another classified in the same species, but yet is not exactly the same. A slight but consistent difference is enough to warrant separating two very similar plants, though they share the same species. Flowers may be fewer but larger, leaves wider, the plant a little shorter. Such differences are not sufficient to merit the variant being given full species rank, but the difference has to be acknowledged. In such cases the plant in question is described by the original species name, and is given a "subspecies" name after that.

SUBSPECIES

A good example is the case of *Lilium canadense*. It was noted that the form growing east of the Appalachian Mountain Range has broader leaves that are not as tapered as others. For this reason, these plants are known as *Lilium canadense* subsp. *editorum*. The word "subsp."—short for subspecies—is not italicized, the other names—genus, species and subspecies—are.

VARIETY

While such a physical difference is given subspecific rank, it would not always be merited just by flower color. The natural reproduction of the species in the wild, by means of seed, can produce

Elegant, free flowering, and full of grace, *Lilium canadense* is a must if you have a woodland setting, where it should be left undisturbed for years.

seedlings of a different color. If this color (color is used as an example—height and foliage form might be other examples) is consistently found, consistently the same, then that variant is known as a *variety* of the species. If the usual color of the flowers of one species was red, but consistently a white-flowered plant was found, then the words "var. *album*" would be added to the name. The *album* would be in italics, but not "var.," which is the accepted shortening of the word *variety*.

Cultivar

Many people refer to a plant as a "variety" of this or that. 'Peace' is called a "variety" of rose, 'Big Boy', a "variety" of tomato. But in both these cases the variety has been man made, and these plants are the result of hybridization. Obviously the same is true of the "varieties" of tulips, gladiolus, dahlias and many other popular bulbs. These are correctly known as cultivars, meaning they were created by humans.

The correct way of writing a cultivar name is within single quotes; it is not italicized. Thus, we have *Tulipa* 'Clara Butt' and *Lilium* 'Enchantment'. The cultivar name is selected by the producer of the new plant, and once registered, the name cannot be used for another introduction in the same genus; it can be used in a different genus. Thus you may well find 'Peace' used for a rose, a lily and a gladiolus as they are all different genera.

Clones and Strains

In the case of the lily 'Enchantment', all existing 'Enchantment' lilies were derived from a single, original bulb by vegetative propagation. This means part(s) of the original bulb were removed and grown on. The resulting plant is known as a clone. Purchase a 'Red Emperor' tulip and you expect a tulip identical to that you purchased under that name in previous years. 'Golden Delicious' apples are the same everywhere, because they are all clones.

Sometimes plants—certain lilies, for example—are sold as "strain." 'Golden Splendor Strain' is a lily strain. Often when a strain becomes well established, the word "strain" is dropped, so you might see the bulbs sold as 'Golden Splendor'. A little variation may be found among plants of the same strain, but the differences will be slight and all would be recognizable as 'Golden Splendor'.

Strains are raised from seed. Selected parent clones are crossed, and the offspring are the strain. As years go by, strains are often improved. Hybridizers constantly upgrade the quality. Deeper color, stronger stems, increased size and number of flowers—such improvements are made by changing the parent clones used to produce the seed from which 'Golden Splendor' plants, for example, are raised. The cost of introducing a new strain into the market is high. Once a strain has been established and has earned a reputation, it pays the grower to continue to market the strain. Over time that strain may be improved in a dramatic way, yet because of name recognition, the name is continued. It is not critical for the home gardener to know whether a plant is a strain or a clone. It is essential for the nurseryman, who might be forcing the bulbs, to know. Why? Clones, identical in every way, will respond in a given way when forced. A strain, made up of individuals, will show variations, perhaps some coming into bloom earlier, or later, or being shorter or taller. Such variations, even slight ones, cause problems when schedules are prepared; greenhouse space is valuable, and such variations can be quite costly.

You will find reference to hybrids in many books and catalogs. We are all hybrids ourselves! We are the result of the crossing of our fathers and our mothers. So it is with plants. New plants derived by crossing two plants are hybrids. When species from two genera are crossed, which happens rarely, we call the result an intergeneric hybrid. One such intergeneric hybrid in the world of bulbs is × *Crinodonna*. This was a result of crossing a *Crinum* with *Amaryllis belladonna*. The hybrid has a bit of both parents' names, and is preceded by a multiplication sign.

HORTICULTURAL CLASSIFICATIONS

Horticultural classifications are needed for a number of purposes. They allow accurate comparison and competition with other plants of the same ilk. You have probably noticed that some dahlias have flowers the size of dinner plates. These large flowers are called decorative. Other

While visiting a breeder of *Alstroemeria*, wonderful plants that are great cut flowers, I came across this specimen, which has good color and great vigor.

flowers are single, others still are shaped in little balls, or are small, medium or large, or ruffled. We classify these differences in order to describe the plants accurately. Obviously to be correct in competition and in our gardens, we want to be able to select the exact type of flowers we want. Knowing that this cultivar (or strain) is of a certain class enables us to obtain exactly what we want. Similar types are classified together.

Not all genera have been refined to this degree, just the larger ones with many different types and forms. Daffodils (the *Narcissus*), tulips, lilies, dahlias, crocus, gladiolus and iris have horticultural classifications. These classifications are compiled by students of the various genera. They are logical and, unlike scientific classifications, horticultural classes are based on criteria plainly visible to the naked eye; understanding them doesn't require great botanical knowledge. Is it really necessary to know much about genera, species, families, subspecies and clones in order to garden? Of course not. If a gardener is going to have a measure of success with plants, he or she must have a love of beauty and of plants themselves. A gardener must be orderly, thought-

Listed in catalogs but not as popular as it should be, *Fritillaria persica* is an easy-to-grow species with flowers and foliage that form a pleasing combination.

The plants know how to grow—we do not need to teach them!

THE FLOWER

There is an obvious need to describe the form and shape of flowers, their colors, petals and sepals. It is a good idea to be acquainted with the various parts of a flower, and their functions, too. When a description is given in a catalog, you want to be able to envision the flower, and then plan for the best location for the plant, and place complementary plants around it.

A flower is made up of several parts. Those essential for reproduction are: the stamens, the male part of the flower that produces pollen; and the carpel, the female part that in the majority of cases is made up of the stigma, style and ovary. The seed is produced in the ovary, and it is the purpose of the flower to produce seed so the plants can reproduce themselves in seasons to come.

Essentially, it is the perianth segments that one commonly thinks of as a flower, and generally there are outer and inner segments. The outer whorl of segments is called the *calyx*, a collective name for the sepals. These protect the inner parts and though they can be green, in most bulbous plants they are another color. When joined together they form a tube, as is the case with crocus flowers. Inside the sepals are found the petals, generally brightly colored, and though the sepals and petals may be of the same color, they are not always so. The collective name for the petals is the *corolla*, and when the petals join to form a tube, as in the daffodil, it is from the end of the tube that the corona extends. It is this corona that forms the mouth of the trumpet in many of the large-trumpet daffodils, and it is an extension of the tube.

Often a trumpet is formed by the sepals and

ful, observant and imaginative. A gardener must have the ability to look into the future and picture the garden that is being created. A given garden may lack form and color, but invariably one finds a plant growing there to perfection, and this excuses many a fault. But achieving a good garden, having plants complement each other in an attractive border, where each plant is in just the right place, does require knowledge. Knowing the relationship of one plant to another, knowing the names, where they come from and the conditions they enjoy in the wild, may not be essential to creating a garden. But it certainly is not a disadvantage to have such knowledge, and the more you know about plants in general, and individual plants in particular, the more enjoyment you will have from gardening. The scientific aspect of horticulture is directed as much toward the improvement of the gardener as of the garden itself. Perhaps one is the reflection of the other. Try to learn and understand as much as you can, but don't worry too much over it.

Iris ochroleuca is a lovely species that remains in flower for a long time, a quality passed to its offspring the Spuria Iris (the other parent being *Iris spuria*). Bold plantings add much interest to a garden.

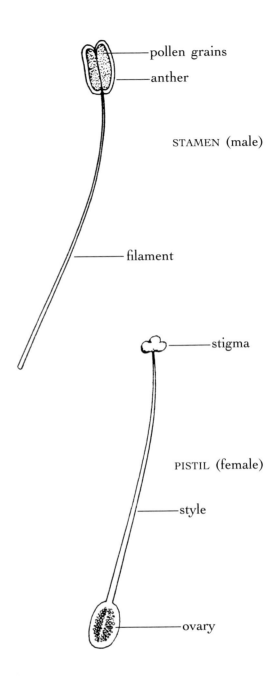

the petals, without it being possible to tell one from the other. This type of trumpet is said to be made up of tepals; trumpet lilies are a good example. It is also impossible to differentiate between sepals and petals in the case of tulips, and for this reason a tulip flower is said to be made up of tepals.

Inside the perianth segments are found the stamens. At the top of the stamens are the anthers, which carry the pollen grains. Usually (but not always) yellow, the grains are the equivalent of human sperm. Anthers are supported by filaments or stalks, and sometimes these emerge from the perianth tube, as can be seen if you cut open a daffodil flower. In those families regarded as relatively primitive, such as Ranunculaceae, there are many stamens; in the advanced families, such as Liliaceae, there are fewer. Stamens are placed so that there is a good chance of pollina-

tion occuring, the transfer of the male gametes (pollen) to the female part of the flower so that seed can develop.

The ovary is found in the center of the flower. Above the ovary is a slender tube, the style, terminating in a structure called the *stigma*. The stigma catches the pollen in various ways. Pollen carried by wind can be caught by a branched stigma or one with feathery appendages. Some stigmas exude a sticky substance that traps the pollen traveling on the hairy legs and bodies of such insects as bees.

The pollen grain germinates on the stigma and forms a tube down through the style. The male gamete travels down the tube, and when the tube comes into contact with the female gamete, the male and female unite, and a seed is formed. This may be a simplistic way to describe what takes place, but it is not inaccurate. Many regard the fluid excreted from the stigma as food for the germinating pollen grain(s), as well as being a substance to trap the pollen.

The purpose of the color and fragrance of flowers is to attract insects. At the base of the petals there may be glands that excrete a sweet substance that is also attractive to them. This substance is nectar, made into honey by bees. It is from these nectaries that scents of flowers are also excreted. Some nectaries are visible to the naked eye, as is the case with lilies, others are visible only with magnification.

These remarks offer insight into the purpose and composition of a flower. There are many adaptations, and the illustrations on pages 8–9 will help in understanding the physiology of various bulbous plants.

FORMS OF FLOWERS

Not all bulbs produce flowers with recognizable petals and sepals. An example is *Haemanthus*, where the color is due to many perianth segments that form a tube from which stamens protrude; there are six stamens per "flower," and many flowers in a flower head. Thus the common name of paint brush is often given to these flowers. Another example is the calla lily, where the female and male flowers are arranged on a spadix that looks like a long cylinder inside the colorful spathe, and which surrounds the cylindrical col-

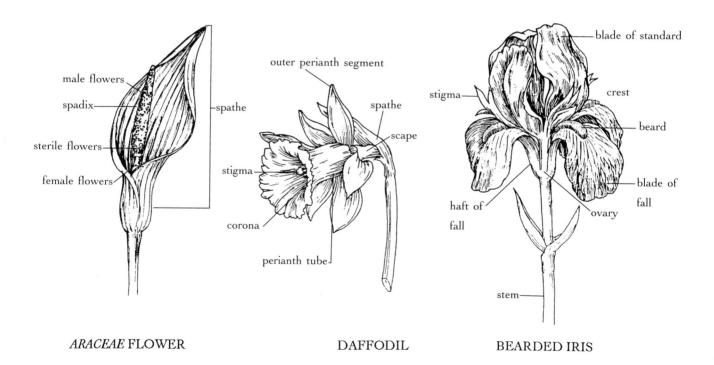

ARACEAE FLOWER   DAFFODIL   BEARDED IRIS

Often when lilies are used in an arrangement, the stamens will be cut off and discarded. This is to prevent the pollen from staining the clothes of the arranger or of someone admiring the flowers. To me this decreases the attractiveness of the flowers, but it is understandable. The stigmas of lilies often produce so much fluid that it drips, and as it is extremely sticky, this can be a disadvantage. Precautions taken to avoid problems include clipping off the stigma. Again, in my opinion, this disfigures the flower.

If pollen happens to stain a garment, allow it to dry, then simply brush it off. If stigmatic fluid drips onto furniture, a little warm water on a clean cloth will remove it easily. If pollen stains petals, it can be removed easily with a ball of cotton dipped in milk.

umn of flowers. Technically this spadix is a fleshy axis on which the sessile (stalkless) male and female flowers are arranged. This arrangement is typical of the family Araceae, the Arum family, and it is the spathe that is colored and attractive. In the case of these flowers, the fleshy axis secretes a sticky substance that attracts insects and thus encourages pollination.

The composition of flowers is a fascinating subject. They are complex and deserving of greater discussion, but that is not the purpose of this book. I do feel that the information in this chapter is basic knowledge essential for all gardeners worthy of the name to understand. Flowers are indeed wonderfully made. It is hoped that the reader will take a minute or two to enjoy exploring the composition and texture of flowers.

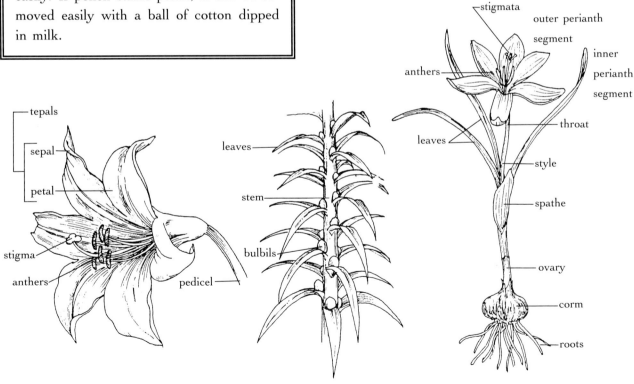

LILY FLOWER   LILY STEM   CROCUS

New hybrids are the result of years of work by hybridizers. We thank Klehm Nursery for this lovely Siberian iris 'Heliotrope Bouquet'. (Photo courtesy of Roy Klehm.)

TWO

Bulbs: What They Are and Where They Come From

Today gardeners and writers of nursery catalogs use the word *bulbs* for many plants that are not, strictly speaking, bulbs. The term has come to include plants with a distinct underground structure that enables them to be lifted out of the ground, stored (and even shipped), and then planted again in the ground to produce foliage and flowers. In most cases lifting takes place during the resting stage of the plant. (Why such resting stages occur is discussed in some detail on pages 47–48.) There are always exceptions. Certain plants generally classed as bulbs are evergreen, and while the greater number of them are plants that prefer warmer climes, such as *Clivia*, *Agapanthus* and certain *Hemerocallis*, they have the attributes of being able to be lifted and transported, and have rootstocks or swollen stems that store food. It is this adaptation, the storing of food in stems, modified leaves or roots, that more accurately describes the broad sense of accepted use of the collective noun *bulb*. Just which forms are taken by various plants, and why, is worth looking at.

Plants develop rootstocks containing stored food and growth buds for both shoots and flowers, in order for them to survive periods in their native habitats when conditions are not suitable for continued growth. Overcoming that check to their growth caused by cold or drought, lack of moisture or searing heat, requires them to adapt their structure to withstand such adverse conditions, and at the same time, retain the ability to grow again when conditions are favorable. They become dormant during that unsuitable growing time.

Burying themselves deep into the soil, forming a hard shell to protect the stored food, adapt-

11

ing their leaves, roots or stems to endure adverse conditions—these are qualities shared by those plants we group under the word *bulb*. The period of time for which bulbs can remain dormant varies. *Anemone coronaria*, which forms a tuber (but is most commonly called a corm—it is often very difficult to distinguish between a corm and a tuber) can easily be stored for two years or even longer. On the other hand, a *Lilium* bulb, being composed of fleshy scales that are modified leaves, will lose turgidity and shrivel unless stored in cool temperatures and surrounded by material that prevents, to a large degree, the loss of moisture. Properly stored, it can be kept for 12 months, and no longer. Corms and hard tubers (a potato is a soft tuber) can be stored for longer periods than a fleshy bulb (such as an onion) or a rhizome (such as the bearded iris), yet all of these would be able to withstand adverse dry conditions better than such fleshy plants as the *Clivia*.

It is important to understand these differences, which can be appreciated by just looking at and handling the various plants. Such knowledge enables gardeners to provide those conditions best suited for overwintering tender bulbs in colder climates. An *Anemone* can be kept dry. A lily cannot, but should be kept moist or prevented from losing moisture. Even as beginners we can, by observation and the application of common sense, begin to understand the needs of the plants. They are, in effect, quite logical.

Before considering in greater detail the differences between the various types of underground storage organs developed by the various plants in the broad grouping of bulbs, let's look at some unusual adaptations of plants.

In certain parts of the world, particularly in grasslands, there is danger of fire during dry seasons. Fire sweeping through such areas is a natural event, and can even be welcome. In fact, certain shrubs need fire before they release seeds,

or the seeds need fire to help break the hard coat that protects the viability of the seed.

In southern Africa there are many species of *Pelargonium*. Among the popular garden plants we grow there in our summer gardens are Martha Washington geraniums and zonal geraniums, both members of the genus *Pelargonium*. While they grow in the wild close to the coast where fire is not common, other species of *Pelargonium* grow in grassland where fires are common. They have developed the ability to form tubers, sometimes just below, sometimes at or just above the surface of the ground. Fires sweeping through the area may destroy the shoots, but the tubers are not damaged. When the fires have passed, new growth emerges.

Other plants take advantage of fire to survive, and afterward find themselves in an area freed—for a time—from competitors for available nutrients. If you walk over an area of the veldt in South Africa that has been scorched by fire, you will be amazed at how many small bulbous plants seem to pop up and enjoy the recently cleared areas. Without fire they remain dormant, or produce just a few leaves in order to maintain themselves, but after the fires have passed, they come into their rightful glory. They have survived when other competing plants have suffered; these other plants have to start again from seed, while the bulbous plants, with established roots and food supplies, can and do take advantage of the situation to flower and seed. That seed will germinate and small bulbs will be formed, but they will wait to flower until the competition has again been reduced to ashes, and the cycle repeats.

But why should such fleshy-stemmed plants as *Clivia* and *Agapanthus* produce their fleshy stems? One might think they do so to provide a reservoir of moisture to take them through periods of drought. In fact, *Clivia* grow in the shade of trees, not in the open sun. The trees consume moisture from the soil, and thus when moisture is in short supply, the clivias survive by using the moisture stored in their fleshy stems.

Agapanthus, on the other hand, grow in full sun, and while they don't compete with other plants for moisture, they live in areas where the amount of moisture available in summer is limited. When water is scarce, they can draw on their reserves. Why does one grow in the shade and the other in sun? I don't know the answer to that, but I can tell you that *Clivia* has broader leaves by far than *Agapanthus*, following the general, and logical, rule that shade-loving plants often have broader and larger leaves than those of plants growing in full sun. With larger leaves to catch or absorb as much light as possible, they are adapted to their preferred locations.

TRUE BULBS

A true bulb consists of leaves modified for storage and a stem compressed into a flattened plate. The leaves are attached to the plate. From the plate, roots are produced. Attached to the plate on the upper side, and surrounded by the modified leaves, is a bud containing the immature foliage and those cells that will develop into the flowers. This bud is the entire growth of the coming season, compressed into a very small area. In some bulbs the embryonic flowers are formed the previous season, as is the case with hyacinths. In others, the stem arising from this bud will produce foliage and buds at the apex; true lilies are examples of this.

Some true bulbs have modified leaves that are closely wrapped around each other, the outer leaves turning color and protecting the inner ones. An example of this type of bulb is the onion, with an outer "skin" (leaves) that becomes dry. Another example is the tulip. (If you cut through an onion, from side to side, you will easily be able to see the "rings" which, if peeled off,

No matter where you aim your camera in the Keukenhof Gardens, you are assured of a pretty picture. Everywhere there is a riot of springtime color.

can be seen to have veins, exactly like those of leaves. This is not the case with tulips.) Other true bulbs are made up of fleshy scales, and given good conditions these remain turgid and contribute to the strength of the bulb. True lilies are good examples of this type of bulb.

How can a gardener profit from such knowledge? When purchasing tulips, you now know that whether the bulbs do or don't have an outer skin isn't of great importance. (Except that, if tulip bulbs are offered for sale with the tunics in place, you can be sure that handling has not been rough, and that unseen bruises are not as likely to be present. Bruising can cause rotting.) If, on the other hand, you see lilies with dried outer scales (modified leaves), you know they have not been kept under optimum conditions and the bulbs have, to a certain degree, suffered. If many scales are dried, it is not a good idea to purchase that bulb. If the home gardener is storing tulips, it isn't necessary to keep them moist, but lilies should be prevented from losing moisture. In our homes we commonly store onions, and no harm comes to them, even if they are stored for a fairly long period; the "skin" holds moisture in. *Lilium* bulbs, not having such a skin, will lose moisture more readily.

The most important part of a true bulb is the basal plate. It is from this that the roots are produced, and the leaves and future flowers and stem also are attached to it. If the basal plate is damaged, then obviously the ability of the bulb to perform is impaired. Check for damage when purchasing bulbs and when you lift and store them. If the plate is badly damaged, it is best to discard the bulb, as such damage will provide an entry point for disease. A sound bulb will be plump and firm to the touch with the basal plate undamaged. True bulbs are generally oval, pear-shaped or rounded.

CORMS

A corm is a stem that is swollen and otherwise modified for storage. Generally, the underground portions of the stem are so modified, and take on a rounded shape, concave on the bottom and flattened on top. Frequently this storage portion

An early hybrid, *Gladiolus* × *citrinus* is still used in breeding. Because it is low growing, it is ideal for the rock garden.

has a brown skin called a tunic—the basis of the stem leaves. In some cases, notably the crocus, the skin (tunic) has a meshlike or woven appearance, which can be an aid in the identification of various species.

Unlike "true bulbs," corms are solid. The roots are produced from the bottom, the shoots from the top. The food for the developing shoots and for the roots is contained in the corm, and by the end of the growing season the original corm is shriveled, and a new corm is usually found on top of the old. Clustered around the new corm will be little cormels, and often, as in the case of *Gladiolus*, the cormels are very numerous.

When you lift a corm at the end of the season, remove the old corm and store just the newly formed young corm. Unless you are going to propagate the cormels and grow them on to flowering size, discard them. It takes some two to four years to raise cormels to flowering size. They should be sown in drills, as peas and beans are sown, but only 1 inch deep. Grow them on for one year, and lift and store over winter. The following spring, sow them again, a little deeper this time. By the end of the second season, they should have reached flowering size and can be planted where you want them to flower. If you live in a warmer climate and leave the corms of gladiolus, for example, in the ground, you will find the cormels will send up shoots that look for all the world like grass. If they are not wanted, just hoe them off.

TUBERS

A tuber is a swollen underground stem or root, but not the base of the stem, as is a corm. It is usually fleshy, rounded and covered with scaly leaves often invisible to the naked eye and concentrated toward the top of the tuber. In the axils (where scales are joined to the tuber) of these scales, eyes (buds) develop, and it is from these eyes that the stems and flowers are produced. There are two basic types of tubers, those formed from the stem, and those formed from roots. The dahlia has tuberous roots on which there are no eyes; the eyes are found at the base of the stem. It is essential that dahlia tubers each have a piece of the old stem with eyes, as the tubers themselves will not produce any new growth, having no buds.

An example of a root-forming tuber is the potato, in which the eyes are quite evident. Most people know that if you leave potatoes in storage for a long time, shoots will emerge from those eyes. A more attractive tuber is the cyclamen, but there is some confusion, as many gardeners call the tubers of cyclamen "corms," however incorrect this may be. Roots can emerge from almost any part of a tuber, but the majority will be from the underside, which is generally rounded, while the shoots emerge from the upper side, which is often concave. In the case of the potato, however, roots arise from the base of the new stems.

That there is a difference between top and bottom is a help when planting cyclamen, but when planting *Anemone coronaria* for example, it does not seem to matter how you plant them—which is fortunate as it is almost impossible to tell top from bottom!

RHIZOMES

A rhizome is a swollen underground stem that has apices (tips) from which shoots emerge. There is generally only one apex that will produce growth at the time of purchase, but after a season or two of growth, the parent rhizome will start to produce side shoots at the end of which shoots will emerge. The roots are produced on the underside of the rhizome. If you cut into a rhizome you'll see it is solid, just like a corm

Long before the flowers of *Anemone coronaria* 'St. Brigid' open, you enjoy the attractive foliage. Few spring cut flowers last as long in water as anemones.

Dietes iridioides is a plant that takes the place of iris in the southern hemisphere. Very free flowering, it is handsome in containers and one of the easiest plants to grow.

or tuber, but the difference between a rhizome and a corm is that only the ends of a rhizome produce shoots. In the case of corms and tubers, growth is from the top. The rhizomes of bearded iris grow with their tops exposed to the sun. While certain plants have rhizomatous roots and spread by producing such, these roots are not swollen and do not act as storage units. Only those roots that are swollen and act as storage units are included in the broad use of the word *bulb*.

WHERE DO BULBS COME FROM?

I doubt if there is a country in the entire world that does not have a bulbous plant growing wild somewhere within its boundaries. Of the some

Dierama pendulum, a graceful plant, deserves to be more widely grown. The flowers atop grasslike stems dance in the faintest breeze.

250 genera that contain bulbous species, 97 of them are found in South Africa. Some of them are not well known, such as the genera *Dipidax, Gethyllis, Hexaglottis* and *Walleria,* but others are well known to gardeners. Among these are *Agapanthus,* so widely grown in the warmer parts of the United States; *Amaryllis; Clivia,* one of the finest bulbs for winter color in warmer climes; the glorious *Freesia;* the popular florist's flower, *Gloriosa;* the pretty *Nerine;* the great container plant *Lachenalia;* and the tough Arum lily correctly called *Zantedeschia,* now found growing wild in many parts of the world, and indeed often regarded as a weed in parts of California.

The beauty of many South African species has yet to be discovered by American gardeners. Some watsonias are known, but more should be grown, and who knows just what new colors will be forthcoming when the full range of *Gladiolus* that grow wild in Southern Africa are more extensively used in breeding programs? The angel's fishing rod, *Dierama,* are worthy garden plants, found in a few gardens, but so very worthwhile they should be grown more extensively. Surely when the unusual colors of such plants as *Ferraria* become known, gardeners will demand they be available commercially. I think it fair to say that we have but scratched the surface of the bulbous plants worthy of commercial introduction. Goodness only knows what marvels of color and form can be created by devoted hybridizers of such genera.

We often think of plants as coming from countries with which we associate them strongly, but often those places are not their true homes. The most popular of bulbs, the tulip, did not originate in Holland but in Afghanistan, China, Crete, Greece, Iran, Turkestan, Turkey and other areas around the Mediterranean. Many of our lilies come to us from China, Japan and Korea, and from species that grow wild in these lands, we have the forebearers of many of our lovely hybrids. True, there are many lovely species native to North America, but these are not as popular as the many hybrids, the progeny of bulbs from other lands.

Some bulbs are found in many different parts of the northern hemisphere, the iris being a good example. Irises are not found in the southern hemisphere. However, the family of the iris is well represented by the genera *Dietes* and *Moraea*, found below but not above the equator. Snowdrops and snowflakes, *Galanthus* and *Leucojum*, are native to Europe, while North America is home to the splendid *Trillium* and the *Calochortus*, commonly known as the Mariposa lily.

With such worldwide distribution it is to be expected that there is a bulbous plant for every garden, no matter what the soil type or the climate. Bulbs are versatile, many having built-in life cycles that enable them to survive and thrive where other plants can't.

In our gardens today, we could—if we had the room—grow several hundred different cultivars of tulip. Yet only a half century ago the exact bloodlines of tulips were unknown. Herein lies a tale. For many years tulips were appreciated in their native lands. Prior to the thirteenth century, Omar Khayyam mentioned them in his writing. The first Mogul ruler of India, Mohammed Barbur, collected them in the early part of the sixteenth century, and Pierre Belon, a French naturalist traveling at that time in Turkey, mentions "red lilies," no doubt a reference to tulips.

In 1529, Suleiman the Magnificent was laying siege to Vienna. The then-Emperor of Austria, Ferdinand I, sent his emissary Augier Ghislain de Busbecq to Constantinople (now Istanbul) to seek peace terms. There the emissary saw fields of flowers, bought some bulbs and shipped them back to Austria, where they came under the care of Carolus Clusius, the court botanist. A little while later, Clusius left Vienna to

---

History

As long ago as 2200 B.C. the Minoans of Crete depicted the lily on their pottery, and irises were painted on the walls of their palaces. Bulbous plants were not unknown to the Egyptians and are depicted on the thrones and tombs of Egyptian pharaohs. Did not Christ refer to the "lilies of the fields"? (Apparently, though, this was a reference to anemones rather than actual lilies.)

Bulbs have long been known and cherished. The Madonna lily is featured in paintings of the Madonna, and has long been the symbol of purity and innocence. It is not surprising that bulbs were used in early medicine. The onion, and its relative garlic, have long been favorites of people wishing to rid themselves of various ailments. Lily bulbs were boiled and used in olden times as external compresses to get rid of tumors, ulcers and inflammations. The symbol of French royalty, the fleur de lis, is a stylized iris. Bulbs have been a part of the fabric of human life, celebrated in art, literature and mythology, and today they themselves are veritable works of art that we can, and should, enjoy in our gardens.

---

take an appointment as professor of botany in Leiden, Holland, and he took his bulbs with him. For this reason alone the tulip industry for many years was centered around Leiden.

During the sixteenth century, the growing of rare and unusual plants was much in vogue in Great Britain. The wealthy vied with each other, not only for the largest houses and collections of art, the most lavish stables and other material ob-

An elegant planting of *Hippeastrum* hybrids in a public park in Durban. The blue delphiniums are a perfect foil for the pink hippeastrums. Later their foliage will separate the petunias and the marigolds. This seems to me a clever use of plants.

jects, but also tried to outdo each other with the magnificence of their plant collections. Plants were imported from all over the world, and among them were many bulbous plants.

In his *Paradisi in Sole Paradisus Terrestris* (1629), John Parkinson mentions daffodils, fritillarias, saffron flowers, lilies, tulips and many other bulbs. Such was the interest and demand for new and unusual plants that seed and bulbs were often transported in diplomatic pouches. Obviously seed was easy to carry, and bulbs, more easily transported than shrubs or trees, were also natural choices for such shipments. During the seventeenth century, many bulbous plants still widely cultivated today were introduced into Great Britain, among them *Agapanthus africanus*, from South Africa, *Sprekelia formosissima*, from Mexico, and *Hippeastrum reticulatum*, from Brazil.

During the eighteenth century, the number of bulbous plants introduced into Great Britain was astonishing, and included such well-known plants as *Zantedeschia aethiopica*, the Arum or calla lily from South Africa; *Crinum asiaticum*, from tropical Asia; *Alstroemeria pelegrina*, from Chile; *Trillium erectum sessile*, from North America; *Tritonia securigera*, from South Africa; *Eremurus spectabilis*, from Siberia; and *Dahlia variabilis*, from Mexico. Bulbous plants were not only in demand but were introduced into cultivation from the four corners of the globe. Throughout the nineteenth century, bulbous plants from the Himalayas, Tibet, Peru, Syria and Uruguay were introduced, and by the early part of this century, there were few genera of bulbous plants not in cultivation. It is indeed unusual to find a new genus of plants, but new species are still being found. (Still, it must be admitted that it is rare to discover a "new" species of outstanding beauty.) Today, we are dependent on the work of hybridizers for new, beautiful cultivars. But such is the gene bank that has been established over centuries that, for the foreseeable future, hybridizers have an almost unlimited number of species with which to formulate lines of breeding.

It is entertaining to read the accounts of the many plant hunters and explorers who roamed the world on their quests. When one realizes the rather primitive modes of transportation, the length of time it took to reach the areas where many of our bulbous plants are at home, one has to admire the courage of these people. Their adventures were many, the hardships endured were almost beyond belief, and yet such was their determination that they willingly went back time and time again to collect new species. Their rewards were not great (many received little monetary reward), but their prestige and the admiration of their fellow plant lovers—who were not as adventuresome—could not have been greater.

Yet these men were humble. It was only after I had known Harold Comber (1897–1969) for a number of years, for example, that he would recount for me his adventures. He explored vast areas of Tasmania, traveling on horseback, carrying cumbersome plate cameras with photographic plates that were heavy and easily broken, nothing so light and easy to use as rolls of film. He and his exploration party had to shoot their food if they wanted meat, and spent weeks and often months on their journeys. As the time for seed gathering is fall, the weather was not always pleasant and balmy.

Plant hunters must have a tremendous knowledge of plants. The explorers who have brought us so much knew the characteristics of the various families, and proper identification of the various species they came across was essential to their work. How crushing it would be to bring back specimens of plants already in cultivation! Because the number of plants that could be handled physically on an expedition was limited, it was critical to spend effort on only new, unknown plants.

Plant hunters had to be knowledgeable about the needs of the species introduced so they could advise how best to cultivate them. It was important that precise records be kept of the latitude and longitude of where each specimen was found—an added chore, especially as maps of many regions explored did not exist. Many men who were sent to remote regions of the world as missionaries had an interest in plants. Two we must thank for many introductions from China—among them the genus *Nomocharis*—were Père Jean Marie Delavay (1838–1895) and Armand

I photographed these *Scadoxus multiflorus* at Victoria Falls in Zimbabwe. Lovely plants, in my garden in San Francisco they remain in flower for six or more weeks.

David (1826–1900). Many plants have been named in their honor. Their writings inspired others to hunt for plants in China, a country that rightly deserves the name "Mother of Gardens," as many fine plants, shrubs, trees and bulbous species were found there.

Information on how to grow the various new plants introduced was often sketchy, to say the least, despite often copious notes by those who discovered them. The lovely Peruvian lilies, *Alstroemeria*, were brought back from South America but for some reason didn't survive in cultivation. Harold Comber was sent out in 1929 to rediscover this lovely genus. It is thanks to his efforts that this plant was reintroduced, and florists the world over owe Harold a deep debt of gratitude, as do all of us who admire these plants in our gardens or arrangements.

Iris pallida 'Aurea Variegata' with *Iris ensata* 'Variegata' in the center. The foliage is attractive, the flowers a bonus.

THREE

Gardening with Bulbs

Where can bulbs be grown? The simple answer is virtually any-where. The great diversity of bulbs available today allows the gardener to select bulbs suitable for every possible type of location. Some bulbs are at home in woodland settings. Some are ideal for extending the interest of flowering shrub borders (when the shrubs are out of flower), while others are superb planted with annuals in display beds, or in containers for decks or patios. Others can be grown indoors, even without soil. Certain bulbs are very effective when grown in lawn areas, and still others are authoritative denizens of the perennial border. Wherever they are grown, bulbs in flower attract attention, and with some planning as to the height and color, time of flowering and scale of planting, dramatic results can be obtained.

Spring gardens can be made to come alive with bold splashes of color. Summer gardens can take on an added dimension with the bold foliage and startling colors of gladiolus and cannas. Well into fall we can enjoy late-flowering lilies. During the winter months in warmer climates, the clivias are at their best. The secret to success is knowing which bulbs to plant where, for while the selection available is vast, not all bulbs will perform well in all locations.

WOODLAND GARDENS

Can there be a more natural home for the English bluebell than a woodland garden? The secret is to plant enough of them to make a noticeable splash of color, and for this reason I don't recommend planting fewer than 50 in any given location, even in a modest woodland garden.

For bluebells to perform at their best, and to show off their colors to advantage, they should enjoy bright light sometime during the day, and not be confined to deep shade. The plantings can be allowed to drift off into shady areas, however, and when this is done the impression is of a greater area planted than actually exists.

Before we continue with bulbous plants for woodland areas, we ought to look at some criteria for such plantings. As mentioned before, the play of light and shade is important in a garden, especially a woodland garden. It affects the perception of color and perspective. Also, sunlight can "spotlight" those plants on which it falls. Plantings of taller plants, such as the lilies, need not be as large as plantings of lower-growing plants. The total volume of a clump of lilies 4 to 5 feet in height can be equated with a planting of a lower-growing plant covering 10 to 15 square feet.

In the woodland garden, it is wise not to plant bulbs that will flower at the same time as such flowering shrubs as rhododendrons and azaleas. Unless carefully sited, the shrubs will dominate the scene. There are always exceptions, of course; one of the most effective uses of bluebells is surrounding and highlighting a planting of azaleas. But exceptions require careful planning.

One doesn't see straight lines in a natural woodland setting. Take that as your cue, and give plantings a free form; "like clouds in the summer sky" is how I remember hearing them described, and this seems to capture the point. Another way to describe the ideal shape of a

Allium triquetrum is an invasive plant, but if there is room, it makes a grand groundcover and requires little care.

planting is to imagine a bucket of water tossed over the ground. There would be a large splash, and several tongues leading out from the main splash. Again, this naturalistic shape makes for an attractive planting.

If the woodland garden is next to a more formal area, then a sort of visual bridge is needed to join the two areas. One approach is to use some of the same plants in each area, but employ them differently. You might wish to line formal paths in one area with regular, even plantings, and then plant, in a less formal way, the same type of bulb in the adjoining forest or woodland. A transition can be achieved by having gaps between groupings, and making the groups themselves different sizes.

Spring seems the natural time to think about and enjoy the woodland garden, but if one restricts oneself to spring, one misses the lilies and the cardiocrinums, and we should always allow space for fall-flowering cyclamen to drift under trees. Cyclamen are low growing, and should be looked up at (try planting them at the top of a bank if at all possible). They are lovely under yew, beech and oak trees, whose noble trunks seem to coddle the dainty flowers and foliage of the cyclamen. One of the loveliest plantings of this type I found quite recently in South Devon, England, on the grounds of a hotel; there the large beds of cyclamen, some 400 to 500 square feet, are a dream come true. Whatever plants are used, keep in mind the style and form of the woodland garden has to be remembered. Is it truly wild in appearance? Is it an area with lots of trees but few shrubs? Obviously there is a difference, but the criteria for plantings are valid in both cases. See to it that there are enough plants to make the desired impact, and that plants shorter than 24 inches can be viewed from close by. It is essential that the character of the woodland setting, vistas and elevations, be studied from all possible angles. Take into account the budget for maintenance of the area so the plantings made can be kept in good condition. It is far better to have fewer, well-maintained plantings than many that are slowly going downhill due to lack of funds or time for adequate maintenance.

Winter aconite, *Eranthis hyemalis*, forms a lovely carpet of bright yellow in February and March, but should not be used if there isn't sufficient room for it to spread without bothering other plants in just a season or two. Trilliums are at home in woodland gardens, but these plants and other plants under 24 inches in height should be planted within easy viewing, perhaps near paths and terraces, not planted at such a distance that they can't be seen to full advantage. Large-flowered daffodils look good on the edge of woodland gardens, just drifting into the woods, but plantings of the smaller types are better suited to, and look more at home in, the woods. It appears as though the trees protect these smaller types. Cultivars of varying colors do not seem quite correct in an informal woodland, but can look great in a contrived or less-wild wooded area. Erythroniums, fritillarias (the Meleagris selections) and practically all the members of the genus *Arum* are ideal for all types of woodland settings. Although *Muscari* (grape hyacinths) are often recommended for woodland areas, in my opinion they are much better suited to the edges of such areas, their habit being a little on the stiff, formal side; in addition to this, they much prefer full sun. The types of bulbs best suited for woodland areas are those that prefer some shade during their growing period. In warmer climes the clivias, the caladiums and *Hymanthus* and their close relatives the *Scadoxus* make ideal woodland plants, as these have rather an exotic appearance, and fit in well with warm-climate trees and shrubs.

This photograph was taken at Monet's Giverny. The artist was a good gardener, and tulips have been "dabbed" here and there to add subtle accents to other spring flowers.

BORDERS

Perennial Borders

Certain bulbous plants are well suited for perennial borders. They must be types that can be left in the ground undisturbed, and still give good displays each year. The summer-flowering bulbs are perhaps best for such locations because they don't leave empty spaces as do spring-flowering bulbs, which tend to die back by early summer. In borders and beds it is essential that the bulbs planted actually contribute to the effect. If a planting is to be viewed only from up close, then 10 to 15 tulips will make a contribution. If it is to be viewed from a distance, then twice that number will be necessary in order for them to have impact. Tall-growing bulbs are best seen against a background. Lilies, for example, need a background such as a hedge, where they will be noticed more than if they are just "floating" in the air. This is more important when the flowers in question are to be viewed from a distance.

Not often are grape hyacinths (*Muscari armeniacum*) used as mass plantings, but they are attractive and effective. They deserve to be boldly planted.

Lilies are wonderful for perennial borders, and cultivars that flower in early summer, mid-summer and into fall all are suitable. *Eremurus*, with its tall spikes, are outstanding even when only three or five bulbs are planted, and they don't leave large, bare areas during the summer months. The dieramas are suitable, too. The effect of their lovely, pendant flowers and arching stems is not easily duplicated, and they add an unusual form to borders. Evergreen plants, among them daylilies, agapanthus and crinums, are also suitable and add much interest. All of the above-mentioned can remain in the border for five to ten years without being lifted. Irises are often used in perennial borders, but successful results require planning to ensure they fit in well. Plant them where late-summer–flowering plants will contribute a good mass of color to the area; with good planning, the swordlike iris foliage will complement these other plants.

Bulb Borders

Few bulbs can be used exclusively to create a border. Dahlias, cannas, irises and daylilies come to mind as candidates for this, but they are all summer-flowering. To extend seasonal interest, spring-flowering bulbs should be interplanted, even if they die down a little later in the year. Consider *Muscari*, species of *Narcissus* and *Anemone* for such a purpose, particularly because all can be left in the ground, and often will multiply. I would even add fall- and winter-flowering crocus and colchicums, to extend the season of interest further.

An effective and attractive border can be composed of lilies, but if care isn't taken to include types that flower at different seasons, or for a long period, the border won't be as attractive as it might be. I remember admiring a border made up entirely of Regal lilies, but could not help thinking it would not be very attractive toward the end of summer, when the flowers had passed. It's a good idea to plant a number of shrubs in the bulb border, selecting those with different flowering seasons. Let the dominant plants be the bulbs, but the shrubs will provide color and form throughout the year.

Shrub Borders

Few shrubs remain in flower for long periods of time. When you add spring-flowering bulbs to the front of the border (the front because they tend to be short), and taller, summer-flowering kinds behind and among the shrubs, you create a border with an extended period of interest. Select bulbs with care. They should add to the interest of the border, but not dominate. Dahlias, for example, dominate more than a clump of lilies or summer-flowering galtonias; in addition to the rather vivid colors of dahlias, their foliage is more imposing. A collection of the shorter bulbs—*Muscari*, *Galanthus*, *Leucojum*, *Trillium*, *Anemone*, *Cyclamen* and *Puschkinia*, which never look untidy—would be better suited to the front of the border than tulips, which don't lend themselves easily to such informal plantings. This, together with the fact that tulips are best lifted each year (as they can't be counted on to perform well the second season), should convince the gardener that bulb selection for a shrub border requires thought and good planning. Shrub borders can't become too dry during the summer; after all, shrubs need some water throughout the year to perform well. Tulips and narcissus, on the other hand, must have a dry resting period in summer. Bear in mind that bulbs selected for the shrub border must be compatible with the cultural conditions the shrubs receive.

Annual Borders

Planting bulbs with annuals is one of the best ways to display the great diversity of their forms and colors, heights and flowering times. A bed of spring color provided by pansies, primulas and, in warmer areas, by *Nemesia* and cinerrarias, as well as forget-me-nots and calendulas, can take on added interest with the contrasting and complementary colors of bulbs. To be honest, I do not regard calendulas as ideal for gardens. Despite claims that certain selections are free from mildew and have great flowers, I am not convinced, and I can't remember seeing a bed of these plants that came even close to the rather lavish descriptions one reads.

However, I do remember with great pleasure the sight of pink tulips hovering above blue forget-me-nots. Another great display was tulips in combination with the large-flowered English daisy, an annual not frequently used, but so easy to grow to perfection. Daffodils leave too many untidy leaves to perform well in formal beds, but almost any type of tulip will give a good account of itself, the exception being some of the species, which are generally too graceful and don't possess the forceful personalities needed to compete with or complement more vigorous annuals. Bold clumps of gladiolus are superb with summer an-

Forget-me-nots are in flower for months. Here at the Butchart Gardens in British Columbia, red tulips grow through them—an added dash of color.

nuals; the tall-growing kinds add a strong vertical accent, even when not in flower, a quality all too frequently not taken advantage of.

Called upon to make a garden pretty for a wedding, I was faced with a narrow border, at the back of which was a fence some 7 feet tall. I planted scalloped rows of pink and white gladiolus, many hundreds of them just 4 inches apart. The owner of the garden became a little anxious as the date of the wedding drew near, and the

Supporters of the University of California will particularly appreciate this blue and gold combination, tulip 'West Point' and forget-me-nots!

glads were not in flower. But right on cue, they started to bloom some six to seven days before the great day. While the weather delayed them from being in peak bloom, there were enough in good flower that the effect was a delight. Having unopened buds on the spikes added to the beauty. If I remember correctly, we planted pink geraniums in front of the glads.

In annual borders, use those bulbs that are best lifted. Thus, lilies are less than suitable, while lower-growing dahlias can be most effective. Cannas, while often not lifted in warmer climates, are good complementary plants for annual beds, and here one should take advantage of those cultivars with colored foliage.

For a very practical summer flower bed, consider chard, petunias and gladiolus, with lobelias as a border. The chard is edible as well as ornamental, and this is true of the gladiolus, too. The blue of the lobelia can be a striking companion to red and white petunias which, in turn, contrast well with the green and white of the chard. In the center a mass of gladiolus. The chard leaves can be used in the kitchen, and un-

An excellent and interesting use of crocus in The Hague, Holland. This type of planting can only be accomplished where winters are cold and the grass remains short.

sprayed gladiolus flowers can be stuffed with shrimp or crab for an attractive hors d'oeuvre. Color, height, form and contrasting textures: what more can one ask of a flower bed?

BULBS IN LAWNS

While the use of bulbs in lawns in not uncommon in Europe, one seldom sees them so used in the United States—a great pity. Crocuses can be most effective in lawns. In late fall, cut and roll back strips of turf, and fork over the exposed earth. Plant drifts of crocus bulbs quite close together, then replace the turf. Mow as usual until the little shoots of crocus start to appear, and don't mow again until the crocuses have finished flowering. As these little bulbs flower very early in spring, they are out of flower by the time the grass needs regular mowing.

Narcissus (daffodils) are used more frequently than crocuses for planting in lawns. Again, it is best to roll back the turf to plant, rather than cut many holes in a lawn. Don't plant the narcissus too close to the house, as it is necessary to delay mowing the grass until the narcissus foliage has started to die back. This style of naturalizing *Narcissus* can be most effective in large areas of lawn, and is even more striking with a backdrop of trees. Take advantage of background trees and weave *Narcissus* through them for a grand and expansive effect. Here, if the grass is quite coarse, digging individual holes is not too hard a task. When planting bulbs in a lawn, make certain the soil is moist; it is much easier to dig holes in moist ground than hard, dry soil.

BULBS IN CONTAINERS

Because they are so versatile—some are happy in sun, some in shade, some are short, others tall and stately—bulbous plants are great for

Before the buds of this Gregii Hybrid tulip open, and after the flowers have passed, the plants' variegated foliage is attractive. The container is perfect for plants of this size.

container growing. Be sure to plant enough bulbs in each container. Too often I see containers with just a few bulbs in them. Much better to have fewer containers, but each choc-a-bloc with bulbs. Any bulbous plant can be grown in a container, as long as the container is of sufficient depth to accommodate the bulbs being planted.

Crocuses and anemones, daffodils and tulips, lilies and gladiolus are marvelous for planting in containers. One container can accommodate more than one type of bulb, too. You can plant daffodils, for example, in a deep (8- to 10-inch) container, cover them with soil, then pop in some of the shorter, earlier-flowering bulbs. Anemones, with their fernlike foliage, and *Muscari*, with their blue flowers, heighten the drama and colors of daffodils. Gladiolus are charming in a container filled with geraniums or petunias. Really, almost any combination is possible. With bulb combinations, bear in mind that those bulbs that

prefer not to be disturbed should not be combined with types that need to be lifted after flowering.

I like clivias in all sorts of containers, and have some that have been in the same containers for more than ten years. Clivias like to be crowded and seem to flower better each year. So far they have not cracked the pots, but they might well do so before too long. There is not much room for soil, so I feed them frequently when they are growing in spring and early summer.

What depth of container should be used for each type of bulb? As a rule of thumb, there should be as much soil under the bulb as above it. If a bulb is to be planted 6 inches deep, you need a container 12 inches deep. It is true you can cheat a little, but not if the bulbs are going to put on the best possible display. Scale is important. A plant 24 inches tall in a low container only a few inches tall does not look right. *Muscari*, for example, look attractive in shallow containers; they are best planted with a minimum of 2 inches of soil over them, so a 4-inch-deep container looks correct.

It really doesn't matter what type of container is used. But I do think daffodils are especially suited to wooden containers, and tulips look their best in terra-cotta, but this is a matter of taste. With a collection of containers, the most important point is that they be of similar design. One each of many different styles and of different materials just looks untidy. The quality of soil used in a container is important. While soil is discussed later (page 39) suffice it to say here that packaged potting soil is just fine for the great majority of bulbs. Don't be tempted to use garden soil, as it can harbor pests and diseases. Drainage is important, too. By far the greater number of bulbs dislike having wet feet. They will not perform if sitting in water. Make certain that any container in which bulbs are grown can drain easily. Add a good layer of broken shards to the bottom of the pot to reduce the chance of

For the effect of a river of color, it is essential that the plants flower at the same time and at approximately the same height. The *Muscari* are an attractive frame for the double early tulips.

the drainage holes becoming plugged. Drill extra holes in large containers, if necessary. I think it is safe to say that containers can't have too much drainage as far as bulbs are concerned.

When considering what to plant, think about where and how you will use the container. A bowl of hyacinths in full flower will perfume

These checkerboard plantings are an effective use of tulips at the Wildlife Sanctuary and Gardens at Port Lympne, England. This garden was designed by the great landscape architect Russell Page, with whom the author had the privilege of working.

the entire home. Just how you are going to enjoy container-grown bulbs in flower will, to a large degree, affect the size of a container, but depth should be a major consideration regardless. No point in planting very large (and, perforce heavy) containers if you hope to move them indoors later—why make additional work for yourself?

Plants that produce several flowers from a single stalk, attractive foliage as well as pretty flowers, long-lasting and fragrant flowers, these can be advantages to remember when selecting just what type of bulb to grow in a container. There are no hard-and-fast rules, and given the great variety of tastes and preferences, it's a good thing we have such a grand selection of bulbs from which we can choose exactly those that please us. In fall, when bulbs are on display in the nurseries, take a moment to look over the selection available. Imagine the various bulbs in containers you already have, and where you might grow them. If these seem to come together in a pleasant way, the depth of the container(s) you want to use is appropriate, and you can give the bulbs the sun or shade they require for good growth, purchase and enjoy them. Don't hesitate to ask questions if the various factors do not seem to come together, and never stop being adventurous!

BEDDING SUGGESTIONS

Experiment with combinations of plants for spring and summer color. Many find it easier to adapt combination suggestions than start from scratch, and for this reason the following planting schemes may be of interest. By all means, use plants better suited for your particular area wherever that makes sense. The purpose of these suggestions is to get the thought process in gear. These planting schemes allow for changes to be made, so go ahead and select the bulb color of your choice. The same applies to annuals where they are called for. I hope that by depicting planting schemes that are a little out of the ordinary, the reader will feel encouraged to experiment.

Added interest to beds can be achieved by changes in elevation. There's no reason why beds have to be flat, and mounded and even hollow areas add a lot of interest to planting schemes of all kinds. Mounding doesn't have to be smack in the middle of the planting but can be planned closer to one end or one side; this way a great deal more color can be seen from a distance. It is best to plan for any slopes to face the point from which the bed will be viewed most.

I have deliberately not suggested certain bulbs, including *Amaryllis belladonna*, *Hippeastrum*, *Nerine* and *Lycoris*, as the cost of bedding them can often overextend the budget. Should funds allow, by all means substitute such species. The only limits on exciting, unusual planting schemes are your imagination and the funds available!

Knowing how many bulbs to plant in a given area is sometimes a mystery. It need not be. If they are spaced 3 inches apart, you would need 4 to a linear foot (12 inches divided by 3 inches). Square this number (4) = 16, which is the number needed for one square foot; for 5 square feet the number of bulbs needed is 16 × 5, thus 80 bulbs.

If the plants are spaced 6 inches apart, you need 2 to a linear foot (12 inches divided by 6 inches = 2). 2 squared = 4, the number per square foot. In each of the following designs, the number of bulbs given is rounded upward to the nearest 5.

The term "interplanted" is perhaps self-explanatory. Plant the bulbs, and then plant the annuals over them. Do not worry if an annual is planted directly over a bulb; the bulb will find its way through. "O.c." means on center, the professional term for distance apart of plants, measured from center to center.

Where bulbs are to be removed after flowering, minimum suggested distances are used (see captions). I recommend that, if the budget allows, the closest distance be used when a bed occupies a prominent position, too. The greater distances might be dictated by budget constraints! However, I advise against spacing bulbs too far apart as then the effect is diluted. Even such bulbs as dahlias, crinums, lilies, cardiocrinums and cannas look more spectacular in groups of 3 or 5 than they do planted singly.

Please note that the diagrams that follow are not all drawn to the same scale.

Spring Planting Schemes

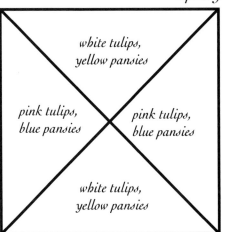

pink tulips	*white tulips*	*red tulips*
white tulips	*red tulips*	*pink tulips*
red tulips	*pink tulips*	*white tulips*

TRIANGLES: *This design, 4 feet square, will need 50 white and 50 pink tulips, about 5" o.c.; interplant with pansies (Viola) or primroses (Primula).*

CHECKERBOARD: *This design should be 6 feet square. Twenty-five tulips, 5" o.c., are needed for each 2-foot square. Alternate red, pink and white and interplant all squares with forget-me-nots (Myosotis).*

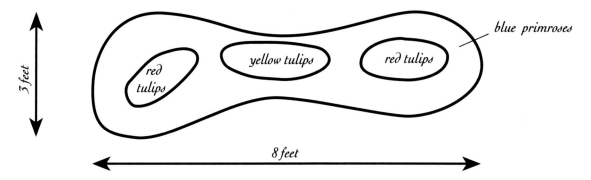

HENRY MOORE: *For this, plant two groups each of 25 red tulips to flank a central planting of 50 yellow tulips. Surround with blue pansies* (Viola) *or primroses* (Primula polyantha).

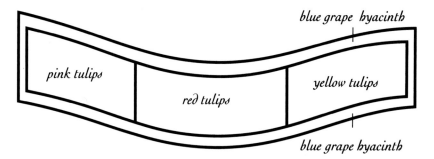

BLUE RIBBON: *The suggested dimensions are 9 feet by 20 inches. Twenty-five of each color of tulip, 4" o.c., and 150* Muscari *3" o.c. are needed.*

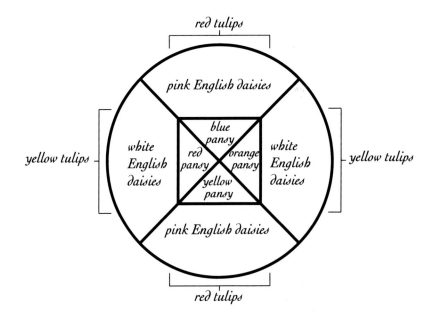

WHEEL OF FORTUNE: *This is a study in the art of interplanting. Opposing quadrants of a 10-foot circle are each planted with 75 red and yellow tulips, 6" o.c. Pansies of different colors are in the central square, and alternating edging of white and pink English daisies* (Bellis perennis) *complete the design.*

Summer Planting Schemes

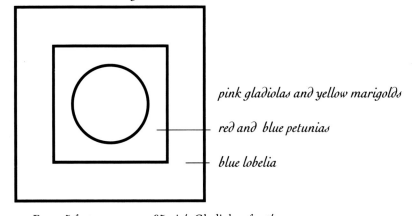

pink gladiolas and yellow marigolds

red and blue petunias

blue lobelia

ALMOST SQUARE: *For a 5-foot square, use 25 pink* Gladiolus *for the circle, 4" o.c., and interplant them with tall marigolds. Surround the circle with a square planted with red and blue petunias, and border the bed with blue lobelia* (Lobelia erinus).

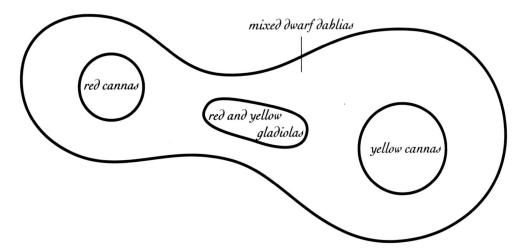

mixed dwarf dahlias

red cannas

red and yellow gladiolas

yellow cannas

SUMMER MOORE: *Fill a kidney-shaped bed with 55 mixed, dwarf dahlias, 10" o.c. Plant 20 red and yellow* Gladiolus *in the center, 5" o.c.; at one end a circle containing 3 red cannas, 12" o.c.; the other end a circle of 5 yellow cannas, 12" o.c.*

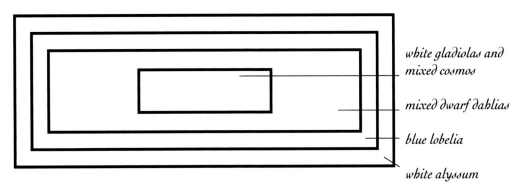

white gladiolas and mixed cosmos

mixed dwarf dahlias

blue lobelia

white alyssum

TRADITIONAL: *For this classic bed, 10 by 4 feet, you will need 25 white* Gladiolus *in the center, 4" o.c. Interplant with mixed cosmos, and surround with 30 mixed, dwarf dahlias, 8" o.c.* Lobelia erinus, *and white alyssum* (Lobularia maritima) *is used to border the bed.*

In superior mixtures of colors, as here, no one color dominates. The 'Hadeco Strain' seen in these *Ranunculus* production fields is one of the finest available.

Four

The Cultivation of Bulbs

PROPAGATION

Most gardeners purchase bulbs each year, and given the great value one receives for the money spent, this is understandable. Propagation is an offshoot of the normal culture of bulbs. Examples of propagation are the necessary lifting and dividing of Bearded Iris, daylilies and agapanthus. These plants increase in size quickly. The older sections of the plants are discarded, and the young, vigorous portions are planted back. Because more young plants are produced by this simple operation, one can say the plants are propagated.

Certain lilies produce bulbils in the axils of their leaves, and stem bulblets on the portion of the stem between the top of the bulb and soil level. Ornamental onions produce bulbils in the flowerheads, and certain species of *Oxalis* produce lots of offsets (progeny) from the parent bulb. Cormels are produced in great number by gladiolus corms, and *Alstroemeria* roots produce

crowns that are easily lifted and divided. But despite these easy methods of multiplication of the plants, few gardeners would say they propagate bulbs.

There are two means of propagating plants: asexual and sexual. The former most commonly involves dividing the plant, taking cuttings, meristem or tissue culture, or bulblet, cormel or scale production. Asexual propagation ensures that the offspring will be identical to the parent, that it is a clone. Sexual propagation involves the production of seed, and results in a hybrid. With a species with established bloodlines, seed will be true to type, but the offspring are not clones. Hybrid seedlings can differ greatly from one another. It is by sexual means that new cultivars are raised by hybridizers and breeders. This, however, is a rather long-term proposition. From literally thousands of hybrid seedlings, only one or two will be worthy of commercial introduction. It takes years to evaluate the offspring fully. For example, about seven years is the minimum time required to raise a new cultivar of tulip or lily; then, stock must be produced in quantity for an effective introduction onto the gardening market. Modern methods of propagation have shortened the propagation period. A worthwhile cultivar can be propagated by tissue culture and thousands of plants produced in a year.

It can be appreciated that, due to the time investment, new and exciting introductions are higher priced than cultivars long in the trade. Unless an avid lover of a particular plant, the gardener is advised to stick with tried-and-true cultivars, and not overspend on new introductions. Raising new plants from seed takes several years. A steady progression of young plants can be had if seed is sown each year. By the time the first plants reach flowering size, others are close behind, and will follow year after year. Some bulbs flower the first year from seed. Among these are *Dahlia*, *Begonia* and *Ranunculus*. If the home gardener wants to try raising bulbs from seed, these three genera should be the first tried.

RAISING PLANTS FROM SEED

There are but three essential requirements for germination: moisture, warmth and air. (Light is required once germination has taken place, and seedlings deprived of light will soon become yellow.) Moisture is required to soften the seed coat, and allow the root and shoot to emerge. After germination, and as soon as the roots have reached into the soil, moisture is needed to keep the plants growing.

A certain temperature is required to activate the seed's cells. The exact temperature for optimum germination and growth varies from species to species. As a general rule, a temperature in the region of 60°F at night and no higher than

75°F during the day is appropriate for a wide range of seed.

It is essential that the plants have air, both for the roots and for the shoots. If the soil mix in which the seed is sown is so dense it does not leave space for air, the roots will not grow. In the wild the seed drops to the ground, and while it might work its way down in the soil a little, perhaps carried there by rains, it will not be far from the surface of the soil when germination takes place, and air is available to it. It is this type of environment that seed needs. Because weed seeds require the same conditions as the desired species, a soil mix formulated for seed should be used rather than garden soil. This will be weed-seed free, either because it has been sterilized or because it is composed of clean and sterile constituents, such as sphagnum moss, vermiculite and perlite. Such soil mixes don't contain much nutritive value, and if such a sterile medium is used, the seedlings should soon be transplanted into a soil mix that contains nutrients, such as any of the potting soil mixes sold in nurseries.

Often seed drops from the seed-bearing plant as soon as it is ripe, but some plants that come to us from colder climates require a certain period of cold temperatures before germination takes place. Among these are *Anemone*, *Camassia*, *Crocus*, *Cyclamen*, *Fritillaria*, *Hermerocallis*, *Iris*, *Muscari*, *Narcissus* and *Tulipa*. In climates where frost is experienced, you can sow such seed in the fall in containers, and place the containers outside where they will obtain the needed cold temperatures. In warmer climates, pop the unsown seed into the freezer for a few weeks, then sow in spring. You will often find seed of bulbous plants listed in catalogs. This seed is sold ready to sow. The ideal is to sow in spring, and keep the plants growing steadily throughout summer and into fall. This isn't difficult, but like time and tide, seedlings wait for no one, and when they need to be transplanted, they must be transplanted. Waiting too long can cause them harm.

Sowing seed is an easy task. The container must be clean, be it a flat or pot. Make certain drainage is adequate, using pieces of broken pot or large gravel in the bottom of the container if necessary. Fill that container with soil mix and firm the surface. The top of the soil should be about 1 inch below the top of the flat or pot. Even firmness is necessary so water will soak evenly downward, without leaving a more firmly packed area dry. Sow the seed over the surface, making certain it is evenly distributed and well spaced. Barely cover with some more of the soil mix, and then lightly tamp the surface so the seed is in good contact with the soil. Seed that is very fine, such as that of *Begonia*, where one ounce can contain several million, should not be covered at all but just firmed into the soil surface. Seed can be difficult to see on the surface of a soil mix, so it's not easy to know when it has been covered. This problem can be overcome easily by placing a dusting of sand over the surface of the soil before sowing the seed. A good rule of thumb is to cover the seed to the same depth as the seed is thick. Water using a watering can with a rose attached to the spout, avoiding drips on the soil surface, as they can dislodge seed. Cover with a piece of glass or translucent, thick plastic. Place the container in a location away from direct sunlight (which can dry out the soil), and keep the temperature even, in the range mentioned above.

As soon as the seedlings start to germinate, remove the glass or plastic. When they are large enough to handle with ease, carefully prise them out of the soil and pot them individually into small pots, or space them 2 to 3 inches apart in another container. A cold frame can be used outdoors in colder climates, but remember, there is no point in sowing seed unless the correct temperatures can be maintained. Better to wait until

Tuberous begonia flowers add a touch of elegance to any garden. Despite a reputation for being a little difficult, they perform well with just a little attention.

overnight temperatures are above 50°F outside than to sow outdoors and see the seedlings damaged or killed. Water as often as needed to keep the soil moist, not wet.

Seedlings should be transplanted the following spring; after two seasons (two years) of growth, they can be planted in the garden. Types that flower the first year from seed—the *Dahlia*, *Begonia* and *Ranunculus*—can be planted out the very first year in the garden. If you live in a cold climate, do not forget to overwinter these plants in a frost-free place. During the overwintering period, keep them barely moist, but never allow them to become too dry, or they will shrivel. Barely damp peat moss is a good storage medium. Treat these young plants the same way you would treat larger plants of the same type with respect to their needs for sun, good drainage and so forth. You may be surprised that, after just one season of growth, the plants will have produced small—but recognizable—bulbs.

Seed from lilies, gladiolus, irises and tulips can be sown outdoors in spring. Good soil preparation is necessary. Make certain the tilth is good and the seedbed quite firm, but not compacted. Scatter the seed over the surface, barely cover with soil, and keep moist. During the first few months of growth, protect freshly sown seed from the sun by using lath (inch-wide strips of wood) or shade cloth. Remove weeds as you see them. After a season (or two at the most), lift the young plants and line them out in rows, planting the young plants about ½ inch deep and 3 to 4 inches apart. Grow them on to full size and treat as you would purchased bulbs of the same type.

Although raising bulbs from seed is easy, it does require quite a bit of time and constant attention. If you need only a few, I would purchase them. However, with cuttings and division—less tiresome procedures—the home gardener should have good success without too much effort.

CUTTINGS

Two popular bulbous plants can be raised from cuttings: dahlias and begonias.

When night temperatures are approximately 65°F, dahlia tubers can be planted in a peaty soil mix in large containers. Barely cover the tubers. Soon each tuber will send up one or more shoots. When they are 3 to 5 inches long, remove them from the tuber with a sharp knife, and place

them at once in a very sandy soil mix. The ideal spot for them is a small cold frame where night temperatures are approximately 55°F. The bottom leaves of the cutting should be removed so that no foliage is placed in the soil. Keep moist, and the air should be humid, so the cuttings do not dry out. A small, clear plastic-covered frame in an area where there is bright light, near a garage window if no greenhouse is available, will work perfectly well. If it isn't possible to make a bed of sandy soil, place the cuttings in small pots containing sandy soil mix. In about 10 days these cuttings will have rooted, and can be repotted using regular potting soil in a container or planted out in a sheltered spot in the garden. Keep the parent tubers moist and additional shoots will be produced, often as many as 10 to 15 from one tuber. Cuttings so rooted will be identical to the tuber from which they were taken; they are clones. I used to raise hundreds of thousands of dahlia cuttings when I worked in France, but there I had a range of greenhouses, bottom heat and many other advantages, such as deep benches filled with sharp white sand, with which I was able to root cuttings in 3 or 4 days. I wouldn't expect home gardeners to root them as quickly, and in fact there is no advantage, but commercial growing is a different proposition; quick rooting, and hence quick production, is desirable.

Begonias present a different problem. You start the tubers off in the same way, but once they start into growth you have two options. You can cut up the parent tuber so that each portion has a young shoot, and grow the pieces on, or you can remove the cuttings when they reach 3 to 4 inches in height, and grow them on, as for dahlias. Production of shoots is not as prolific from begonia tubers as from dahlia tubers. The maximum number is usually four or five, but sometimes they produce only two or three.

DIVISION

Bulbs left in the ground year after year will, at some time, need to be lifted and divided. Bulbs that require such treatment include lilies, daylilies, *Agapanthus*, clivias, alstroemerias, *Iris* (bearded types), *Narcissus*, scillas, crinums, *Dieties*, *Moraea*, and all small bulbs. Lifting and dividing should not be done until the clumps show signs of becoming overcrowded, with a consequent loss in flower production. Overcrowded plants produce many small shoots rather than fewer, large ones. If the plants are still performing well each year, do not lift and divide, unless propagation is the objective.

The time to lift and divide is after flowering and when the foliage has started to die back. In the case of such evergreen species as clivias and agapanthus, lift and divide at the end of summer, but allow the divisions sufficient time to become reestablished before the onset of colder temperatures. Plants need six to eight weeks to reestablish themselves before they can face harsher conditions. If this is not possible, wait until spring. Some gardeners advocate waiting until all the foliage has died back, but I find that having some foliage attached to the bulbs allows for easier location of the bulbs to begin with, a distinct advantage.

Bearded irises are an exception, and should be lifted and divided in the middle of summer, July at the latest. If you delay the operation, the plants will not suffer, but flowering the following year will be greatly reduced, if not entirely lacking. With many of the smaller bulbs, overcrowding seldom seems to occur. Masses of bluebells in the woods never get lifted and divided—they flourish! If the plants are flourishing, they don't need to be lifted and divided.

Having lifted the plants, shake the soil from the roots. Pry the clumps apart. If this is difficult,

use a clean, sharp knife. Cut with care, and try to avoid destroying good plants by working the blade between the stems. Discard older stems. The smaller plants with roots attached can be planted in nursery rows, and grown on for a season or two until of flowering size. Larger plants can be replanted, spacing them a good distance apart, depending on the type of plant, so as to allow them several years of good growing before this lifting and dividing has to be done again.

After replanting small plants, water them well, keep them moist and give them a feeding of a balanced fertilizer (equal parts of nitrogen, phosphorous and potassium) as soon as they have started back into growth. If they are dormant, then plant them at the correct time for the species, and give them a feeding as soon as growth starts in spring. Do not allow these smaller plants to flower; cut off any flower spikes they produce until the bulbs have reached a good size, of a size that you would purchase; you can gauge the size of bulbs in the ground by the size of their shoots.

Bear in mind when planting small plants that good soil preparation is a very sound investment. A good soil has the ability to produce good plants. Poor soil will not; even if plants tolerate poor soil, they will not grow as well as they would in good soil. There is a difference between tolerance and good growth!

When lifting lilies, you will find many bulbs of good size, and many more of a smaller size, clustered around the larger (older) bulbs. These smaller bulbs will include stem bulblets. Carefully remove bulblets from the stem and from around the parent bulb. Plant them in nursery rows, and grow them on for a season or two before planting them into their permanent locations. Many of the early-flowering Asiatic upright lilies, such as 'Enchantment', produce a great number of stem bulblets each year. Lifting each year is not necessary. Should you wish simply to reduce the growth of the clumps, pulling off the young (smaller, less sturdy) foliage will reduce the growing potential of these small bulblets. Perhaps this is a lazy way of tackling the problem, as it isn't a long-term solution to overcrowding, but this stopgap method can sometimes postpone the need for lifting and dividing.

Whenever you tackle division, take all the bulbs out of the ground; do not remove just a portion of the clump. Then, select from the material at hand the plumpest and healthiest bulbs for replanting. Discard all damaged plants and those that show signs of rotting.

Some cultivars are more vigorous and faster growing than others. Keep this in mind or you may end up with lots of the same plant, and lose colors that are not such strong growers. For this reason it is a good idea to label the clumps when in flower. Then you will be able to plant back a good and varied selection.

One can almost feel the great texture of the petals of *Ranunculus* 'Hadeco Pink' and know the flowers will last a long time.

SCALES

Lilies can be propagated by taking some of the other scales from large bulbs and sowing them in a flat, using potting soil with added sand. Little bulbs will form at the base end of the scales, and these can be grown on to flowering size. But I would recommend home propagation be confined to using those bulblets produced on the stems or found upon lifting the parent bulbs. Why? The removal of scales and the time it takes to look after them until they are of good size doesn't seem worthwhile in the case of a few bulbs.

SCORING

Hyacinths are commercially propagated by taking large bulbs and making a series of slashes across their bottoms. Small bulblets form on the edges of the cuts, and these are removed and grown on. Again, not a job for the home gardener, at least not in my opinion.

While I would suggest that a keen gardener try his or her hand at raising dahlias and ranunculus from seed, I feel that raising other bulbs from seed should only be undertaken after considerable thought. Raising bulbs from bulblets presents far fewer problems and disappointments.

CULTIVATION AND PLANTING

The potential for any bulb can be reached only if correct cultivation is provided, and if it has been correctly planted. The majority of garden soils are suitable for the majority of bulbs. Where bulbs are to be grown, it is important that the soil be cultivated to a depth of 12 inches. The addition of well-rotted organic material is an advantage, of course. Good preparation that includes soil amendments is essential if the area to be planted has been used for growing annuals for several seasons; such areas are often only shallowly cultivated, the soil has not enjoyed uniform moisture, and compaction may well have taken place. In compacted soil, roots have a hard time growing, and proper soil aeration and movement of moisture through the soil are impossible.

Good Soil

If your soil is sandy, organic matter will increase its moisture retention. If yours is a clay soil, organic matter will increase air circulation and allow for easier passage of moisture. If the soil has not received any fertilizer in the form of organic matter or commercial products for six months, the application of a balanced fertilizer — equal proportions of the major "food" elements nitrogen, phosphorous and potassium — should be applied at least 7 to 10 days prior to planting. Follow the directions for rates at which to apply. Do not think that giving an extra-heavy application will be beneficial, and note that if you have a heavy clay soil, less fertilizer is needed than for a sandy soil. The rates of application listed on the package are generally for a soil that is neither heavy nor light, but in between. Apply accordingly.

The halfway point between clay and sand is ideal, and such soils are called loams. (If they lean toward sand, then they are sandy loams; if they lean toward clay, they are heavy or clayey loams.) Gardens that have soils with a high percentage of organic matter are generally older gardens, where farmyard manure (f.y.m.) has been used for many years. The soils are very dark, easy to cultivate, rich in plant food, and suit most types of plants, including bulbs. For hundreds of years f.y.m. was the principle fertilizer used in gardens. There was a limited use of sulphate or muriate of potash, superphosphate, bone meal and dried blood. It seems we have almost come full circle, as today it is recognized that such organic, or natural, products are indeed best for the great majority of crops, and to maintain healthy soils.

Ask an old gardener in the British Isles the secret of his success and you might well receive the reply, "dung under 'em," and in my opinion, we should return to such natural culture. I am not against special formulas for various plants, but I think the gardening public has been exploited to the point where it has become almost *de rigeur* to purchase special formulas for many different types of plants. Some would have you believe even if you have only a small garden that it is necessary to have a half dozen different fertilizers. This is just not true. Gardeners have succumbed to hype, and forgotten the basic facts, which follow.

Three elements comprise the major plant foods: nitrogen (N), phosphorus (P) and potassium (K), and it is these three letters that appear with percentages on product labels. Nitrogen encourages growth; phosphorous thickens plant cell walls, adds color to fruit, encourages bud set and makes for sturdier plants; potassium is used in the translocation of food inside the plants to the growing points, where it is needed and used. In spring we want our plants to get off to a good start. We can give them nitrogen to encourage growth, but at the same time, because we don't want the plants to produce unbalanced growth, we also give them phosphorous and potassium. A formula in the range of N10–P5–K5, that is, 2 parts nitrogen to one each of phosphorous and potassium, is suitable. The exact formula can vary some, as long as there is a higher percentage of nitrogen. Nitrogen is more easily washed or leached from the soil than the other two elements, so to give the plants a little spring boost, when there is often a good deal of rain, keep the nitrogen percentage higher. During summer months we want the plants to grow steadily, so we give them a "balanced" feeding with roughly equal percentages of N–P–K. In fall, to help plants get ready for winter, it's best to eliminate the nitrogen but keep the phosphorous and potassium available in goodly amounts, and 0–10–10 is the fertilizer to apply. Plants use a number of other foods, including zinc, iron and magnesium, and others of which only a trace is needed. Thus, especially in spring, it is best to apply the needed N–P–K with a product that also contains minor and trace elements.

Soil is a living thing, filled with all sorts of organisms that break down materials into forms plants can absorb. In early spring soil can be cold, and bacteria in the soil are often not very active; they, like us, need a pleasant temperature to perform at full potential. Hence, while phosphorous and potassium are seldom missing in an average soil, the plants are waking from their winter sleep and need food that encourages growth (nitrogen). Nitrogen is not readily available to plants until bacteria have worked on it. Thus we apply it in a form that is readily soluble.

This may sound all too simple, but that's the way it is! Now, what about lime? Lime is not a fertilizer. It can be used to correct the pH of the soil, and it also works to make fertilizer and/or food in the soil more readily available to plants, because organisms that break down substances into food plants can absorb work best in a certain pH range. PH is measured on a scale where 7 is neutral; purified water has a pH of approximately 7. Soils that are acid, or "sour," have a pH below 7. Alkaline or "sweet" soils have a pH above 7. Most arid soils have a pH above 7. Soils high in organic matter are in the 6 to 6.5 pH range, which is where the great majority of plants are happy. Substances used by plants as food tend to be most available to the plants in this pH range. In acid soils, certain ingredients of a well-balanced diet for plants are missing. Still, certain plants, called "acid loving," have

adapted to this and thrive when the pH is low, say in the 5 to 6 range. A classic example is rhododendrons. As for bulbs, those that love woodland settings—such as trilliums, eranthis and fritillarias—are at home in the woods because that is where trees drop their leaves, contributing much organic matter to the woodland soil, resulting in a lower pH. There are plants that like a neutral or slightly alkaline soil, among them many of our desert plants. Irises can grow well in such soils, but as they also thrive in soils with a pH of 6 to 6.5, we do not have to provide them with an alkaline soil, just a good soil. It is true, however, that the addition of a pinch of lime when planting Bearded Iris is a good, but not essential, thing.

I should mention here that inorganic fertilizers, and for that matter a mulch such as sawdust, are broken down into formulas plants can use by bacteria that occur naturally in soil. Constant use of inorganic fertilizers can deplete the soil of these organisms, but the use of organic fertilizers does not cause such depletion. For this reason (there are others, too), organic fertilizers are better for container feeding, where there is but a limited amount of soil available, and thus a limit to the essential organisms. If you use sawdust as a mulch, you should add some nitrogen to the mulch to help break down the sawdust. Where containers are concerned, the watchword should be "feed weekly weakly!" And I suggest that you will have greater success with container plants if you use a liquid organic fertilizer each week, but apply at only half the strength recommended. This is about the only time manufacturer's directions should be adjusted to accommodate a special circumstance. (If the product label instructs to feed weekly anyway, there is no need to dilute.)

If you are feeding a plant, make certain the food gets down to its roots. Water your nutritional supplement into the soil if there is no rain to do the job for you. When it comes to bulbs, there are a couple of special considerations. To be honest, we do not fully understand them, but they are worthy of attention. Bulbs seem to require some of the minor elements found in bone meal and/or "hoof and horn," an old type of fertilizer we used when I was a boy. These are slow-acting fertilizers, which means they take a while to break down into the phosphates they contain. Because they are slow acting, they aren't the food we give bulbs when planting them. If you plant bulbs without adding such a product as hoof and horn or bone meal, or one of the bulb fertilizers available, you will get good flower production if the soil is good, but it will be just a bit better if you do use bone meal or hoof and horn. Just a pinch should be mixed into the soil at the bottom of the hole. Note, please, that you must mix it well into the soil; never let any fertilizer come into direct contact with the plants, whether it be foliage or the roots. Wash off any fertilizer that accidentally spills onto a plant, as it is caustic.

For spring-flowering bulbs, add some hoof and horn or bone meal at planting time; then, in spring, as soon as shoots from the bulbs appear above the surface, give them a feeding of 15–10–10 fertilizer and make certain it gets down to the roots. Give summer-flowering bulbs the same treatment. Treat fall-flowering bulbs when the foliage starts to appear. In the case of those bulbous plants you are going to let stay in the ground—lilies in most parts of the country, dahlias and agapanthus, for example, in warmer climes—give a balanced feeding in midsummer. Then, some four weeks before the weather becomes cold, say in late September or early October, give them a feeding of 0–10–10. This is a good idea because the plants are still active; these two ingredients will toughen them and help them start into fall and winter in the best of shape.

Soil well worked, soil in good heart, with goodly amounts of organic matter worked in, is ready for planting. With bulbs, depth of planting is most important. Many bulbs that do not give a good performance are planted in soil that is not well cultivated, and perhaps for that reason, they were not planted deeply enough to begin with. Every bulb entry in the Alphabetical Listing of Genera provides the depth at which the bulb should be planted. Do remember this is for average soils. If you have a sandy soil, do not hesitate to plant a little deeper. In a heavy clay you may plant a little closer to the surface, but always err on the deeper side if in any doubt. Why? That is worth explaining, as knowing why certain things happen can be as important as knowing the right and wrong way to do things.

PLANTING

At a lower depth the soil temperature is more constant, less likely to vary greatly. For tulips, *Narcissus*, hyacinths, Dutch iris, *Galanthus* and *Muscari*, constant temperatures are conducive to root production, and good roots result in good flower production the following spring. Slow and steady growth is what is wanted, and that can be achieved by planting deeply. Close to the soil surface, frost lowers the temperature dramatically. Similarly, even though the sun may be weak in winter, it still warms the soil surface. So, up and down, up and down goes the temperature of shallow soil, where the risk of damage to new growth is much greater. Certain bulbs such as ranunculus and anemones like to be planted only an inch or so deep. The fluctuation of soil temperature doesn't seem to cause them problems. I'm afraid I do not know exactly why this is, but will hazard it may be because these plants are not only fast growers, but tough, sturdy plants, too. Even if some of their roots are damaged, it doesn't seem to be a problem, as many are produced. Look at the number of roots produced by an *Anemone*, and you will be amazed.

What is the best way to plant? First of all, the soil should be moist—it makes planting so much easier. Second, if you have a great number of bulbs to plant in an area, it will be easiest to excavate the area to the depth required, and work some bone meal into the soil. Place the bulbs gently, but firmly, into the soil, then fill in

the area, perhaps stopping as needed to place any other bulbs that are not so deeply planted at their correct depth. Then, fill in the entire area and water in. Watering in is important, as it makes certain the bulbs are in direct contact with the soil. We do not want any bulbs that aren't snugly planted, or they may suffer from drying out. Watering well eliminates air pockets. If you are going to plant annuals over the bulbs, use a board to kneel on, to avoid compacting the soil. Do not worry a bit about planting directly over bulbs; they will find their way through without any problem. Trowels, spades and bulb planters are all good, but I prefer a trowel. Use the tool with which you are most comfortable.

Many books recommend that labels be used so you know where you have planted a certain bulb. I do not think that is truly necessary, but do recommend that a note be made of the name and type of the bulb(s), as it is quite annoying to be asked the name of a plant and not know it. Somehow saying that it is a tulip or a narcissus is

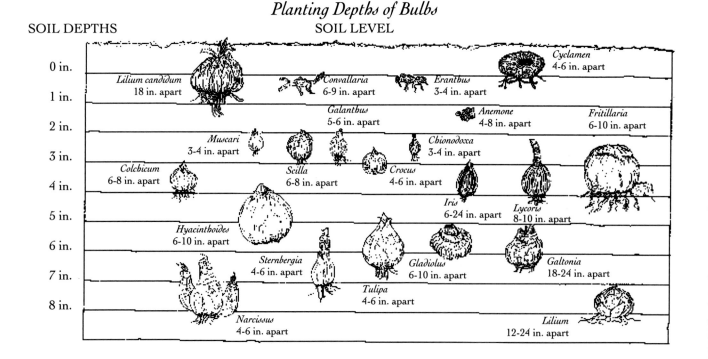

Planting Depths of Bulbs

SOIL DEPTHS   SOIL LEVEL

0 in.

Cyclamen
4-6 in. apart

Lilium candidum
18 in. apart

1 in.

Convallaria
6-9 in. apart

Eranthus
3-4 in. apart

2 in.

Galanthus
5-6 in. apart

Anemone
4-8 in. apart

Fritillaria
6-10 in. apart

Muscari
3-4 in. apart

3 in.

Chionodoxa
3-4 in. apart

Colchicum
6-8 in. apart

Scilla
6-8 in. apart

Crocus
4-6 in. apart

4 in.

Iris
6-24 in. apart

5 in.

Lycoris
8-10 in. apart

Hyacinthoides
6-10 in. apart

6 in.

Sternbergia
4-6 in. apart

Gladiolus
6-10 in. apart

Galtonia
18-24 in. apart

7 in.

Tulipa
4-6 in. apart

8 in.

Narcissus
4-6 in. apart

Lilium
12-24 in. apart

Planting Depths of Bulbs

Planting depths are indicated for average soils. In sandy soils, plant a little deeper; in heavy or clay soils, not as deep. Soils should be well cultivated, moisture retentive but not waterlogged. If fertilizer is to be applied, do so as the shoots emerge from the soil.

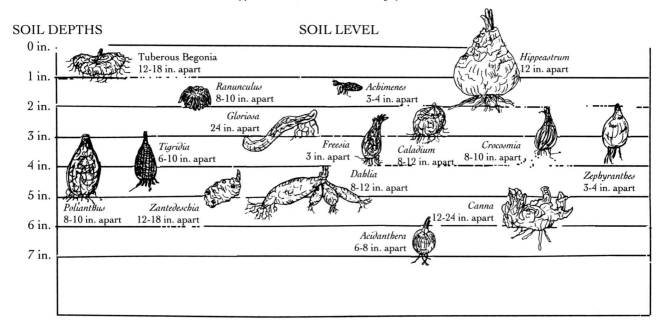

SOIL DEPTHS   SOIL LEVEL

0 in.
Tuberous Begonia
12-18 in. apart
Hippeastrum
12 in. apart
1 in.
Ranunculus
8-10 in. apart
Achimenes
3-4 in. apart
2 in.
Gloriosa
24 in. apart
3 in.
Tigridia
6-10 in. apart
Freesia
3 in. apart
Caladium
8-12 in. apart
Crocosmia
8-10 in. apart
4 in.
Dahlia
8-12 in. apart
Zephyranthes
3-4 in. apart
5 in.
Polianthus
8-10 in. apart
Zantedeschia
12-18 in. apart
Canna
12-24 in. apart
6 in.
Acidanthera
6-8 in. apart
7 in.

not quite satisfying. People like to know the name of the cultivar! "It is a Darwin hybrid named 'Appledoorn'," or "*Narcissus* 'Mount Hood' " does answer the question.

MULCHES

Without a doubt, the use of a mulch after planting makes the area look neat and tidy. In addition, mulches keep down weeds, conserve moisture, help reduce fluctuations in soil temperature, and can, if the right materials are used, improve the quality of the soil. There has been far too much use made of bark chips. While they may look fine when first applied, they soon lose their color, and scatter and look untidy. The large chips can hardly be counted on to conserve moisture to the same degree as finer material does; there are just too many large air spaces between the chips. Cultivation and future planting are difficult without first removing the

chunks of wood and all in all, I do not feel they have a place in the garden. I have doubts about the smaller chips, too.

I use Redwood Soil Conditioner, which is mostly organic matter. It looks more like soil than a conditioner, and contains some chicken manure or similar product. When applied to the soil after planting, it provides a kempt appearance. As the texture is quite fine, it doesn't inhibit the penetration of moisture into the soil, yet seems to impede moisture loss. Any weeds that manage to germinate and grow through it are easy to remove, and as time passes and this product works into the soil, it improves the texture and quality of the soil. It can hardly be used too heavily, and I have found this type of material to be the best.

Shredded fir bark looks untidy to me, and while it will break down over a period of time, it isn't a soil conditioner. Sawdust, with added nitrogen to help it break down, is used extensively by commercial firms, as are wood shavings (again, with extra nitrogen provided). While some advocate shredded newspapers, I prefer to use them on a compost heap and apply them to the garden only when no longer distinguishable from other ingredients in the compost. Grass clippings can be used, if not applied in a thick layer, but the clippings should be left on the lawn anyway. Some recommend sphagnum peat moss as a mulch, but it can be very difficult, if not impossible, to get moist. I recall using some on a border in my garden and, months later, I would come across pockets of the material still bone dry, and this despite making it moist before applying it. Either I did not moisten it enough, or it dried out quickly, and it never became sufficiently moist again. Rain often beads up on peat moss and runs off. There are numerous other mulches, but I have yet to find one that serves the soil, the plants and the gardener as well as a good soil conditioner used as a mulch. You can't go wrong with a soil conditioner.

If no mulch is used, then it is beneficial to keep the surface of the soil lightly cultivated. This deters weed growth, and any weeds that germinate are quickly dealt with. Keeping the surface friable allows easy penetration of rain and stops any moss from growing. All types of plants seem to thrive with light cultivation. Be careful not to disturb roots, and take extra care when shoots are beginning to emerge from the soil. A three- or four-pronged cultivator allows a large area to be cultivated in a short period of time, and if cultivated on a regular basis, the garden looks neat and tidy.

STAKING

There are a few bulbs that require support, among them lilies, dahlias and gladiolus, especially if they are grown in a windy area. The trick here is to use supports that are of the same type throughout the garden. Few things look as untidy as a mishmash of different types and colors of stakes. Simple bamboo canes are easy to insert into the soil, and last for many a season. I think they are much preferable to metal or fiberglass canes, which never look right in the garden. In the old days we used to use raffia to tie plants to their supports, but now plastic tape is often used. Make sure that the knots are hidden behind the cane, not exposed to view. The canes themselves should, if at all possible, be placed behind the plants. A good support should be in place, but not seen. Ties should support, not strangle, and allow for a season's growth.

The time to put a support in place is when the plant has grown 12 to 18 inches tall. At that point the roots will not be too greatly disturbed by the introduction of a cane, and you can position the cane close to the stem. If you wait too long, you'll have to place the cane several inches away from the plant, where it will be more conspicuous and less attractive. The cane should always be shorter than the plant it supports; there is no point in having a cane that extends inches above the stalk of the plant it supports. If necessary, you can trim the cane to the correct height once it's in place, but it is far better to use a cane of approximately the correct height in the first place. You can always push the cane down into the soil, providing your soil is well cultivated.

Tulips and hyacinths grown in Zones 8 through 11 should be precooled before planting. If they have not been, place the bulbs in the vegetable section of the refrigerator for at least 6 to 8 weeks prior to planting (store them as described below). Do not store with apples, as they produce ethylene gas, which is harmful to bulbs. You should ask whether bulbs have been precooled when purchasing them.

There are temperature variations in all zones, and if your area adjoins a lower zone, then obviously you should plant a little earlier than if you are near a higher zone. There is some leeway in the planting dates, but they give the gardener a general idea of when to plant. However, do not miss the opportunity to purchase bulbs in advance of planting time. The best selection is to be had when bulbs are first offered for sale, and you can take advantage of "specials," too. Store bulbs in the refrigerator prior to planting as the temperature remains constant there, and they can wait 8 or even 10 weeks.

Lilies can be planted in fall or spring. If planted late in spring, the bulbs may not perform very well the first year, or come into flower a little later than expected. They will flower as scheduled their second season. If lily bulbs arrive and you cannot plant them right away because the ground is too wet, or for any other reason, store them in the vegetable section of the refrigerator, in woodshavings in a plastic bag left open a little. Except these fleshy types, all other bulbs are best stored in paper bags, not plastic; poke holes in the bags for air to circulate.

Spring planting of summer-flowering bulbs should take place some two weeks before the last expected frost, in those areas where frost occurs; in warmer areas, plant so the bulbs enjoy temperatures of approximately 45°F at night. If you plant too early, they will just wait for the right temperatures to arrive. There is little advantage in planting dahlias, tuberous begonias or cannas outdoors until temperatures reach the mid- to low 50s at night. When summer-flowering bulbs are planted, we want them to grow slowly but steadily, not in fits and starts, which will be the case if they are planted out too soon.

LIFTING AFTER FLOWERING

While species tulips can be left in the ground year 'round, and will return for years, the majority of tulip cultivars cannot be relied on to perform well the second year. However, it is well

---

When to Plant

The following chart will give you the best planting time for spring-flowering bulbs.

USDA Zone	MONTH TO PLANT
1–3	Early to mid-September
4	Mid- to late September
5	Late September to early October
6	Early October
7	Mid-October
8	Not after late October
9	Not earlier than late October to early November
10	Not earlier than mid- to late November
11	Not earlier than early December

---

worthwhile saving the bulbs. Don't fail to label them correctly so you aren't confused when it is time to replant them. As soon as the foliage starts to turn brown, lift the bulbs with the foliage remaining attached. Spread the bulbs out in a dry, airy location, away from the direct rays of the sun. The foliage will soon dry completely and can then be easily detached and discarded. Clean the bulbs; the soil will be dry and easy to remove. Discard any damaged and the very smallest bulbs. Store the remainder in old panty hose or nylon sacks, suspended in a dry, well-ventilated, dark place. Check stored bulbs periodically and discard any that show signs of rotting. If rotting has occurred during storage, dust the bulbs with a fungicide. Eight weeks before planting time, place the bulbs in a paper sack with holes and place in the vegetable section of the refrigerator. (Do not put fungicide-dusted bulbs in the refrigerator, however.) At the correct planting time, plant the bulbs, but quite close together as they will then put on a show and can be cut for the house. Should you wish to save all bulbs, including the smallest, then plant those that are smaller than a large acorn in nursery rows, and do not allow them to flower. They can be lifted the following spring and treated as outlined above. Planted again the following fall, they should produce flowers the following spring.

Narcissus can be left in the ground, but make certain they have a dry spell in mid- to late summer, so they can ripen. If rains are the norm in mid- to late summer, and the ground is constantly moist, it is best to lift the bulbs and replant them. If the area they are growing in is going to be watered, then lift them as soon as the foliage starts to die down, and treat as for tulips (above). The same applies to hyacinths, but seldom will you see the same size or number of flowers per bulb in subsequent years as you did the first season of flowering. The bulbs may put on quite a display and be well worth growing, but don't expect them to be as great as in their first season.

Summer-flowering bulbs such as begonias, gladiolus, cannas and dahlias can be left in the ground in warmer zones where little or no frost is experienced. If they must be lifted, then do so shortly after the first frost, which is normally enough to kill the top growth but not harm the bulbs. Begonias, cannas and dahlias shouldn't be allowed to dry out. Place them in barely moist peat moss, making sure the entire root is covered. Keep the peat moss barely moist during the winter months, at approximately 40°F. Replant them when planting time comes around. Keep an eye out for storage rot, and discard any plants that show signs of rot. Or, cut out and discard the portion of rotted bulb, and dust the cut surface with a fungicide.

Gladiolus can be lifted, and the old, spent corm separated from the newly formed corm, as soon as the foliage has died back. When the new corms are clean, put those the size of a quarter and larger into paper bags and store them in a dry area at about 45°F to 50°F. Corms smaller than a quarter can be saved and planted back the following year in nursery rows and grown on; some of the larger ones may flower, and you can cut them for use indoors, or simply remove the flowers to strengthen the corms. Here again, unless you really don't mind a lot of work, I would suggest that saving small corms is not worth the effort.

Water Requirements

While some of the rare species have specific moisture requirements, the majority of bulbous plants the home gardener will grow have rather simple ones. Some plants, such as the Louisiana iris, like to have their feet in water. This genus is the exception for bulbous plants, and water requirements for the rest are very much the same: During the period of root development and the growing period, the plants should be moist but not in soggy soil that never has a chance to dry. As soon as the foliage begins to wither, the amount of moisture made available should be reduced, and as soon as all foliage has dried, withhold water, supplying only that amount needed to prevent the dehydration of the bulb.

Thus watering of bulbous plants is, for the most part, a simple affair. Where there are special requirements, as in the case of the hippeastrums, they are noted in the plant portraits that begin on page 61. All summer-flowering bulbs like adequate moisture, but lilies, dahlias and gladiolus don't appreciate standing in water; indeed, such conditions cause the rootstocks to rot. While some bulbs may be able to withstand being dry, then moist, then dry again, the moisture content of the soil is better kept even. That way, the growth of the plants isn't checked; such checks can result in lower (and poorer quality) flower production.

You may have read it is better to water plants in the morning or evening. It matters not. If the plant is dry, water it, no matter what the time of day. If summer-flowering bulbous plants are wilting, and you know they have adequate moisture available to them in the soil, the reason for the wilting is more than likely to be because the demands on the roots by the stems and foliage is greater than the roots can supply. Such conditions can occur when temperatures are very high, especially if there is some breeze as well. It will reduce the stress on the plants if they are given an overhead shower. This will lower the surrounding temperature, cool the plants, and give the roots an opportunity to satisfy the decreased demand. A leaf will lose more moisture in a dry atmosphere than in a humid one. If we are overheated, we appreciate a cooling shower. Plants are the same!

GROWING BULBS OUT OF SEASON

We all have seen bulbs in flower out of their normal flowering seasons in the florists' shops. If bulbs are ahead of their season, they are said to have been forced into flower. If they are late into flower, they are said to have had their growth retarded. The commercial nurseryman will have any number of bulbous plants in flower at various times of the year. Perhaps the most popular of bulbs, the Easter lily, has to be forced into flower, as the normal flowering time for this plant is August. Another popular indoor bulb is hippeastrum, which flowers in late spring to early summer outdoors, but is offered for sale in fall and preplanted, so that these lovely flowers can be enjoyed around Christmastime. Tulips, daffodils and hyacinths are but a few of the bulbs available out of season.

It is a well-known fact that tulips need pre-cooling prior to being planted. What takes place inside the bulb? The development of the embryo continues during the rest period. This is true not only of tulips, but of all true bulbs. But the treatment is not just a matter of providing six to eight weeks of temperatures in the neighborhood of 40°F.

Before cooling, tulips should be warmed for two weeks at temperatures between 68° and 72°F. For very early flowering, warming for a week at 94°F prior to this is necessary. Such a series of treatments is known as curing the bulb. Exactly what takes place inside the bulb to trigger this preparedness for flowering is not fully understood, but suffice it to say that it is required. Even if not forced and simply planted in the garden, bulbs that have been cured flower earlier than those that haven't been.

Curing a number of bulbs for a simultaneous show is rather a tricky process because they must all be at the same development stage before curing, and they must all have received the same culture. Bulbs from Holland, the area around the Wash in England and from the American Pacific Northwest are good bulbs for forcing. The cultural conditions received during the growing season will be almost, if not exactly, identical. Bulbs from Japan, where there are apparently greater climate variations within even a small geographic area, do not force as well. Though they are ideal for the garden, they are not for growing under greenhouse (forcing) conditions, because all the buds inside the bulb are not at the same stage of development, and forcing accentuates any such differences. The standard process for preparing bulbs for forcing is:

1. Curing by warming for short or long periods
2. Cooling for varying periods, according to the needs of the genus, from 4 to 9 months, generally in the range of 48° to 50°F

Warming followed by cooling prepares a bulb for forcing. If only warm treatment is given, flow-

A new selection of *Crocus chrysanthus* sent to me for trial, 'Ard Schenck', will soon be listed in catalogs, and is well worth growing. It flowered for several weeks in my garden in San Francisco.

ering is delayed. Certain cultivars within a genus will need slight variations in the length of warm and cool treatment, and between genera there are even greater differences. Narcissus, for example, need temperatures of 68° to 72°F for at least two weeks, then precooling. This goes some way in explaining the need for these bulbs to be planted in an area that will be dry in August, where the natural warmth of the soil will provide this temperature for the prescribed period. The Dutch iris, a very popular flower that commercial growers force in great quantity, needs some three weeks at 83°F, followed by about a month at 50°F, prior to planting. Thus, by manipulating the temperatures bulbs receive, they can be made ready for forcing by growers, and/or be planted late to provide flowers out of season. Research is ongoing, but I think it will be clear to home gardeners that the preparation of many bulbs for forcing out of season is not something that can be undertaken without adequate facilities and precise knowledge.

The forcing of bulbs for the home is not so complicated a process. Unlike the case of the commercial grower who has to have plants available for a given date, if home-forced bulbs are a few days, or even weeks, early or late, they can still be enjoyed. There is one essential point the home gardener must keep in mind: Bulbs for forcing must be of tip-top quality, free of any damage, and top size. The costs involved in obtaining first-class bulbs isn't much greater than for bulbs of slightly smaller size. The amount of work, containers, and hours spent will be the same, so why not obtain the best possible results?

Allow some 13 to 18 weeks of cool temperatures before the bulbs are given warmer temperatures. This includes the time spent in the refrigerator as well as in the container in a cool spot in the garden. After the bulbs are planted in the containers, they should be placed in a cool area, below 50°F and, if possible, in the range of 45° to 48°F. In cooler climates such temperatures can be given by digging a trench in the garden and covering the base with sand. Set the containers in the trench, and cover them first with sand, then soil. In other climates it is enough simply to place the containers against a north wall. In all climates, necessary temperatures can be maintained by placing the containers in an old, but still functioning, refrigerator. At no time should the temperature to which the bulbs are exposed fall below 35°F. And, if necessary, protect the containers against rodents by using chicken wire; surround them with chicken wire above and below so they are in a sort of cage. When the bulbs are well rooted, in six to seven weeks, they can be brought indoors and flowering can be expected in some three to four weeks. (You can check for roots by looking under the container, or by knocking the root ball carefully out of the pot.)

FORCING WITHOUT SOIL

Certain bulbs can be coaxed to flower without being planted in soil. Moisture must be provided, of course, even though the bulbs produce their own food. Bulbs that assure success are 'Paperwhite' narcissus and their yellow counterpart 'Soleil d'Or', and the 'Chinese Sacred Lily'.

Select a water-tight container. Place a layer of gravel, glass marbles or similar material an inch deep on the bottom of the container. Use a glass container, as it is interesting to see the roots develop. Nestle the bulbs into the material, spacing them no more than an inch apart. Fill the container with more of the same anchoring material until it reaches the necks of the bulbs. (You can see you need a container at least 3 inches deep.) Put in water until it just reaches the bottom of the bulbs. While the bulbs are growing, the water level must be maintained; frequent topping up will be necessary. Some gardeners place charcoal in the container to keep the water "sweet," but I don't think this is necessary.

Place the container in a dark area, ideally at 45°F, but up to 50°F is acceptable. The temperature should not be much higher than that. In three to four weeks, the bulbs will produce a lot of roots, and foliage will start growing. Bring the container into the light and slightly higher temperatures. (At too high a temperature, you will end up with a lot of foliage in which the flowers will be hidden and the entire container looks untidy.) Tie string around the foliage to keep it under control, if necessary.

Another bulb that can be grown in this way is the hyacinth. Purchase bulbs that have been prepared. This simply means they have received adequate precooling, etc. These bulbs can be grown in hyacinth glasses or vases, which have the same shape today as they did many years ago, and which Rousseau depicted in one of his paintings. Fill the vase until the water just touches the bottom of the bulb, and place it in the dark as described above for the narcissus for some four to ten weeks. When the roots have filled the container, and the tops have grown three to four inches, gradually expose

Forcing Schedules

To have bulbs in flower by a certain date, remember:

To flower in January, plant in the first two weeks of October.

To flower in February, plant in the middle of October.

To flower later, plant in the first part of November.

Keep records of the cultivars planted and when the bulbs come into flower. After a few seasons it is possible for the home gardener to have bulbs in flower by a given date.

the plant to warmer temperatures and more light. Again, the water will need topping off from time to time. As the hyacinth bulb seals the water from the air, here it is a definite advantage to add a piece of charcoal to the water to discourage slime from growing on the glass.

Crocus vases exist, but they are not easy to find. They are miniature forms of the hyacinth vase. To grow crocuses this way, follow the procedures outlined above. I recall a dinner party where every guest had a crocus at their place setting. (I must have been very impressed, because I can remember the crocus perfectly, but not the food we enjoyed—unusual for me!)

Do remember that when you force bulbs out of season, you are subjecting them to a certain amount of stress. These bulbs cannot be expected to perform again, unless allowed several years to recuperate. I would simply discard them. The same applies to any bulbs you receive as presents or purchase out of season. Enjoy them while they are beautiful, then discard them. Such, unfortunately, is life. However, if you have room, plant them at the correct depth in the garden, and after several seasons they may bloom.

A narrow border is made attractive for the entire summer by dwarf cannas, not at all demanding of attention.

FIVE

Pests and Diseases

A goodly number of pests and diseases can attack bulbous plants, but fortunately it is likely the home gardener will encounter only a few of them. The reasons for this are that growers exercise great care in the production of their crops, and those bulbs purchased from nurseries and mail-order catalogs are in tip-top shape. In addition, spring-flowering bulbs are in flower before many pests and diseases are active, and modern cultivars are vigorous plants. If the home gardener follows good cultural practices, a most attractive flower production is almost assured. I say "almost assured" as there may be the occasional problem with such perennial pests as slugs and snails, and later spring–flowering and summer-flowering bulbs can be subject to attack by aphids, but seldom will such pests decimate the entire crop.

I would be remiss if I did not touch on problems that may occur. The question the home gardener should ask is, just how much damage will be done if no controls are followed? Far too frequently, chemical measures are used to control an attack of aphids, when a harsh jet of cold water will dislodge them from the plants and they will not come back. Many pests can be squashed between the fingers, and if the plants are looked at on a regular basis, such infestations can be eliminated before they get out of hand. The negative effects on the environment of toxic chemical use is becoming appreciated today. Milder controls such as insecticidal soaps should be the first controls used, and then only if the attack is getting out of hand and a definite loss will be sustained. I understand that commercial growers need to protect their crops carefully or else face economic loss of harmful proportions but I feel the milder controls have their place in commercial culture too, and are the first line of defense before harsh controls are used.

The control of weeds, the removal of debris from the garden, constant vigilance to detect the very first sign of a problem can, and should, eliminate the need for chemical controls. Keeping the plants healthy and growing well will reduce attacks, just as if we keep in good health we are less prone to medical problems. Today an increasing number of biological controls are available, and it is hoped that these will replace the use of toxic substances to an even greater degree. It is of the utmost importance, whenever a product is used in the garden or in the home or on indoor plants, that the label be read, and the directions and any precautions listed be followed to the letter. Dilutions and frequence of application must be adhered to. In addition, it is essential that the product used is appropriate for use on the plants being treated. Read the label and follow directions.

ANTS

Generally they are not much of a problem, but sometimes they can be a nuisance. Ants tend to be found when other pests are present, such as aphids (which the ants use as milk cows!). If you have ants on your plants, check for other problems. Boiling water poured onto an ant nest will destroy the ants; if the problem persists, then professional help may be in order. In more than 45 years, I have not noted any damage to bulbous plants that can be attributed to ants. Indeed, ants are used by certain bulbous plants to distribute the seed.

APHIDS

Aphids, or greenfly, are common pests. They reproduce at an alarming rate, as many as 20 generations in a year. Thus the need for constant vigilance and eradication at the first sign of their presence. They come in a variety of colors—green, black and many shades in between.

These insects suck the sap from the tender parts of the plants. They can cause distortion of the buds, and in severe cases, stunting and a loss of vigor. They are often found on summer bulbs, but will prey on late-spring–flowering bulbs too. Aphids can infest the bulbs themselves, working their way between the tunic and the bulb in the case of tulips—something to watch for, if you lift and store your bulbs at the end of the growing season.

As mentioned before, a good, hard jet of water, crushing them between the fingers, and the use of insecticidal soaps are the first lines of attack. If these measures fail, then an insecticide can be used, but do make certain it is warranted. Aphids often attack roses, and while I recommend the use of nontoxic products, if you are spraying your roses, the product can probably also be used on lilies, gladiolas, dahlias and daylilies (but again, check the label), so you may wish to spray your summer-flowering bulbs at the same time.

CORN BORERS (*Ostinia nubilalis*)

If you live in an area where a great quantity of corn is grown, there is a chance that the corn borer will attack those plants in your garden with stalks similar to those of corn, the dahlias and gladioli. The nocturnal female moth that lays the eggs is yellow-brown in color—hard to see, difficult to control. The larvae are ¾ inch long and pink. If you find these on your summer-flowering bulbous plants, it is best to destroy the plants—at the minimum, the above-ground portions.

STALK BORERS (*Papaipema nebris*)

Late-flowering lilies, irises and dahlias can be attacked by this 1-inch-long, pale yellow caterpillar with a purplish band. Unfortunately, there are few nontoxic controls. Obviously hand-picking can help a great deal, but if there is a severe attack, chemical controls may be necessary.

JAPANESE BEETLES (*Popillia japonica*)

One of the advantages of living in the western part of the United States is that this beetle is not a problem. There are few regions east of the Mississippi that are free of this pest. The ½-inch-long grub overwinters in the soil and moves toward the surface in spring, devouring the roots of grasses as it travels. In early summer the adult beetle emerges and chomps away on buds, flowers and soft stems of such bulbous plants as cannas, dahlias and lilies. Bronze in color, and of a size that can be readily spotted (about ½ inch in length), hand picking and trapping are good controls. Chemical controls may be necessary for overwhelming infestations.

WIREWORMS (*Melanotus* species)

Few gardeners have seen these little wriggly pests, often golden in color, the larvae of beetles. You will find them infesting the roots of dahlias and *Narcissus*, boring into the bulbs. They can actually devour bulbs! Cultivating the soil to expose them to natural predators, such as birds, will provide some control. Using baits such as carrots to bring them to the surface can also be effective, but cultivation, which seems to discourage the laying of eggs, is no doubt the best natural control.

NEMATODES

There are many species of nematode, not all of them harmful. Some cause root decay of a good number of bulbs. Nematodes are not visible to the naked eye, but if you have deformed foliage and much browning of the bulbs, then chances are that nematodes are the problem. Removal of the infected plants is about all you can do, except for sterilization of the soil—not a feasible solution in the majority of gardens. Dig up and discard infected bulbs, and do not plant bulbs again in that location for several years.

WHITEFLY

While in colder areas these common pests are more frequently found in greenhouses, they can be a problem outdoors in warmer climes. The adults are what we see flying around like a cloud of dandruff. They lay pale-yellow eggs on the undersides of plants, and some summer-flowering bulbous plants such as dahlias are frequently attacked. It is the nymphs, which hatch from the eggs, that cause the problems. They wander around on the undersides of leaves, determine a spot where they wish to remain, and complete their life cycle. They pierce the leaf and feed on the sap. The plants are weakened by such attacks. Their leaves become lighter in color and eventually can become quite dry and withered if the attack is severe.

This pest can be quite easily controlled by spraying the plants, particularly the undersides of the leaves, with a fine but forceful spray of cold water. This not only disturbs the adults, but cleans off the nymphs that are doing the damage. As soon as you notice the adults flying around, check the undersides of the leaves of plants. If they get a good start on you, they can be difficult to control. As is so often the case, observation and prompt action are good ways to control these pests.

THRIPS

There are a number of thrips, and they feed on foliage. Their rasping mandibles pare away the surface of the leaves so the thrips can get to the juicy cells underneath. Thrips that attack onions, including the ornamental onions, and gladiolus are the ones most likely to be encountered. The damage is distinctive. Look for light-colored striations in the foliage; from a distance it looks almost as though the foliage is mottled. Eradication is not difficult. If there is a problem, dusting the bulbs with an insecticide prior to planting will take care of thrips, and this is especially important if thrips have caused problems in past seasons.

MITES

Few living things are exempt from attacks of mites of one sort or another. The problems that can be seen with bulbous plants are attacks by red-spider mites. Cyclamen are especially prone. Mite webs can be found on the undersides of the leaves, and if you hold a piece of white paper under the leaves and tap them, small, moving dots (the spiders) will fall onto the paper. Leaves become yellowish and mottled, and the vigor of the plants is greatly diminished.

These pests are particularly prevalent during the dry summer months. A very simple control is to spray the undersides of the foliage with cold water. (This is a good cultural procedure to follow with cyclamen anyway, as it makes growth sturdy, not lanky.) If plants are severely attacked, it is best to discard them.

SLUGS AND SNAILS

Is there a garden where slugs and snails are not known? I doubt it. Hygiene is one of the best ways to keep these pests under control. Baits can be used. Try setting out the shells of half grapefruits, placed upside down on the soil; they will attract these pests, and can be gathered in the morning and destroyed. Snails do like beer, but it was only just recently that I found a most effective bait for slugs. One of my Corgie dogs did not finish all of her kibbles, which remained out on the deck overnight in her feeding bowl. When I went out to retrieve the bowl the next morning, I found it had been invaded by slugs. I sent them to their deaths immediately. The next night I deliberately left out some kibbles, and again the following morning I found slugs eating them. Now, I hadn't noticed any damage from these pests to the plants on the deck, but obviously the garden is better off without them around. You might try this bait, but wear gloves because the mucus from slugs can be hard to remove from the fingers, as I found out.

GOPHERS, MOLES AND MICE

Just how many different ways to control these pests I have read, I do not know. The mixing of detergent, castor oil and water; the use of flares; the planting of so-called "gopher plants"; poisoned grain; miniature windmills that are supposed to emit sound that disturbs these persistent pests. I don't think any of these really works. Trapping seems to be the only certain way of getting rid of them.

Planting bulbs inside wire cages protects them, but the cages must be made of small-mesh wire (½-inch gauge is fine). This keeps the bulbs safe until they become large clumps, when the bulbs outside the cage will be consumed. Rodents are not easily discouraged, but you will prevail if you keep at it, using cages and traps, and planting each year!

VIRUSES

There is not a living thing that is not susceptible to attack by one or more viruses. There is an interesting relationship between tulips and virus diseases. Way back, when the breeding of tulips was in its infancy, bulbs that produced flowers with many different streaks of color were much sought after. High prices were paid for these bulbs, and when they rotted, gardeners would smear sound bulbs with rotted bulbs, in the hope that the magical power of streaking would be transferred from one bulb to another. The "magical" streaking was often transferred, we know now, by a virus. Today, 'Rembrandt' tulips exhibit this streaking. Streaking of the flowers, severe mottling and white streaks on the foliage and distortion of the buds are the results of virus attack. There is no cure, and affected plants have to be discarded.

Some viruses are less potent and not lethal, but smaller flowers and sickly-looking plants are to be expected when the plants are infected. Some vigorous cultivars exist infected for several years, the plants slowly declining in strength. The virus gets them in the end, but many put up a good struggle before they succumb. Such problems can be passed from one plant to another by sucking insects such as aphids. It is best to discard any plants showing symptoms of virus infection.

The decline of the lily 'Enchantement' was something of a mystery, and while at first clonal breakdown was thought to be the cause, it was found that a virus was present. In affected plants the petals were not as large, and the individual tepals not as wide. By removing only the growing tips of the plants, it was possible to obtain cells that were not contaminated by the virus. These cells were grown on in the laboratory and later planted out in fields far removed from other plantings of lilies. The flowers of these new plants—uninfected, with broad, large tepals, and clean stock, free of virus—were again available to the public.

Keeping weeds under control, keeping an eye open for attacks from sucking insects, and immediately destroying any unhealthy plants will enable the gardener to maintain the garden largely free of viruses. All gardeners should be aware of such problems, even if they will never face them.

DISEASES

As with pests, it is not likely that the home gardener will have to face severe disease attacks of many varieties, if any. Two diseases are nevertheless worth mentioning.

BOTRYTIS (*Botrytis* species)

During the cooler months, when humidity can be quite high, small yellow-to-brown spots may appear on the foliage of summer-flowering bulbs. The spots turn gray as the problem spreads. Bulbs that prefer some shade, such as the tuberous begonias and lilies, are particularly susceptible. Good air circulation and the avoidance of wetting the foliage when watering can reduce the problem. Fungicides can be used as controls, but good cultural procedures go a long way to keep botrytis from occurring in the first place.

MILDEW

The most common mildew to be found in gardens in the western parts of the United States is downy mildew. This fungus attacks the leaves, and leaves cottony-looking circles. Expect mildew when the temperature is low and humidity high. Powdery mildew is distributed by the wind, and there is seldom a summer when plants, particularly roses, are not attacked in the western United States.

The first sign of attack is small white spots on the undersides of leaves. These quickly expand, and soon the entire undersurface is covered with a weblike structure. Affected leaves curl, turn yellow and wither if the problem is not checked. Here too, plants that like the shade, where air circulation is often restricted, are often attacked. Fungicides can be used as a control, but more than one application may be needed.

The gardener should not be discouraged by the rather extensive listing of pests and diseases. The chance of bulbous plants being attacked by more than a very few of the problems is remote, and the possibility of severe damage to plants, to the point of having them destroyed, is most unlikely. Good cultural procedures, attention to first signs of a problem arising, with prompt remedial action being taken, will greatly reduce the likelihood of great harm being done to the plants. I doubt whether any one group of plants suffers less from pests and diseases than bulbous plants.

Clivia nobilis was very popular, and deserves to be again. It is a superb pot plant in cooler climates, a great garden plant in warmer climates.

SIX

Lessons Learned, Experience Gained

I must have had the pleasure of visiting several hundred gardens, and I hope to be able to visit many more. Many gardens make excellent use of bulbs. No garden can compare with the Keukenhof, near Lisse in the Netherlands. This is a paradise for all plant lovers, and a pure delight for those who love bulbs. Acres of spring-flowering bulbs are most attractively displayed. If you have a chance to visit this garden, seize it! April and May are the best months—there is always a grand display to be enjoyed. The latest introductions are on show, as well as hundreds of older favorites.

It is possible to get ideas for your own garden by visiting Keukenhof, even if thousands of bulbs is beyond the scope of your own garden. While open for but two or three months of the year, Keukenhof should be visited if you love bulbs; no, I will say it is a must for all who appreciate these marvels of nature.

I am willing to bet all our gardens can profit from having more bulbs in them, and gardeners should consider planting some in unexpected places. I once visited a small garden in Marin County, just north of San Francisco. The owner remarked what a pity it was that her rose garden was not of great interest in early spring. As her garden was not at all large, I had to admit that the rose beds, occupying as they did a fair proportion of the garden, did look bare. Still, I regard roses as one of the best values for summer color. I suggested that small clumps of *Muscari, Galanthus, Crocus* and the small species of *Narcissus* would provide variety of color, and as these plants flower early, they would not clash or compete with the roses. These bulbs were planted throughout the rose bed and have been a delight to the owner of the garden every year. The individual clumps were formed by planting 15 to 20 bulbs in each. They were scattered at irregular intervals, and this proved better suited to the location than planting them in rows or having clumps at regular spacings.

In designing another garden, I was faced with a rather difficult spot to plant. Facing north, it was damp and close to a door that led into the garden.

A flowering quince provided the area with color in the winter months, but I wanted an interesting groundcover underneath it. It occurred to me this area was well suited to lily of the valley, a choice that turned out to be a good one, as these plants have taken over the area. The fragrance in late April to early May is a pure delight. This small area is now an interesting one, and while not very colorful later in the year, this hardly matters, as by summer the garden is full of flowers.

I often wonder what builders have in mind when they leave a border just a few inches wide between a house and a path. What do they think will grow in such a confined area? Gravel seems to be one solution, but in such spots I am always willing to try one or more of the many small bulbs available. I filled one narrow border with a mixture of autumn- and spring-flowering crocus. They have persisted for a few years now, and though I will have to replant the area soon and change the soil, I think I'll use the same types of bulbs. They have provided color and interest, and appreciate the warmth during the cooler months, and the rather dry summer months that must make them feel at home.

Sometimes there doesn't seem to be a reason why certain bulbs just don't perform well. One of my clients loved tuberoses. I had tried them in many different locations in the garden, but was not able to establish a planting. When confirmation that yet another batch of these lovely, fragrant bulbs would arrive soon came last year in the mail, I wondered whether I would find a suitable spot for them. I mention this because, even with a lot of experience, one is not always successful. I had other plantings of the same species in gardens in the same neighborhood, but still covered my bets by planting some lycoris, which filled in nicely. Was I planting these tuberoses too early? They are, after all, native to Mexico. I waited until the nights got warmer before I planted the tuberoses, when the soil was

more pleasant for them. I hoped they appreciated my concern for their comfort, and they did! When I think back, I should have known the reason for my failure. Knowing the natural habitat of bulbs is one thing, but letting this knowledge dictate planting times is another. I still have much to learn about even my favorite plants. The answers, when they come, are always logical!

Frequently I am asked if one can run into problems when handling bulbs or working with them. While I have not experienced any problems, I know there are always exceptions. Allergies, for example, are a very personal thing. The home gardener probably will not be handling hundreds of hyacinth bulbs. I have handled a fair number, and one year obtained a particularly large number for a display garden and mentioned this to a friend whose family had worked with bulbs. "Make sure you wear gloves," he told me. He explained that when the skin of the bulbs is dry, crystals form on the surface, needle shaped and quite sharp. They pierce the skin, and cause it to itch. Scratching drives the crystals deeper into the skin, and they become more irritating. Washing removes the crystals, but as they are very fine, they can blow around and land on any exposed skin. If lots of hyacinth bulbs are to be handled, an ounce of precaution is worth a pound of cure. In Holland, those who handle thousands of hyacinths apply a sort of petroleum jelly product to the skin before setting to work. Should you itch when handling hyacinths, wash your hands and don't scratch.

Workers in the bulb fields of the Netherlands, and I am sure those working in the production fields in other countries, develop a problem known as "tulip finger." Remember, we are talking about handling tulips day in and day out. This particular problem seems to attack the fingers around the cuticles, causing swelling and irritation. People who take great care of their hands, keeping them soft and so forth, seem to suffer more from this than gardeners whose hands are a little tougher. Again, the wearing of gloves is suggested if you handle many bulbs and have very sensitive skin. I do not like wearing gloves when working with plants; indeed, even when pruning roses I don't wear them, and consequently my hands are not exactly soft.

If you have ever cut a good number of daffodils, you will no doubt remember that your hands become covered with the sap from the cut stems. Constant exposure to this can cause swelling of the fingers. Please note that I say "constant exposure." Cutting flowers for the home is not likely to cause any problem, but if you have sensitive skin you might wish to wear gloves and wash your hands as soon as the job is done.

Constant handling of one type of plant will often cause some irritation, as it would appear that most plants exude or contain some irritant. The most common case I suppose would be the *Primula,* and most gardeners know about the stinging nettle!

I wish I could say I have invariably come up with good ideas, but such is not the case. Upon reflection the majority, if not all, of my mistakes could easily have been avoided! Looking at a woodland garden I thought that drifts of daffodils would look perfect. They were planted, the rains came and the area was wet. The daffodils gave a very poor showing, and the owner of the garden mentioned that perhaps he should have told me that area was one of the wettest in the entire garden. Actually, as the supposed expert, I should have asked, should have known there was a reason why the groundcovers were a little thin, why there was moss on the soil. The signs were there, and I should have interpreted them. Correcting the problem by raising the level of the soil and putting in some drainage tiles was not a big job, but having been a student in Scotland, it hurt me to know I had needlessly wasted my client's money. No matter

Chemical Headaches

When herbicides have been worked into the soil, they can have a harmful effect on bulbs. Ascertain if such products had been used, and then make sure that sufficient time has passed to render them innocuous.

how much money there is for the garden, I see no need to waste even a penny.

Bulbs can contribute to the effect of so many garden situations. Adding of spring-flowering bulbs to shrub borders can bring interest to sections of the garden before they would otherwise be interesting. Adding lilies to borders of spring-flowering shrubs adds summer color. Planting a bulb of contrasting color, say, bluebells near drifts of daffodils, *Muscari* to edge a border of tulips, *Anemone blanda* drifting away from a brick path, can be far more effective, at modest cost, than you might think possible. Don't be complacent when you look at your garden. Never stop trying new plants, new combinations. The result will be new pleasure, new joy and new excitement each and every season.

I always question it when people tell me that this or that plant will not grow in a particular part of the country. When I first arrived in California, I had the opportunity to plant some *Eremurus.* "They will not grow here," I was told. Well, I tried, and I must admit they did not grow. I learned later that these plants need some frost during the winter months. As I had grown them quite well just a few miles away, I thought the climate would have been much the same, but no, the spot was a warmer one and didn't get frost. (Herbaceous peonies also need frost, so if you have peonies in your garden and they grow well, then you can grow *Eremurus.* Make certain the peonies are the herbaceous kind, as many tree peonies do not need any frost in order to flower.)

Achimenes 'Paul Arnold' is an excellent plant perfect for hanging baskets, as they flower for a long time. Refer to the plant portrait on page 62. (Photo courtesy of International Bloembollen Centrum.)

SEVEN

Alphabetical Listing of Genera

I have included in this section both well-known genera and some that deserve to be more widely cultivated. For each there is at least one reputable commercial source in the United States; a list of sources is given on page 249. Those genera that are not well-known are offered in catalogs by firms I have indicated as "suppliers of rare and unusual species," but I hasten to add this is no guarantee a given species will be available each and every year. Obviously if there is little or no demand for a cultivar, firms are not going to continue to offer it. I would encourage gardeners to try species presently unknown to them. The suppliers may well be encouraged to increase their listings of new and less-known species. Only in this way will the selection available increase. The rule of supply and demand applies to plants as much as to anything else.

Many plant names have interesting derivations, and where such are known, I mention them. As you know by now, I feel it important to be aware of where the plants occur in the wild, so I include their places of origin in the information that follows. Depth of planting, distance apart, time of flowering, height, and the special needs of individual species are also given. It is only when all such details are known that an optimal place for each plant can be selected. If there is a special place in the garden where I think the bulbs should be planted, I mention it. Finally, I include comments about many plants; these are my thoughts, and you may not always agree with me, but they may be of interest.

A note regarding flowering times:

The flowering times given for various genera in this listing are approximate, and would be typical of areas with some frost and moderate snowfall, but not areas where snowfall is heavy and where snow persists through much of the winter.

In very cold areas, the bulbs will flower later than the months indicated. In warmer areas, where little or no frost is experienced, flowering times will be a little earlier. Use the flowering times given as a guide.

Bulbs that are not able to withstand frost and are grown in warmer areas will flower at the times mentioned. Where such tender bulbs are grown in cold areas, being planted in late spring after danger of frost has passed, the bulbs will flower in the summer.

There will be differences in flowering times from garden to garden, and even within one garden. Bulbs in a protected location will flower before those in an exposed and therefore colder location. Such differences in flowering times are very difficult to determine with great accuracy, and specific flowering times can only be achieved when temperatures and amount of light received by the plants can be controlled, as, for example, when they are grown in a greenhouse.

ACHIMENES
Gesneriaceae

Some think the name is derived from *achaemenis*, a word used by Pliny and which means "a magic plant." Others believe it comes from *cheimaino*, which means "to suffer from cold." I am inclined to the latter, as these plants require warmth. They come to us from Central and South America. While there are some 30 species, the plants grown in our gardens are hybrids or selections.

Few plants are as well suited for light shade, and *Achimenes* are lovely when grown in hanging baskets or other containers where they can droop over the sides. I do not recommend them for planting in the garden border. They come into bloom some 12 to 14 weeks after the scaly tubers are started into growth. The showy flowers appear sometimes in clusters, sometimes solitary, and they are always pretty and among the finest

and longest-flowering of summer bulbs. The flowers have a very narrow tube, terminating in a five-petaled flower often more than 2 inches in diameter. Plants will reach some 15 inches in height and as wide. While *Achimenes* are often offered by color—blue, pink, red and white—some firms list them by such names as 'Fairy Pink', 'Rosy Red' or 'Violet Night'. A much older selection, 'Paul Arnold', was named after a specialist of *Achimenes* from Binghamton, New York, and another great selection is the 'Cascade' type, making use of the plant's cascading habit. These are great indoor plants, happy in a well-ventilated place, not confined in close quarters.

If you live in a warm (frost-free) climate, start the plants in February or March in a regular planting mix. Space the tubers 3 to 4 inches apart and cover them to a depth of 1 inch. If you are growing them in wire hanging baskets, plant on the sides of the baskets and on top, pushing the tubers through the sphagnum moss until well embedded in the soil. Keep them moist, and make certain they enjoy temperatures consistently in the upper 50s or low 60s. When they reach 4 to 6 inches in height, pinch out the growing tips to make the plants bushy (not essential, but preferred).

In cooler areas (where frost occurs), start individual tubers in peat pots filled with potting soil, and keep them in a warm, well-lighted area with night temperatures in the upper 50s. Start them 6 to 8 weeks before night temperatures outdoors are in the 50s. For most colder areas this would mean planting in early April. The plants will flower in July, so you might wish to try a patriotic combination of red, white and blue! If you wait until temperatures outdoors are warm, the plants will be late into flower, so it is best to start them indoors or in a greenhouse or frame. Plant pots in containers when roots appear through the sides of the peat pots. Planted almost touching, they then form bold and beautiful clumps. The plants should never be exposed to bright sunlight, but always filtered light. Fertilize with weekly waterings of a weak liquid fertilizer; *Achimenes* love to be fed.

Toward the end of summer, you will notice that flower production is reduced. When this occurs, stop feeding, and gradually reduce the amount of water given so that by the time the first frost arrives and kills the top growth, you will be able to retrieve the tubers, now much bigger of course. Store them in peat moss that is on the dry side, but not completely dry, in a location where the temperature will not drop below 50° F. The following spring you can start them into growth again.

When starting them into growth, you can break the tubers into pieces each about ½ inch long, so you can give some to friends who have admired the plants. You might be tempted to start them from seed, but given their hybrid background you will more than likely end up with a mixed bag of nondescript colors. Seed will take at least two seasons to reach flowering size, and is not worth the effort, in my opinion.

About the only pests that seem to bother these lovely summer-flowering plants are red spiders. Discourage them by giving the plants a spray with cold water every once in a while during the growing season. Make sure you use a very fine spray when doing this. This also discourages thrips, which have been known to bother them.

Botanical Name: Achimenes
Family: Gesneriaceae
Common Names: Magic flower, nut orchid, widow's tears
Flower Colors: Blue, pink, red, white
Flowering Time: Summer
Height: 15 inches
Spread: 15 inches
Native Habitat: Central and South America

Hardiness: Not hardy; will not stand frost or cold temperatures below 50° F
Depth of Planting: 1 inch
Distance Apart: 3 to 4 inches
Containers: Excellent for all types, good in hanging baskets
Light Requirements: Filtered light, needs shade
Soil Type: Regular planting mix
Special Conditions: Must have warmth at all times, not below 50° F
Comments: One of the loveliest summer bulbs for shade. Nip out growing tips of young plants to make bushy. Once well into growth, feed weekly with weak solution of organic liquid fertilizer.

ACIDANTHERA
Iridaceae

If you look at the anthers of the flowers, you will see they are pointed, and it is this characteristic that gives the plants their name, *akis* (point) *anthera* (anther). There are some nine species, but only one is cultivated and offered in catalogs. This is *Acidanthera bicolor* var. *murielae*, which is at home in Ethiopia. Other species are found in tropical and southern Africa. The common names, Ethiopian and Abyssinian gladiolus, are understandable, as the plant was first introduced as a gladiolus, and certain botanists regard this genus as rightly being included with *Gladiolus*. However, this genus has straight perianth tubes, whereas in *Gladiolus* they are bent. In addition, *Acidanthera* are fragrant, not a common feature of *Gladiolus* (though some species have a slight fragrance).

A number of catalogs list these plants with a note to the effect that they are imported from Ethiopia. It is hoped that they are not collected in the wild. Gardeners might inquire of the publishers of catalogs where such is noted, and let conscience be the guide regarding responsible purchasing.

Allied to *Gladiolus, Acidanthera bicolor* are pleasantly fragrant, unusual and striking, and deserve more recognition than they presently receive.

These plants are grown as gladiolus: same culture, same planting instructions. In areas where winters are mild and frost seldom experienced, this means they can be left in the ground. Where there is frost, they should be planted a few weeks before the last frost is expected, and lifted at the end of the season. The flowering time is late summer. The flowers each have a long tube, often 4 inches in length or even longer, and are up to 3 inches in diameter. The white petals have chocolate-colored blotches at their bases. Although the plants can reach a height of 36 inches, they are generally shorter. The flowers, up to eight or more per stem, are carried above the straplike foliage. They should be planted in good garden soil, in full sun. Plant 6 inches deep, spacing 6 to 8 inches apart. In warmer climates where they can be left in the ground; space them a little farther apart, as they will multiply. In good garden soil no fertilizer will be needed. In poorer soils, feed with a balanced fertilizer just after they emerge from the ground and again about six weeks later. Plant *Acidanthera* where their fragrance can be enjoyed. Superb cut flowers, they are also fine in containers, but do use a deep one so that you can place 6 inches of potting soil both over and under them. I would plant them closer in a container, about 4 inches apart.

They do have one drawback, and that is they take quite a while to come into flower, so do not delay planting. In fact, I suggest you err on the earlier side and, should a late frost be expected, protect them. Otherwise they may not finish flowering before the first frost; this is especially true in areas where frost is expected in September or early October. In such areas plant them near the protection of a south-facing wall; they will enjoy the additional warmth provided. Keep moist, but not wet. In fall, as the flowers fade and the foliage starts to turn brown, reduce the amount of water given. Lift and allow to dry, all the time protecting them from temperatures in the low 40° F range. Place the corms in dry sand to overwinter. They will produce many little cormels which can be grown on in nursery rows; they will reach flowering size in 2 seasons of growth. I find *Acidanthera* a delight, especially in areas with a long growing season, and for the cool greenhouse. If you have a sunny border near a window, these plants are ideal. I would hesitate to grow them among annuals—far better to give them their own space in a mixed border. They are practically trouble free. An arranger's delight, just a few spikes will perfume the home.

Botanical Name: Acidanthera
Family: Iridaceae

Common Names: Abyssinian gladiolus, Ethiopian gladiolus

Flower Colors: White with chocolate blotch

Flowering Time: Late summer

Height: to 36 inches

Spread: Upright growers

Native Habitat: Ethiopia, tropical and southern Africa

Hardiness: Will not withstand frost

Depth of Planting: 6 inches

Distance Apart: 6 to 8 inches, closer in containers

Containers: Good; must be deeper than 12 inches

Light Requirements: Full sun

Soil Type: Average garden soil

Special Conditions: Must be planted in good time to finish flowering before first frosts in cool areas. After season is over allow to become dry (do not water), lift and store dry and warm.

Comments: Well worth growing, especially if you like to have flowers in the home. Very modestly priced for the beauty they provide. Be patient, as they take a while to come into flower. Plant in bold clumps.

AGAPANTHUS
Amaryllidaceae

The name is derived from the Greek *agape* (love) and *anthos* (flower). Possibly the name was given because Xhosa brides would wear pieces of the root to ensure fertility and easy childbirth. The plants are native to southern Africa, where the Xhosa live. One of the common names is lily of the Nile, even though *Agapanthus* grow far from the Nile (the source of the Nile was unknown when the plants were first grown in Europe). It was listed in a catalog of plants at Leyden Botanic Gardens in 1687. No doubt it was introduced into culture in the Netherlands because of the association the Dutch East India Company held with southern Africa. Another common

Lovely plants, *Agapanthus walshii* are often labeled 'Albus'. They are trouble free, easy to grow and great in containers.

name is Harriet's flower, named after Harriet Meyer, an American horsewoman who rode extensively in South Africa.

The flowers have long been admired in their native land. The roots were used extensively in tribal medicine, providing treatment for a number of disorders. (I often wonder why such uses are not tested and compared with manufactured drugs.) I have seen both the lovely blue and white flowers growing wild. They make a spectacular show of color at the Cape of Good Hope, the species here being *Agapanthus africanus*. *A. praecox* ssp. *orientalis* is most commonly listed and sold as *A. africanus;* the white form is regarded as a separate species, *A. walshii*, but is commonly sold as *A. africanus* 'Albus'. One good thing about these name changes is that it does not change the beauty of the flowers.

There are both evergreen and deciduous species, the latter being a little hardier, surviving to 26° F and even lower if given the protection of a south-facing wall and mulch. *A. inapertus*, which is deciduous, comes from the Transvaal in South Africa. In the wild this species is subject to temperatures that fall below freezing, and at times, it may even be covered with snow. This is a lovely plant, as indeed are all the *Agapanthus*, with pendulous, deep blue flowers. This is the species I would try in a colder climate, as I think it would grow well in areas where the temperature drops to 25° F, and perhaps even lower with some protection. I have seen it growing in Brittany in France, and it grows well there without protection.

Agapanthus are versatile. They grow well in containers and in ordinary soil in sunny borders. They will increase in size quite quickly and should be left undisturbed for years. They require little or no moisture other than what nature supplies. The rather thick, wide leaves are fleshy, and the rootstock looks like an elongated leek. Plant so the green portion of the stem is above ground level, the white part not completely buried. Space 18 to 24 inches apart, a little closer in containers. In the border, one feeding with granular fertilizer is enough, applied early in spring. In containers, feed during the growing season with organic liquid fertilizer about once a month. In colder areas protect from frosts, except as noted above. There are smaller-growing plants available, among them *A. praecox* 'Peter Pan' and *A. praceox* 'Rancho Dwarf', reaching only 24 inches in height. This makes them more manageable than the species, as both *A. inapertus* and *A. praecox* will have foliage up to 36 inches in length and flowers on stems reaching 48 inches or more in height if in a fertile soil or when fertilized. Such height, however, is not, in my opinion, a good thing, as the plants look too lush and lose their attractiveness, which I feel is at its best when the foliage is shorter and the flowers carried well above it.

Certain nurseries offer plants with yellow stripes in the leaves or otherwise variegated, and some forms with double flowers. Do not be surprised if you see forms offered with dark blue or light blue flowers; there is considerable variation, especially when raised from seed, which is a slow process and not recommended for the home gardener. It's far better to lift and divide established clumps if additional plants are desired.

Botanical Name: *Agapanthus*
Family: Amaryllidaceae
Common Names: Lily of the Nile, Harriet's flower
Flower Colors: Blue, white, often with variegated foliage
Flowering Time: Summer, sometimes in late spring and into fall
Height: Up to 48 inches; dwarf forms 18 to 24 inches
Spread: Will form large clumps in time
Native Habitat: South Africa
Hardiness: Do not expose to prolonged periods of low temperatures. Protect if temperature drops below 25° F by bringing indoors if in containers, heavy mulch if in borders.
Depth of Planting: Plant so white part of rootstock is not completely buried
Distance Apart: Tall types, 18 to 24 inches; low types, 12 to 18 inches
Containers: Yes
Light Requirements: Full sun
Soil Type: Average garden soil; potting soil if grown in containers
Special Conditions: Fertilize occasionally. After season is over: indoors, keep barely moist but in good light; outdoors, protect from slugs and snails.
Comments: When well grown and in flower, these lovely plants provide good color in borders and containers. Very easy to grow, but watch the hardiness. Great cut flowers and also interesting when flowers are past, thus good for dried arrangements. If growing well, do not disturb.

Allium moly is a grand species, not invasive, but showy and deserving a place in all gardens. The foliage makes a splendid foil for the flowers. (Photo courtesy of International Bloembollen Centrum.)

ALLIUM
Liliaceae

Allium is ancient Latin for garlic. Onions belong in this genus together with leeks, shallots, spring onions and chives, which tend to be confined to the kitchen or vegetable garden. Any gardener who has seen onions in flower knows the ornamental value of the genus. While the bulbs and foliage are largely used in cooking, it should be remembered that the flowers are also edible (when unsprayed), and the small flowers of chives dropped onto soup add a great deal of interest. *Allium schoenoprasum*, chives, is an attractive border plant, pretty when lining a path or used in the front of a mixed border; as few of the leaves are used at a time in cooking, this is a very good use of the plants.

Through the ages the medicinal value of the various onions has been extolled. People are again turning to plants and using them medicinally, and the onion is among the leaders. Quite apart from their edible virtues, the flowers of alli-

ums are very attractive. There are more than 350 species, all from the northern hemisphere. A few of the species have escaped from gardens in the southern hemisphere and become naturalized. This is not surprising, as they are easy to grow and quite hardy. With the exception of just a few species, they prefer fertile soil and like the sun. Many species will naturalize and, if not checked, colonize a large area.

Gardeners are sometimes hesitant to plant alliums, being a little apprehensive about the typical onion smell. This shouldn't be of concern as the species grown for their ornamental flowers give off an odor only when crushed or bruised;

When in flower, *Allium giganteum* are conversation pieces. Let the spent flowerheads stay on the plants, as they are also quite attractive. (Photo courtesy of International Bloembollen Centrum.)

even then, the odor is often very mild. One species, *Allium neapolitanum,* is in fact grown for its pleasantly fragrant flowers. Sadly, this species is not the hardiest and can withstand temperatures to 20° F, but not lower without protection of a mulch, and the added warmth of a south-facing wall. Most other species (but not all) withstand temperatures down to −20° F and even lower with mulching. But *A. neapolitanum* has another good point: it grows well in containers, so even those living in cold areas can enjoy this lovely species. It can also be forced into flower earlier than spring, its normal flowering time.

Allium neapolitanum grandiflorum, which has larger flowers than *A. neapolitanum,* is a frequent catalog listing; the form 'Cowanii' is considered the best, often incorrectly listed as a separate species. All the species listed below are well worth growing in the garden. Select the species to suit a particular spot in your garden.

Travel in southern England in late April or May and you will see in the hedgerows and in sylvan glades lots of white flowers. Look a little closer and you will find they sit atop triangular stems about 12 to 18 inches in height. This is *A. triquetrum,* an invasive plant (proving, I suppose, that one can have too much of a good thing). It is pretty and, if you can keep it confined, well worth growing. Unlike most other species, it needs some shade and good moisture, especially in very early spring. Close inspection reveals the flowers are striped with green.

Anybody who has seen *A. giganteum* will remember it. The flowerheads are carried on 48-inch stems and are often more than 6 inches in diameter. Eye-catching, to say the least, the lilac-blue blooms flower in midsummer and are prettiest contrasting with summer annuals. Even after flowering, these giants are attractive and great for use in dried arrangements. I find, however, that while they are truly spectacular, the foliage is often untidy and unattractive—another good

reason to plant with annuals, so the foliage is partially hidden.

Allium moly, a lovely plant, will naturalize slowly and should be located so the brilliant yellow flowers can be seen from many angles. The blue-green foliage is attractive, and though the flowering time is midsummer, when there is much else in flower, it will stand out and give a good account of itself. A species with attractive foliage is *A. karataviense,* generally with two leaves, up to 5 inches wide and with a distinctly bluish hue, that stay low to the ground. The large, globular, pinkish white flower heads are carried 6 inches above the ground, making this a compact plant. (It flowers in late spring and early summer.) Both of these species are perfect at the edge of a path and at the front of the border.

One expects to find blue and white alliums, and I have mentioned the yellow flowers of *A. moly,* but I would be remiss if I did not mention *A. oreophilum,* often listed as *A. ostrowskianum.* This is a dwarf species only 4 to 6 inches in height, with attractive carmine-pink flowers. If you ever see these plants with *A. moly,* you are in for a pleasant surprise; the colors combine beautifully, and who imagines carmine and yellow when thinking of onion flowers? Try this combination—it will delight you.

While the tall spikes of *A. giganteum* are eye-stoppers, I think you would be delighted with the 24-inch stems of *A. caeruleum* (sometimes listed as *A. azureum*) and *A. christophii* (sometimes listed as *A. albopilosum*). Both flower in early to midsummer, *A. caeruleum* with the brightest blue flowers in dense heads, and with so many, the blooming period seems to last and last. *A. christophii* has up to 100 little starlike flowers carried in a perfect ball. Both excellent plants deserve a place in the garden, but they must have full sun and well-drained soil.

There is a great difference in size between

the bulb of an onion and a shallot, something we can all appreciate. There is a great difference in size among the bulbs of ornamental onions as well. The taller the plant, the larger the bulb, it seems, with the bulbs of *A. giganteum* being very large, often 4 or more inches in diameter. When planting, do not set the bulbs too deeply into the soil; they appreciate having their tops warmed by the sun. Distance apart varies according to their height, but even the tallest should not be planted more than 10 to 12 inches apart. Be sparing with fertilizer, as they don't require much feeding, almost none if the soil is fairly good. Alliums grown in pots are the exception, and they appreciate a weekly weak feeding of a liquid organic fertilizer while making leaf growth. Do not overfeed, or bulbs will not be firm and hard, which they should be in order to overwinter well and produce good flowers. The bulbs are best planted in fall, but spring planting is acceptable, and bulbs should be left in the ground if possible. Those used in summer bedding should be lifted after the foliage has died down, in late summer; try to give the bulbs a dry period prior to lifting. Some natural increase from bulblets is common, and the bulblets can be grown on for a season or two, by which time they will reach flowering size and can be planted out in the garden.

Allium aflatunense: Reaching up to 36 inches in height, it blooms in late spring or very early summer, producing purple flowers with a hint of lilac in a dense, rounded head 3 to 4 inches in diameter. A great cut flower, it is very showy in the border. The selection 'Purple Sensation', often listed, is a little shorter and violet-purple in color. The foliage is quite wide (4 inches is not unusual) and as much as 24 inches long.

A. atropurpureum: The color is difficult to describe—maroon-purple, deep wine-red or just purple—but no matter, you will love the small

spheres just over 2 inches across, carried on very strong stems 20 inches high, sometimes taller when well established. With many flowers in each head, these plants are of interest for a long time, flowering in early summer. Some catalogs list *A. nigrum* var. *atropurpureum*, and it would appear this is the same species.

A. caeruleum (syn. *A. azureum*): As one would expect from a plant native to Siberia, this is a hardy species and easy to grow. In a few seasons you will have large clumps, as it multiplies easily. It boasts dense flower heads of bright blue, stands 24 inches tall, and flowers in midsummer.

A. cernuum: This species is at home in the Allegheny Mountains and other parts of the eastern United States. The light pink flowers are pendulous, on stems from 8 to 18 inches tall. It flowers in early summer. The dwarf selection 'Early Dwarf' is an excellent plant for rock gardens, under 12 inches tall with deep lavender flowers. The common name is nodding onion.

A. christophii (syn. *A. albopilosum*): The common name is star of Persia, and this plant certainly is a star, with the largest flower heads of the genus, often more than 12 inches in diameter. Flowering in early summer, the pale, bluish purple flowers have a metallic sheen and glisten in the sun. A good cut flower; when dried the flower heads last several years. Height varies from 18 to 24 inches, sometimes taller when established. Often still listed under the former name *A. albopilosum* in catalogs, this is one of the most spectacular species.

A. flavum: There are several variants, and while the species seldom grows taller than 12 inches, some of the forms available are often only half that height or even shorter. Lemon yellow, it flowers in midsummer.

A. giganteum: This is the tallest species, with purple-violet flowers (or are they lilac-blue? The color does vary a little). 48 inches tall, sometimes even taller, it flowers in midsummer. This makes a good cut flower, but it seems a shame to take such striking stems from the garden; it might be better to grow some in an area specifically for cutting. The foliage is attractive when young, but by flowering time often becomes ragged, so grow with plants that will hide the leaves. The flower heads are handsome in dried arrangements. This is a great plant to grow if you have children, as they are fascinated by the height these plants reach.

A. karataviense: Worth growing for the foliage alone, this species produces two glaucous blue leaves up to 5 inches wide and 9 inches long. White with a hint of pink, the flowers reach up to 6 inches in height in early summer.

A. macleanii: For many years this species was known as *A. elatum*, and it is still sometimes listed under this name. Similar to *A. giganteum* but not as tall, the foliage is more attractive, a clean, shiny green. Lilac-purple flowers are produced in late spring.

A. moly: Perhaps the most popular species and deservedly so, *A. moly*'s brilliant yellow flowers are carried on 12-inch stems above attractive, bluish, wide leaves that remain close to the ground. Early- to midsummer flowering, this plant naturalizes with comparative ease, so place it where it can do so. A great plant for any garden.

A. neapolitanum: The white flowers have a pleasant fragrance. The individual flowers will reach 1 inch in diameter, and there will be many in a flower head, giving the overall impression that the plant remains in flower for a long period of time. The common name, Naples garlic, denotes its origin; the garlic smell is missing unless the leaves are crushed. Flowers appear in late spring, 24 inches in height. *A. cowanii*, a species sometimes listed in catalogs, appears to be a form of Naples garlic with perhaps larger flowers. Another selection listed is 'Grandiflorum', with reportedly larger flowers.

A. oreophilum (syn. *A. ostrowskianum*): A dwarf plant, well suited to the rock garden, it is only 4 to 6 inches in height with carmine-pink flowers that appear in midsummer. Pleasantly fragrant, perhaps the finest of the dwarf alliums.

A. rosenbachianum: The dark violet flowers with white stamens appear on 24-inch stalks in early summer. This species is vigorous. A white form, 'Album', is sometimes available, and both are well worth growing.

A. roseum: The flowerheads, 3 or more inches in diameter, are bright pink and produced in early summer. The height is quite variable, from 10 inches to more than 24. Quite often you will find a listing for 'Grandiflorum', which has larger flowers and a slightly larger flower head.

A. schubertii: This species, occasionally listed, has very large flower heads of rosy pink. It reaches 18 to 24 inches in height and flowers in summer. This is not a hardy species, but it can be grown in containers, and then the many-flowered umbels can be appreciated indoors.

A. sphaerocephalon: This easy-to-grow species produces purple-crimson flowers atop stems that reach up to 36 inches in height. An attractive species and great garden plant, it has the common names of drumsticks and roundheaded leek. It is very popular with bees.

A. triquetrum: A native of much of Europe, it grows in damp, shady places and is quite invasive. It does not have as many flowers in the umbels as most species, often only 7 to 20 of pure white with greenish stripes. The individual flower stalks are quite long, and the flower heads are not really rounded, but often one-sided. An interesting point about this plant is that the seeds have a coating attractive to ants. The ants carry the seeds around and help distribute them, one of the reasons this plant can become invasive. If you have the space and can confine the planting, it is well worth growing.

A. unifolium: Native to northern California and southern Oregon, this species reaches 15 inches in height and flowers in late spring to early summer with blossoms that are pink tinged with white. It is unusual in that the young bulbs are produced on short rhizomes. Not fully hardy, this species must have winter protection where temperatures fall below 20°F.

Botanical Name: Allium
Family: Liliaceae
Common Names: Various: giant onion, Naples garlic, ornamental onion
Flower Colors: Shades of blue and violet, yellow, pink and white
Flowering Time: Varies by species: most spring and early to midsummer
Height: Can grow 4 feet or taller, but most are shorter
Spread: Many species can form large clumps in a short time, while other, invasive ones require containment
Native Habitat: Northern hemisphere; many from Europe, some from North America

Hardiness: Quite hardy, with the exception of a few species
Depth of Planting: Close to the surface, so they can ripen
Distance Apart: Varies by species: tall-growing types to 12 inches, dwarf species 4 to 6 inches
Containers: A neapolitanum makes a good potted plant.
Light Requirements: Most prefer full sun, although certain species prefer shade; see individual species above
Soil Type: Average garden soil; regular potting soil should be used if growing in container
Special Conditions: With few exceptions, alliums require well-drained soil. Unless grown in poor soil, they require little fertilizer, but do feed if grown in pots. Moisture needed during the growing season, but do not overwater.
Comments: There are many wonderful species and at least one will be right for your garden. Alliums are very interesting plants when in flower. If you have a large garden and need a good groundcover, consider A. triquetrum, especially if you have plenty of room for it to spread and yet can confine it to the desired area. While many gardeners oooh and ah over the large flower heads of certain species, the smaller and daintier types are more garden worthy and will give greater pleasure to the discerning gardener. Alliums are good cut flowers, and after the flowers fade, many are excellent for dried arrangements. While certain species grow well in containers, remember that the length of time these plants are in flower is measured in weeks, not months, and so they are less than ideal if the number of containers is limited.

The Peruvian lilies are superb cut flowers and great garden plants, best left undisturbed when growing well. Here is *Alstroemeria* 'Ligtu Hybrid'.

ALSTROEMERIA
Liliaceae

This wonderful genus has become popular in recent years, providing cut flowers of outstanding quality, and it has rightfully received a great deal of attention from hybridizers. Alstroemeria were especially popular garden plants in the twenties and thirties, fell a little out of favor, came back somewhat in the fifties and sixties, and now are again enjoying popularity with new hybrids. They play a strong role in the commercial production of cut flowers, often undertaken in greenhouses, especially in Europe.

Linnaeus named the genus in honor of his friend Baron Clas Alstroemer (1736–1794), a Swedish botanist. While the common name Peruvian lily is used, this genus is perhaps even better known as alstroemeria. Justice is being served, perhaps, as few of the same 50 species are native to Peru; most are native to Chile and Brazil.

You will read about 'Ligtu Hybrids' in catalogs and indeed in many books, which are, with

Alstroemeria aurantiaca, the hardiest species. *A. ligtu*, reintroduced into culture by Harold Comber, is itself a very variable species and without a doubt selections offered are without any hybrid blood. I have discussed this matter with several people, the most knowledgeable being Judith McRae, of Oregon. After much research Judith finds that even using the most modern techniques, including embryo culture, it is not possible to cross any larger-flowered species with *A. ligtu* or *A. aurantiaca* to make plants hardier and produce fertile plants. Crosses between *A. pelegrina* and *A. violacea* have resulted in the many large-flowered cultivars grown in greenhouses, and are responsible for the often startling colors and patterns in the flowers. These plants are not hardy, and are exceedingly difficult to transplant; any bruising of the roots causes them to rot. Though not as hardy, they will withstand much warmer temperatures, and this makes the plants well suited to greenhouse growing. (On the other hand, if you grow the relatively hardy *A. ligtu* in a greenhouse at temperatures above 70°F, flower production is reduced and dormancy is encouraged; the plants become progressively shorter, until they stop growing and are dormant.)

Another interesting fact Judith discovered is that the roots of *A. ligtu* will often grow down 36 inches and there form their tubers. To say the least, this is quite a depth. Because of that depth, the plants are able to withstand cold temperatures. Any books that tell you to plant *A. ligtu* 2 to 3 inches deep might be regarded with suspicion, but it must be remembered that these plants produce sinker roots and will find their ideal depth themselves. Much work needs to be done to unravel the complex genetic composition of these great plants. Fortunately, we do not have to do this in order to appreciate their charm and great garden value.

These plants need good drainage and sun. Though the fleshy roots can withstand periods of drought, they like moisture during their growing season; when established they can survive with a minimum of attention. In the warmest of climates—where temperatures are consistently above 85°F for days or weeks at a time—some shade is appreciated during the heat of the day, especially when the air is very dry. They will thrive in average garden soil. The only times they need fertilizer are during the first season after planting, when you should feed as soon as growth appears above ground, and again in midsummer. Do not over-feed. Give dressings of a well-balanced fertilizer in the 10–10–10 range. Container-grown plants (and they will perform well in containers more than 18 inches deep, in regular potting soil) appreciate occasional feedings of a liquid organic food.

Plant 8 inches deep, spacing 12 inches apart, and leave undisturbed for years. Lift and divide only when beds become overcrowded or when you wish to increase your stock by dividing the crowns. In most climates this is best done in early fall, as soon as the foliage starts to die back. Although it can be done in spring, fall is preferred, except in the colder areas (where frost persists during the day), where fall-planted tubers are more likely to be harmed by cold temperatures.

Plants start to flower in midsummer. Some support may be needed, as many plants become quite tall, and are prone to being knocked over by wind. Mulching is suggested to give added protection against the cold and to conserve moisture. When well established, these plants will smother weeds. *A. aurantiaca* and *A. ligtu* are hardy to 0°F, but with a good mulch and when established, will withstand even colder temperatures. In areas where temperatures are lower during winter months, grow in containers and move into protected quarters. About the only problem gardeners may face is disappointment if they try to grow greenhouse selections outdoors.

These are just not well suited for garden growing; they lack vigor, and attacks by snails and slugs finish them off. Thrips may bother the foliage in dry climates, but frequent spraying with fine, forceful jets of cold water will keep them under control.

Alstroemeria aurantiaca: The flower heads reach heights of 36 inches and more. They are freely produced, each with many flowers. The outer petals are tinged red with green tips; the pointed inner petals are orange streaked with red. Selections offered in catalogs include 'Orange King' and 'Lutea', which is yellow. All selections of *A. aurantiaca* are great garden plants.

A. ligtu: This species doesn't have quite as many flowers in each flower head as *A. aurantiaca*, but has a far greater color range. The flowers vary from pale lilac to reddish to white, and the inner petals most commonly have some yellow, variously striped with purplish tones, but the overall appearance of the flowers will be pink, salmon, orange and so on, all attractively marked and shaded. Known as St. Martin's flower, it is generally 36 to 48 inches tall but, as with color, the height can be quite variable. Listings in catalogs of 'Ligtu Hybrids' contain a grand mix of colors and are selections from the species; no hybrid blood is actually involved, just crossings within the species itself. The plants are summer-flowering, remaining in flower for a long period of time.

A. pulchella: Sometimes called the parrot alstroemeria, these flowers are more funnel-shaped and don't open as wide as other species. The exterior of the flower is a dull red, the interior variously patterned with yellow-green. Generally 24 to 36 inches tall, and later-flowering than others, this species comes into flower in midsummer, often lasting well into fall.

Cultivars: A number of very attractive selections are offered in catalogs: 'Dr. Slater's Hybrids'; 'Butterfly hybrids', which are mixed colors some with white picotee edges, not quite as tall growing; 'Meyer Hybrids', 'Ashia Strain', mainly in tones of lavender-violet; 'Pacific Strain', solid colors with yellow or white throats; 'Pink Pearl', pink with lightly striped white centers. I would strongly suggest that gardeners stick to 'Ligtu Hybrids' or *A. aurantiaca* selections for trouble-free plants, and try the other offerings, which are often quite expensive, only when the temptation is too great. Remember Oscar Wilde's advice, that the only way to deal with temptation is to yield to it.

Botanical name: Alstroemeria
Family: Liliaceae
Common Names: Peruvian lily, St. Martin's flower (*A. ligtu*)
Flower Colors: Many: yellows, violets, pinks, rose, reddish tones, some with green shadings (all brightly colored), whites
Flowering Time: Summer, some into early fall
Height: Most garden-worthy plants are 36 inches tall
Spread: Will form large clumps in 2 to 3 seasons, a comparatively short time
Native Habitat: Brazil, Chile, Peru
Hardiness: Quite hardy but good mulch protection if temperatures drop to around 0°F; see notes above, as not all species are hardy
Depth of Planting: 8 inches or deeper
Distance Apart: 12 to 18 inches
Containers: Pots must be deep, staking may be necessary
Light Requirements: Full sun, some shade in hottest areas
Soil Type: Average garden soil. In containers use well-draining potting soil.
Special Conditions: Provide good drainage. Little or no fertilizer is needed. Provide moisture dur-

ing the growing season but do not overwater. If plants are growing well, leave them alone!
Comments: Remember that there are lovely colors available in the *A. ligtu* and *A. aurantiaca* species. Avoid planting florists' offerings, as you might be disappointed. Great garden plants and superb cut flowers. Ideal to plant on a slope where they control erosion when well established, especially the 'Ligtu' types, which send down very deep roots and form their tubers at good depths. Always handle the roots with care. As these plants should remain for long periods without disturbance, select the area where you plant them with care. As they are good garden plants and cut flowers, and free from pests and diseases, alstroemerias should be considered even for small gardens.

AMARYLLIS
Amaryllidaceae

Amaryllis is a Greek feminine proper name. It is a monotypic genus, there being but one species, *A. belladonna.* The specific name means beautiful lady, and has nothing to do with the belladonna used in medicine, a compound derived from the nightshade. The common name for these plants is naked ladies, and I offer no comment about this.

Unfortunately, there is confusion about this name. Amaryllis is the common name given to the various selections of *Hippeastrum,* often seen in flower at Christmastime. These plants have very attractive and large flowers too. The true *Amaryllis,* however, has trumpet-shaped flowers, not as wide at the opening nor as flat, for want of a better word, as the true *Hippeastrum.* Some catalogs list *Amaryllis papilio.* This is an incorrect name. If you look closely, you will see the plant is a *Hippeastrum.* The flowers are not trumpet-shaped and foliage (evergreen) appears with the flowers. I question the name of this plant, and feel it is a hybrid. Confusion was compounded by the movement of some 15 species of *Amaryllis* to the genus *Hippeastrum* and the genera *Cybistetes, Lycoris* and *Nerine,* all of which have similarly shaped flowers. This left but one species in *Amaryllis,* so perhaps it is a "naked" species in another way, too.

If you visit California in late summer you might be quite startled to see towering spikes of lovely pink flowers with reddish-pink stalks growing to a height of 36 inches in parched soil and without leaves. These are the true *A. belladonna,* as much at home in California as they are in their native land, South Africa. The flowers are sweetly scented, and there is some variation of color, some almost white, others very deep pink. After the flowers have faded, the straplike leaves emerge and persist during winter into spring, when the bulbs become dormant until late summer and the cycle starts over again. The bulbs become very large and will form large colonies. They should be left undisturbed unless you wish to propagate them; if you lift, divide and replant, you might wait a few years before you again enjoy the lovely flowers.

The bulbs must be allowed to become absolutely dry during summer, and I mean dry! The eighties and early nineties, when California had years of drought, saw the best flower production from these bulbs. I have had no luck with them in my garden in San Francisco for two reasons: We do not have high summer temperatures for long periods of time, and drips from trees, even though caused by fog condensation and not rain, were enough to stop the ripening of the bulbs essential for bud formation. To grow these flowers, protect them from even the slightest moisture by placing a glass table 10 to 12 inches over the bulbs. (I should heed this advice myself!)

Plant in May or early June with the neck of the bulb at, or slightly above, soil level. The soil must be well drained, and the site selected

In late summer the flower spikes of *Amaryllis belladonna* thrust their way through parched soil and put on a fantastic display. A lovely plant for dry warm areas. (Photo courtesy of International Bloembollen Centrum.)

in full sun. In areas where there is some frost but temperatures remain above 10°F, plant a little deeper and protect with several inches of fine mulch, so the top of the bulb is buried some 5 to 6 inches; couple this with the protection of a south-facing wall, and you should be able to grow these lovely plants. When the leaves are green and growing, give the plants moisture if rain doesn't provide all they require. Taking the time to amend the soil with sharp sand from the builder's yard is a good thing to do, and a little balanced fertilizer given when the leaves emerge (rain or applied moisture can wash it down to the roots) will keep these plants happy. Warm, moist winters and hot, dry summers exactly describes the climate *Amaryllis* require.

If you find some seed of these plants, sow in a sandy soil mixture in spring. The seed germinates without much trouble, but keep the natural cycle of these plants in mind; as soon as seedlings show signs of dying back, stop watering and let them follow their cycle of growth. It will take 3 to 5 seasons for bulbs to reach flowering size.

These lovely plants can be grown indoors in colder climates. Use a potting soil, and add a good measure of sharp sand. Follow the watering schedule outlined above, giving water only when the flower spike has started into growth. When brought indoors, give as much light as possible, and keep temperatures around 45°F (or higher) at night. The reward for all this trouble? If you are lucky, as many as 12 grand trumpets per stalk, with a delightful fragrance that will make you forget the little extra work these bulbs may require. We may see commercial production of these plants for cut flowers; they last quite a long time in water.

A. *belladonna* offers fragrant pink trumpet flowers in late summer. The leaves, produced after the flowers, may reach 18 inches long and up to 2 inches wide. Sometimes one sees A. *belladonna* 'Spectabilis' listed. This has rose-colored flowers that are whiter on the inside. A selection called 'Lady Godiva' is described as "blushing pink," which fits perfectly with the common name, naked lady. (This is a plant I have not seen, but some PR company did their homework!)

Botanical Name: Amaryllis
Family: Amaryllidaceae
Common Names: Naked ladies, belladonna
Flower Colors: Pink shades varying from light to dark
Flowering Time: Late summer
Height: Up to 36 inches
Spread: If left undisturbed for years, will form good-sized clumps
Native Habitat: South Africa
Hardiness: Give protection where temperatures drop to 10°F, and if possible, plant near a south-facing wall.
Depth of Planting: In frost-free (or nearly so) areas, the top of the bulb should be just level with the surface of the soil; where some frost is experienced, plant 3 inches deep and cover with mulch for added protection.

Distance Apart: 6 to 10 inches
Containers: Use a porous soil mix
Light Requirements: Full sun, perhaps a hint of light shade where extreme heat is experienced
Soil Type: Average garden soil with excellent drainage. Add sharp sand if needed to improve drainage.
Special Conditions: Where summer moisture will be experienced, protect with a sheet of glass placed 10 to 12 inches above the bulb, so air can circulate freely.
Comments: Worth growing in all gardens in warm areas where the necessary dry conditions can be provided without much effort. Lovely fragrance, a fun bulb to grow and a great cut flower.

Anemone
Ranunculaceae

The genus name is derived from the Greek word for wind, *anemos*, but if you are romantically in-

All cultivars of *Anemone blanda* are great for the garden ('Bridesmaid' is pictured here). Make sure you plant enough to put on a show, as they look better crowded.

clined you might agree with certain authorities who maintain the name is derived from the Syrian *nama'an,* the cry for the dead Adonis, whose spilt blood sprang up from the earth in the scarlet form of these plants. The common name is wind flower, but I am at a loss as to why; although these plants are very hardy and can withstand winds, they grow better without them.

Not all members of the genus are bulbous; many of the more than 50 species are perennials, and deserving of space in the borders, but not in this book. The tuberous species are lovely plants, and among their virtues is a relatively low cost. *Anemone coronaria,* its forms and selections, are superb cut flowers. If I had to name a very "clean" color, I would immediately think of the blue found in certain selections, and the red. The petals shine, and while almost delicate in appearance, they are in fact tough, long-lasting flowers. These plants are easy to grow. While growers will tell you the species, with the exception of *A. nemorosa,* prefer soil on the alkaline side, and suggest adding a little lime at planting time, I have found that almost any good garden soil will suit these plants, but they appreciate sun and good drainage. Most garden soils are not truly acid, but if your soil is high in organic matter, a dressing of lime would not be amiss, as a high proportion of organic matter generally indicates the soil will tend to be acid, not neutral, and certainly not alkaline.

A. nemorosa, a woodland plant, does like acid soil. This dwarf plant inhabits woodland areas in much of Europe. I love to see it along the roadsides; for some reason it reminds me of an aunt of mine, frail-looking yet tough, not demanding, but making certain it has the right location. While the flowers are not powerful in appearance, they survive the vagaries of spring in Europe, sun one day, rain or even snow the next, and are always dependable and charming.

Not all bulbs have pleasant-looking foliage,

but anemones do. Some describe it as "fernlike," but I think *A. coronaria* and derivatives of this species have foliage like parsley—curly and pleasantly green. Even before flowers appear, anemone foliage makes an attractive contrast when planted with primulas, for example. We think of anemones as spring flowers, and indeed this is their natural flowering time, but you can plant in spring for summer flowering in cold areas (where hard frost occurs and temperatures seldom, if ever, climb above 40°F during the winter months), and in summer for late summer and fall flowering. The tuberous rootstocks are easily kept in paper bags in a dry, well-ventilated location. Some people like to soak the tubers for 24 hours before planting them. I think this is advantageous for late spring and summer plantings, but there's not much point if you are putting them into soil that is moist in the first place, as it often is early in spring.

There are single and double forms of *A. coronaria.* Both are lovely, but I prefer the appealing simplicity of the singles. Grow both and make up your own mind. If these plants have one disadvantage, it is that they do not seem to be as free flowering after two years of good growth. When you see the flower production decline, get rid of them and plant a new stock, but not in the same spot too frequently, or the plants will not thrive; rotate their location.

Another charming plant is *A. blanda.* A border of these little wonders in front of tulips or other bulbs, or a large planting of them in an informal shape, is a most attractive sight. There are several color forms available, and I list some below. Make sure you plant enough, not one or two here, one or two there, but 50 in one place or in a line along a border. Be bold when planting anemones; you will not regret it. Plant anemones 2 inches deep and set them 6 to 8 inches apart; set shorter plants such as *A. nemorosa* (only 6 inches in height) closer together. If you wish to grow just for cut flower production, purchase the smallest size tubers available and sow them in drills (miniature furrows only 2 inches deep), spacing them 2 to 4 inches apart. I don't remember ever seeing any anemones attacked by pests or disease, but I would not be surprised if late-summer flowers were afflicted with aphids; these little pests seem to have good taste. Wash them off with cold water before bringing the flowers indoors, as some might not appreciate seeing aphids crawl over the dinner table!

Anemone blanda: In warm (frost-free or nearly so) climates this species will flower very early in the year, but elsewhere it flowers in early spring. Flowers are single, 2 inches in diameter, and a rich blue (other colors have been noted). It is best to select from one of the many named strains. Often listed are A. *blanda* 'Alba', a white form, A. *blanda* 'Atrocaerulea', a deep blue, and A. *blanda* 'Rosea', pink. Some catalogs simply list by color, or offer a mixture. Well-known, reliable selections are: 'Charmer', with deep pink flowers; 'Radar', one of my favorites, with bright red flowers and white centers; and 'White Splendour', with clean white flowers perhaps a little larger than some of the others.

A. coronaria: Sometimes called poppy-flowered anemones, they do look a little like poppies. They are hardy to about +10°F, so in very cold areas plant in spring when temperatures are rising and well above this, and then plant more a little later for summer bloom. These have long been grown commercially as cut flowers; in the late eighteenth century, they were produced in and around Caen and Bayeux in northern France. I have no proof that the 'de Caen' anemones offered in catalogs, and grown for many years, are so named because they were from Caen, but it is a good bet this was the case. The

following named selections are reliable plants: 'His Excellency', bright scarlet and very large flowers; 'Mr Fokker', a good blue; 'Sylphide', a deep violet; and 'The Bride', true white. But handle the flowers with care, as they are easily bruised.

The other race of these plants are double-flowered, known as 'St. Brigid', and for years I wondered about this name. In *All About Flowering Bulbs* by T. A. Weston, published in 1931, I read they were an Irish introduction. Saint Brigid was an Irish saint who founded two important monasteries that became the city of Kildare; she was a friend of Saint Patrick, and her festival is observed on February 1. The selections available are old favorites, and have been grown for many years. They are: 'Lord Lieutenant', a bright blue; 'Mount Everest', a pure white; 'The Admiral', the violet of cyclamen; and 'The Governor', a vermillion-scarlet. Some are of the opinion that the 'St. Brigid' forms are a result of crossing A. *stellata* with A. *fulgens multipetala*, both native to southern Europe. When next in Cornwall, I should visit one of the experimental stations to find out more about these lovely plants.

A. nemorosa: Native to much of Europe, this plant is at home in woodlands, where it finds the moisture, shade and rich humus it needs. This species will naturalize as its rootstock is rhizomatous, so give it room to spread. The flowers are white tinged with pink, about 1 inch in diameter; if you examine them closely you can't help seeing a hint of blue. The form *allenii* (often written with one *i*) has lavender-blue flowers (rose-lilac on the backs of the petals). 'Robinsoniana', a selection found at Gravetye Manor in Sussex, is sometimes listed, and has lavender-blue flowers with prominent golden anthers. If you have a shady area, I suggest you try this species.

A. ranunculoides: Known as the buttercup anemone, this species has yellow flowers and glossy foliage. It spreads by means of shallow rhizomes, and can be quite invasive where there is good moisture, as it likes a soil rich in water-holding humus. Only 6 inches tall, it flowers in April/May. This is a plant well worth growing, but only if you have room for it to spread; it is too pretty to keep corralled.

Botanical Name: Anemone
Family: Ranunculaceae
Common Names: Wind flower, wood anemone, buttercup anemone
Flower Colors: Many, often two-toned; blue, red, white, pinks and shades between. Yellow is rarest color.
Flowering Time: Mostly spring, but anemones can be planted to flower at other times of the year.
Height: Woodland types and *A. blanda* selections under 8 inches, others to 12 inches
Spread: Will form large clumps, and *A. nemerosa* and *A. ranunculoides* can become invasive.
Native Habitat: Those commonly grown are European; certain species are native to North America
Hardiness: Hardy to 10°F
Depth of Planting: 2 inches
Distance Apart: 4 to 8 inches
Containers: Yes
Light Requirements: Full sun except in the very hottest areas (where temperatures remain higher than 80°F day after day), where light shade should be provided. The woodland types prefer high shade.
Soil Type: Average garden soil for most. Some species may prefer soils that are not very acidic. Woodland types like an acid soil. Good drainage necessary.
Special Conditions: Anemones appreciate moisture when growing. Woodland types shouldn't be allowed to become dry for long periods. Little or no fertilizer required. Older plants become shy bearing (produce fewer flowers), and when flower production drops off, replace with new stock but remember to rotate planting location.
Comments: If you like clean-looking colors and cut flowers in the home, then these plants are for you, especially the *A. coronaria* selections. Their foliage is also very attractive and a mixed planting of anemones and primulas is a knockout in spring. Except for cut flower needs, spring flowering is best in warmer climates where there is little or no frost, and summer flowering should be encouraged in colder areas. *A. nemorosa* deserves wider planting, especially if you appreciate "dainty" flowers. Do not worry about planting the tubers the right way up! I like to scatter them over the surface and then just push down into soil to the correct depth.

ANOMALESIA
Iridaceae

The name is derived from the Latin *anomalus*, meaning irregular. The flowers are indeed most unusual, each with three upper lobes forming a spoon shape over the anthers and stigma, the other two lobes affixed, winglike, on the sides of the upper lobes. The color of the flowers is a brilliant coral red, the stems a lovely glaucous blue—a stunning combination, yet *A. cunonia* is rare in cultivation. You may be lucky to obtain a bulb or two from M & C Willetts, Moss Landing, California. If you do, you will be in for a treat, but do not try to grow it if you experience temperatures below about 26°F.

I can remember when I first saw these plants flowering in the wild, at the side of the road along the Garden Route in South Africa. They were stunning, seeming to glow against a green backdrop of various grasses. The stems are

Anomalesia cunonia is a lovely plant waiting to be discovered. The brilliant, coral-red flowers seem to jump out at you, and are bound to give pleasure to discerning gardeners. I took this picture in the wild.

18 to 24 inches in height, with flowers in early spring. The foliage is narrow and grasslike, but it grows thickly with a bluish tinge. Set the corms 3 inches deep and 10 inches apart in full sun. Keep the plants on the dry side except when the foliage is growing; reduce water when the foliage begins to dry. Each corm will produce lots of cormels. When lifted after flowering, separate them from the corms and grow them on for a year or two until they reach flowering size, about the size of the bulbs you purchased. Often I feel such work is not worthwhile as the price of the bulbs isn't high, but *Anomalesia* is an exception because it is a rare plant. Do your part to see if we can get it going in our gardens. There are often 10 or more flowers per spike, each 2 to 3 inches long. This plant grows well in containers, I am told, but I have only seen this plant flourishing in the wild, and so can't give you much more advice than to say take a shot at growing it. Your gardening friends will envy you such a rare beauty.

Botanical Name: Anomalesia
Family: Iridaceae

Common Names: None known
Flower Colors: Brilliant coral red
Flowering Time: Early spring
Height: 18 inches
Spread: Will form small clumps after three full growing periods (three years)
Native Habitat: Cape Province, South Africa
Hardiness: Not hardy; where hard frost occurs, lift and replant in spring.
Depth of Planting: 3 inches
Distance Apart: 10 inches
Containers: Yes; grows well with light feedings of liquid fertilizer.
Light Requirements: Full sun
Soil Type: Average garden soil, must be free-draining
Special Conditions: Keep as dry as possible when foliage dies down; give moisture only when in active growth, and then sparingly.
Comments: Stock available is limited, but this plant is worthy of greater recognition as it is unusual in form and has a lovely color. These qualities will be appreciated by all gardeners who like the challenge of growing something different. Accept the challenge and grow it, and you will have a lot of fun showing it off.

ARISAEMA
Araceae

The name is derived from the Latin *aris* and Greek *aron*, meaning arum, and wake robin, and *haima*, meaning blood-red. Many members of the "Arum family" produce bright red berries from late summer into fall. A woodland plant, the well-known jack-in-the-pulpit is *Arisaema triphyllum*. I must admit these types of plants did not interest me when I was a boy, but I did not like cheese then, either! I am now appreciative of the rather complex flower arrangement of this family, and have become quite fascinated by the colors and forms of the spathe—they are remarkable. The flowers, small and crowded together, are found on the spadix, the cylindrical column in the center, and the spathe surrounds it. "Jack" is the spadix, the pulpit is the spathe, frequently with a rounded section that hangs over, much like the sounding boards above many pulpits. In this family, the spadix has the function of attracting pollinators, as the flowers are devoid of color.

The rootstocks are tuberous, fleshy and quite large. Of more than 100 species of *Arisaema*, few are in cultivation. They are native to Japan, North America, Malaya, India and tropical Africa. It seems this genus is the European counterpart to *Arum*, which is found in Europe and around the Mediterranean, but not in the Americas or Asia. The difference between the two is that *Arisaema* is monoecious, which means the spadix has either male or female flowers on it, whereas the spadix of *Arum* has both, with a band of sterile flowers between them.

A. triphyllum is native to the eastern seaboard of the United States, from Florida all the way to Quebec Province in Canada. Hardy and easy to grow, it is a great plant for damp, shady areas; it can grow in almost swamplike conditions. The spathe is green to purplish brown and interestingly marked with purple inside. The spadix is brown. While the 18-inch plants are not very striking in spring—the flowering time in warmer climates—the brilliant red berries that appear in late summer and are carried into fall are striking in woodland settings. Simply set the tubers 3 to 4 inches deep and 12 inches apart. Once established, they should be left undisturbed. They are pretty along the banks of a stream, and while they like shade, a little dappled sunlight will not harm them. In early fall you can lift and divide the tubers; it is best to replant them as soon as possible, but if you have to keep them until spring, store in damp peat moss and protect from frost.

A lovely woodland plant, *Arisaema triphyllum* is native to the eastern United States. It is hardy and easy to grow, and the red berries that follow the flowers are a bonus! (Photo courtesy of Virginia R. Weiler.)

I noticed *A. sikokianum* listed in a recent catalog. From Japan, it is able to withstand temperatures to −20°F. The spathe is chocolate-maroon outside, shading to white on the inside, surrounding a pure white spadix. The "sounding board" above the "pulpit" is green streaked with white. Quite an attractive plant, flowering in early summer, growing to a little over 12 inches tall. If you purchase seeds, I would sow them in spring using a sandy soil mix with peat moss added. Barely cover the seeds, keep moist, and provide night temperatures around 45°F. Put the seedlings into individual pots as soon as they are large enough to handle and place them outdoors in a shady area. I would plant them out the following spring, giving them some protection over their first winter. The Japanese name for the plant is "snow rice-cake plant." I have not seen this plant "in the flesh," but it sounds most interesting.

Botanical Name: Arisaema

Family: Araceae

Common Names: Varies by species: jack-in-the-pulpit, snow rice-cake plant

Spathe Colors: Green and purple, chocolate and white

Flowering Time: Spring, early summer; berries in fall.

Height: most 8 to 18 inches

Spread: Will form clumps of a moderate size over a period of time

Native Habitat: North America and Asia

Hardiness: Most quite hardy to −20°F

Depth of Planting: 3 to 4 inches

Distance Apart: 10 to 12 inches

Containers: No; plants fare better in woodland settings

Light Requirements: Dense shade, or shade with dappled sunlight

Soil Type: Rich in humus and moist throughout the year

Special Conditions: Ideal woodland plants and for best appearance should be given such a setting, but can be planted in shady shrub border.

Comments: These aren't plants for everyone, especially if space is limited, as stronger spring colors might be enjoyed more. However, if you like unusual plants, dignified and quiet, then these should be considered. No woodland area should be without representatives of the arum family. The plants have a certain subtle merit.

ARUM
Araceae

Theophrastus used the name *aron* for these plants, which are at home in Europe and around the Mediterranean. The roots of these plants, after quite a lot of preparation, were ground and mixed with honey to form cakes, to be eaten when other food was in short supply. A common

With the light behind them plants of *Arum italicum* appear "cheeky", and bring a smile to my face, reminding me of a Punch and Judy show. Superb woodland and shade plants, they are trouble free and reliable.

plant of the hedgerows in many parts of Europe, it was commonly cooked and eaten in Albania, and the leaves were eaten by Greeks. Arrowroot was produced from the roots, and many years ago there were commercial production fields. This should not be surprising as taro, the diet staple of many Pacific Islands, is closely related.

The common names of *Arum maculatum* are Lords and Ladies, and cuckoopint. I would guess that the names came into being because the flowers, with a little imagination, could seem like a Lord or Lady enrobed in a cape, the spadix representing the person, the spathe the cloak. As for cuckoopint, possibly because it appeared at the same time the cuckoo was heard. My copy of *Mawe's Dictionary of Gardening*, which dates from 1748, gives the common name of wake-robin; this is seldom used, and few modern books list this as a common name. Jack-in-the-pulpit appears only in books printed in more recent times.

The plants are interesting as *Arum maculatum* is actually a flytrap. Flies are attracted to the carrion smell of the spadix, and slip down its smooth sides. A crown of stiff hairs keeps them from escaping. At the bottom is nectar mixed with rainwater. After the flowers are pollinated (the flies' job), the spathe soon shrivels; any flies still alive can escape. Inside the flower, the temperature is a little higher than outside, due to the high metabolic activity of the tissues, so if they can survive, the flies are kept warm and fed!

In fall the flower stem is topped by bright red berries. The spathe is pale yellow-green, and as the plants grow in the shade, you can easily miss them unless you are looking closely. Generally they are found among grasses and other hedgerow plants. While the leaves are 12 to 18 inches long, sometimes spotted with purple, it is when the berries are ripe and red that it is most easily spotted. It flowers in spring, a time of much lush growth in its habitat. Much more noticeable, and for that a better garden plant, is *A. italicum,* found in many places in Europe but originally from Italy. It has the common name wild ginger and produces attractive orange-red berries. The creamy white spathe is produced in spring. When these features are combined with the pretty foliage with white markings, which is with us from fall through much of summer, you can appreciate that this is a worthy plant to consider for naturalizing in the garden. If you grow it, give it room to spread.

The genus is indeed variable. *A. pictum,* from Spain, Corsica and Sardinia, produces its flowers before the foliage. The spathe is purple, reaches up to 18 inches in height and flowers in fall. After that, green leaves with yellow veining appear. I wish I had room to grow these species in one location, as together they would provide interest for many months. On the spadix the male flowers are above the females. The poor male flowers dry up, and the top of the spadix withers so that the berries crown the spike. Matriarchal plants these, deserving of consideration.

No matter which species you grow, set the tubers 3 inches deep and 12 inches apart. Shade

and moisture are required, but the species from Italy, Spain, Corsica and Sardinia can stand some sun where summer temperatures are not above 80°F. Still, it would be better not to push your luck; if in doubt, give them shade.

Arum italicum: This species is often listed in catalogs, but you might actually receive one of the subspecies, as these are perhaps more garden worthy. Some suppliers list all the plants as *A. italicum* as the species is very variable; the spathes may have more or less yellow and foliage markings may differ. Flowering in spring, the spathe is yellow or yellow-green and reaches 18 inches in height. Orange-red berries appear in the fall.

A. maculatum: Flowers occur at the base of a club-shaped spadix, which is enclosed within a greenish white bract. The spathe holds male flowers above the female. But this description doesn't do justice to the plant. The bright red berries in fall are most attractive.

A. pictum: Despite coming from warmer areas of the Mediterranean, this is a hardy species. It is often described in catalogs as the black calla but is not black, rather a deep purple, and of course it is an *Arum,* not a *Calla.* It grows up to 18 inches in height, with leaves a little taller and 4 inches wide. Flower spikes are produced in fall.

Botanical Name: Arum
Family: Araceae
Common Names: Lords and Ladies, jack-in-the-pulpit, wild ginger, black calla
Flower Colors: Spathes: green, yellow, purple; Spadix: yellow, white. Foliage also attractive
Flowering Time: Most species in spring, *A. pictum* in fall
Height: Most from 18 to 24 inches

Spread: Will naturalize and spread comparatively quickly if site agreeable

Native Habitat: Much of Europe and around the Mediterranean

Hardiness: Hardy to 0°F with protection

Depth of Planting: 3 inches

Distance Apart: 12 inches

Containers: Not recommended

Light Requirements: Prefer shade, although certain species can take some sun

Soil Type: Rich in humus; woodland type of soil

Special Conditions: If given woodland settings and moisture when growing, no fertilizer needed

Comments: Perhaps these should be grown by gardeners who appreciate the subtleties of nature as it is, not for those who like bright colors and large, showy flowers. In woodland settings the plants will provide much interest, and I would try to establish more than one species for even longer periods of interest. Hardy plants, in very cold areas they will appreciate a thick mulch, but it should be loose and not form a mat, or shoots may have a hard time getting through.

BABIANA
Iridaceae

I wish every gardener could see these lovely plants in flower in the wild in South Africa. I have had the good fortune to see them, and they always give me great pleasure. It is unfortunate that of the 30 or so species in the genus, only one is offered in catalogs. This is *Babiana stricta*, and you will also find selections, generally in shades of blue. The species itself is quite variable, ranging from cream to crimson to lilac. I suspect that if you purchase the species, you will receive corms that will produce mostly blue flowers, but some other colors would probably be in the mixture. A great way to welcome spring!

There are a number of selections of *Babiana stricta*, all great garden plants. 'White King' is pictured here. At home on Table Mountain overlooking Cape Town, South Africa, they were so named because baboons love their rootstocks. (Photo courtesy of International Bloembollen Centrum.)

Unfortunately the plants are not hardy, and while I feel they are worth a try in areas where temperatures remain above 20°F, I would certainly give the protection of a thick mulch and plant near a south-facing wall where temperatures around 20°F are experienced. Where temperatures fall lower than that at any time, grow them only in a heated frame, or in containers that can be moved to a protected area. They are worth such trouble, I assure you.

Apart from the long-lasting flowers, which with any luck will be yours to enjoy for as long as five weeks, you might become intoxicated by the perfume. It can be quite strong, but is very pleasant. In their native habitat the corms are dug out of the earth by baboons, who love to eat them. The botanical name comes from the Dutch diminutive of baboon, *babiantje*. (The Dutch make diminutives of many words, it was explained to me, when I lived in Holland, because their country is so small!) Ordinary garden soils are fine for these plants. They must have good drainage, and they need sun in strong doses; these are not plants for the shade. Provide moisture during their growing period; afterward they can be allowed to dry out. If I had a garden with a slope and I lived in California or another warm part of the country, I would plant a lot of these corms among grasses. They would think they were at home, with moisture during fall and winter, and into spring, followed by dry summers. Once they are established, leave them alone, lifting only when you wish to divide the clumps and plant other colonies.

Babiana stricta: The leaves are stiff and have the appearance of being pleated. They are not very long, lanceolate (slightly pointed) to sword shaped, up to 1 inch in width, and covered with fine hairs. The flowers are carried on sturdy stems reaching up to 18 inches in height, with several flowers per stem, and as the corms can produce more than one stem, they assure good value for the money spent. In average soils plant the corms 5 to 6 inches deep and 6 inches apart. In sandy soils set them a little deeper. The selection 'Purple Star' is the color of cyclamen, with a darker color in the throat, 'Tubergen's Blue' is more of a violet, with white markings on 2 petals; this is a vigorous plant, and it can carry as many as a dozen flowers on a stem, each about 1½ inches across, just a little larger than the species.

Botanical Name: Babiana
Family: Iridaceae
Common Names: Babiantje
Flower Colors: Shades of blue, may vary from cream to crimson to lilac
Flowering Time: Spring
Height: Up to 18 inches
Spread: Individual plants are upright, but will form colonies over time
Native Habitat: South Africa
Hardiness: If you live where frost is experienced, protect with a deep mulch, or lift and store over winter and plant again in spring.
Depth of Planting: 5 to 6 inches
Distance Apart: 6 inches
Containers: Good

Light Requirements: Full sun
Soil Type: Average garden soil; use potting soil in containers, and ensure good drainage.
Special Conditions: Must have good drainage. Give moisture while growing. Appreciates a dry period from summer into fall.
Comments: I do hope you will try some of these lovely plants. If you have a warm and sunny corner of the garden, then these plants are for that place. Even in cooler climates, I would suggest you try a few; they are worth the work of moving them into a protected place when frost arrives. If you obtain a mix of colors, you might wish to save the seed and grow them on to flowering size. Sow in late summer in warm areas, in spring in cooler climes. Use a sandy soil mix and barely cover the seed; keep it moist, not wet, while growing. You should have some flowers to enjoy after two seasons—worth the wait.

BEGONIA
Begoniaceae

The genus is named in honor of Michel Begon, a patron of botany and one-time French governor of Santo Domingo. This is a very large genus with hundreds of species. Among them are some lovely plants, often with striking foliage and grand flowers, in a wide range of colors. Begonias are at home in the warmer regions of China, South Africa and India, but mostly are from South America. There is only one true bulb in the genus, *Begonia socotrana*, introduced by the Scottish botanist Sir Isaac Bayley Balfour of the Royal Botanic Garden in Edinburgh. It is rare in cultivation. The begonias that interest us today are the tuberous begonias. The bedding begonias, known as "Semperflorens" begonias, are not bulbous plants, but great garden plants nevertheless. Straightaway I must say that, while these

Tuberous begonias are excellent for growing in containers, but are not appreciative of exposure to the wind.

temperatures with a good winter mulch for protection. Flowering in late summer and into fall, it reaches 36 inches in height when well established, producing cascades of pink flowers above lush foliage that appears quite succulent. This is a good plant to leave undisturbed in a shrub border, which I think is the right place for it, as it prefers to remain for many years in one spot. In the perennial border, it would either have to be moved every 2 to 4 years, or you would have to work around it when lifting and dividing other perennials.

I always feel that a garden that has beds of tuberous begonias or hanging baskets of these lovely plants is richer for their presence. They have a sumptuous look, implying that the gardener in charge knows his or her plants, for it seems hardly possible that such luscious flowers can be of comparatively easy culture. I would rank them as one of the most lovely of summer bedding plants for areas with some shade; they do not take kindly to full sun, but warmth is something they not only appreciate, but need.

With such a large genus as *Begonia*, some additional classification is called for based on horticultural differences, not necessarily botanical subtleties. Although there is some dissent, and while every show committee will have some variations to accommodate any special classes they might feel essential, the 13 groups that follow are those generally accepted for show purposes, and for listing cultivars in catalogs. (I appreciate the kind permission of the Royal Horticultural Society to reproduce this classification.)

divisions are quite logical, the results of modern hybridization are that clean-cut distinctions are becoming blurred. There have been numerous crosses between types and groups. In the seemingly always-changing world of the tuberous begonia, known as *B. tuberhybrida,* a few points might help the home gardener.

In addition to the famed tuberous begonias, there is *B. grandis,* sometimes listed in catalogs, and most correctly referred to as *B. grandis* ssp. *evansiana.* Also tuberous, it enjoys the common name of hardy begonia. It withstands temperatures down to −10°F, and perhaps even colder

1. **Single group.** Flowers large, tepals 4, usually flat.
2. **Crispa or Frilled Group.** Flowers large, single, tepals frilled or ruffled.
3. **Cristata or Crested Group.** Flowers large, single with frilled outgrowth in center of tepal.

4. **Narcissiflora or Daffodil-flowered Group.** Flowers large, double, central tepals spreading-erect, resembling corona of *Narcissus*.

5. **Camellia or Camelliflora Group.** Flowers large, double, tepals regular, resembling a camellia flower, self colored (of one color), not ruffled or fimbriate (fringed).

6. **Ruffled Camellia Group.** As (5), but with tepals ruffled.

7. **Rosiflora or Rosebud Group.** Flowers large, with center resembling rosebud.

8. **Fimbriata Plena or Carnation Group.** Flowers large, double, tepals fimbriate.

9. **Picotee Group.** Flowers large, usually double, camellia-shaped, with tepals edged with different shade or color, or blending with main color.

10. **Marginata Group.** Flowers as in (9), precisely edged with distinct color.

11. **Marmorata Group.** Flowers as in (5), pink, marbled with white.

12. **Pendula or Hanging-basket group.** Stems trailing or pendulous, flowers many small to large, single or double.

13. **Multiflora Group.** Plants low, bushy, compact, flowers many, small, single to double.

Nonstop Begonias are the result of intensive breeding undertaken in Europe between large-flowered doubles and the Multiflora group, resulting in extremely floriferous plants with flowers somewhat smaller than those of the typical large-flowered types. But this loss of size is more than made up for with the great vigor and the large number of blossoms, making them garden plants. The selections offered are the ones the home gardener should purchase.

"Double Rose Form" and "Camellia Form" are both listed in catalogs, and the distinction today is almost academic. I would choose the cultivar with the description that sounds best to you! Picotee Begonias are chiefly yellow or white

The wide range of colors of Tuberous begonias available allows for single-color or mixed plantings, adding fullness to the partly shaded border.

(or shades of these), with a narrow band of red or pink at the end of the tepals. The only difference between Picotee Begonias and Bicolors is the width of the band of color, a judgment call at best. Lace Form flowers are edged in white and are very ruffled.

Many catalogs offer various selections of different forms, generally by color, but some named selections are also listed. These are most commonly from strains such as the Blackmore & Langdon Strain, and 'Alan Langdon', 'Jean Blair', 'Sea Coral' and 'Tahiti' are examples of variously colored tuberous begonias.

Pendula Begonias also are frequently offered by color. Grow them where they can tumble over the sides of a container and show off their lovely form.

I think this is enough about classification, forms, etc., and it is time to say something about growing these lovely plants. I cannot emphasize enough the need, if ordering by mail, to make sure that you obtain the tubers from a good, well-known firm. Frequently the cost of the tubers is low, and you always get what you pay for. You want to start with tubers more than an inch in diameter, so you might check the size offered first; if not listed, it might be worth a telephone call to the firm offering them. Often Belgian tubers are offered at lower prices, but they have little else to recommend them. California tubers are reasonable in price, and the named cultivars are generally superb, but will have been produced by cuttings and are thus more expensive.

If you purchase from your local nursery, select tubers that are plump and firm, avoiding those that are mushy. I should mention that by late spring some might have a spongy feel. This indicates some loss of moisture, but hopefully not too much. If you find tubers with small pink or white buds, select them. Most tubers will probably sprout, but those with buds are just a step ahead. One or two sprouts is about right, except for Pendula types, in which case the more buds, the better. Avoid tubers with sprouts longer than 1 inch, as they may not develop sturdy stems. Handle them with care because the buds (sprouts) are quite easily damaged.

The proper time for starting tubers is five to six weeks before setting them outdoors. This means five to six weeks before the nighttime temperatures stay above 50°F. (Tubers can be started any time if being grown in a greenhouse.) Light isn't necessary for starting the tubers, but it is essential when the shoots are 2 inches or more in length. In poor light the shoots will be spindly. If the available light comes from one direction only, rotate the containers so the stems don't grow crooked.

The starting mix should be 2 parts (by volume) coarsly ground sphagnum peat moss to 1 part each perlite and vermiculite, with some slow-release fertilizer added. Or, use ordinary potting soil and add lots of peat moss. You need containers 4 inches deep. Flats are best for large numbers of tubers. If using pots, make certain there is adequate drainage; pots should be 12 inches in diameter, as anything smaller won't allow for good root development. Space the tubers 6 inches apart. Make a depression in the mix for each tuber and place it concave side up (the side with sprouts), and cover with ½ inch of soil mix. Roots will develop from the top of the tuber too. Keep the soil moist, never soggy. The ideal temperature is 60° to 70°F. When the shoots are 4 to 5 inches tall and night temperatures are 50° to 55°F, they can be moved outdoors. Acclimate them outdoors for a few hours each day before planting them (you "wean" them), so they can better take being outdoors permanently.

Work over the beds where you are going to plant. Add well-rotted compost, peat moss and, if your soil is heavy, some sharp sand. Plant so that the root ball is even with the top of the bed, and water it well. A week later, water with a water-soluble fertilizer in the 20–20–20 range, then repeat two weeks later. After that, fertilize every three to four weeks with a 15–30–15 formula.

Some say you should pinch the shoots to encourage branching. In my opinion, this isn't necessary, and it will delay flowering. As these plants are inclined to take their time flowering anyway, pinching doesn't seem advantageous. But what is essential is to remove carefully the first two or three buds. You may be tempted to leave some buds on so you can enjoy flowers sooner, but you would get smaller flowers toward the end of the season.

In borders, space plants 18 inches apart. As the plants grow, you may notice that some of the lower leaves develop brown spots or brown edges. Cut them off, as any leaf that turns color has finished contributing to the vigor of the plant. Some plants produce a good number of shoots, and in some cases can become quite crowded in the center of the plants. One of the essential conditions for good flowering and good health of the plants is good air circulation. This may require a judgment call. If you do not remove the offending stem, you may have problems with rotting or mildew; if you do remove it, you may lose some flower production. Upright-growing types may require some staking. When the plant is 8 to 10 inches tall, place a cane behind it and use a plastic (nonsticky) tape to tie the stem to the support. Don't secure the plant with a material that will cut into the stem.

Contrary to popular belief, tuberous begonias do not appreciate dense shade. The beds are at their best in filtered sunlight or strong overhead light, such as on the north side of a house. Avoid direct sunlight except that of the early morning or late afternoon.

Begonias are not temperamental, but if you find buds dropping, check to make sure you are not overwatering, or that the plants are not too dry. Overfeeding will also cause a loss in flower production, as will too much shade. During summer, remove spent flowers; pinch them off, leaving about an inch of the stem, which will soon dry and drop off. When you cut to bring flowers indoors, use the same technique.

As the days become shorter, plant growth will slow, so stop fertilizing. When the frosts arrive or rains start to beat the flowers to pieces, it will be time to lift the tubers. First cut the stems back to about 5 inches above the tubers. Lift the tubers with a small root ball of soil and place where they can dry. Then, brush off the dry soil and protect the tubers from frost. After four to five weeks the remainder of the stem will drop off, or can easily be removed (do not force it). When dry, store the tubers in a frost-free location where the temperature is in the 40° to 60°F range, placing them in barely damp peat moss or wood shavings. Keep an eye on them through the winter until it is time to start them into growth again.

Tuberous begonias can be raised from seed—quite a process, and I would suggest that for most home gardeners tubers are best purchased. Propagation should be confined to cutting the tubers, each piece with a bud attached, or taking cuttings. Seed should be sown in February in sifted peat moss. There are some 2 million to the ounce—it is very fine seed. Scatter seed over the surface of the moss and water very gently, using a watering can with a fine nose. Place a piece of glass over the container and keep in temperatures around 65°F with full spectrum light (such as Gro-lux) provided for 14 hours a day. As soon as the seed has germinated, remove the glass during the day, replacing it at night. After about five weeks you will be able to transplant the seedlings into individual containers. Grow on slowly, making certain they have good, but not direct, sunlight, and keep moist (not wet). Started in February, seedlings should be ready to plant out in June, when outside temperatures are around 50°F at night. Remember to ensure good air circulation, constant temperatures at all times, and good light.

If I have gone into detail regarding the culture of these lovely plants, it is because they are well worth the effort to grow well. Even so, I am not of the opinion that the average gardener should propagate these plants from seed. Too many things can go wrong, and I would hate for any gardener to be discouraged from growing tuberous begonias—they are such grand plants.

Begonia grandis: Correctly *B. grandis* ssp. *evansiana,* the "hardy begonia" reaches a height of up to 30 inches when well established, producing cascades of pink flowers in late summer into fall. Hardy to −10°F and even lower with the protection of a good mulch. Leave undisturbed. Plant

4 inches deep, 8 to 10 inches apart, in light shade but where some sun is enjoyed.

B. tuberhybrida: There are two basic types, pendulous and upright, and many different forms. Height varies, but is generally 18 to 24 inches; pendulous forms droop 18 to 24 inches. Start into growth 6 weeks before outside temperatures are around 50°F at night. Plant 18 inches apart, or grow in pots at least 12 inches in diameter using well-draining soil mix rich in humus. Place in dappled shade. They bloom in summer and into fall. There are many colors and interesting flower forms, including bicolors and doubles. Monoecious flowers, the males are showy, the females not as showy; often the males are located between two females. Lift the tubers in fall and store in frost-free areas over winter.

Botanical Name: Begonia
Family: Begoniaceae
Common Names: Tuberous begonia, begonia, hardy begonia
Flower Colors: Many (no blues or purples), often bicolors or tips of tepals have a lighter color
Flowering Time: Mid- to late summer into fall
Height: Tuberous begonias to 18 inches; hardy begonias, 4 inches
Spread: Tuberous begonias 12 inches, hardy begonias to 36 inches when well established
Native Habitat: Tuberous begonias derived from South American species, hardy begonias from China.
Hardiness: Tuberous begonias are not hardy; hardy begonias take temperatures down to −10°F.
Depth of Planting: Tuberous begonias just at soil level or slightly below; hardy begonias, 4 inches
Distance Apart: 12 to 18 inches
Containers: Yes, splendid in hanging baskets
Light Requirements: Dappled shade; morning and late afternoon sun are acceptable
Soil Type: Rich, well-drained soil

Special Conditions: These plants need humidity during the summer months, so in dry areas, spraying with water may be necessary. Must have temperatures around 50°F at night to grow well. Should be fertilized regularly.
Comments: Begonias are regarded by some as difficult plants, but I disagree. Selections from the many types available, especially 'Nonstop', are superb and give class to any garden in which they are grown. You will seldom see a more beautiful sight than a hanging container of well-grown tuberous begonias in full flower.

BELAMCANDA
Iridaceae

This genus is said to be named for the Indian word for this plant, yet it is native to eastern Asia, China and Japan. Some authorities feel there is but one species, *Belamcanda chinensis,* with irislike leaves that surround flowering stems that reach 24 to 36 inches in height. The flowering stem seems to zigzag as it grows and bears many flowers, which while individually not long-lasting, provide interest for several weeks in late summer; up to a dozen or more flowers are produced in a loose head. Color in *B. chinensis* is variable, most commonly in the orange-red tones, with darker spots of reddish brown on the petals.

Another point of dissention is whether the rootstock is a tuber or a rhizome. I am inclined to think it is a tuber, but one thing is certain: After the flowers fade, the plants take on another look as the seed pods develop and open, exposing the black seed loosely arranged and resembling blackberries, hence the common name blackberry lily.

The other species is *B. flabellata,* which differs from *B. chinensis* only in color or height. It is yellow and seldom taller than 24 inches. As it is consistently yellow with the red-brown spots, and not as tall, I feel that there are indeed two species. Both forms (or species) are attractive plants. They appreciate full sun, with light shade in the hottest areas (where temperatures remain at 80° to 90°F day after day). It is not fully hardy, needing protection where temperatures drop below 15°F, and in colder areas should be lifted at the end of the season and replanted in spring.

These attractive plants like a well-drained soil, on the sandy side but with good humus. They need moisture during their growing season. As the plants will form colonies if left undisturbed, I feel this plant is better off in the shrub border or in another area where it can remain undisturbed, rather than in a perennial border. I hear this plant has escaped from gardens in the eastern United States and has established itself in the wild in various areas. This would bear out the claim that it is easy to grow. (So many of our garden plants seem to do quite well without too much attention, a point all gardeners should keep in mind.) Set the rootstocks 1 to 2 inches deep and 12 to 15 inches apart. Lift only to increase the stock, best done in fall in moderate climates (where little or no frost occurs), in spring in colder areas.

I am not a great lover of dried flower arrangements, but understand that if the flower heads are cut just as the seedpods open, they can be dried and add interesting color and form to arrangements. The seed can be saved and sown in a sandy mix in spring; this provides another way to increase the stock. A yellow selection, *B. flabellata* 'Hello Yellow', is listed in catalogs. It has the spots on the petals, and I wonder if it is indeed a selection, or just a variant of the species. Some gardeners may be tempted to cut the flowers for use in fresh arrangements, but they are not long lasting. It is far better to enjoy them in the garden and use just the opened seedpods in dried arrangements.

The flowers of *Belamcanda chinensis* are unusual, attractive and freely produced. With bursting seed pods, the plants are sought after by flower arrangers and are favorites for use in dried arrangements. (Photo courtesy of International Bloembollen Centrum.)

The old name for the genus was *Pardanthus*, which enjoyed the common names blackberry lily and leopard flower. A well-known catalog lists seed of *Belamcanda* 'Leopard Lily Mixed', showing flowers of yellow, orange, salmon, purple and lilac hues. Another firm lists × *Pardancanda norirsii*, with the same basic colors. I suspect these are selections made from crossing the variable species *B. chinensis* with selected seedlings of the same species to obtain the rich color mix offered. I found reference to leopard flower in *Bulbs and Tuberous Plants*, by C. L. Allen, copyright 1893 by Orange Judd Company, New York City. The text mentions that the Chinese leopard flower "was formerly very common in gardens, but like many other deserving plants, has given way to the universal craze for novelties." An interesting comment from one hundred years ago!

Botanical name: Belamcanda
Family: Iridaceae
Common Names: Blackberry lily, leopard flower

Flower Colors: Varies by species: tones of red and orange, yellow

Flowering Time: Late summer into fall

Height: Varies by species: 24 to 36 inches

Spread: Will form colonies in time

Native Habitat: China, Japan, eastern Asia

Hardiness: Not fully hardy; protect in areas where temperatures fall below −15°F by overwintering in frost-free area, lifting in fall, and planting again in spring. Store in peat moss.

Depth of Planting: 1 to 2 inches

Distance Apart: 12 to 15 inches

Containers: Not recommended

Light Requirements: Sun; light shade in hottest areas, where summer temperatures are 80° to 90°F day after day

Soil Type: Well-draining, sandy soil with humus.

Special Conditions: Give good moisture while plant is growing.

Comments: Easy-to-grow plants with the added attraction of being late flowering, and handsome seedpods good for dried arrangements. Plant where they can be left undisturbed. Perhaps not for the garden where space is limited, but should be considered for the sizeable shrub border. Not a plant to be regarded as essential for every garden, mainly because it has little value as a cut flower. Listings in some catalogs of various color mixes mostly available as seed could well mean that a greater color range of rootstocks will become available; this would make these plants of greater value for smaller gardens. It is said the roots are an antidote to cobra venom, but I shouldn't like to be the one to prove this.

BRIMEURA
Liliaceae

Marie de Brimeur was a keen gardener who lived in the sixteenth century. There are only two species in this genus that commemorates her, and

While *Brimeura amethystina* looks like an English blue-bell, it prefers sun, not shade. The tepals are fused to form a tube, which is one of the differences between *Brimeura* and *Hyacinthoides*. (Photo courtesy of Van Tubergen UK.)

you will only find *Brimeura amethystina* listed in catalogs. For years it was known as *Hyacinthus amethystinus* although it doesn't look like a hyacinth but more like a bluebell. Differences between *Brimeura* and *Hyacinthus* can be appreciated with the naked eye. In *Brimeura* there is a prominent bract under each flower stalk; almost transparent when the flowers are open, this bract hardly exists in *Hyacinthus*. The tepals of *Brimeura* are joined to form a tube; in *Hyacinthus* they are not joined, but free.

The bulbs are small, less than 1 inch in diameter. Grasslike foliage appears in spring. The flower spike that follows reaches 10 inches in height, and in April–May, as many as 15 pendant, bright blue flowers appear. In cooler areas where frost occurs, the flowers may be produced later, and as the plants are hardy to 15°F, it will be appreciated that flowering time in such areas will be later than in parts of California.

Plant in full sun in average garden soil, 1 to 2 inches deep and 4 to 5 inches apart. Select the spot with care because you should not disturb the plants, but allow them to form little colonies, which they will do quickly if they like their home. They seem to like the rock crevices, where they receive winter and spring moisture, then a dry period during summer; this may approximate their home around the Mediterranean. They are fine in containers, but do leave them in the same ones for a number of years; use ordinary potting soil (these are not fussy bulbs). A white form can be found listed as *Brimeura amethystina* 'Alba'.

Botanical Name: Brimeura
Family: Liliaceae
Common Names: None known
Flower Colors: Blue, white
Flowering Time: Late spring
Height: 10 inches
Spread: Will form colonies over time
Native Habitat: Pyrenees
Hardiness: Quite hardy, to 10° to 15°F
Depth of Planting: 1 to 2 inches
Distance Apart: 4 to 5 inches
Containers: Good in containers
Light Requirements: Sun
Soil Type: Ordinary garden soil with good drainage
Special Conditions: Appreciates moisture during winter and spring, prefers dry conditions in late summer.
Comments: Do remember that the bulbs are small and this great little plant doesn't take up much room. Plant where you can get close to them. In

containers they can be used indoors as decorative pot plants, but take them outside again, as otherwise they are inclined to become lanky and fall all over the place. Some catalogs still list them under *Hyacinthus amethystinus* with such cultivar names as 'Alpine Hyacinth', which is quite accurate, as they do come from the Pyrenees. Perhaps this should be the common name for these plants.

BRODIAEA
Liliaceae

The genus is named in honor of James Brodie, a Scottish horticulturalist who specialized in non-flowering plants, mosses and such. There is a famous pub in Edinburgh (and a good one, I must admit) called Brodie's, and while this may not have anything to do with James Brodie, I would suggest you visit it and ask!

If ever there were a genus examined by botanists, this is it. Over the years it has been di-

Flowering in early summer when blue is much appreciated, *Brodiaea laxa* are tailor-made for the front of a mixed border. (Photo courtesy of International Bloembollen Centrum.)

vided, and species formerly in *Brodiaea* are now to be found in *Tritelia, Bloomeria, Dichelostemma, Ipheion* and *Muilla*. (This last genus is *"Allium"* spelled backward, perhaps appropriate as brodiaeas are sometimes called California onions.) They seem the counterparts of alliums in Europe, and inhabit deciduous woodlands along the west coast of the United States, just the type of habitat the alliums enjoy in Europe. The other common name is fool's onion, but how it got this name I do not know. Controversy surrounds the family to which *Brodiaea* belong. The ovary is superior, thus the plants belong in Liliaceae, but the flowers grow in umbels, so some say the family should be Amaryllidaceae. Still others think they should be in Alliaceae. Thank goodness the plants do not change with the discussion that surrounds them. There seems to be general agreement that *Brodiaea* has three fertile stamens, which distinguishes it from the other genera mentioned.

There are five species that can often be found in catalogs. All have grasslike foliage. The corms, which resemble those of *Gladiolus* but are smaller, should be planted 5 inches deep and 6 inches apart. The foliage is often on its way toward being dry and withered by the time the flowers are produced. It is best planted in groups and left undisturbed. The species from California, generally those listed, need moisture during winter and spring, then a dry period during late summer and early fall, just as they enjoy at home. They must have excellent drainage at all times. They are hardy to around 20°F, withstanding lower temperatures with the protection of a mulch, but not fully hardy. In colder areas, lift and store over winter and replant in spring. Frequently mention is made that these are good rock garden plants; I do not agree. For the most part they are found in grassland, and while the soils will get quite warm, they are not baked as they are frequently in a rock garden, where heat re-flected off the rocks is a factor not to be ignored. In nature *Brodiaea* can be found growing near rocks, but only where there are trees to provide some shade. These plants look fine on the edge of a woodland, where good moisture is available during their growing season and any excess moisture will be taken up by the trees later, ensuring the needed dry period in late summer.

Brodiaea californica: Native to northern California, growing in grasslands most frequently at the base of hills, it is the largest and tallest of the *Brodiaea*, reaching up to 24 inches in height and, when well established, having as many as 12 to 15 flowers. The tubular flowers are quite large, an inch in diameter, and while the color can vary from pale to intense blue to pink shades, it is generally the pink forms that are listed in catalogs. Flowers in early summer.

B. lactea: Sometimes listed as *B. hyacinthina* and *Triteleia hyacinthina*, this species is found from British Columbia all the way south to California. It reaches up to 18 inches in height, and as the species name suggests, is milky white with the flower heads in tight umbels. The individual flowers are quite large and held on wiry stems. It flowers in early summer and is one of the easiest to grow. The flowers are touched with a hint of blue that heightens their whiteness, and when this color is more pronounced you might find it listed as *lilacina*.

B. laxa: Strong, wiry stems reach some 24 inches. The large umbels, as much as 6 inches in diameter, bear flowers of a deep blue. The selection 'Queen Fabiola' is a favorite of catalogs and a good plant. The individual flowers are tubular, flaring away from the base. Flowers in early to midsummer. This species is at home in Oregon and California. I must make mention of the common name "Ithuriel's spear," unusual, to say the least. This is the name of the angel in Milton's *Paradise Lost*. Whoever gave it this name must have been an interesting character.

B. pulchella: Often listed as *Dichelostemma congestum*, this plant is at home in Washington, Oregon and California. The very tight umbel of flowers is reminiscent of onion flowers, violet-rose in color, crowded together. The stems always seem to have a curve in them. They grow up to 24 inches in height, and flower in summer.

B. × tubergenii: A hybrid raised by the firm of Van Tubergen, this is a strong grower, to 24 inches in height. It flowers in early to midsummer with pale blue flowers. Makes a good cut flower.

Botanical Name: Brodiaea
Family: Liliaceae
Common Names: Fool's onion is applied to many species, Ithuriel's spear to the species *B. laxa*
Flower Colors: Blue, white and rose shades
Flowering Time: Summer
Height: Up to 24 inches
Spread: Will form large colonies if left undisturbed
Native Habitat: Those most commonly grown are from the west coast of the United States
Hardiness: Quite hardy, but where temperatures drop below 20°F, lift and store over winter as for *Gladiolus*.
Depth of Planting: 5 inches
Distance Apart: 6 inches, but can be spaced as far as 10 to 12 inches apart
Containers: Not good in this formal setting
Light Requirements: Sun, some light shade in dry, hottest areas; never deep shade
Soil Type: Well-drained, average garden soil
Special Conditions: Moisture is needed during spring and into early summer for later-flowering species, but a dry period is needed at end of summer. Best grown where they can be left undisturbed; lift only to propagate. Each corm will produce many small ones.

Comments: While they are great plants, and have potential as cut flowers, I doubt if they will ever become popular as such. It seems a pity that more work has not been done on these plants; it would seem possible that a greater color range could be developed, as well as larger flower heads. If you want something a little on the unusual side, these plants are for you. Not difficult to grow, but there must be a reason why they are not more popular. While they will not disappoint, I doubt if they will overpower you with their beauty, which must be regarded as subtle.

BULBOCODIUM
Liliaceae

Among the hardiest of bulbs, this genus contains two species; only one, *Bulbocodium vernum*, is found in catalogs. The name is derived from the

Perhaps the hardiest of bulbs, *Bulbocodium vernum* does not like moisture and should enjoy a dry period in summer. This is a fun species as it is so dependable. (Photo courtesy of British Alpine Garden Society.)

Greek *bulbos*, bulb, and *kodoum*, wool or woolly covering, a reference to the rather unusual covering of the bulbs. That they have need of some insulation is understandable, as they are at home in the Alps and Caucasus, and mountains in Spain, where it gets very cold. No matter where you live in the continental United States, you should have no problems growing this bulb in the garden, and I would think it would not be killed even outdoors in Alaska!

The common name is mountain saffron, and while *Bulbocodium* is not *Crocus*, the genus of the bulb from which saffron is gathered, the plant looks much like a crocus. However, *Bulbocodium* has a superior ovary, and six stamens instead of three. In cold climates it blooms in March, in warmer areas in February, and in very, very cold areas, in late March or April. Wherever it grows, it seems to lead the other bulbs as one of the first to flower.

Despite being hardy, it does not like to be in wet areas, preferring good drainage and sun. It isn't fussy as to soil, being quite happy in almost any type except the heavy clays. It is best planted in fall, 3 inches deep and 4 to 5 inches apart. The flowers appear before the grasslike leaves, which die down in early summer. If you want to increase your stock, this is when the bulbs should be lifted and divided. They can be planted again right away, or stored until fall, and this is helpful if you cannot give them a dry period toward the end of summer. They will form colonies, but seem to benefit from being lifted and divided every 4 to 5 years. This is a plant for the rock garden, and it is agreeable in containers with ordinary potting soil.

I like this plant because it is tough and will not disappoint. It gives interest to the garden early in the year, often with the snowdrops and winter aconites. Plant at least three in a group or better yet a greater number, so they make a splash of color even though only 4 inches tall.

Botanical Name: Bulbocodium
Family: Liliaceae
Common Name: Mountain saffron
Flower Colors: Shades of purple, white
Flowering Time: Early spring
Height: 4 inches
Spread: Will naturalize into small colonies
Native Habitat: The Alps of Europe
Hardiness: Hardy
Depth of Planting: 3 inches
Distance Apart: 4 to 5 inches
Containers: Plant close together in containers to make a good splash of color.
Light Requirements: Sun
Soil Type: Ordinary garden soil; must have good drainage.
Special Conditions: Not a fussy bulb, but at no time should it sit in water. It must have dry conditions at the end of summer.
Comments: Every garden should find a spot for this early-flowering bulb—it lifts the spirits and gives a taste of good things to come. I am a little skeptical of it being able to grow well in those areas with no frost in winter, but it is worth trying; in such areas, it is essential that it have a dry period in late summer and early fall. The flowers open wide and they last quite a long time.

CALADIUM
Araceae

The name is derived from the South American Indian word *kelady*, but I do not know why. The rootstock is a tuberous rhizome, and the main reason for growing these plants is for their attractive foliage.

All caladiums listed in catalogs have as their forebears species from South America, and they share the need for warmth. They don't appreciate temperatures much below 70°F, which makes them ideal for summer color in warm climates,

With foliage that can be any combination of colors, caladiums add a tropical look to the summer shade garden.

but this heat must be combined with humidity and shade, as well as protection from strong winds. This may sound like a lot of trouble, but if you see these plants when well grown, you will appreciate that they are exotic, exciting and elegant. If not well grown, they look miserable.

There are many different shapes to the foliage—strap-, heart- and lance-shaped leaves. Those known as fancy-leaved are taller and tend to have broad, heart-shaped leaves. The leaves come in a multitude of colors—green with red, white with green veining, speckled white on green with red veins, lighter- or darker-colored edges to the leaves—the selections seem endless. They are of thin texture, and the leaf stalks are often varied in color. The flowers are in a spadix, a cylindrical cone, the yellow-gray, male flowers on top. Below them is a segment of light gray, sterile flowers, then the female flowers of light yellow. The spathe is hooded, with the lower portion rolled. Again, the flowers are of little interest; it is the foliage that is of value.

There is no point in trying to grow these plants if humidity is low and temperatures aren't above 55°F or so all the time. They are ideal as indoor plants for a well-lighted and warm bathroom, where humidity is high for periods of the day. But let the temperature drop, and the plants soon show they disapprove. All caladiums are great container plants, not fussy as to soil as long as heat and humidity are provided. If grown outdoors in pots or borders, caladiums should be fed often with organic liquid fertilizer, at least once a month to six weeks. Plant the tubers 2 inches deep, spaced 8 to 12 inches apart; the distance apart will vary with the cultivars, dwarf types being planted closer together. Toward the end of summer, reduce the amount of water and gradually allow the plants to become dry. When the foliage has died down, lift the tubers and store them over the winter in a dry, well-ventilated area with temperatures around 70°F.

While you might be tempted by beautiful catalog illustrations, I feel you are wasting your money and time if you can't give these plants the warmth they require. Given warmth and humidity, they are easy to grow. In the case of most plants, temperatures that are too warm result in their rotting. With caladiums the opposite is true: Give them cold temperatures and they will rot.

Don't order them too early or the tuberous rhizomes could be damaged in the mail. The names given to the selections often will indicate the color of the foliage. 'Brandy Wine' is a dark red, 'White Christmas', a white with dark green veining, and 'Scarlet Beauty' has scarlet leaves with a hint of green at the edges. In the case of selections with such names as 'Fannie Munson', 'Festiva' and 'Frieda Hemple', you have to read the descriptions.

Botanical Name: Caladium
Family: Araceae
Common Names: Caladium, fancy-leaved caladium

Flower Colors: Grown for their colored foliage, which varies greatly, often with interesting color combinations. The leaf stalk and veining are also variously colored. Shades of greens and reds in varying combinations.

Flowering Time: Summer

Height: Some are dwarf, others reach up 24 or more inches

Spread: One plant can be quite wide spreading, up to 24 inches; depends on age of plants, length of growing season

Native Habitat: Most are hybrids from South American species of Brazil, Trinidad, Peru, Ecuador, and Colombia

Hardiness: Will not withstand frost, even when dormant

Depth of Planting: 2 inches

Distance Apart: 8 to 12 inches

Containers: Good houseplants

Light Requirements: Bright, indirect light; exposed only occasionally to direct sunlight

Soil Type: Soil rich in humus that holds moisture but does not become soggy

Special Conditions: These plants need tropical conditions: warm soil, warm temperatures and humidity. Avoid planting where wind could damage the leaves. Should be fertilized with liquid organic fertilizer on a regular basis.

Comments: You will seldom see any plants with such attractive foliage and in such a great color range as can be found in caladiums. They are ideal for bright summer shade. They bring an exotic look wherever they are grown and when used indoors, but if you cannot give them the conditions they need, they soon become unhappy and show it.

Camassia leichtlinii, native to the West Coast, is a great garden plant, perfect for growing near water. The color varies a little, but is always pleasing.

CAMASSIA
Liliaceae

When I first came to the United States I lived in Oregon. One day, while driving near Sandy (which lies east of Portland), I saw in a field, close to a stream, a very large group of striking blue flowers in full sun. It was a large colony of *Camassia leichtlinii,* commonly known as camass or quamash, and sometimes as wild hyacinth. At times the roots of these plants provided an important food for Native Americans, who boiled and roasted them. (The boiled roots yield a sort of molasses, used on festive occasions.)

While *Camassia* are found in many areas of the Pacific Northwest, most commonly in or near the foothills of mountain ranges, they are at their shining best when near a stream, as they require good moisture through midsummer. They seem to have no objection to a drier period after that. Many books say they require some shade, but this is not the case if they have enough moisture; if you can't supply the moisture they want, shade is the substitute. Examine their habitat in the wild and you will note the bulbs are above the waterline, but the roots have easy access to a plentiful supply of moisture.

Related to the English bluebell, this plant is sometimes called the American counterpart. This stretches the point; they are for the most part blue, but are not found under deciduous trees as English bluebells are. At home in almost any garden soil, the plant produces flowers in long racemes, which open to almost flat, generally narrow petals on flower stalks that vary between horizontal and upright. As there are many flowers on the flower heads, and they provide color over a long period of time, blooming in late spring and early summer. These plants are quite hardy, with the exception of a species from South America, not listed in catalogs. All the species and selections listed in our catalogs are from North America, and principally the Northwest. The species from the Midwest and the South, *C. scilloides*, I have yet to come across in a catalog, but it is a less attractive plant compared with the other species.

The bulbs of *Camassia cusickii* can weigh in at 4 to 8 ounces. The other species have bulbs of good, but not large, size, except in plantings that remain undisturbed for years. Plant 4 to 5 inches deep and 10 inches apart in fall. I do suggest that you plant in groups of five or more; they seem to like one another's company. Do not lift unless you have to, but if you must, lift in late summer, divide the bulbs and plant them

back as soon as possible. You will probably run into trouble if you plant too late in fall. The bulbs need time to become established before the onset of cold weather.

Where to grow camassia is a good question. Obviously not many gardens have streams running through them, but do plant near water if you can. Otherwise, choose an area that remains moist, especially in the early months of the year, until about May. Planted among shrubs, in grassland, in a bed by themselves—all such locations are suitable, but I would avoid putting them where you will have to lift them after just a few years. I understand that seed germinates quickly, and that it is not at all difficult to raise seedlings. They flower in about 3 or 4 seasons, but should be of sufficient size to set out in the garden in the second season.

Camassia cusickii: Native to Oregon, this species reaches up to 30 inches in height, has 2-inch-wide leaves and an excellent bud count on each stem. Variable in color, the flowers are generally pale blue with perhaps a hint of green, but deeper blue forms are sometimes listed; all are great cut flowers.

C. leichtlinii: This species is widespread over much of the western United States and into British Columbia. Leaves are not as wide as those of *C. cusickii*, but the flower spikes are often taller than 36 inches. Color is variable. Generally the white forms *C. leichtlinii* 'Alba' and deep purplish-blue *C. leichtlinii* ssp. *suksdorfi* are offered. Semi-double forms can also be found. All forms and selections are great garden plants.

C. quamash (syn. *C. esculenta*): Of the species native to the western states, this has the widest distribution; in addition to the coastal states, it is found in Montana and Utah. Not as tall as the other species, it rarely reaches more than 24 inches. It is hardy and perhaps the easiest species to grow. The flower color varies from white to pale and deep blues. Check the listings in catalogs when ordering, as some nurseries feature blue, and others violet, flowers. It flowers a little earlier than the other species.

Botanical Name: Camassia
Family: Liliaceae
Common Names: Camass, quamash, wild hyacinth
Flower Colors: White through shades of blue to violet-purple
Flowering Time: Late spring to early summer
Height: Varies by species from 24 to 36 inches
Spread: Plants will form large colonies if undisturbed; not considered invasive
Native Habitat: Species available in catalogs are from western North America
Hardiness: Quite hardy, to −40°F
Depth of Planting: 4 to 5 inches
Distance Apart: 10 inches
Containers: Not recommended
Light Requirements: Sun; if moisture supply is short, give light shade.
Soil Type: Good garden soil
Special Conditions: It is essential that the plants have a good supply of moisture through the flowering period and for a month or so afterward; then, they do not mind being on the dry side. In average soil there is no need for fertilizer.
Comments: While not bulbs for small city gardens, they should be considered for gardens of modest to large size. Planted with later-flowering azaleas or rhododendrons, they provide blue that seems to heighten the colors of these shrubs. Not at all difficult to grow, they are essential plants if there is a water feature in the garden. If you have a grass-covered slope that has good moisture for much of the year, these plants would be ideal, as this would give them a habitat very similar to their native one.

While many gardeners do not like plants with variegated foliage, cannas have their merits and let their presence be known.

CANNA
Cannaceae

The name is derived from the Greek *kanna*, meaning a reedlike plant. The common name, Indian shot, was given because the seed is black and very hard, resembling the shot or pellets fired from early firearms. But at once I must point out that the plants don't look reedlike, nor do they come from India.

There are some 50 species, most of which are seldom grown today. One, *Canna flaccida*, is native to Florida and has been much used in producing the many hybrids listed in our catalogs. The other species come from South America and the West Indies, and several have been used to produce the vivid blooms and colored and striped foliage of these summer-flowering plants. Few plants can be as spectacular, and I always enjoy the very large beds filled with cannas in the Botanic Garden in Durban, South Africa. Cannas have been growing for years there and, as it is a subtropical climate, they are left undisturbed. Gardeners in all parts of our country can enjoy cannas. Where there is little or no frost, the tuberous rhizomes can be left in the ground. In areas where frost is experienced, these rootstocks should be lifted and stored over winter in a frost-free location and kept just moist enough to prevent dehydration.

When next you have the chance, look closely at the flower of a canna. You will find it is made up of three sepals that are most commonly green, three long petals (that are often not very wide, but have good color), and five broad stamens that are colored and look like petals. Generally only one stamen is fertile, and this is often petaloid (having the appearance of a petal) on one side. There is a single style leading to an inferior ovary. The flower seems devoid of a logical arrangement of the various parts, but their combination is spectacular. The foliage is also of interest. Many have dark green foliage, some bronze, and still others have a mixture of bronze and green. As if this were not enough, one or two cultivars produce yellow and green foliage. I have yet to see yellow, green and bronze foliage on one plant, but no doubt it will be on the market one of these days.

Cannas are usually tall plants, some reaching more than 6 feet, and have been in cultivation since the seventeenth century. In 1893, C. L. Allen, the author of *Bulbs and Tuberous Plants*, wrote that the French had to be thanked for introducing a distinct new class of dwarf plants, known as Crozy's Dwarf Cannas. But Allen also mentions he had found a listing in Loddiges' *Botanical Cabinet* of a dwarf plant known as *Canna aura-vittata*, which was very similar to the cultivar listed as Madame Crozy. Allen goes on to say that the selection 'Star of 1891' is an American introduction worthy of special notice, as the height of that plant does not exceed 18 inches.

I mention this because recently great attention has been given to the cannas introduced by Mr. Wilhelm Pfitzer, a German hybridizer. Often in catalogs, these are great plants that reach about 30 inches in height. You will often find them listed as 'Pfitzer's Chinese Coral', 'Pfitzer's Primrose Yellow', and so forth. I wonder if Mr. Pfitzer managed to get hold of some of the older selections. There are very few cannas as short as 'Star of 1891' mentioned in Allen's book. The one that seems to come close is 'Ambrosia', a rich pink; 'Star of 1891' was a bright orange-crimson. Judging from photographs of 'Ambrosia', I think orange-crimson is not far from the actual color.

Hybridizers will often introduce new strains and give them names such as the already mentioned 'Pfitzer Selections'. The 'Liberty Series' is on the market now. All such plants are good, and from the many listed, you will find colors you like.

Cannas are quite versatile. Some gardeners like them in mixed borders, others in beds by themselves, while still others will plant large clumps close to a shrub border or even among the shrubs. I think that in colder climates their place is in the mixed border along with annuals and perennials, because lifting and storing them for winter would just be a continuation of work undertaken in that border anyway. In warm climates I like to see them in a bed by themselves, bold plantings of strong colors. Cannas grow well in containers, but the container must be at least 18 inches in depth or the plants will not look at home. Cannas, even the dwarf types, seem to look best in solid-color containers, perhaps because of the strength of their own colors. In containers and in the border, cannas appreciate a good soil rich in humus and regular feedings with a liquid organic fertilizer. Never let them stand in water—they just do not like it; make sure that drainage is good.

While I appreciate variegated foliage, I prefer that foliage be of a solid color in cannas. To me, leaves streaked with yellow look as though there is something wrong. I am not quite as much against bronze mixed with green, but good, clear flower colors, above solid foliage colors, is for me. While most gardeners will be able to select colors and plants that reach desired heights from the various catalogs, the following information may be of some assistance. Three cultivars are really tall, reaching 6 or more feet in a season, with flower production that is not heavy. These are 'City of Portland', deep pink with green foliage; 'Orange Beauty', orange with green foliage; and 'Red King Humbert', red with reddish foliage (this cultivar has been around for a number of years). The selection of plants that vary between 4 and 6 feet is greater, and includes: 'Florence Vaughn', orange-red with green foliage; 'Los Angeles', coral pink with green foliage; 'Mohawk', a good bronze color with bronze foliage; 'President', red with green foliage; 'Richard Wallace', a lovely canary yellow with green foliage; and 'Rosemund Cole', a bicolor with red and gold flowers and green foliage. Those plants under 30 inches are mostly the Pfitzer type, and you would not go wrong with these or the 'Ambrosia' I have mentioned.

One of the great things about cannas is that they are practically trouble free, and seldom will you have any pest or disease problems. The trick to growing them is not to be too hasty in setting them outdoors. They like warm nights; although they are not as fussy, by any means, as the caladiums, put them outdoors only when nights are warm, above 50°F, and then they will grow steadily. Give them cold nights and they seem not to budge, and even if warm nights come along, they never seem to grow as well as plants set out when the nights are warm.

Storage can be tricky, but with just a little care you can avoid losing any plants. When lifting, cut them down to about 6 inches above soil level after the first frost has blackened the foliage. Shake off as much of the soil as you can, then store in a frost-free area with good air circulation. When the plants are dry, clean off the remaining soil, then store them in damp peat moss. Check every once in a while that the moisture level is at a point that stops dehydration of the tubers—not wet, but only barely moist. To start them into growth, you can cut the rootstocks into smaller sections to increase your plants, but each must have one or more buds.

Botanical Name: Canna
Family: Cannaceae
Common Name: Indian shot
Flower Colors: Wide range of yellow, pink and red tones, with some bicolors. Foliage may be green, bronze or a mixture of these, as well as green striped with yellow.
Flowering Time: Mid- to late summer
Height: From 23 inches to more than 6 feet
Spread: 2 to 3 feet per plant, as plants form bold clumps over a few seasons.
Native Habitat: C. flaccida is native to Florida. The other species come from tropical and subtropical regions of America.
Hardiness: Must be lifted and stored over winter where there is severe frost.
Depth of Planting: 4 to 6 inches
Distance Apart: Dwarf types 12 inches, taller types to 24 inches
Containers: Grows well in containers
Light Requirements: Full sun
Soil Type: Good garden soil with high organic content
Special Conditions: Appreciate being fertilized on a regular basis and like to have good moisture during summer. Well-established plants withstand drought well.
Comments: One of the brightest mid- to late-summer-flowering plants. Even a small garden

would benefit from a selection of the dwarf types. A garden of fair size should grow these plants, but I think they look best if viewed with lawn in front of them. I prefer the moderate-sized plants to the dwarf and very tall ones. Fertilize only when not growing well. Many a garden in California owes its summer color to these plants. They will not let you down, and if you can leave them undisturbed, do so!

CARDIOCRINUM
Liliaceae

The name is derived from the Greek *kardia*, meaning heart, and *krinon*, a kind of lily, in reference to the shape of the leaves. I wish all gardeners could see this plant in flower. It is magnificent. For many years it was named *Lilium giganteum*. It has all the grace of a lily, including strong fragrance, but the growth habit, the shape of the leaves (which can be 12 inches long and as wide), and the form of the bulb, a few overlapping scales, all combine to make this genus separate from *Lilium*. Even so, the common name remains giant lily. A curious point: This is the only bulbous genus that provides us with a musical instrument. The hill people of Nepal, where *Cardiocrinum giganteum* is at home, make musical pipes from the hollow stems.

There are three species, but you will find only *Cardiocrinum giganteum* listed in catalogs. *C. cathayanum* from China and *C. cordatum* from Japan are rare plants, but nevertheless beautiful. *C. giganteum* is the ideal woodland plant. Clothed with striking foliage, it often reaches well over 6 feet in height when it flowers, which it will do only when the bulb is some five years old. Each year it will send up strong stems that die back to the ground in fall. Then gathering strength over the years, it sends up a stem, the top several feet of which carry lovely trumpet-

It may take seven years for *Cardiocrinum giganteum* plants to flower, but even without flowers, they are not unattractive, and perfect for shady areas.

shaped flowers of pure white, each 6 inches in diameter, as many as 20 to a stem. This is a wonderful sight in late summer, and in the evenings the surrounding air will be laden with the most delightful perfume.

So strong are the stems produced and so vigorous is the plant that the diameter of the base of the stem will often be 6 to 8 inches. After the flowers fade, very large seedpods with many seeds are produced—necessary, as after flowering the plant dies. It is monocarpic. But not to worry, as over the years that it has been growing it will have produced young plants at its base. These will now take over and will, in turn, flower.

I like the giant lily best with a backdrop of rhododendrons and a mass of primulas at its feet. The short primulas make the imposing stems over them seem even larger. Obviously such a plant is not for every garden. These plants should not be imprisoned in containers. They may exist under such conditions, but will not perform well. They love a rich soil with plenty of organic matter, and require moisture throughout summer. They do come, after all, from areas where it is almost constantly raining. But don't try to grow them in areas where they will stand in water for more than a few days, for they may object strongly.

Just how hardy these plants are is debatable. Certainly they will withstand temperatures down to −20°F, with the protection of a good mulch, and I think even colder temperatures can be withstood with a good thick mulch and snow-cover. What will harm them is freezing and thawing.

If you have a friend with a woodland garden, I can think of no finer gift than 3 or 5 of these bulbs. It would be thoughtful to take along at the same time a large bag of leaf-mold, so the soil can be well prepared for them. Plant in fall or early spring. Plant in enough time for the bulbs to make some root growth in fall, or protect them from severe cold and plant in spring. Set the bulbs with their necks just breaking the soil surface, then cover them with leaves. Some feel the plants should be lifted after one stem has flowered, then divided and planted back, to prevent overcrowding. I feel they are best left undisturbed. Let the young plants fight it out for room; nature has a way of looking after such crowding. Space the bulbs some 18 inches apart. Protect the plants from slugs and snails. At all costs avoid foot traffic over the bulbs; the soil should not be compacted. Despite their great height there is no need to stake the stems, which will be strong enough to withstand any but the most extreme winds that come along.

Botanical Name: Cardiocrinum
Family: Liliaceae
Common Name: Giant lily
Flower Colors: Pure white trumpet flowers, some purple shading at base
Flowering Time: Late summer
Height: Can reach 8 feet or more when in flower
Spread: Will form colonies at base of stalks
Native Habitat: The Himalayas, parts of Nepal and Upper Assam and upper Burma to parts of southeastern Tibet
Hardiness: Hardy to −10°F with protection
Depth of Planting: Neck of bulbs should just break the soil surface
Distance Apart: 18 inches
Containers: Not recommended
Light Requirements: Light shade
Soil Type: Rich woodland soil
Special Conditions: Must have adequate moisture throughout the summer months. No feeding needed, but top dressings of rotted leaf mold are advantageous. Firm soil but not compacted is best.

Comments: If this is not the finest bulbous plant for the woodland, I know none better. Once you have seen it in flower you will remember it for years and recall the lovely fragrance. Lilies have been called the aristocrats of the garden, and this plant is first among equals. Worth walking several miles to see!

CHASMANTHE
Iridaceae

The name comes from the Greek *chasme* meaning gaping, and *anthe,* or flower. The flowers are indeed tubular, a couple of inches long, with upper petals longer than the lower ones and thus forming a hood over the protruding anthers. Very free-flowering, the plant is distichous on a branched stem—the flowers face in opposite directions and are arranged in two rows on either side of the stem.

There are several species but only one, *Chasmanthe floribunda,* is found in catalogs, and that rarely. This is a great pity, as these are striking plants and easy to grow. Sadly, they are not hardy, but neither are *Gladiolus,* yet these are commonly grown in our gardens. *Chasmanthe* corms can be left in the ground in frost-free (or nearly so) areas. Plant them in spring, lift in the fall and store them over winter in colder climates. They are well worth this little extra work.

The flowers are closer to orange than red. Produced in late spring, they tower above the sword-shaped foliage, which can be as much as 2 inches wide at the base. The flowers may be carried on stems reaching 36 or more inches in height. It is not uncommon to find well over 30 flowers on a stem, and as they last a long time when cut and placed in water, I think one day they will be grown for commercial flower production. They are easy to grow.

Chasmanthe floribunda grows wild just north of Cape Town, South Africa, a striking sight. The soil in this region is not particularly rich and *Chasmanthe* will grow in any garden soil. Plant the corms 3 to 4 inches deep and 10 to 12 inches apart. Planted in fall in warmer (frost-free) climates, they will be in flower in late spring or early summer, a little later when planted in spring. Make sure they receive moisture in winter and spring; after flowering they do not require much moisture, and the

Despite being easy to grow, *Chasmanthe floribunda* is not as frequently found in gardens as it ought to be.

foliage soon dies back. At this point the corms will be dormant, suitable for lifting in fall and planting in spring in colder areas.

There has been much discussion during recent years of the need to furnish our gardens with plants that are drought-tolerant. If ever a plant was designed with this in mind, it is *Chasmanthe.* Combine this attribute with the ease of culture and the fact that it is a good cut flower, and I think we have a winner. These are not common garden plants, but they most certainly deserve to be. The other species offer bright red flowers and yellow flowers with red stripes, and it would seem certain that many interesting interspecific hybrids could be obtained. To my knowledge, no one is undertaking such work—a pity.

Chasmanthe floribunda: 36 or more inches in height, with orange-red tubular flowers with protruding stamens, sword-shaped foliage, flowers early to midspring. *C. f.* var. *antholyzoides* has reddish-orange flowers, *C. f.* var. *duckittii* has soft yellow flowers.

Botanical Name: Chasmanthe

Family: Iridaceae

Common Name: None to my knowledge, but plantsman Richard Doutt refers to them as pennants or pennant flowers.

Flower Colors: Red-orange and yellow

Flowering Time: Spring

Height: Up to 36 inches, sometimes more

Spread: Will form colonies in warm climates if left alone

Native Habitat: Cape Province, South Africa

Hardiness: Not hardy; withstands only a little light frost.

Depth of Planting: 3 to 4 inches

Distance Apart: 10 to 12 inches

Containers: I would suspect these plants would fare well in containers, but I have not seen them grown this way.

Light Requirements: Sun or very light shade

Soil Type: Good garden soil

Special Conditions: Not difficult to grow, but must have moisture during their growing period, and prefer to be a little on the dry side when foliage dies down.

Comments: Why these plants are not more widely grown where drought-resistant plants are needed is a mystery. Even in cold climates they are deserving of consideration and well worth lifting and storing over winter. Good cut flowers. A genus that deserves to be discovered by hybridizers and it is certain many interesting colors and forms could be forthcoming. Near my office in Sausalito these plants flourish without care and without water (they are practically weeds).

Chinodoxa luciliae is a pure delight, and as it flowers early in the year, it is always a welcome sight, truly a "glory of the snow." (Photo courtesy of International Bloembollen Centrum.)

CHIONODOXA
Liliaceae

These are the popular glory-of-the-snow bulbs. The name is derived from the Greek *chion,* meaning snow, and *doxa,* glory. It is apt, as these plants are at home in the high mountain regions of Turkey, Crete and Asia Minor, appearing as soon as the snows start to melt. They are perforce very hardy, probably seen at their best in short grass, but to be effective they must be in bold plantings.

Chionodoxas must be numbered among the finest of early flowering bulbs. The flowers are mostly in shades of blue with various splashes of white, but pink and white forms are not uncommon. Related to *Hyacinthoides,* they differ in that their petals are joined at the base to form a very short tube, and then flare, resulting in a cup at the center of the flower. Foliage is sparse; often only two leaves are produced, thick, narrow and dark green. There are some nine species, but catalog listings generally offer four species. Many selections of *Chionodoxa luciliae* are to be found, this being the species most commonly grown and the finest. The genus should be examined in depth, as some authorities feel the *C. luciliae* of commerce is in fact *C. forbesii;* fortunately this need not be of concern to gardeners, but something for the purists to worry about.

Plant the bulbs in fall, putting them 3 inches deep in a sunny area, and plant many in one spot so they will be noticed. Space them 3 to 4 inches apart and leave undisturbed for years, lifting and dividing if and only when the plantings become overcrowded. When you do lift, you will find many small bulbs have been produced, and you will be able to make other bold plantings with the production from the original ones.

Chionodoxa gigantea: This species has large flowers of light to medium blue, and stands up to 8 inches tall. Some nurseries offer a white form. I am skeptical of some listings, as I feel that what is offered is a large-flowered form of *C. luciliae* and the name has been coined to accommodate this form. This is unfortunate, as there is another species correctly called *C. gigantea.*

C. luciliae: By far the best species, and the most commonly grown and listed. It carries as many as 10 flowers on a 6- to 8-inch stem, the flowers, 1 inch in diameter and well spaced. The color is a good blue with a white center. Various forms are listed, including: 'Alba', white; 'Blue Giant', sky blue with a white center; 'Pink Giant', which is most likely the same as 'Rosea', a bright pink with a white center.

C. sardensis: This species comes from Turkey and flowers a little later than the others. A good, deep blue, rather rare, and a little shorter in height. Some catalogs list such selections as 'Deep Blue' and 'Gentian Blue', but I suspect these are not much, if any, different from the species.

C. siehei: This is the largest growing of all the species and can reach 12 inches in height, with flowers that are almost purple. With such a deep color I would be inclined to grow this where snow can be expected at flowering time; seen against a dark soil, the color is not always appreciated. Possibly the latest flowering of the species, it deserves as much attention as *C. luciliae,* but does not get it.

These bulbs make good plants for indoors when grown in small pots in ordinary potting soil; crowd the bulbs together, and make certain they are well rooted before giving them additional warmth and placing them in a sunny window.

Botanical Name: Chionodoxa
Family: Liliaceae
Common Name: Glory-of-the-snow
Flower Colors: Blue, with white and rose selections; also purple
Flowering Time: Early spring
Height: Usually 6 to 10 inches
Spread: Will form colonies if left undisturbed, but not invasive
Native Habitat: Turkey, Crete and Asia Minor
Hardiness: Fully hardy
Depth of Planting: 3 inches
Distance Apart: 3 to 4 inches
Containers: Can be grown in containers and brought indoors, but should have good rooting period outdoors before being given warmer temperatures.
Light Requirements: Sun or very light shade
Soil Type: Average garden soil
Special Conditions: They like moisture while growing, but don't like to be too wet. When "forced" into flower the bulbs are best discarded after they have finished blooming, or they can be planted out with no expectation of flower for a season or two.

Comments: These plants are quite charming, but if you just have a few you may not notice them, so plant in very bold groupings. Great little plants for bringing indoors for a breath of spring early in the year; the secret is to give them bright light as well as warmth, or they can become a little lanky and then look untidy.

CHLIDANTHUS
Amaryllidaceae

The name is derived from the Greek *clideio*, meaning delicate, and *anthos*, meaning flower. This is not a common genus, but I am pleased to say a number of nurseries are listing *Chlidanthus fragrans*, and discerning gardeners will be able to enjoy the delightful yellow flowers and the lovely fragrance. *Chlidanthus* flowers in midsummer with trumpet-shaped flowers in a loose umbel, one umbel per stem. The flowers appear before the leaves, on stems 10 inches tall.

The unfortunate thing about these bulbs is that they are not hardy, and in areas where temperatures fall below 26°F they must be lifted, stored over winter and planted again the following spring. In frost-free areas and where there are only minor frosts, they can be left undisturbed and will form bold clumps in just a few seasons. These plants like sun, or very light shade, in the hottest areas. This is not unexpected, as they are at home in Mexico (*C. ehrenbergii*), Peru and Chile (*C. fragrans*). Some authorities feel there is only one species, and that all the plants are *C. fragrans*. The main difference between the two species is that *C. ehrenbergii* has flowers on stalks that are 1 to 2 inches in length, while *C. fragrans* has flowers that are sessile, or very nearly so.

They are not fussy as to soil, but prefer well-drained, sandy loams with a little compost or organic matter worked in, so that moisture is re-

Pop a few *Chlidanthus fragrans* into a small container and bring them indoors to enjoy the wonderful fragrance. It is good to see these plants listed, so well worth growing. (Photo courtesy of Helen Crocker Russell Library.)

tained and available to them during their growing period. They make good container plants. Plant with the noses of the bulbs (they are not large) just at soil level, three bulbs to a 6-inch pot. The ideal soil mix is equal parts good topsoil or potting soil, sharp sand and peat moss. You can get by just adding some sharp sand to regular potting soil. Once they have flowered and the foliage has started to die down, put the pots on their sides and let them become dry. Then, remove the bulbs, and clean them off and store them. Repot each spring in a fresh soil mixture;

they don't seem to like the same soil in successive seasons. You will find a few offsets produced around the bases of the older bulbs. These should be removed and, if of fair size, they can be planted or repotted with the older bulbs.

While no fertilizer is required if grown in borders, *Chlidanthus* in pots appreciate some liquid organic fertilizer. Wait until the flowers have finished, then feed as long as the foliage remains green; stop feeding as soon as the foliage starts to die down.

Give *Chlidanthus* a prominent place in the front of the border where you can keep them moist until the foliage starts to die down, when they prefer to be on the dry side. In colder areas, lift when dormant and store in nearly bone-dry sand or peat over winter in a frost-free area, protected from temperatures below 40°F, and keep them dry.

When storing over the winter, make certain the bulbs are not suffocated. Keep them well ventilated, but dry, or rot will set in. These plants seem free of most problems, except that slugs and snails seem to like the emerging flower stems. Despite their rather limited height, these are great cut flowers. However, for the house I think it preferable to grow them in pots. Just one or two will make their presence known by their fragrance.

Botanical Name: Chlidanthus
Family: Amaryllidaceae
Common Name: None known
Flower Color: Yellow
Flowering Time: Midsummer
Height: 10 inches
Spread: Will form colonies if left in the ground
Native Habitat: Peru and Chile; *C. ehrenbergii* from Mexico
Hardiness: Not hardy
Depth of Planting: Plant with nose of bulb just exposed

Distance Apart: 12 inches in the garden, much closer in pots
Containers: Excellent
Light Requirements: Sun, light shade in warmest areas where summer temperatures remain 80° to 90°F day after day
Soil Type: Not fussy, but good drainage is important.
Special Conditions: Moisture is needed while the plants are in growth, and afterward a dry period is best. They must be dry when stored over winter.
Comments: Reading about these plants in an old book, I was amused to learn the bulbs should be planted in the same manner as *Gladiolus*, but in a dry and well-drained soil, as they are impatient of water. I wonder how they grew, as the bulbs should be at soil level, not deep as *Gladiolus*, and they need moisture while growing. If you can grow *Chlidanthus* indoors in pots, do so, as their fragrance is a delight and their color so cheerful and bright. Deserving of a place in even quite small gardens, they give great value for the space they occupy.

CLIVIA
Amaryllidaceae

Many people think this plant was named after Clive of India, an English colonialist, but it was named for the Duchess of Northumberland, whose maiden name was Clive. There are four species of evergreen plants in this genus, all native to South Africa. While the rootstock is not strictly a bulb (it is barely modified for storage), it is so called when the term *bulb* is loosely applied. The plants are listed in bulb catalogs and regarded as bulbs by most, but this is stretching the point a little. Only one species is available, *Clivia miniata*.

Some books list this as having the common

Clivia miniata are lovely plants for the shade, and good container plants. In my garden in San Francisco they are in flower from November to March, marvelous value!

wall; it is quite protected, and while temperatures have dropped to 32°F, it has survived without any problem. But I made the mistake of not having it right against the wall, and thus exposed to sun for a period of about a week in summer. The result was that the tips of the broad, deep green leaves were exposed to the sun and burned.

These plants of mine have been in the same large pots for more than 10 years now. They are thriving and as yet have not cracked the pots, but they will soon. These plants thrive on not being disturbed for many years.

One of its merits is that it produces large umbels of 10 to 20 or more flowers, each bell-shaped and opening to 2 inches in diameter, so the umbel is often more than 8 inches in diameter. Flowers appear in winter and into spring, and occasionally at other times of the year. The color varies a little from red to orange, some plants having flowers more orange than others. There is a lovely yellow form known as *Clivia miniata* var. *citrina*, much sought after, and commanding a very high price. In addition, a form known as *striata* with variegated leaves exists, but it is not an attractive plant.

Plant so the white part of the stem is almost buried, and set the plants 12 inches apart. In pots, plant one bulb to a 12-inch pot; it may look a little lost for a while, but will quickly form offsets and fill the pot. Use ordinary potting soil. No fertilizer should be given until after the plants have finished flowering. Then, feed every six weeks until the end of summer, then stop. Moisture must be given at all times, even when the plants are grown in containers and the pots are filled with nothing but roots. I just pour water into the center of the plants—they seem to appreciate it! I have never had a problem with pests or disease. Snails and slugs seem to leave the plants alone, but keep an eye open for them nevertheless.

name Kaffir lily, now a derogatory term. In its native land it is called *boslelie*, meaning woodlily, as it is found growing in damp shady places in woods, forest and bush. Though this plant is not hardy, there is consolation in that it makes an excellent houseplant, and indeed is frequently listed as such. In areas where there is even a touch of frost it should be indoors during winter, then placed outdoors in shade during the summer. I live in San Francisco and have grown this plant in a pot outdoors against a north-facing

My plants reach some 24 inches above the

pots. I doubt they will ever grow taller than this, and when I have seen them in the wild they are shorter, but have formed very large colonies. If you plant them out in a warm climate, give them room to spread. In an old book I read, "Clivia, a very pretty genus, represented by one species only, *C. nobilis*, a greenhouse plant, the flowers are drooping, from 40 to 50 on a well furnished spike, of a delicate flesh-color throughout the greater part of the tube, heightening to a deep red." This is quite a good description of *C. nobilis*, a species unfortunately not found in catalogs.

Botanical Name: Clivia
Family: Amaryllidaceae
Common Names: Often called Kaffir lily, bush lily or woodlily
Flower Colors: Orange to orange-red; yellow forms also known
Flowering Time: Winter to spring
Height: Seldom more than 24 inches
Spread: The wide, arching leaves spread 8 to 10 inches on each side of the plant when well established. Will form large colonies.
Native Habitat: South Africa
Hardiness: Not hardy
Depth of Planting: Almost cover the white parts of the stem; the top of the white and all the green should be above the soil.
Distance Apart: 12 inches
Containers: Excellent
Light Requirements: Must have shade; never direct sunlight or leaves will burn
Soil Type: Good garden soil, use potting soil if growing in containers.
Special Conditions: Provide moisture throughout the year. Fertilize a little after flowering is finished and for the rest of summer. Let plants become crowded; they like to be that way. Protect from frost by bringing indoors, but do not place in a sunny window.

Comments: Lovely plants; others in the genus also deserve to be grown. Wide, shiny green leaves make this an attractive plant even when not in flower. One of the finest plants for the shade in warm climates. As it flowers from winter into spring, it is a valuable plant and doesn't seem to have problems with pests or diseases. I hope the yellow flowering form becomes popular.

COLCHICUM
Liliaceae

In Armenia there is a city called Colchis, known both as the birthplace of Medea and for its poisonous plants. Horace wrote, "Every baleful juice which poisonous Colchian globes produce." The genus is widespread, found in Iran, Turkestan and other parts of the eastern Mediterranean, as well as in much of Europe and Great Britain. The most commonly grown species is *Colchicum autumnale*, and there are several forms of this spe-

It is wonderful to see the flowers of *Colchicum autumnale* just pop out of the ground. To preserve the flowers, protect them from rain with a sheet of glass.

cies listed in catalogs. There are more than 50 species, and they flower in fall, winter and spring. They are sometimes confused with *Crocus*, but they are in a different family. A quick way to tell the difference between the two genera is that *Crocus* has three anthers, *Colchicum* has six.

Colchicums have been used for medicine, and the extract colchicine can be used to cause dwarfing in plants and to change the chromosome count in the pollen and egg cells of plants. *Colchicum* seeds are covered with a sugary substance when ripe, and appreciative ants help to distribute the seeds. The ants eat the sweet coating, but the essential parts of the seed are protected by colchicine and not eaten.

The corms of colchicums can be quite large and irregular in shape. The fall-flowering species can burst into flower even when not planted, and to avoid this they should be planted in July, 5 inches deep and 6 to 8 inches apart. There is not quite such a rush to plant the winter- and spring-flowering species, but they should be planted as soon as you receive them, and while you space them. As for the fall-flowering species, you can set them just a little shallower. Autumn-flowering species flower before the foliage is produced, which follows in winter and lasts well into spring. The winter- and spring-flowering species produce their foliage at the same time as the flowers. Moisture should be given while foliage remains green; then, as it dries, reduce the amount. All colchicums like the sun and seem to do just fine in ordinary soil. Bulbs should be left undisturbed; lift only if you wish to propagate. This is best done when the foliage has died down. Separate and replant the bulbs; the smaller ones will flower in about two seasons, the larger ones the following season. I think the best use of these plants is in the front of the shrub border where they provide interest and color when many shrubs are dormant. The flowers are inclined to become floppy and untidy,

and this makes them unsuitable for growing in containers.

Because it consists of so many species, with three distinct flowering times, the genus has been divided into three sections.

1. Autumn-flowering species.
2. Winter- and spring-flowering species. Only one of this section is generally available, *C. luteum*, the only yellow-flowered species.
3. Tessellated species. These are species that have a crisscross pattern of dark and light mauve on the petals. I have not seen any of these offered in catalogs, but one day they may be. In the past, one species (*C. bowlesianum*) was sometimes listed.

Colchicum autumnale: Native to much of Europe, it produces as many as six pale pink flowers from one corm. Often in flower by late August, the plants reach up to 6 inches in height but soon flop over. It will flower on the shelf if not planted quickly enough. Nurseries offer various forms such as: 'Album', a white-flowered single; 'Alboplenum', a white-flowered double; 'Plenum', a double form of the species with pale pink flowers; and 'Pleniflorum', with amethyst-violet, double flowers. All of these plants produce their leaves after the flowers have finished.

C. bornmuelleri: This species from northwest Turkey has very large flowers of bright mauve and the added attraction of a white throat. Not very tall, reaching only 4 inches, it flowers in September. Foliage is produced after the flowers.

C. byzantinum: This is a species that has long been in cultivation, and has an interesting history. It was named by Clusius, court botanist to Emperor Ferdinand I of Austria, and sent from Constantinople to two ladies in Vienna in 1588. The corms are very large and can produce a great number of flowers, more than a dozen not being unusual when well established. The lilac-to-purple flowers appear in September. The foliage is a bit unusual, as much as 4 inches wide and more than 12 inches long. This species does not set seed. E. A. Bowles, a great authority on many of the smaller bulbs, felt this was because it had for years been propagated vegetatively. I suppose this is possible, but somehow doubt it. Sometimes incorrectly listed as *C. autumnale major.*

C. cilicicum: Much like *C. byzantinum,* this species has large, deep-purple flowers enhanced by brilliant golden filaments (the stamen stems), and it has a little fragrance. It flowers in September.

C. luteum: This species from northern India produces 3 or 4 small flowers that are a lovely yellow and stay almost flat on the soil. Leaves appear with the flowers in late winter–early spring, and continue to grow long after the flowers have passed. These plants have a very long flowering period, often as much as three months, but even just a few flowers put on quite a display. Not commonly listed, but well worth having.

C. speciosum: This species from Turkey and the Caucasus is regarded as one of the finest for the garden. In the species, the white throats add an almost bicolor look to the flowers. Flowers have a tulip form, reach a height of 8 to 10 inches, and are pale to deep reddish violet. They appear in September or early October. A white form is offered under the name 'Album'. The foliage appears late, sometimes not until spring.

Cultivars: In catalogs frequently there are listings of such named forms as 'Giant' and 'Waterlily'. These would appear to be selections from

the species *C. speciosum,* selected for their large flowers and height.

Botanical Name: Colchicum
Family: Liliaceae
Common Names: Autumn crocus, meadow saffron
Flower Colors: Pinks, violets, whites and one yellow species
Flowering Time: Some in autumn, others winter and early spring
Height: 4 to 12 inches
Spread: Will form good-sized clumps in 2 or 3 seasons
Native Habitat: Eastern Mediterranean, Iran, Caucasus, Turkey, India and much of Europe, depending on species.
Hardiness: Fully hardy
Depth of Planting: 4 inches
Distance Apart: 6 to 8 inches
Containers: Not recommended, as they are a bit untidy
Light Requirements: Full sun or light shade
Soil Type: Average garden soil
Special Conditions: Allow the foliage to grow and mature in order to strengthen the bulbs. Keep them moist during the growing season.
Comments: These plants occupy very little space, and the care needed is minimal. For these reasons they are plants for all gardens and all gardeners. However, if you like flowers that remain tidy, they are not for you as they flop around and don't retain their shape for long. Still, their color and effectiveness are undiminished.

The famed lily of the valley (*Convallaria majalis*) is a grand plant for a cool, shady area, and the fragrance is a delight. (Photo courtesy of International Bloembollen Centrum.)

CONVALLARIA
Liliaceae

Convallaria majalis is the only species in this genus to be found growing wild in much of Europe and North America. The name is derived from *convallis*, meaning a valley, and this much-loved plant is commonly known as lily-of-the-valley. It has a scaly, rhizomatous rootstock, and while not strictly a bulb, I mention it here because it is included in lists of bulbous plants nurseries offer. The rootstocks are called "pips" in the trade. The flowers are lovely little white bells on sturdy stems that reach up to 9 inches in height, surrounded at the base by two fresh green leaves. The native habitat is under deciduous trees and shrubs, where it can enjoy a soil rich in humus, and also moisture, especially during the spring and early summer months. It is not found in the wild in areas with dry summers, and indeed is difficult to grow in warmer climates, with little or no frost. A great pity, as the fragrance and the plants' ability to spread make it a superb groundcover; in cooler areas, where considerable frost and even snow occur, it is hard to imagine a more delightful one. It is charming in small containers and is grown commercially in this manner.

It used to be a tradition in Europe for young men to search the forests and woods for these flowers in order to be the first to bring them to their girlfriends. Today it is easier to purchase them, and it is better to preserve the species in the wild. I can think of few greater pleasures than to sit, in the warm evenings of springtime, near the edge of a wood, enjoying the fragrance of a mass of lilies of the valley, with the companion of one's choice.

I can't quite decide whether these are, or are not, difficult plants to grow. I have had both good luck and no luck at all in getting them established. The same care was given each time, the plants were good, and the location seemed ideal. Why did one batch grow while the others did not? I do not know. The plants are worthwhile trying several times if the setting seems right. But what is the right setting? A shady place where these plants can spread, a woodsy soil with plenty of humus, a climate that can provide good moisture through much of the year, and temperatures rarely much higher than 85°F. Set the crowns of the plants (or the "pips") 3 inches deep and 6 inches apart. Firm them gently in the soil; the earth should not be compacted. If they like their location the plants will thrive, this to the point where in a few seasons you can dig the plants up in early fall, divide them and expect the largest of them to flower the following spring.

As might be expected, there are some selections offered. 'Fortins Giant' flowers a little later in June and has larger bells and glaucous foliage. 'Rosea' has a hint of rose in the flowers. The double-flowered form is known as 'Flore-plena'.

Botanical Name: Convallaria

Family: Liliaceae

Common Name: Lily-of-the-valley

Flower Colors: White; a pink form is also grown

Flowering Time: Spring

Height: 6 to 9 inches

Spread: Can be an effective groundcover

Native Habitat: Europe and North America

Hardiness: Hardy

Depth of Planting: 1 inch

Distance Apart: 6 to 9 inches

Containers: Very nice

Light Requirements: Shade

Soil Type: Woodland type rich in humus

Special Conditions: Seem to require a cool winter and do not take kindly to warmth. Must have good moisture during the growing season and never let go completely dry.

Comments: One of the great woodland plants of Europe, thriving in deciduous woods and forests (but never under beech trees, *Fagus* species). It can be found in quantity in those areas where shade is constant, the winters cool and moisture present throughout the year. They should be planted close to the house so the lovely fragrance can be frequently enjoyed.

The large flowers of × *Crinodonna* are elegant. They make good container plants, quite attractive even when not in flower. (Photo courtesy of International Bloembollen Centrum.)

× CRINODONNA
Amaryllidaceae

These lovely plants are the result of crossing two genera, *Crinum* and *Amaryllis*. The cross took place in two different countries in the same year, Italy and the United States of America, in 1920. The American hybridizer named the progeny × *Amarcrinum howardii* (F. Howard, of Los Angeles, made the cross), but the description was first published in Italy, by the hybridizer Dr. Ragioneri of Florence. Hence the Italian's name, × *Crinodonna corsii* established preference.

The two species involved are *Amaryllis bella-donna* and *Crinum moorei*, the *Amaryllis* being the seed parent. All crosses between these two species result in × *Crinodonna*. They all flower in fall, with the persistent green leaves of *Crinum* and the pink, funnel-shaped flowers of *Amaryllis*. Like the parents, these bulbs are not very hardy. However, they perform well in containers, so gardeners in colder climates can grow them if they can provide protection over the winter months.

These plants are great in climates where frost is seldom experienced. The evergreen foliage is never unattractive, and the flowers are carried aloft on strong, 30-inch-long stems. The flowers will often measure 4 inches in diameter; there are many, and as they do not open all at once, the plants are in flower for a long period from late summer into fall.

Ordinary garden soil suits these bulbs well. Plant with the neck of the bulb just above the surface of the soil and space 10 to 12 inches apart. They appreciate sun but do well in light (not dense) shade. Keep them moist, and give a little organic liquid fertilizer in early summer if the soil is not very fertile. These plants should remain undisturbed, and if grown in containers, this will mean some feeding will be necessary for the plants to maintain their vigor. However, do not feed too heavily, or the result will be good foliage production at the expense of flowers.

Botanical Name: × *Crinodonna*
Family: Amaryllidaceae
Common Name: None to my knowledge
Flower Color: Pink
Flowering Time: Late summer into fall
Height: 30 inches
Spread: Will increase by producing offsets, but not quickly
Native Habitat: Human-made hybrid
Hardiness: Not hardy
Depth of Planting: Neck of the bulb at soil level or just above
Distance Apart: 10 to 12 inches
Containers: Performs well
Light Requirements: Sun or light shade
Soil Type: Good garden soil
Special Conditions: Should have moisture throughout the year. Will not withstand any frost.
Comments: I would hesitate to say this is a "must" for any garden, but it should be high on the list of those with large gardens in a warm climate. In colder climates, I think it is not a plant for home gardens, but well worth growing in gardens open to the public, as when in flower it is bound to attract attention. A number of selections are listed in catalogs, but the merits of these may owe more to descriptive writing than anything else.

CRINUM
Amaryllidaceae

Krinon is Greek for lily, and if *crinums* were hardier plants, I think they would rival the lilies as garden plants. While they can be grown in containers, and thus in colder climates with protection over the colder months, I would hesitate to plant them in borders where the temperatures drop into the high teens. Even then I would give them the protection of a south-facing wall and a thick mulch.

No one can deny the beauty of *Crinum*. The flower forms vary, from trumpet-shaped to flat-faced flowers with narrow petals. The colors vary

These *Crinum macowanii* were photographed in the wild. Planted close together in a garden, they are sensational. Try some!

from white through pink into red. Color can be found in the center of the petals or over the entire flower. The fragrance is most pleasant, but a little elusive to my nose, as I have found plants strongly scented in late afternoon and into the evening, but return the following evening to find the scent almost gone. The bulbs are large. Sometimes their necks are very long, sometimes short. Sometimes the foliage is held almost erect, while in other plants it spreads out over a large area. It is always attractive and dark green in color. The height of *Crinum* varies. In Zimbabwe I have seen *C. macowanii* only 12 to 18 inches in height, far less than the 48 inches it "normally" reaches.

The distribution of *Crinum* is quite wide, from the warmer parts of Africa to the cooler regions of the Cape, from the tropical parts of America to parts of Florida and westward into Texas, in China, and in India to the mountains of Abyssinia. No wonder it has attracted the attention of hybridizers, and today a great number of hybrids are to be found. Some of these are, to say the least, expensive.

While I would grow several of the species without hesitation, I am a little leary of some of the hybrids—not that they might not grow well, but because I have noticed from photographs that the number of flowers they produce can't compare with the species. If and when the hybrids have 20 or more flowers I will change my mind, for then they would compete with the species.

Crinums are tolerant of a wide range of soils but prefer those with a good organic content. They like moisture throughout the year. While they prefer full sun, they are tolerant of light shade. Once planted they should remain undisturbed for years, and when grown in containers they should receive regular feedings of liquid organic fertilizer starting in early spring, and ending when they come into flower. While never invasive, they form good clumps after a few seasons.

Crinum bulbispermum: This species is native to South Africa where it is known as the Orange River lily. The flowers are trumpet shaped, 3 to 4 inches long, fragrant, and white to pale pink with a rose stripe through the center of each petal. More than 20 flowers are carried on a stem that reaches 36 inches in height. Early summer flowering. An attractive feature of the foliage is that it arches up from the bulb, then curves back to the ground—dramatic, as the leaves are several feet in length.

C. macowanii: This South African species is not a popular one, but in my opinion it deserves to be. Easy to recognize with its black anthers, it reaches a stately 48 inches in height with large, white, trumpet-shaped flowers, with crimson stripes down the center of each petal. There is also a pink form, a very pretty plant that flowers in late summer; after flowering, the seed produced is irregular in shape.

C. moorei: Known as the Cape Coast lily and found along the coast of South Africa, this plant has been grown for a great number of years in cool greenhouses and conservatories. The leaves are 4 inches wide, the flowers pink or white. These plants reach 48 inches in height, flowering in mid- to late summer. Unlike other species, this is often found in forested areas, and needs some shade in the hottest areas of the country.

C. × powellii: This is an interspecific hybrid between *C. bulbispermum* and *C. moorei*. It is hardier than either parent, but I would hesitate to expose it to really cold weather. As many as 15 fragrant, trumpet-shaped flowers bloom per stem. This plant is shorter than its parents, only some 30 inches tall, with flowers white to light pink in color. This vigorous plant is the one to grow first if you have not grown *Crinum* before. A number of selections are offered in catalogs, enabling the gardener to select light or dark pink forms.

Other species listed in catalogs include *C. asiaticum,* with white trumpet flowers tinged with pink along the edges of the petals, a great species but one that must have temperatures that never drop below 40°F. *C. americanum,* native to Florida and west into Texas, likes swamp conditions (generally not available in most gardens), and while they may offer some interesting characteristics breeders might use, they are not likely to become typical garden plants.

Botanical Name: Crinum
Family: Amaryllidaceae
Common Names: While some crinums have common names in their native lands (such as orange river lily, Cape Coast lily), there is no common name given to them in the United States.
Flower Colors: White, pink and red
Flowering Time: Spring or summer
Height: 36 to 48 inches
Spread: Will form good-sized colonies in a short time
Native Habitat: Various parts of the world: Florida to Texas, warmer parts of South America, Africa, India, Australia, Peru, etc.
Hardiness: Not hardy
Depth of Planting: Plant so the necks are at soil level or a little above.
Distance Apart: 12 to 18 inches
Containers: Suggested for cold climates
Light Requirements: Sun; tolerates light shade in certain warm areas. One species, *C. moorei,* should have shade.
Soil Type: Good garden soil with organic matter
Special Conditions: When growth is apparent they appreciate some fertilizer, especially when grown in containers. Never let the bulbs become com-

pletely dry, but never sopping wet, either. One species rare in cultivation, *C. campanulatum,* grows in water, while *C. americanum* grows in swampy areas.
Comments: If you live in a warm area where frosts are rare, and seldom does the temperature stay below 32°F all day, try *Crinum.* In colder areas, I would grow them only if you can easily look after the containers in winter and protect the plants from the cold. They are not difficult to grow. While I read they will withstand quite cold temperatures and that they have survived under quite severe conditions, I would not risk these plants being always able to survive. There is a great difference between survival and growing well. I like plants to grow well.

CROCOSMIA
Iridaceae

The names of plants often surprise me. This name is derived from the Greek *krokos* or Latin *crocus,* meaning saffron, and *osme,* meaning smell, the reason being that when dried and immersed in warm water, the flowers smell strongly of saffron. I wonder how this became known in the first place, as how many people go around immersing dried flowers in warm water and then smelling them?

The genus is well known to gardeners, or perhaps I should say, used to be well known, as it contains the Montbretia hybrids that were once in great favor but now seem to have lost some of their popularity. A pity, as they are lovely plants, so easy to grow and surprisingly hardy considering that their parents came from South Africa. The parents are *Crocosmia aurea,* with golden yellow flowers, and *C. pottsii,* with flame-colored flowers, yellow flushed with red and orange. Could it be that because they are so easy to grow they have lost their reputation?

Crocosmia flowers open often to 2 inches wide,

Years ago *Crocosmia* were popular, and they are becoming so again. They perform well with little attention. A number of selections are listed, all worth growing. (Photo courtesy of Dr. Alfred Byrd Graf.)

space in the garden but adequate space for containers, as they require so little care and only ordinary potting soil. Plant the corms 2 to 3 inches deep and 8 to 10 inches apart in full sun. They like average garden soil, with a preference for sandy soils with organic matter. Select the site with a little care as you will want to let these plants stay in the ground and multiply. Give them room to expand. In areas where temperatures fall below 20°F, treat the corms as you would gladiolus, lifting them at the end of summer, storing over the winter and planting in spring. *Crocosmia* are very clean plants. I have yet to see one harmed by any pest or disease. With all the good things going for them, I just wish that more gardeners would plant them.

The listings in catalogs are almost entirely hybrids. 'Firebird' is a good orange, 'Jenny Bloom' a deep yellow, 'Lucifer' an intense red. The latter is claimed to be a bigeneric hybrid between *Crocosmia* and *Curtonus*, and hardier than straight *Crocosmia* hybrids.

Botanical Name: Crocosmia
Family: Iridaceae
Common Name: Montbretia
Flower Colors: Reds, yellows and orange
Flowering Time: Summer
Height: Up to 36 inches
Spread: Will form good-sized colonies quickly
Native Habitat: Parents of most hybrids from South Africa
Hardiness: Hardy to 10°F with mulch
Depth of Planting: 2 to 3 inches
Distance Apart: 8 to 10 inches
Containers: Yes
Light Requirements: Sun
Soil Type: Average garden soil, preferring light, sandy soil with humus
Special Conditions: Provide moisture during early summer. Mulch well in colder climates where

with the lower part of the flower a tube about an inch in length. There are many flowers on each spike, which reaches up to 36 inches in height, sometimes a little more when well established. It is not unusual for each spike to carry as many as 50 flowers, which start opening in midsummer and carry on flowering well into late summer. They are excellent cut flowers. The flowers are carried well above the sword-shaped, green foliage. *Crocosmia* grow well in containers, consolation for those gardeners with limited temperatures drop into the teens or lower, or lift in fall and replant in spring.

Comments: I doubt whether many plants are easier to grow than *Crocosmia*, so deserving of a place in all gardens. Superb cut flower, pest and disease free, good flower production, and yet with all these good points, still graceful plants. Why they are not more commonly grown is a mystery. If overwatered and overfertilized, these plants can become too lush with fewer flowers, but you will have to work harder at making them perform poorly than getting them to perform well.

CROCUS
Iridaceae

This genus includes some 80 species and, surprisingly, more of them flower in fall and winter than in spring. The spring-flowering species

An advantage of crocus is that they flower when the weather is quite cold, and so they last for a long time. This cultivar, *Crocus* 'Zwanenburg Bronze', is an unusual color.

have received the attention of the hybridizers and, together with their selections and hybrids, they outnumber the others.

Crocus is a Chaldean name for saffron given to the genus by Theophrastus. One autumn-flowering species, *Crocus sativus*, produces the saffron of commerce, which comes from the orange-red stigma that is so long it often protrudes from the closed flower. This is one spice that had a town named after it, Saffron Walden in Essex, England, because at one time *C. sativus* was raised in the environs, the climate providing the hot summer weather these bulbs need to flower well. While this species is native to Italy and eastward to Turkey, today the majority of saffron comes from Spain. It takes more than 4,000 flowers to produce an ounce of saffron. This requires much hand labor, and it is no wonder that saffron is so expensive.

Any gardener wishing to learn more about these plants should read E. A. Bowles' *A Handbook of Crocus and Colchicum*, first published in 1924 and revised in 1954. Brian Mathew (Timber Press, 1983) writes extensively and well about the genus in his book, *The Crocus*. His "Informal Key to Crocus Species" is invaluable in helping understand the species.

The corms of *Crocus* are covered with small scaly leaves, and the various forms and patterns of tunic the scales form are, of help in identification. The styles of *Crocus* also are used to identify them, as they vary in shape and number of lobes. The flowers are usually carried singly, and when they first appear they are wrapped in spathes. There are three inner and three outer segments to the flower. They close at night and in dull weather, but will open in the sun to give blossoms several inches in diameter. The ovary is at the base of the flower, at the end of a tube, and thus well protected from harsh weather.

While *Crocus* tolerate a wide range of soils,

and perform well in average garden soil, they must have good drainage. If you wish to grow *Crocus* well and increase their number, prepare the soil well before planting. Add several inches of sharp sand or gravel below where the bulbs will be set, to ensure they keep their feet dry. The corms should be planted 4 inches deep. In warmer areas, where temperatures don't fall much below 20°F, do not expect plantings to be long-lived. They will grow and flower, but they need cold winters to flourish and form large colonies. In warmer areas they will persist for a few years, then disappear.

While seldom more than 6 inches tall, *Crocus* make a great display when in flower, and they are versatile, being good for the border, in containers and when planted in lawns. This last use of spring-flowering types is not often practiced in the United States, but is not uncommon in Europe. In fall, the turf is cut and rolled back. The soil is lightly cultivated, the crocuses set in place 3 to 4 inches apart, and then the turf is replaced. Mowing is discontinued at the very first sign of the *Crocus* emerging, and resumes only after they have finished flowering and the foliage has started to die back. At that point the grass is again mown in the usual manner. The carpet of color is well worth the untidy look while the foliage is maturing.

To grow spring-flowering crocus in containers, use ordinary potting soil and make certain the drainage is good. Place the corms quite close together, burying them 2 to 3 inches deep. Set the containers in a cool (40°F is ideal), shady location for 6 to 8 weeks so the roots develop, then move them into a sunny area indoors to enjoy when the foliage is barely emerging.

The foliage of *Crocus* is grasslike, the edges rolled, exposing a white or silver streak along the midrib. The foliage nourishes the corms, so it is necessary to allow it to grow. Remove it only

Crocus are little flowers that add a lot of interest to the garden. Try to plant in clumps; they are more effective this way.

when it has died down. While most crocus species have some foliage evident at flowering time, others produce their foliage after flowering. Once planted, crocus are best left undisturbed. I suggest bold plantings of considerable numbers of bulbs, but not mixing forms or species. This makes cultivation and removal of the foliage easier, as all plants will be at the same stage of development.

Here are the species, cultivars and selections found in catalogs.

AUTUMN-FLOWERING SPECIES:

Crocus cancellatus	*Crocus ochroleucus*
Crocus goulimyi	*Crocus pulchellus*
Crocus kotschyanus	*Crocus sativus*
Crocus laevigatus	*Crocus serotinus*
Crocus medius	

Crocus ancyrensis: A dwarf only 2 inches tall, with lovely golden yellow flowers produced very early in the year, often in January. A selection often listed is 'Golden Bunch'.

C. biflorus: The Scotch crocus, given this name because it escaped from gardens in Scotland and naturalized in the countryside. White flowers with a prominent purple stripe on the exterior of the segments, and a deep yellow in the throat. Fragrant, 4 inches tall. Flowers in February or March, perhaps a little earlier or later, depending on location.

C. biflorus ssp. *alexandri:* The same as *C. biflorus*, but the throat is not yellow.

C. biflorus ssp. *weldenii:* Pure white without any stripes or yellow in the throat, otherwise same as the species.

C. cancellatus: Flowering time varies from September to December. 2 to 3 inches tall, pale to mid-lilac blue. The stigmata are orange and showy.

C. cartwrightianus, correctly *C. sativus* ssp. *cartwrightianus:* A pure white form of *C. sativus* with striking red stigmata. Flowers in September or October.

C. chrysanthus: The flowers are bright orange, feathered with bronze. Flowering in February or March, this species often produces as many as five flowers from each corm. This is a good performer and the parent of many hybrids; it stands 3 inches tall and the offspring are generally the same or a little taller.

Cultivars

'Advance': yellow inside, violet outside, very free-flowering.

'Blue Bird': dark blue exterior, white margin to the petals and white inside.

'Blue Peter': inside a soft blue with a golden throat, exterior purple.

'Cream Beauty': free flowering, soft, creamy yellow.

'E. A. Bowles': named in honor of E. A. Bowles, who contributed much to the knowledge of *Crocus* throughout his lifetime. A lovely plant, free flowering, butter yellow with bronze feathering.

'E. P. Bowles': another fine plant, bronze with a hint of purple.

'Goldilocks': golden yellow, feathered with brown-purple, long lasting; seems to withstand inclement weather well.

'Jeannine': a striking plant with flowers of light yellow with crimson featherings.

'Ladykiller': has a white interior; the exterior is rich purple edged with white.

'Princess Beatrix': a pleasing light blue with a golden yellow base.

'Saturnus': a very striking plant with petals dark purple on the outside, dark yellow inside—a regal combination.

'Snow Bunting': a great introduction, having outer petals that are cream with dark lilac feathering, and white interiors.

'Zwanenburg Bronze': one of the introductions of Van Tubergen, a well-known firm of the Netherlands. Bronze on the outside with a yellow interior; quite stunning.

C. corsicus: A late-flowering species, often not opening until March or early April. 2 to 4 inches in height, outer segments pale lilac with deep purple feathering, inner segments mauve, white throat with a hint of yellow.

C. etruscus: The foliage has a distinct white band. Large flowers of lavender-lilac are striped with deeper lilac, and have yellow throats. March flowering. Though seldom listed, *C. meuscus'* selection 'Zwanenburg' is the one most often available, a vigorous plant, and well worth growing.

C. fleischeri: Flowers very early, often in January. White flowers striped with purple at the base, anthers orange-red.

C. goulimyi: The flowers are a soft lilac and 3 to 4 inches in height; they are produced in October and November. This species quickly forms a large colony.

C. korolkowii: Deep yellow, with the outer segments feathered with dark bronze. It flowers in February-March, reaching 4 inches in height.

C. kotschyanus: One of the finest of the autumn-flowering species. The flowers are large and pale lilac, with an orange band on the inside base of the petals. A great plant for naturalizing, as it produces many cormels. The var. *leucopharynx* is sometimes listed incorrectly in catalogs as *C. karduchorum*; this differs slightly from the species as it has no orange ring at the base of the petals, and is such a vigorous plant it increases even more quickly than the species.

C. laevigatus: Flowers appearing in late fall or early winter are a deep violet-blue, with deep lilac-mauve feathering and a yellow throat. The stigmata is orange, the stamens white. A grand combination of colors.

C medius: A light lilac with deeper veining, the flowers appear in late October or early November. 3 to 4 inches in height, with a white throat and red stigmata, this is an attractive species.

C. ochroleucus: Not as showy as many October-flowering species, reaching 3 inches in height. It has small flowers of creamy white.

C. pulchellus: One of the taller species at 6 inches, flowering in September. Pale lilac with deeper veining, orange stigmata and white anthers. The selection 'Zephyr' is a little shorter and pure white, with a golden yellow throat.

C. sativus: Saffron is produced from the orange-red stigmata. Lilac-purple, deeper color in the throat, flowers in September. A form known as 'Cashmerianus' produces more flowers and is sometimes incorrectly listed as *C. cashmerianus*.

C. serotinus: Pale to deep lilac, flowers in October or November. Three to 4 inches in height. Brian Mathew proposes that many of the autumn-flowering species belong in this species. The subspecies *clusii* is different from the species because of the tunic of the corm. With the exception of ssp. *salzmannii*, the forms in this species are fragrant.

C. sieberi: Bright lilac with an orange throat, tipped and striped with purple-maroon, a color unique to this species. Add orange stamens and scarlet stigmata, and it is no wonder it is regarded as one of the most beautiful of the species. Spring-flowering in March to April. Several selections are offered in catalogs: 'Atticus', white with purple streaks; 'Bowles White', a pure white form; 'Firefly', rich lilac with a yellow base. All are fragrant.

C. speciosus: Perhaps the easiest autumn-flowering *Crocus* to grow. If it likes where it is planted, it will seed itself and soon occupy a large area. The plants stand 5 to 6 inches in height, with large flowers of deep violet blue with deeper veining, yellow anthers and orange stigmata. A variable species, and a number of selections have been made, enabling gardeners to enjoy the best of the variations. Flowering in September or October. Among the selections are:

Cultivars

'Aitchesonii': a pale blue, somewhat later to flower

'Artabir': with a hint of white under the lavender-blue inner petals and a creamy white throat, deep orange stigmata

'Cassiope': with perhaps the largest flowers of a good blue with a yellow base, somewhat taller, reaching 7 inches. Flowers open very wide to show the orange stigmata

'Conqueror': a lovely, deep blue

'Oxonian': a good Oxford blue, large flowers

C. susianus: Sometimes called *C. angustifolius* in catalogs, this is a deep yellow, tinged with mahogany on the outside. Orange-scarlet stigmata. Flowers in March.

C. tommasinianus: Reaches 6 inches in height, with a pale lavender interior and silver-gray exterior. March flowering. A number of selections are offered, including: 'Barr's Purple', large flowers of rich purple-lilac; 'Ruby Giant', almost plum in color, large flowers, a good selection; 'Whitewall Purple', reddish purple.

C. vernus: This species, at home in the Alps and Pyrenees, is a variable species that has spawned many selections. Colors in the wild may be anywhere from pure white to deep purple. Flowering time is similarly varied, from February to April, but the height is quite constant—around 3 inches. The following are just a few of the selections listed:

Cultivars

'Grande Maitre': an old selection but still a good one, lavender-violet

'Jeanne d'Arc' or 'Joan of Arc': with this name, it has to be white!

'Peter Pan': not the largest of flowers, but many fine white blooms are produced; orange stamens

'Pickwick': white and lilac, perhaps the best striped form

'Purpureus Grandiflorus': cup-shaped flowers of exceptional size, great for containers and in the garden

'Queen of the Blues': large blue flowers, long lasting

'Remembrance': earlier flowering than most, silvery purple flowers

'Yellow Mammoth': the biggest yellow-flowered selection, also listed as 'Dutch Yellow', 'Large Yellow' or a similar name, there apparently being a few yellow selections made

From the above list you should be able to find the color and form you wish, as well as plants that will flower at the desired time. Make sure you purchase a good number of each selection; just five of each will hardly make a showing.

Crocus are free from most pests and diseases, but one word of warning for gardeners who live near open fields: Mice like to nibble on the corms, so it might be a good idea to protect any *Crocus* planting with fine-mesh chicken wire. Surround the corms with it, both under and above. Or, I suppose you can train your cat to watch over your plantings!

Botanical Name: Crocus
Family: Iridaceae
Common Names: Generally known as "crocus." Scotch crocus is the name given to *Crocus biflorus.*
Flower Colors: Whites, purples, violets, blues, yellows and orange, many striped and feathered with interesting color stigmata.
Flowering Time: Varies by species: fall, winter or spring
Height: Few more than 6 inches, most in the 4-inch range.
Spread: Certain species will form quite large colonies in a few seasons.
Native Habitat: Regions around the Mediterranean, the Alps, Pyrenees, Turkey and Iran
Hardiness: Hardy
Depth of Planting: 3 to 4 inches
Distance Apart: 4 to 6 inches, closer in pots
Containers: Wonderful, especially in special pots with holes in sides
Light Requirements: Sun
Soil Type: Average garden soil, potting soil in containers.
Special Conditions: It is essential that *Crocus* enjoy good drainage. Removing the soil and placing several inches of sharp sand or gravel mixed with the soil under the planting is an advantage, especially in colder climates where these plants will stay undisturbed for years. Allow foliage to mature before removing it.
Comments: The selection of species and cultivars is almost overwhelming, but avoid the temptation to buy a few corms of several types; instead, pur-

chase a good number of a few types. A minimum of 25 is necessary to make a good display. *Crocus* should be in every garden. Start with spring-flowering ones, and take advantage of any "special offers," as even small corms will perform well in the garden. If you intend to grow them in containers, select the largest sizes available. In all but the warmest climates, you will get more than one season of flowers from the corms. Remember they like cold winter temperatures. If you live in a warm (frost-free) area where they do not come back, avoid any gaps in the border by planting some *Crocus* each year. You may find one species performs better than another. If this happens, try all the selections of that species. If your garden has drainage problems, you live in a warm climate, and you enjoy moisture through most of the year, *Crocus* may not be for you. Try some in pots anyway—they are well worth the money.

CYCLAMEN
Primulaceae

To my knowledge *Cyclamen* is the only genus in Primulaceae that contains plants with bulbous rootstocks. Strickly speaking they are tubers, but I have always referred to them as corms, as they have the shape of a corm; you will find other gardeners, and references in many books, to the "corms" of cyclamen.

The genus name is derived from the Greek *kyclos,* meaning circular, in reference to a peculiar habit of the flower stem twisting, after the seed is set, and drawing the seed capsule down to the ground. There are some 20 species in the genus. The florist's cyclamen is an important potted plant, *Cyclamen persicum,* which can be grown outdoors in frost-free areas. The smaller species are great plants for colder climates; even though all are at home in the Mediterranean region,

Cyclamen pseudibericum grow well in containers, and would they not add sparkle to any room, or even the dining room table?

some grow in mountainous areas where cold temperatures are experienced.

One of the attributes of the hardy species is their ability to grow and flourish beneath conifers, where many plants have a hard time even surviving. Soil with a high organic content, such as that found in woodlands, is what these plants appreciate, with a good moisture supply in fall, winter and spring. While they will survive where there is poor drainage, they much prefer a well-drained area. A light covering of leaves and similar debris should be scattered over a planting, but it must not be heavy or the plants will be smothered.

The flowers are produced one per stalk. The five petals are reflexed with their lower parts forming a tube. Flowering time varies with the species. The flowers may be white to pink to red, with the tube's interior often very dark. Fragrance is present sometimes, absent at others even among plants of the same species; no one knows why, as all other characteristics can be

identical, even to the plants having the same number and type of chromosomes. Fall- and winter-flowering species should be planted in July, and those that are spring-flowering should be planted in October. Plant the tubers at soil level or just a little below, but breaking the surface. The smooth side (the bottom) of the tuber should be firmly in contact with the soil. Tubers will increase in size, but the plantings will increase in size by seeding, not by offsets of the parent tubers. For this reason space them only 4 to 6 inches apart. It is a good idea for gardeners who wish to increase the size of plantings to help nature by hand-pollinating the flowers in order to obtain good seed production.

Cyclamen grow well in containers. Use potting soil and add a little leaf mold to the mix. Shallow pots or pans are ideal as cyclamen are not deep-rooted. In containers or in borders they should enjoy shade, the exception being *C. cilicium*, which prefers some sun. While we pay attention to the beauty of the flowers, we should not forget the foliage, which often has attractive markings and warrants consideration as a groundcover for this factor alone. Problems with cyclamen are, fortunately, rare. Those that occur are generally due to not paying attention to their needs, overwatering or their being smothered by debris—certainly through no fault of the plants themselves. The only fertilizer I would consider using on established plantings would be bone meal, given in spring. It is best to mix it with some soil first and apply it as a top dressing.

Cyclamen africanum: This species will not withstand frost, but in warmer climates is well worth growing under pines where often little else thrives. Foliage is often 6 inches wide, with undulating margins. The flowers are rose with deep carmine patches at the bases of the petals. It grows to 6 inches tall, and flowers in September to October.

C. cilicium: A lovely little species, quite hardy, and in flower from September into November. The flowers on 4- to 5-inch stems seem to hover above the heart-shaped leaves. Light pink with a deeper band at the base, the flowers have a lovely fragrance. A form even more dwarf than the species, 'Alpinum', is sometimes listed.

C. coum: This species is hardy to 0°F, and is found in the Caucasus, in Europe, Iran and parts of Asia. It is quite variable, and sometimes the geographic forms are given species rank, such as *C. ibericum* and *C. caucasicum*. Both the leaves and flower stems creep for a short distance underground before emerging. The plants reach 4 to 5 inches in height. Flowering between December and March, the blooms vary from light pink to crimson. The leaves are dark green on the upper side, sometimes with a few markings; the undersides of the leaves are a dull crimson. These are great garden plants. 'Album', white, and 'Roseum', a good pink, are forms sometimes listed.

C. cyprium: An autumn-flowering species from Cypress, with large white flowers with crimson-red blotches at the bases of the petals. 2 to 3 inches tall.

C. europaeum: One of the longest in flower, from late summer into fall, this native of northern Italy and Yugoslavia (it grows in the Alps) is very hardy. The leaves are rounded, sometimes with markings. Flowers vary from light to dark red with a band of more intense color at the base. Very fragrant. A white form is known, but is rare in cultivation.

C. graecum: Unusual in that the tubers are often found several inches deep in the soil. It is native to Greece and western Turkey. September flowering, with carmine blooms and distinct swellings around the mouth. The leaves are large,

with a margin that is rough to the touch; in young plants the undersides are a dull red that turns green with age. Leaves often persist.

C. neapolitanum (syn. *C. hederifolium*): This species has tubers more than 3 inches in diameter and produces roots from the upper surface only. Native to Europe. The leaves vary greatly, some ivy-leaved, others lance shaped, margins smooth to crinkled, many with attractive markings. Foliage persists from August through May, then disappears for a while. The most free-flowering species, with more than 20 flowers from a tuber not uncommon, on 3- to 6-inch stems in late summer, before the leaves appear. It is hardy and spreads quickly. The white form 'Album' is often listed, while the species will have flowers that range from near white to deep shades of carmine.

C. persicum: The florist's cyclamen, despite its name, is a native of Cyprus, not Iran (Persia). Not hardy, but good plant for light shade in frost-free areas. The leaves are variegated and often the markings are most attractive. There are many named selections. The color range is very wide, from white to pink to red shades, with very large petals and darker rings of color in the centers of the flowers. When these plants have finished flowering indoors, if you plant them in the garden they will sometimes (not always) perform well for a couple of seasons. It is worth a try in frost-free areas. Do not bury the tuber but leave it half in, half out, of the soil.

C. repandum: Known as the ivy-leaved cyclamen, this native of Europe (from southern France eastward to Italy and the Greek Islands) is not as hardy as many species and needs protection from temperatures below the mid 20s. One of the last to flower in spring to early summer, it stands 4 to 6 inches tall. The color varies from rosy white to deep carmine, with a zone of much darker color around the mouth. Small leaves, nicely mottled with very dark green and dull carmine on the undersides; this color does not change as it does in many other species.

Botanical Name: Cyclamen
Family: Primulaceae
Common Name: Cyclamen
Flower Colors: White, rose through pink to deep carmine red
Flowering Time: Varies by species
Height: Under 6 inches; often only 3 to 4 inches
Spread: Can self-seed and cover large areas
Native Habitat: Around the Mediterranean and the Alps
Hardiness: Most are hardy; see above
Depth of Planting: Just at soil level; *C. graceum* a little deeper
Distance Apart: 4 to 6 inches
Containers: Excellent
Light Requirements: Shade; one species, *C. cilicium*, likes some sun.
Soil Type: Woodland type, free-draining but with moisture in fall, winter and spring. In containers use potting soil with added leaf-mold.
Special Conditions: Cyclamen like a light scattering of leaves over them. Spreads by self-seeding, so do not cultivate soil between plants; hand pull any weeds.
Comments: One of the prettiest sights I have seen was an entire slope of *C. neapolitanum* under a magnificent yew tree in South Devon, England. Seedlings were popping up in other places in the garden, almost to the point of becoming weeds! If plants of one species are doing well in an area, try another close by, and you might try some cross pollination and see if any hybrid forms develop. Lovely in woodland settings where they can be seen both from a distance and at close range. The fragrance of certain species is a delight, and the beauty of the foliage when the plants are not in flower should not be over-

looked. No matter where you live, try some of these plants.

DAHLIA
Compositae

These popular garden plants were named in honor of Dr. Andreas Dahl, a Swedish botanist and pupil of Linnaeus. The species are at home in Mexico, Central America and Colombia. They were long cultivated by Aztec gardeners, and the

You will find dahlia flowers with interesting color breakings, as seen here. Some feel this is a genetic weakness, others find such flowers attractive. What do you think?

roots used as food by the natives of Mexico. The roots are fleshy tubers, and hold considerable amounts of food and moisture. (They also contain inulin, used in the manufacture of certain chemicals, and are also used in the testing of liver and kidney function.) In an Aztec herbal, the *Badianus*, dating from 1582, it mentions that they were used in the treatment of urinary disorders. This use, based on the doctrine of signatures, wherein a plant having the appearance of a part of the body, or being able to function in a similar way to a part of the body, was thought to have properties that could cure the depicted part. The stems of the tall-growing *Dahlia imperalis* were used by the Aztecs to convey water from mountain springs to their dwellings; one of the Aztec words for *Dahlia* is *cocoxochitl*, meaning water pipes.

Introduced into Europe toward the end of the eighteenth century, dahlias did not enjoy great success. Grown as a possible food source, they were not at all well received, the taste described as bitter and nondescript. Some gardeners persevered nonetheless, and by the middle of the nineteenth century dahlias were in great demand as garden plants—to the point that "dahliamania" of the mid-nineteenth century matched the "tulipmania" of the seventeenth.

The first plants introduced were *D. coccinea*, with single red flowers, *D. rosea*, with single rose flowers, and *D. pinnata*, with red flowers with a hint of bluish purple in them and with an inclination to produce "full" flowers. Just these three, through the efforts of skilled hybridizers, have given the public a plethora of colors, shapes and sizes. To keep order among the many forms, it was necessary to develop a horticultural classification. Today, with more than 20,000 cultivars listed in the *International Register of Dahlia Names*, adherence to an orderly classification is essential. The plants are grouped by flower shape. In talking to various dahlia societies, it became clear

One of the great advantages of single dahlias is that they produce many flowers throughout the summer.

to me that, while they adhere to the principal categories, each society adjusts the divisions in the groups to accommodate local traditions and needs. The following will help gardeners understand how the flowers differ from one group to another.

Single-flowered. Open-centered bloom with one or two complete outer rows of florets surrounding a disc. These plants are great for growing in beds because they fill in gaps. Most grow to a height of 12 inches. Often produced from seed.

Dahlia garden forms (a) Single (b) Anemone-centred (c) Collerette (d) Ball (e) Pompon (f) Decorative (g) Decorative (fimbriated) (h) Waterlily (i) Cactus (j) Semi-cactus (k) Peony-flowered (l) Star (m) Orchid-flowered

From *The New Royal Horticultural Society Dictionary of Gardening*. Reproduced with kind permission of the Royal Horticultural Society and The Macmillan Press Ltd. and Stockton Press, New York. Illustration by Vana Haggerty.

Anemone-flowered. Not commonly grown, and only a dozen or so names have been registered. The flower has one or more rows of ray florets surrounding a dense group of upward-pointing tubular florets. The height is in the 24- to 36-inch range, with flowers 3 inches in diameter.

Collarette. The flower has an open center surrounded by an inner ring of short florets composing the "collar," and one or two complete outer rows of (usually flat) ray florets. These have a good color range and are great cut flowers. The height is just under 4 feet, with flowers 4 to 6 inches in diameter. These are often listed in seed catalogs, as they are easily raised from seed.

Waterlily- or Nymphaea-flowered. These have flowers that resemble waterlilies, fully double, with broad and generally sparse ray petals that are flat or slightly incurved. They stand 36 to 48 inches, with flowers 4 to 5 inches in diameter.

Formal Decorative. The flowers show no central disc and are fully double. Broad, flat or slightly involute (rolled inward at the edges) ray florets, sometimes slightly twisted at the apex, usually obtuse. The height can vary from 3 to 6 feet. The difference between Formal and Informal Decorative is that in the Formal, the ray florets grow in a regular arrangement; in the Informal, the rays are long and twisted or pointed, and irregular in arrangement.

Informal Decorative. See Formal Decorative, above.

Ball. The flowers are ball shaped or globose, sometimes flattened at the top, with ray florets blunt or rounded at the tips and cupped for more than half the length of the florets. There are often subgroups to the Ball category, based on the size of the flowers, Small Ball being 4 to 6 inches in diameter, and those under 4 inches known as Miniature Ball.

Pompon. Quite similar to the Ball types, but the flowers are more globose, with the florets involute for their entire length on flowers up to 2 inches in diameter and reaching a height of up to 3 feet.

Cactus-flowered. These, and the semi-cactus group that follows, are largely derived from *Dahlia juarezii,* including crosses with other species. Fully double flowers show no disc. The long ray florets are finely quilled (strongly revolute) for more than half their length. Flowers are 4 to 6 inches in diameter. Often divided into the straight cactus types and slightly incurved or recurved rays and incurved types whose pointed rays curve toward the centers of the flowers.

Semi-cactus-flowered. Flowers fully double, with slightly pointed ray florets that are broad at their base, revolute for less than half their length, and either straight or incurving. Generally about 48 inches in height.

Peony-flowered. The flowers have two or more rows of flat, broad ray florets and a center that is open or partly covered by small, twisted floral rays around the disc.

Miscellaneous. This covers a number of different types, for example the Orchid Cultivars, similar to the single dahlias except that their petals are revolute for at least two thirds of their length.

Star Dahlias have small incurving flowers, formed by two or three rows of scarcely overlapping pointed rays surrounding central discs.

Chrysanthemum types have flowers resembling large, incurved chrysanthemum flowers.

In many cases subdivisions are made according to the size of the flowers. While the various dahlia societies differ in their graduations of size, the following will give an idea of typical divisions.

Giant: flowers more than 10 inches in diameter

Large: flowers between 8 and 10 inches in diameter

Medium: flowers between 6 and 8 inches in diameter

Small: flowers between 4 and 6 inches in diameter

Miniature: flowers less than 4 inches in diameter

In addition, there are divisions by color. Fourteen colors have been recognized:

White
Yellow
Orange
Bronze
Flame
Red
Dark red
Light pink
Dark pink
Lilac, lavender or mauve
Purple, wine or violet
Blends of two or more colors intermingled
Bicolored (ground color tipped with another
    color)
Variegated (several colors striped or splashed
    in one flower)

The reader will appreciate that while seeming rather complicated, the groupings are in fact quite logical. If you visit a flower show where dahlias are exhibited, the above groupings will make a lot of sense. The drawings of the different types will also make understanding the classifications easier.

Dahlias are popular because they are easy to grow. They must be given a sunny location, and like a rich, but well-drained, soil that contains good amounts of organic matter.

In warm climates the tubers can be planted in March or April. Set them 4 inches deep and 24 inches apart. In colder areas where frost is experienced, they should be planted a week or 10 days before the last frost is expected; set them at the same depth and distance apart. Plant when there is no chance of young growth being harmed by frost. As it will take 10 days or longer for the shoots to emerge, I suggest 7 to 10 days be allowed. If the young plants and/or tuberous roots have shoots on them, delay planting until all danger of frost has passed.

After a month, when the shoots are about 12 inches in height, pinch out the growing tip to encourage the plants to become bushy. Tall cultivars will need some support, and the canes for this should be inserted at this time. As the shoots develop, tie them gently to the supports. Some 8 to 10 weeks after planting, the first blooms will appear. From earlier plantings in warmer climates, flowers will be produced somewhat before midsummer.

Fertilizer should be given after the growing tip has been removed, and an ongoing fertilizer program should then be instituted. This can be either with granular fertilizer applied every 4 to 6 weeks, or organic liquid fertilizer each week. Keep the plants moist; never let them dry out. At the top of the flower stalks, several buds will be produced. If large flowers are desired, remove all but one bud. If it is just color that's of interest, and the size of flowers is of minor importance, no disbudding is required.

Dahlias used as bedding plants (that is, the shorter cultivars) require regular feeding but no disbudding. Dahlias can be propagated by seed, by cuttings and by division of the tubers. Remember that the tubers themselves have no buds or "eyes," and it is essential that a piece of the stem with an eye be planted. Seed can be sown in a regular potting soil mix, and well-decayed organic matter can be added to the soil mix when transplanting the seedlings. The seed should be given a temperature of 60°F for good germination. The seedlings are best transplanted into individual pots as soon as they are large enough to handle with ease. Make sure that they are gradually exposed to lower temperatures, a process known as "hardening off," before setting them out in their permanent beds when all danger of frost has passed. Remove all spent flowers from the plants. Keep the plants well supported by tying them to their stakes. If well-rotted compost or manure becomes available, apply it as a mulch.

In fall, the first frost will kill the foliage. Label the plants, noting type, color and name. Cut the foliage down, leaving some 6 inches of stalk. Dig the tubers with care and place them in a frost-free area with good air circulation. When the soil on the tubers has dried, brush it away. Store the cleaned tubers in sharp sand (builder's sand, not sand from the seashore, which contains harmful salts), and keep them at around 40°F. Check periodically during the storage period, and remove any tubers that rot. If rotting has occurred, dust the remaining tubers with fungicide to prevent the spread of the problem; you can use fungicide as a preventive measure, before any rot is noticed, if you like. The tubers should be planted the following spring.

In warmer climates where the temperatures hardly ever reach the freezing point (or seldom do), the tubers can be left in the ground. Where moderate frosts are experienced, tubers in the ground can be protected by a heavy mulch, but if in doubt, lift them.

The number of cultivars listed in catalogs is so great that you should, without any difficulty, be able to select color, form and height that suit you. The following are great plants, in many cases tried-and-true, superior performers. Many of the older cultivars are less expensive than recent introductions. They have withstood the test of time and, in my opinion, are better suited for the home gardener. Recent introductions are for the specialist; but, if you see a cultivar that interests you, do not hesitate to acquire it, as all dahlias are easy to grow.

Cultivars

Formal Decorative

'Alabaster': pure white, 5 feet tall

'Duet': crimson with white petal tips, 3 feet tall

'Lavender Perfection': lavender-pink, 3 to 4 feet tall

'Orange Julius': bright orange edged with yellow, 4 feet tall

Informal Decorative

'April Dawn': white flowers edged with lavender, 4½ feet tall

'By Golly': rosy red, 4 feet tall

'Croydon Ace': outstanding—a bright, non-fading yellow, 3 feet tall, vigorous

'Gay Princess': pink with cream center, 4 feet tall

Ball

'Nettie': soft yellow flowers, 3 feet tall

'Nijinsky': glowing purple, 4 feet tall

'Rothsay Superb': a great red, superb cut flower, 3 feet tall

'Swiss Miss': good, true pink with cream center, 3 feet tall

Pompon

'Amber Queen': golden amber-bronze, 4 feet tall

'Chick-a-dee': combination of wine and pink, 3 feet tall

'Mary Munns': deep lavender, good cut flower, 3 feet tall

'Zonnengoud': canary gold, 3 feet tall

Single-flowered

'Bambino White': 10 inches tall

'Chessy': bronze-yellow, 10 inches tall

'Irene van der Zwet': soft yellow, 1½ feet tall

'Siemen Doorenbosch': light magenta, 1½ feet tall

Anemone-flowered

'Brio': deep orange, 12 inches tall

'Honey Honey': bronze petals, golden yellow center, 1½ feet tall

'Roulette': lavender-pink, 12 inches tall

'Snow Country': pure white, 2 feet tall

Collarette

'Cherubino': white with a yellow center, 4 feet tall

'Jack O'Lantern': very free-flowering, light orange, 4 feet tall

'Mickey': deep red with yellow center, superb plant, 3 feet tall

'Rosy Wings': bright pink, 4 feet tall

Waterlily-flowered

'Lisa': white with lavender tips, 3 feet tall

'Purple Splash': variegated lavender with purple, 4 feet tall

'Rose Marie Webb': good pink, good cut flower, 4 feet tall

'Sweet Sixteen': dark pink, 3 feet tall

Cactus

'Brookside Cheri': salmon pink, 4 feet tall

'Estralata': lovely white flowers with hint of lavender, 4 feet tall

'Juanita': rich ruby red, 4 feet tall

'Tequila Sunrise': caramel orange with golden highlights, 5 feet tall

Semi-cactus

'Amanda Jarvis': old rose, 3 feet tall

'Andrie's Orange': soft orange, good cut flower, 5 feet tall

'Bella Bimba': apricot pink, very free-flowering, 4 feet tall

'Hamari Katrina': sulphur yellow, great cut flower, 4 feet tall

Peony-flowered

'Japanese Bishop': dark orange, very popular and rightly so, 3 feet tall

'Jescott Julie': orange with burgundy reverse, 3 feet tall

Dahlias from Seed

'Redskin': mixed colors, double and semidouble, 12 to 14 inches tall

'Rigoletto': mixed colors, doubles, yellow, red, pink, white, 12 inches tall

Botanical Name: Dahlia
Family: Compositae
Common Name: Dahlia
Flower Colors: Wide range, all colors except true blue
Flowering Time: Midsummer to frost
Height: Varies from 12 inches to more than 5 feet
Native Habitat: Mexico and Central South America
Hardiness: Will not withstand frost; lift and store over winter in cold areas. Leave in the ground in areas that are frost free or nearly so.
Depth of Planting: 4 inches
Distance Apart: Varies by species: plant dwarfs 8 to 12 inches, taller types 24 inches
Containers: Small or dwarf cultivars are appropriate; others not very well adapted (grow too large or too tall, or occupy too much space), but possible
Light Requirements: Sun
Soil Type: Rich, well-drained soil
Special Conditions: Fertilize on a regular basis. The taller types may need staking. When 12 inches in height, taller growing plants need growing tips removed to promote bushiness
Comments: Among the loveliest of the summer-flowering bulbs. Look after dahlias and they will give you lots of color and good cut flowers for the house. When harvesting, it is best to place cut stems in hot (160°F) water for an hour, until the water cools. Remove all old flowers as soon as they have passed. Watch for slugs and snails when the shoots first emerge. Protect from gophers, who seem to like the tubers, by planting in wire-mesh baskets.

DIERAMA
Iridaceae

The name is derived from the Greek *dierama*, meaning like a bell or funnel, appropriate as the flowers are bell shaped. This is a lovely genus of evergreen plants, with arching, thin stems from which hang the bell-shaped flowers. I love to see these plants in the wild. From the distance you can see the pink flowers, but the stems are so thin that the flowers seem to float on air. The common names are angel's fishing rod and wand flower.

There are several species, but only one, *Dierama pulcherrimum*, has received the attention of hybridizers. Selections are sometimes listed in catalogs. This plant flowers in mid- to late summer for many weeks, and is the hardiest of the species, withstanding temperatures to 10°F if given ample mulch and a warm location. In colder areas they should be grown in large containers and moved indoors for protection in the winter. This species will grow to 6 (or even more) feet tall, the stems towering above the sword-shaped foliage that reaches only 24 inches. Another species, *D. pendulum*, is also very beautiful. Not quite as tall, it seldom grows to much over 36 inches, and flowers in late spring. Both species are superb when planted near a pond, so that the reflections of the flowers can be seen.

Being native to South Africa and the Mediterranean climate zones they like moisture in

I wish more catalogs would list these lovely *Dierama pulcherrimum*, seen here in their native habitat. They are easy to grow, increase slowly but steadily and are quite unusual in form.

winter and spring. *D. pulcherrimum* appreciates some summer moisture too, and as it is at home in that intermediate zone between Mediterranean and tropical climates, it thus receives some summer rain. Good drainage, good garden soil with plenty of organic matter and full sun are the conditions these plants appreciate.

The rootstock is a corm. Any foliage attached to the corm might well disappear after you have planted the corms, but it will come back after they have had a chance to become established. Plant them 3 inches deep and 18 to 24 inches apart; they will take perhaps a year to become established. Feed container plantings with liquid organic fertilizer in spring up to the time the flower stalks appear. In the garden, with good soil, little fertilizer is required. If you can bring yourself to cut the long stems, you will find *Dierama* to be a great cut flower, with unique charm and grace. However, I don't recommend harvesting them unless you have quite a colony

established; they are too beautiful and, obviously, last longer in the garden.

Dierama pendulum: The flowers, about an inch in length, hang from a thin stem that can reach 36 inches (and perhaps a little more). Bell shaped, mostly pink, but darker and lighter forms are known. Late-spring flowering, evergreen.

D. pulcherrimum: Later into flower than *D. pendulum* and much taller, with stems reaching well over 6 feet when well established. Strings of pink, bell-shaped flowers sway in the slightest breeze. Evergreen, swordlike foliage reaches 36 inches in height. There is some variation in the color, and selections have been made, ranging from light pink to very dark, wine red.

Hybrids between the two species, intermediate in height, are sometimes listed. They are produced by the Sleive Donard Nurseries of County

Down, Northern Ireland. If you have an opportunity to obtain some, do so; they are a delight, and come in a wide range of colors, from fuchsia pink to carmine-purple to strawberry.

Botanical Name: Dierama
Family: Iridaceae
Common Names: Angel's fishing rod, wand flower
Flower Colors: Shades of pink, from very dark to light
Flowering Time: Varies by species: late spring or midsummer
Height: Varies by species: 3 feet or more than 6 feet
Spread: Will form clumps after a settling-in period, but never invasive
Native Habitat: South Africa
Hardiness: To 10°F with protection of a deep mulch and south-facing wall
Depth of Planting: 3 inches
Distance Apart: 18 to 24 inches
Containers: Yes
Light Requirements: Sun
Soil Type: Rich, well-drained, average garden soil
Special Conditions: If grown in containers, feed with liquid organic fertilizer from early spring up to flowering time.
Comments: One of the loveliest bulbous plants, unusual because of the very thin, strong, flowering stems that shiver in the slightest breeze. It is unfortunate that these plants are not more widely grown and more readily available. Be patient, as it might take a season or two for them to settle in.

DIETES
Iridaceae

No irises are native to the southern hemisphere. Instead there are genera such as *Moraea* and *Dietes*. *Dietes* is derived from the Greek *dis*, mean-

The "wild iris" (*Dietes iridioides*) is in flower for a long time. Drought resistant and fool-proof, this is a "must have" plant for warmer areas.

ing twice, and *etes*, meaning an associate, in reference to the petals. There is discussion regarding the genera *Dietes* and *Moraea*. Some regard them as being the same, and advocate combining them. I feel there are two major differences: *Dietes* species have rootstocks that are rhizomes, whereas *Moraea* species have rootstocks that are corms. *Dietes* have evergreen foliage, and the foliage of *Moraea* is deciduous.

Dietes species seem to thrive on neglect. They are frequently used in landscapes around industrial developments in California, around parking lots and around office complexes, as they are tough plants that need little or no attention. While the rootstocks are rhizomes, *Dietes* are most commonly sold as container plants, in one-gallon cans. Vigorous, they quickly become established and form large clumps. Individual flowers last for only a day, yet these plants are seldom without a flower as many flowering stems, each carrying many blooms, are produced in abundance. They flower most heavily in spring, but throughout the summer these plants are pleasant. The foliage is swordlike, tapering to a sharp point.

These plants like full sun. They are not fussy as to soil, but do not like poor drainage. *Dietes* perform well in containers and can be left for many seasons without being lifted and divided. They are hardy to 20°F; in colder areas they must be moved indoors over the winter. The two species available commercially are *D. bicolor* and *D. iridioides*, both native to the eastern Cape Province of South Africa.

If rhizomes are obtained, set them just below the surface of the soil. If planting from a container, the soil level in the container should be at the soil level of the border. The plants are best set at least 18 inches apart, and if you have plenty of room, set them 24 inches apart. Grow them only in large individual containers or in planters, as they will soon crowd any pot that isn't at least 12 inches in diameter.

No fertilizer is needed. Ensure they have moisture in winter and spring only. Once established, they are drought tolerant, and I have yet to see any of these plants suffering in California, despite severe droughts over a number of years.

Dietes bicolor (syn. *Moraea bicolor*): The common name is peacock flower. Of the two species commonly grown, this has the prettier flowers, light cream with a brown blotch at the base of the broader petals. Many flowers are carried on the branched flower spike to a height of 24 or more inches. The sword-shaped foliage, quite wide at the base, is held in a fan—very tidy in appearance.

D. iridioides (syn. *D. catenulata, D. vegeta, Moraea catenulata, M. iridioides, M. vegeta*): It is commonly known as the wild iris. Slender stems carry the irislike white flowers, with bluish, petaloid styles, to a height of 24 inches, rising above the sword-shaped leaves held in a fan. Flower stalks not as branched as those of *D. bicolor*. There would appear to be two separate types, one flowering earlier than the other, but of the same species. The foliage is quite tough, and the Bantu weave mats from it.

Botanical Name: Dietes
Family: Iridaceae
Common Names: Peacock flower (*D. bicolor*) and wild iris (*D. iridioides*)
Flower Colors: Varies by species: cream with brown blotch, white with blue
Flowering Time: Throughout the year, heavier in spring, early summer
Height: 24 inches
Spread: Will quickly form large clumps
Native Habitat: South Africa
Hardiness: To 20°F
Depth of Planting: Rhizomes set just below soil level; from containers, set soil level of containers at soil level
Distance Apart: 18 to 24 inches
Containers: Yes
Light Requirements: Full sun
Soil Type: Average garden soil
Special Conditions: Dietes appreciate moisture in winter and spring.
Comments: These are tough plants. While they will thrive for years without assistance I feel they should be lifted and divided after 3 or 4 years, the reason being that the foliage becomes dirty looking, and the plants look healthier and prettier with clean, young foliage. If you have an area in full sun that needs filling, these plants will do it.

Eranthus cilicia is a nice low-growing plant for woodland areas. Scatter some seed and you will have another colony. (Photo courtesy of International Bloembollen Centrum.)

ENDYMION
Liliaceae

See *Hyacinthoides*. For many years the English bluebell and the Spanish bluebell were included in this genus, having been moved there from *Scilla*, where they had been for many years. Now they have found their final home (I hope) in *Hyacinthoides*. In certain catalogs the older names *Scilla* and *Endymion* are sometimes listed. The several species still in *Scilla* are from the southern hemisphere.

ERANTHIS
Ranunculaceae

This is a genus of tuberous buttercups, and in very early spring the woods of many parts of Europe have a golden groundcover, *Eranthis hyemalis*. The name is derived from the Greek *er*, meaning spring, and *anthos*, meaning flower. *Eranthis hyemalis* translates into "flower of spring," a most apt description. There are several species, but only this one is commonly grown.

The rootstock is very small, not much larger than a pea, yet the plants quickly cover a large area, so it should be planted where it has room to spread. The shiny green leaves form a rosette and hug the ground. The flowers are bright yellow and reach only 3 to 4 inches in height. The plants are found in deciduous woods, and they must have at least filtered sunlight in the early months of the year; they don't do well under evergreens.

Loose, friable soil with organic matter is what they like, with good moisture during winter and spring. By midsummer the plants will have disappeared. They are attractive among deciduous shrubs, where they will stifle many other, less desirable, plants; make sure the shrub won't rob them of needed light. Plant the tubers 1 inch deep and 3 to 4 inches apart in bold, informal clumps, not in unnatural-looking lines. Surprisingly, they can be grown in containers. Crowded together in a 6-inch pot they can be brought indoors to be enjoyed, but after they have finished flowering they should be placed outdoors. Save the seed and scatter it in other locations. Germination is quite rapid, and you will soon have another colony of these small but delightful plants. Sometimes there is a listing in catalogs for *E. cilicica*, which has a bronzy green foliage and is often regarded as a variant of *E. hyemalis*. If you see a listing for *E. hyemalis* with such a description, it is likely to be *E. cilicica*. All these plants are good ones.

Botanical Name: Eranthis
Family: Ranunculaceae
Common Names: Winter aconite, flower of spring
Flower Color: Golden yellow
Flowering Time: Very early spring: February, March
Height: 3 to 4 inches
Spread: Will soon cover a large area
Native Habitat: Much of Europe

Hardiness: Very hardy
Depth of Planting: 1 inch
Distance Apart: 3 to 4 inches
Containers: Yes
Light Requirements: Light shade; will not accept shade of conifers or evergreens
Soil Type: Woodland type with good organic matter; in containers, regular potting soil
Special Conditions: Must have moisture during winter and early spring
Comments: If you have a woodland area, you should grow this plant, placing it where it can be seen from a distance. Give it room, but at the same time contain it; if it is happy, it can become invasive, but not difficult to control. These are easy to grow, and it is fun to have them in small containers for indoor enjoyment.

EREMURUS
Liliaceae

Stately plants, *Eremurus* demand and receive much attention, yet are suprisingly easy to grow. This is 'Shelford Hybrid'.

It is the tall flower spikes that earned these plants their botanical name, from the Greek word *eremos,* meaning solitary, and *oura,* meaning tail. The flower spike towers above the foliage, and the tip often is bent, so that it resembles the tail of a fox. Indeed, one of the common names is foxtail lily, another is desert candle.

The first time I saw the rootstock, a very thick tuber shaped like a starfish, I wondered what the flowers would be like. Even the bud is an odd shape, an egglike dome arising where tubers meet. Always handle *Eremurus* with great care as the tubers are brittle, one of the reasons these plants should be left undisturbed. They are among the most striking of the early-summer–flowering bulbous plants. It is amazing how in but a few short months they can reach heights of 6 feet or even more, yet they need staking only in exposed areas.

There are many species, only three or four of which are commonly found in catalogs. They are at home in Afghanistan, Iran, northern India, Turkestan and Siberia, and one species is from China. *Eremurus* are hardy, withstanding temperatures down to 0°F, and even colder with a good mulch during winter. Remove any mulch in spring so the emerging foliage has plenty of room. If it is covered, rot can set in. The foliage is held in a cluster, rather fleshy in appearance, often 3 inches or wider in some species. The flower spike rises from the center of the foliage, and it grows quickly. The height depends on the species, but in most cases half the spike is covered with many small flowers in shades of pink, orange, white or yellow.

Provide well-drained, sandy soil with good

organic content. The plants need full sun and good moisture during winter and spring until they have finished flowering. After flowering, the amount of moisture can be reduced. Given the fragility of the roots, leave them undisturbed. It is best to plant by removing the soil to a depth of 6 to 8 inches and forking over the bottom of the hole. Then, set the roots on the loose soil so that at least 6 inches of soil will cover them. Firm them into place with care. Set the plants at least 36 inches apart; some gardeners like to place the shorter species closer together, but if they are planted well apart, one never has to worry about over-crowding. They are wonderful accent plants, but I would not grow them in containers—they never look quite right nor seem to be happy.

A word of warning: Remember the height of these plants, as you want other plants in the area to be in scale. *Eremurus* are eye-catching, but will not look right if not surrounded by plants of moderate size. Do not plant it, for example, with dwarf shrubs, which would be overpowered. They look beautiful against a dark background, where the color of the flowers will more easily be seen.

Eremurus robustus: This is one of the tall species, reaching to more than 6 feet with as much as 4 feet covered with small, deep pink flowers. Early-summer–flowering, with foliage as much as 48 inches in length and 4 inches wide. This species rightly deserves the name *robustus.*

E. × shelford: This is a cross between *E. olgae* and *E. stenophyllus,* made in the garden of Sir Michael Foster at Great Shelford in Cambridge, England. The color range is a wide one, from white to shades of pink and yellow. Coming into flower in early summer, the plants are strong growers, reaching heights of 3 to 4 feet. Several selections can be found in catalogs, all well worth growing.

E. stenophyllus (syn. *E. bungei*): This species from central Asia is one of the shorter ones, reaching up to 36 inches tall. 12 to 15 inches in length, the narrow leaves are produced in abundance. The species has bright yellow flowers covering as much as three-quarters of the spike; the lower flowers having quite long stems. The flowers open slowly, and this species (and the selections in various shades of yellow made from the species), remains in flower for a longer period than others, starting in early summer.

Botanical Name: Eremurus
Family: Liliaceae
Common Names: Foxtail lily, desert candle
Flower Colors: White, orange, pink, yellow
Flowering Time: Early to midsummer
Height: Varies by species: 36 inches to over 6 feet
Spread: Some foliage quite long; will slowly form clumps
Native Habitat: Western and central Asia, Afghanistan, Iran, northern India, Turkestan, Siberia and China
Hardiness: To 0°F and below, if well mulched and in a protected border
Depth of Planting: 6 to 8 inches
Distance Apart: 36 inches
Containers: No
Light Requirements: Sun
Soil Type: Rich, well-drained, sandy soil
Special Conditions: Will not grow well in areas where there is little or no frost; must enjoy cold winters to perform well.
Comments: Once you see these plants at their best, you will long remember them. They seem to me a little temperamental, and while they are spectacular, I hesitate to recommend them for every garden. I do think they are well worth trying, but take great care when handling them, as the roots are brittle. Once they are planted and growing, leave them alone!

Erythronium 'Pagoda' and *E. tuolumnense*: 'Pagoda' has more and larger flowers, but the color is not as intense as that of E. *tuolumnense*. It is, however, the better garden plant.

ERYTHRONIUM
Liliaceae

One might expect these plants to have red flowers, given that the name is derived from the Greek *erythos*, meaning red, but this is a reference to the red mottling often found on the foliage. These are among the most graceful of spring flowers, pendant and quite lilylike. It is to be hoped that more will be listed in catalogs. Only three of more than 20 species are generally found, but certain growers do list more, and in time perhaps more gardeners will enjoy the beauty of these plants.

Many erythroniums are native to the West Coast of the United States. The species most commonly grown is native to Europe, the dog's tooth violet, *E. dens-canis*. The name is given not for the shape of the flowers but for the shape of the corm, which is quite pointed. The size of the corm varies with the species. Erythroniums enjoy several common names, most having to do with their habitats and foliage; it seems the beauty of the flowers takes second place in such things. It is called avalanche lily because it appears as snows melt, trout or fawn lily because of the markings on the foliage, and adder's tongue and lamb's tongue because of the shape of the leaves. It is surprising that the foliage receives such attention, as usually only two leaves are produced!

The plants are quite tough and hardy—they have to be to survive in their native habitats. The western species are found in areas where there is snow in winter and hot, dry conditions in summer. The European species is widespread, growing even in Siberia. Certain species grow in rich soil, others in poor soil. They all have one requirement: ample moisture in winter and spring. In the wild you will frequently find the species growing near shrubs, and thus a little protected from the hot summer sun. In the garden they all seem to thrive in good soil with a high organic content, and in the hottest areas, with some high shade. Like many lilylike flowers, they seem perfect for woodland settings.

Plant the corms, preferably in early fall, 3 inches deep in good, well-drained soil, 6 to 8 inches apart. Water them well so the soil is well packed around the corms, and keep it moist through spring; after that, they can stand dryer conditions. These plants do not take too kindly to being grown in containers. Early in spring the leaves emerge. Then, from between the two leaves, the flowering stem rises. The number of flowers per stem depends on the species, but each flower has 6 segments that recurve, the stamens becoming prominent.

Erythronium dens-canis: Native to Europe. Leaves marbled brown to bluish green. One large flower per 6-inch stem, with recurved petals, bluish or purple anthers. The color of the petals varies from white through pink to deep purple; at the mouth of each flower where the petals recurve is a ring of purple markings. Plant a good number of these, as they flower over a long period and you will want to have more than one in flower at a time. A number of selections are listed: 'Frans Hals', with petals of deep purple and attractively mottled leaves; 'Lilac Wonder', purple with chocolate-purple markings; 'Pink Perfection', clear, bright pink; and 'Snowflake', pure white.

E. revolutum: This species grows along the Pacific Coast where there is either summer rainfall or fog. As many as 5 large flowers per 10-inch stem appear in late spring. The color varies from white to rose-pink, with yellow or almost orange centers. The individual flowers can be quite large. Selections such as 'Citronella', 'Rose Beauty' and 'White Beauty' allow you to select the color of your choice.

E. tuolumnense: This species is found growing at the base of the Sierra Nevada in eastern California. The leaves are not mottled, and the deep golden yellow flowers carried on 12-inch stems flower in mid- to late spring. This is an easy species to grow. Selection 'Pagoda', with larger flowers than the species, is generally the only catalog listing. I find the flowers to be a little lighter in yellow than the species and not quite as shiny, but it is an outstanding selection.

Botanical Name: Erythronium
Family: Liliaceae
Common Names: Dog's tooth violet, avalanche lily, fawn lily, trout lily
Flower Colors: White, shades of pink, yellow

Flowering Time: Mid- to late spring
Height: 8 to 12 inches
Spread: Will form quite large colonies
Native Habitat: Europe, many species found in the United States along the Pacific Coast
Hardiness: Hardy
Depth of Planting: 3 inches
Distance Apart: 6 to 8 inches
Containers: No
Light Requirements: Will withstand sun but seems to prefer dappled shade
Soil Type: Rich well-drained soil
Special Conditions: After the foliage has died down, in mid- to late summer, the plants appreciate having leaves spread over the area.
Comments: One of the loveliest of the woodland species, ideal for the front of the shrub border or on the edge of woodland areas. Plant them where they can remain undisturbed. If you must lift them, do so as the foliage withers; divide and replant at once.

EUCHARIS
Amaryllidaceae

The Greek word for very graceful is *eucharis,* an appropriate word for the flowers of this genus. While there are some eight species, only one—*Eucharis grandiflora*—is listed in catalogs and grown for the flowers, which are superb and much admired for both their beauty and fragrance. Native to Colombia and known as the Amazon lily, *Eucharis* looks more like a daffodil than a lily. It has white petals and a cup in the center of the flowers formed by the expanded bases of the stamens. The stamens rise from the cup. The flowers are up to 5 inches in diameter, and 4 or 5 are carried to a height of 18 to 24 inches on each sturdy stem. The strong-stalked leaves are several inches in width and are waved at their edges.

Appreciated by florists, the clean-looking and fragrant flowers of *Eucharis grandiflora* require warm temperatures.

These evergreen plants need temperatures around 60°F at night in order to grow well. Thus they are suited only for the warmest parts of Florida and Hawaii, and of course warm greenhouses. Flowering can be induced by lowering the temperature in the greenhouse, holding back on the amount of water given, then after a period of some four months, increasing the temperature again. Copious amounts of liquid fertilizer should be applied during the period of higher temperature, and humidity must be kept high. Plant the

bulbs with their necks just at soil level. Space them 8 to 10 inches apart if growing them outdoors, and crowd them in containers, spacing them 3 to 4 inches apart if growing them in a greenhouse. Use a soil mix with much organic matter, and never allow the bulbs to become dry. Give them bright shade.

This said, I must reveal that the *Eucharis* I have seen growing in Mexico were in very little soil in an old container. The temperature was high, but the humidity was low. The bud count was good, the fragrance lovely and the quality of the flowers was very good, as witness the illustration! It will be a waste of time to try to grow these bulbs if you cannot give them the warm temperatures and humidity they require. If you have a collection of orchids that require these conditions, then this bulb would make a good companion plant for the orchids. Once they are potted in a container, allow them to stay there for several seasons. After each flowering period, replace some of the top soil with well-rotted organic matter mixed with some soil. Completely repot every three to four years, removing any offsets the parent bulbs have produced; grow offsets on to flowering size.

Botanical Name: Eucharis
Family: Liliaceae
Common Name: Amazon lily
Flower Color: White
Flowering Time: Being tropical, it will often flower twice a year, the primary display generally from April through November.
Height: 24 inches
Spread: Will form large clumps over a period of time
Native Habitat: Colombia
Hardiness: Must have warm temperatures and high humidity
Depth of Planting: Neck of bulb at soil level

Distance Apart: 6 bulbs to a 12-inch pot, 8 to 10 inches apart in borders

Containers: Yes

Light Requirements: Bright, indirect light

Soil Type: Rich, well-drained soil

Special Conditions: Giving periods of lower temperatures, around 60°F, followed by higher temperatures, will induce flowering.

Comments: Consider *Eucharis* only when warm temperatures and humidity can be provided. This is a long-lasting cut flower, but is more economically purchased than grown, as providing the right growing conditions will incur much expense.

The "pineapple flower" (*Eucomis comosa*) is attractive in the garden and an excellent, long-lasting container plant. (Photo courtesy of International Bloembollen Centrum.)

EUCOMIS
Liliaceae

The flowers are in a cylindrical column topped by a flurry of leaves. The individual flowers are small and resemble the markings on a pineapple, so it is easy to appreciate the common name pineapple flower. The word *eukomes* is Greek for beautiful headed, an apt description.

While some 10 species grow in the wild in tropical Africa and South Africa, only one species, *Eucomis comosa* var. *comosa*, is to be found in catalogs. The bulbs are large, producing broad leaves up to 24 inches in length that arch up and away from the bulb, then curve back to the ground. The foliage is spotted with purple at the base. The flowers cover as much as half of the 24-inch flower spike, and have violet-purple ovaries, light green petals and prominent stamens. The flower color can vary a little, sometimes tinged with pink. Flowers appear in early summer and, because of the number of flowers and attractive seedpods that follow, remain of interest for a long time.

Eucomis like a rich, well-drained soil, and prefer light shade during the heat of the day although they need morning and afternoon sun, especially in spring and early summer. Plant 5 inches deep and 12 inches apart. They can be grown outdoors where temperatures never remain below freezing throughout the day. In cold areas they can be grown in containers, three to five plants in a 12-inch pot. These bulbs must have moisture in spring and through flowering; thereafter they appreciate a dryer resting period.

Rather unexpectedly, these flowers last a long time when cut. They are more beautiful in the garden, though, especially with the background of a rock to offset their stockiness.

One species which to my knowledge is not in cultivation, *E. pole-evansii*, reaches a height of 6 feet, the top 24 inches (or more) covered with flowers. I cannot help thinking that one day hybridizers will work with these plants and some very interesting colors will become available.

Botanical Name: Eucomis
Family: Liliaceae
Common Name: Pineapple flower
Flower Color: Greenish
Flowering Time: Early summer
Height: 24 inches; some species much taller, but not available
Spread: Will form good clumps if left undisturbed
Native Habitat: South Africa
Hardiness: Will withstand some frost, but should not be grown in areas where frost lingers throughout the day. Protect with mulch and plant in a protected border.
Depth of Planting: 5 inches
Distance Apart: 12 inches
Containers: Yes
Light Requirements: Some sun mornings and evenings in spring, shade during the hottest parts of the day
Soil Type: Rich, well-drained soil
Special Conditions: Provide moisture in winter and spring until flowering has finished. Protect from slugs and snails as foliage and stems are succulent.
Comments: A wonderful bulb to grow if the climate allows, but hardly worth the effort of growing in containers and moving them in and out of protection. Has potential for commercial production as the plants are unusual in color and form, and quite attractive. In warmer areas they should be grown if the garden is of moderate to large size; they are not for the small garden. I think they look best against the background of a large rock.

Renowned for their fragrance, freesias are superb container and garden plants, deserving of greater recognition.

FREESIA
Iridaceae

This genus was named by an apothecary, C. E. Ecklon, who was born in 1795 in Northern Schleswig and who did much plant hunting in South Africa. The name honors Friedrich Heinrich Theodor Freese, a doctor who was a student of Ecklon's. There are some 11 species, all native to South Africa. The species *Freesia refracta* was introduced into culture in 1816, but it was not until it was crossed with *F. armstrongii*, some 70 years later, that freesias became popular. This cross gave the wide range of colors available today.

The plants are not hardy, but can be grown outdoors in frost-free climates. In colder climates they can be planted after the danger of frost has passed; then the corms should be lifted and stored over winter in a frost-free location, and planted out the following spring. They grow well in containers and are great cut flowers. The flowers are zygomorphic (having one plane of symmetry), and are carried on a one-sided spike that turns at right angles just below the lowest flower, and thus all the flowers are upward facing. While the species seldom have more than six flowers, twice that many are not uncommon in the hybrids. The foliage is grasslike, and shorter than the flower spikes that reach 12 inches or more. It continues to grow after the flowers have finished, and should be allowed to remain growing as long as possible. Lift the corms only when the foliage has started to die down.

In warm climates, the corms can be planted 2 inches deep in September and spaced 3 inches apart. These plants will flower in spring. During their growing season, apply liquid organic fertilizer, stopping when the flower spike is well evident. Keep moist until the foliage dies down, then let them have a dry resting period. These corms will often start back into growth in late summer and produce another crop of flowers in fall, fewer in number than the spring production. In cooler climates, plant corms as soon as the danger of frost has passed, and again about a month later. This will assure a good supply of cut flowers for the home.

Light, well-drained soil rich in organic matter and a sunny location are required for these plants. If growing indoors, place six corms in a 6-inch pot, and use regular potting soil. Keep them moist and warm, and never overwater. As soon as growth appears above the soil, apply liquid organic fertilizer. Do not try to move any plants from one pot to another; they resent being moved while in growth. When you lift the corms after a season of growth, you will find a great number of cormels around the bases of the older corms. These can be grown on, but given the rather inexpensive cost of fresh stock, I wonder whether this is worthwhile. It may be better to purchase new corms for each crop. The attention given to these plants by hybridizers is consider-

able. Many fine selections are available, including double-flowered forms. Among those you will find listed are the following:

Cultivars

White

'Alpine', a double

'Ballerina'

'Marie'

'Matterhorn'

'Snowdon'

Yellow

'Aurora'

'Gold Crown', a double

'Helios', a double

'Royal Gold'

'Wintergold'

Orange

'Princess Marijake'

'Talisman'

Reds and Pinks

'Adonis Rose', double

'Bloemfontein', pastel pink, a double

'Florida', rose-pink

'Oberon', flame red with yellow center

'Pimpernel', flame scarlet

'Rose Marie', dark pink, a double

Purples and Blues

'Blue Navy', deep purple

'Blue Wimple', violet-blue

'Royal Blue', campanula blue, white throat striped violet

'Silvia', blue, a double

Botanical Name: Freesia
Family: Iridaceae
Common Name: Freesia
Flower Colors: Many: whites, yellows, blues and violets, reds and rose
Flowering Time: Depending on planting time, can be in flower many months of the year; fall planting yields flowers in spring, spring planting yields flowers in summer.
Height: 8 to 12 inches
Spread: Will slowly form clumps
Native Habitat: South Africa; today mostly hybrids are grown.
Hardiness: Will not withstand much, if any, frost
Depth of Planting: 2 inches
Distance Apart: 3 inches
Containers: Yes
Light Requirements: Full sun
Soil Type: Average, well-drained garden soil
Special Conditions: Fertilizer should be applied from when plants emerge from the ground until flower spikes appear.
Comments: One of the loveliest flowers, but as they can be temperamental, I question their worth in the small garden. Well worth a try in containers in all climates so the fragrance can be enjoyed indoors. Select with care, as some hybrids are not as fragrant as others.

FRITILLARIA
Liliaceae

The name of the genus is derived from *fritillus,* meaning a dice box, probably because many species are checkered on the exterior of the flowers. A genus of more than 80 species, found in the northern hemisphere, around the Mediterranean and eastward to China and Japan. Certain species are also found in North America, particularly along the West Coast of the United States. These plants are closely related to other members of the family Liliaceae.

Most of the species produce unbranched flowering stems. The foliage is sometimes in whorls, as with *Fritillaria imperialis,* the crown imperial; this is one of the most striking species, unique in that the flowers are bunched together at the top of a strong stem, with a tuft of leaves above them. All other species have flowers distributed along the stems. The flowers are bell shaped and have a nectary at the base of each petal, there being six petals of equal size (or nearly so). The bulbs of this genus must be han-

Native to Siberia, *Fritillaria pallidiflora* is a very hardy plant. Situate the plants where you can easily tilt the flowers to admire their red-crimson interiors.

dled with care as they are brittle, and must be packed so that moisture loss is kept to a minimum. While the European and Asiatic species are often larger than the American species, they are made up of fewer (but larger) scales. The American species with a greater number of scales can be propagated by removing some of the outer scales, much the same way lilies are propagated.

Despite the variety of their habitats in the wild, the cultural requirements of these plants is quite similar. Plant them 3 to 4 inches deep. The distance apart will vary by species, but most are set 8 inches apart; the tall-growing *F. imperialis* bulbs are placed 18 inches apart. All species like a rich, well-drained soil with a high organic matter content. Moisture must be provided during their growing period and over the winter, and with the exception of *F. imperialis*, which likes the sun, all species prefer filtered shade. Once planted, the bulbs should remain undisturbed for years. Lift and divide only if the bulbs become overcrowded or if an increase in stock is desired.

All the species will perform quite well in containers. If you grow them this way, you might want to bring them indoors when they have started into growth and, with the additional warmth, they will come into flower earlier. If you do grow them indoors, make certain they have bright but indirect light. When they have finished flowering, take them outdoors to grow for a couple of seasons there before you use them indoors again.

One of the problems with these plants is that they will often take a year to settle in. Many gardeners are impatient, and if the bulbs do not give a grand performance the first season after planting, they are branded as difficult. Poor performance is far more often due to incorrect handling than any fault of the bulbs. It is for this reason that the location where they are to grow must be selected with care, and then, once planted, the bulbs should be left alone.

Fritillaria acmopetala (syn. *F. lycia*): This species is native to Cypress, Syria and Lebanon. Over the years nurseries have selected sturdy, vigorous plants, and the bulbs offered in catalogs grow taller than those in the wild, often to more than 24 inches. The flowers are olive green and streaked with brown or purple on the exterior, while the interior is a shiny olive green. The petals are quite pointed and recurve; there are as many as three flowers to a stem, appearing in late spring.

F. biflora (syn. *F. agrestis, F. grayana, F. roderickii, F. succulenta*): The common name for this Californian is mission bells. It is also found in the southern part of Oregon. It flowers in early spring with brownish, unmottled flowers with some green shading, 12 inches tall.

F. camschatcensis (syn. *F. kamtschatensis, Lilium camschatcense*): Quite variable in height, from 6 to more than 12 inches, which is not surprising considering the very wide distribution of this species; it is at home in Japan, Alaska, Washington and Oregon. That it was at one time considered to be a lily speaks of its beauty. The leaves grow in whorls on strong stalks. The flowers may be the darkest of all the species, deep maroon to almost black. Where it grows determines the flowering time, blooming quite early in warm climates, and not until midsummer in Alaska.

F. davisii: This is a rather rare species from Greece, and it is pleasant to see it is being listed in catalogs. A deep chocolate brown, pleasantly checkered, 6 to 10 inches tall, it flowers in early spring.

F. imperialis: The crown imperial, this native to the western Himalayas has been in culture since the sixteenth century and is one of the most popular species of the genus. Tolerant of a very wide range of soils, it likes the sun. Give it time to settle in, and when it is established, leave it undisturbed. The stems are strong, the bell-shaped flowers clustered at the top with a tuft of leaves above them. The nectaries are quite prominent, but often not seen, as the flowers are pendant on stems 48 inches tall. Very showy and long lasting, coming into flower in April and lasting well into May. When well established it will often produce a double ring of flowers, one above the other, but this can make the head a little untidy. A great number of selections of this species are listed in catalogs, among them: 'Aurora', with orange-red flowers; 'Lutea', with strong yellow flowers; 'Lutea Maxima', even stronger than 'Lutea', forms good heads but can be untidy; 'Rubra', orange flowers with a hint of brown. It is unfortunate that some nurseries list selections with fanciful names very much like and easily confused with those listed above, which have stood the test of time. Look at the photographs when selecting to make certain you obtain the ones you like, and do not be misled by names such as 'Orange Giant'. Something to remember with *F. imperialis* is that the flowers stink like rotten mutton, so do not plant these bulbs where their aroma will cause dismay.

F. meleagris: The snake's head fritillary, a favorite in European gardens for many years. It must have shade and moisture throughout the year, and is at home in woodlands in much of Europe. Strong stems carry the flowers 15 inches tall. The flowers are pale or dark pink with hints of purple and checkered with blackish dots, while the interior is greenish yellow. A remarkable combination of colors, and so variable it has led to a number of selections: 'Alba', a pure white; 'Artemis', checkered purple with green; 'Saturnus', violet with a reddish hue. Some nurseries offer a mix of colors, which means you'll

obtain a mix of the many forms available, but probably not the pure white forms.

F. michailovskyi: A lovely species I admired at the 1992 Floriade in The Hague, with a reddish purple bell with a bright yellow mouth. It reaches 6 to 8 inches and flowers in April. It is good to see such a comparatively rare species listed in catalogs.

F. pallidiflora: If you have any doubt about how hardy these plants are, then grow this species from Siberia! The foliage appears in two whorls. Above the leaves, pale yellow flowers spotted inside with reddish crimson appear in May. The plants reach 15 inches; I suspect in moderate climates they might grow a little taller.

F. persica (syn. *F. arabica*, *F. eggeri*, *F. libanotica*): This lovely species comes from southern Turkey, Iran and Cypress. It is one of the taller sorts; I have seen it in the garden at Minau on Lake Constance topping out at 36 inches, the upper 24 inches covered with the dark-plum-colored flowers, providing a grand contrast to the bluish foliage. This was most likely the form known as 'Adiyaman', which does grow a little taller than the species.

F. purdyi: A native to northern California and seldom more than 6 inches tall, it forms a rosette of leaves at the base of the flower stalk. This species can surprise you. While there is often only one flower per stalk, it sometimes will carry as many as six. The flowers are white with broad chocolate-crimson stripes and dots on the interior of the petals. Flowers in late spring.

F. uva-vulpis: This is the correct name for the plant often listed as *F. assyriaca*. A recent introduction, it was found in 1974. The flowers are outstanding, being pendulous and maroon with golden bronze interiors, and appear in late spring. A strong grower, the plant reaches 12 to 14 inches in height. Do not be put off by the name—this is a grand species and produces a number of offsets. If the budget allows, do try some; once they are established, you will look forward to seeing them in flower year after year.

Botanical Name: Fritillaria
Family: Liliaceae
Common Names: Fritillary, crown imperial, mission bells, checker-lily, snake's head fritillary
Flower Colors: Wide range of colors: orange, yellow, white, many checkered on the outer petals, many bicolors
Flowering Time: Varies by species; early to late spring
Height: Some species reach more than 36 inches, others are in the 6- to 12-inch range
Spread: Will form large colonies if left undisturbed
Native Habitat: Mediterranean regions, eastward to China and Japan, the Himalayas, North America
Hardiness: Hardy; in coldest areas (where frost is heavy and prolonged) it appreciates a mulch in order to avoid repeated freezing and thawing
Depth of Planting: 3 to 4 inches
Distance Apart: Low-growing species 6 to 10 inches, taller species 18 inches
Containers: Yes
Light requirements: Most species prefer light shade; *F. imperialis* prefers sun.
Soil Type: Average garden soil; most species prefer well-drained soil with good organic content.
Special Conditions: Some taller species may require support in very exposed areas.
Comments: Some of the loveliest of bulbs. *F. persica* pleases me with its long flowering period and unusual color. Crown Imperials always are attractive, and given the beauty of the flowers of the species, I encourage all gardeners to try one or more of these striking plants. Take care when handling, do not be impatient, and give them time to get settled in. They will not disappoint you—in fact, I am certain they will delight you.

GALANTHUS
Amaryllidaceae

The name of the genus is derived from the Greek *gala*, meaning milk, and *anthos*, meaning flower, and these flowers are indeed milky white. The common name is snowdrop. All the species are hardy; no matter how cold the weather, they seem impervious. Native to the eastern Mediterranean, these early flowering plants are popular, but only one species (*Galanthus nivalis* ssp. *nivalis*) is commonly listed in catalogs. While species in a genus are often distinguished by the difference in the flowers, it is the difference in foliage that distinguishes one species of *Galanthus* from another. The leaves vary in length, in the juxtaposition of one to another, and in their width and color.

Snowdrops are not unlike snowflakes, which belong in the genus *Leucojum*. The difference between the flowers is that in *Galanthus* the segments are not of equal length as they are in *Leucojum*. (I can remember this because *Leucojum* starts with *L*, for "level," and petals of equal length are level with one another.) In *Galanthus* the inner segments are shorter and notched at the tips, with green markings around each notch. The flowers tend to be solitary and drooping.

While tolerant of many soils, *Galanthus* prefer one with lots of organic matter. They like

Because *Galanthus nivalis* are easy to grow, their beauty is often overlooked. They are good for spaces in shrub borders and to fill odd corners in the garden. (Photo courtesy of International Bloembollen Centrum.)

some direct sunlight for part of the day, and are unhappy in constant shade, except in the very hottest areas, when high shade is appreciated. Plant the bulbs 3 inches deep and 5 inches apart, and leave them undisturbed for years, in fact until they become overcrowded and show signs of decline (which may not occur). They grow well in containers, but do not accept forcing; they should be almost in flower before being brought indoors. These are great plants to grow among shrubs, but as they are dwarf, keep them where they can be seen. Plant in bold groupings in an irregular pattern. They make a good show when planted around the bases of trees in lawns, and like *Crocus* they can also be planted under lawns, but mowing schedules have to be adapted so the foliage can mature.

While the common snowdrop flowers early in the year, certain species flower in the winter months — *G. caucasicus*, for example. If hybridizers gave attention to this genus (which seems unlikely), I would be surprised if cultivars could not be produced that would be in flower for many months of the year, and perhaps other colors might be forthcoming. Moisture is needed from fall until the foliage dies back, and while some bone meal is appreciated (applied in late fall), these plants are not demanding. They give good value for the money.

Galanthus nivalis **ssp.** *nivalis:* Native to much of Europe, and one of the finest species. 4 to 8 inches in height, with flowers of pure white, and notched inner segments with green color around the notch. They bloom from January through February, and the gray leaves are pressed together at the base. A number of variants have been selected and are listed in catalogs. Among them are: 'Flore Pleno', with double flowers; 'Viridapics', the outer and inner segments with green tips; and 'Simplex', with flowers somewhat larger than those of the species.

Botanical Name: Galanthus
Family: Amaryllidaceae
Common Name: Snowdrop
Flower Color: White
Flowering Time: January–February
Height: 6 to 8 inches
Spread: Will form colonies if left undisturbed
Native Habitat: Much of Europe
Hardiness: Very hardy
Depth of Planting: 3 inches
Distance Apart: 5 to 6 inches
Containers: Yes
Light Requirements: Sun for part of the day; high shade tolerated in very warm climates

Soil Type: Average, well-drained garden soils, preferably with humus

Special Conditions: The plants appreciate some bone meal at planting time. Moisture is needed in winter and through spring until foliage has died down.

Comments: Delightful little plants well worth growing—just pop them in the ground and enjoy them year after year. I have seen them growing in lawns; it's a different look, but I am not sure it is worth the work involved. Crowded in a pot, they look marvelous indoors, but remember not to force them. They must be almost in flower before being brought indoors.

GALTONIA
Liliaceae

This genus was named in honor of Francis Galton, a British scientist who traveled widely in South Africa, and wrote *A Narrative of an Explorer in South Africa*. Galton was also an advocate of the fingerprint method of identification. These plants are closely related to *Hyacinthus*, and one species of *Galtonia*, *G. candicans*, has the common name of summer hyacinth. This is the only species worth growing, and it is often listed in catalogs. The other two species are rare in cultivation and should remain so.

The bulbs are not hardy, and where winter temperatures fall below 20°F they should be lifted in fall, overwintered in a frost-free area and planted in spring when all danger of frost has passed. The bulbs are large and should be planted 6 inches below soil level and spaced 18 to 24 inches apart. Average garden soil with good drainage is ideal. *Galtonia* should receive sun for most of the day.

The pendulous flowers are carried on long

Galtonia candicans flower for a long time. Permanent residents of gardens in warmer climates, they are well worth lifting and replanting in other areas.

flower stalks well away from the stem. As many as 30 to 40 will be found on a stem that can reach 4 feet in height. Pure white, they start to flower in late July and will often still be flowering in September, making this plant an attractive one for a long time. The leaves are 2 inches wide, carried at the base, upright and pointed, about 24 inches in length.

Galtonias do well in large containers. Though they are supposed to be fragrant, I have yet to appreciate it, and at the moment I regard these plants as having "little" fragrance. (Having said this, I expect the next plants I look at will knock me over with a delightful perfume!) If you live in a mild climate, use these bulbs in the mixed border. They remain tidy and add a texture and form to a border quite different from those of most other plants.

I have often wondered if color could be bred into these plants. One species has green flowers, *G. viridiflora*, and the other species, *G. princeps*, has cream-colored flowers; if there are genes with other colors on them (they would be recessive), I do not know. If the lovely towering spike of the summer hyacinth came in as many colors as the spring hyacinth, then these plants would be a sensation. Perhaps one day we shall see such marvels.

Botanical Name: Galtonia
Family: Liliaceae
Common Names: Summer hyacinth, in South Africa called the berg lily
Flower Color: White
Flowering Time: Late summer
Height: 48 inches
Spread: Will form small colonies, but very slowly
Native Habitat: South Africa
Hardiness: Will survive down to 20°F, a little lower with heavy mulch and when planted in a south-facing border
Depth of Planting: 6 inches
Distance Apart: 18 to 24 inches
Containers: Yes
Light Requirements: Sun; some shade in hottest areas (never continuous shade)
Soil Type: Average, well-drained garden soil
Special Conditions: If growing in containers, make

certain they are large. A half wine or whisky barrel is ideal, planted with 3 or 4 bulbs.
Comments: These easy-to-grow plants have a form, appearance and long flowering period that makes them a good addition to a mixed border. I just wish these lovely spikes of summer purity were available in color. They are always fun to see, but I question whether these plants are of value in any but the larger gardens.

GLADIOLUS
Iridaceae

It is no surprise to learn the name is derived from the Latin *gladius*, meaning sword, because the foliage is distinctly sword shaped, sharply pointed and rather coarse. It is the lovely flowers, however, that demand attention. There are some 150 species (few of them in cultivation) and many hundreds of cultivars. Today's catalogs are filled with all the colors of the rainbow—except blue. Gladiolus have quite a history, and the breeding of contemporary hybrids was begun in the early nineteenth century. An Englishman crossed two South African species, *Gladiolus cardinalis* (red with a white blotch on the lower segments) with *G. tristis* (a very sweet-smelling species, pale yellow with crimson markings). The name given to this cross was *G. × colvillii*, and the progeny were the first hybrids used as cut flowers and forced for early flowering. These hybrids were not as tall as modern hybrids, and the flowers not as large; the petals are loosely held and frequently have color blotches on three of the segments. You will find them listed sometimes as "winter hardy gladiolus" or under *G. nanus*. They are wonderful garden plants. Named selections will be listed, in white, pink, orange and red tones, with some interesting bicolors.

The species used to produce the large-flowered, taller hybrids we grow today including *G. cardinalis, G. natalensis* (syn. *G. psittacinus*) and *G. papilio* (syn. *G. purpureo-auratus*). Among those involved were Max Leichtlin (Germany), M. Lemoine (France) and Arthur Kundred (United States), all during the latter part of the last century. Many large-flowered selections were brought onto the market, for the most part in hues of yellow or red.

Then, in 1904, Mr. Frank Fox of Wimbledon, England, was working on the bridge that spans the Zambesi at Victoria Falls. He discovered *G. primulinus*, a good yellow, and it was this plant that unlocked Pandora's box and made possible the great range of colors we enjoy in these great plants today. I have walked over this bridge—it is the border between Zambia and Zimbabwe—and have seen *G. primulinus* flowering in the wild in this area.

Gladioli have rootstocks that are corms. Plant them 6 inches deep and 6 to 10 inches apart. They like a rich, well-drained soil and enjoy the sun. The "winter hardy gladiolus" can be left in the ground in all climates, but the tall hybrids are not hardy, and while they can be left in the ground in frost-free (or nearly so) areas, in others the corms should be lifted and cleaned, the old corm detached from the new, and the new corms stored in a dry, well-ventilated area with temperatures around 50°F. On lifting, many little corms can be seen clustered around the larger ones. While these can be grown on, this process will take several years. Corms about the size of a quarter are worth saving and will no doubt flower the following season. Corms should be planted after all danger of frost has passed.

More than one crop of flowers can be obtained by staggering the plantings. Allow the earliest spring plantings some 120 days to come into flower. Those planted in early July should be in flower 90 days later, early October. This is about as late as you can get them to flower in the gar-

Available in myriad colors, gladiolus bring a striking accent to summer gardens.

den, as soon after that the cooler temperatures will slow growth and frost will be experienced in all except the warmest climates. In warm, frost-free areas planting can continue throughout the year.

Gladioli are best planted in bold clumps all of the same color, in the perennial or mixed border, or to provide a striking contrast among annuals. Where wind is a problem, taller cultivars may need some support. Deeper planting allows the plants to withstand the wind better, but if this is done, make certain the soil is cultivated down to at least 14 or more inches.

Gladioli make great container plants, but the containers should be large and at least 10 to 12 inches deep. Plant the corms a little closer together here than in the border, spacing them just 4 inches apart. Use ordinary potting soil and make certain that the drainage is good. If you wish to grow Gladioli for cut flowers, line them up in rows, plant with the corms almost touching each other. Allow at least 36 inches between each row.

Although they are seldom attacked by pests or diseases, you may find that thrips have caused the foliage to streak. The damage is caused by the insects' gnawing on the fleshy parts of the leaves. The majority of such problems occur because the stock was not clean. If you experience thrips, ask your supplier if other customers have had the problem. Dusting with an insecticide is simple and effective, but it is best to purchase from quality firms that supply only top quality corms in the first place. If you treat the corms or the plants with an insecticide, follow the directions on the label.

Gladioli should not be allowed to become dry during their growing period. If your soil is not very rich in organic matter, give them a feeding of liquid organic fertilizer twice a month, starting as soon as they poke their noses above the ground and stopping when the first hint of the flower spike appears. After flowering has finished, you can let them dry out a little, and as soon as the foliage starts to die back, you can stop watering altogether. Where Gladioli have been grown, you might find in the following season what looks like a crop of grass. This could be the little cormels sending up their foliage, which happens in warmer areas. If they are a nuisance, just jerk them out.

Gladioli are superb, long-lasting cut flowers. Cut them early in the day when the stems are filled with moisture, or cut them late in the day, but never in the heat of the day. The time to cut is when the lower buds show signs of color; the flowers will develop fully if the stems are cut at this stage. Do not cut before you can clearly see the color, or you may find that the buds do not develop well. A few species are to be found in catalogs. They are fun to grow, but do not expect them to be as luscious as the hybrids. Still, they have an air of gentle refinement about them, better suited for certain interiors than the powerful colors of some cultivars.

Gladiolus byzantinus: Native to the Mediterranean area, this is a tough plant I have seen in full glory in the stony ground of Malta. Flowers are distributed around the stem, facing at least three directions. Deep burgundy red, as many as 10 to 15 flowers per 24-inch spike, early summer flowering. The foliage is sparse, held in a fan-shaped cluster, with seldom more than five leaves per plant. The plants can withstand some frost, more with the protection of a mulch, but they are not hardy plants.

G. carneus: The nomenclature of this South African species is, to say the least, confused. It appears that red forms of *G. blandus* were named *G. blandus* var. *carneus*. Later, some raised the red form to specific rank, calling it *G. carneus*. This is a valid name. The species has a wide color range, from white to cream with purple blotches on the lower segments. The plants are 18 inches tall, small but quite showy, as the individual flowers are of good size (but not many per stalk), flowering in early summer.

G. × citrinus: One of the earliest hybrids ever produced, still used in breeding new cultivars. Short (only 8 to 10 inches tall), pale yellow and flowering in June. This is not the same plant as *G. citrinus*, a very rare species native to South Africa.

G × colvillii: One of the very first hybrids made (the cross is described above), it is still to be found today. A selection can be found sometimes listed under *G. nanus,* mostly in the red and yellow colors, with the blotch on each of the lower three segments.

G. undulatus: This rather rare species is native to South Africa. The cream-colored petals are undulated, tapering to a rather sharp point and twisting. The plants reach 24 inches and flower in early summer.

You might see other species listed, and if you enjoy flowers that are rather subdued but with a classy look to them, yield to temptation and purchase a few. I doubt you will be disappointed. The number of cultivars available is vast. Recently named series have been listed under such names as 'Cathedral Gladiolus' and offer colors with such names as:

'St Patrick's', ruffled, green, with hints of cream and yellow

'Sacred Heart', rich burgundy red with a yellow throat

'Canterbury', blue with a white throat

'Dreaming Spires', orange

Some catalogs list various collections under such names as 'Royalty' and 'Royal Collection'. These are also offered under such names as 'Candy Cane', 'White Friendship', 'Cherry Flip' and 'Lemonade', where it is quite easy to determine the color of the flowers from the names.

Rather than give a list of cultivars that may well be out of date even just one year from now, I suggest you select from the catalogs exactly the colors you wish and take advantage of any specials. There is no need to purchase the largest size corms offered. The second and third sizes flower well, and there is no great advantage in planting such large corms—it just makes for more work digging larger holes! I like to see about 25 corms of one color planted together, feeling that such a planting makes a statement, and if you cut a few they will not be missed. But some gardeners like a mixture of colors in a group. You make the choice, but please, keep the tall cultivars with other ones; mix colors perhaps, but heights? That is a no-no!

Botanical Name: Gladiolus
Family: Iridaceae
Common Name: Gladiolus
Flower Colors: Very wide range, some bicolors
Flowering Time: Early summer and midsummer; the planting time can be staggered for flowers throughout summer into fall.
Height: Varies by type; most 3 to 4 feet, but some cultivars are 18 to 25 inches
Spread: Will produce offsets that take a while to flower; count on them to give you large clumps.
Native Habitat: South Africa and around the Mediterranean
Hardiness: Some are hardy, the *G. nanus* types or those listed under "Hardy Gladiolus." Large and tall types can't withstand much, if any, frost.
Depth of Planting: 6 inches, although more would not hurt
Distance Apart: 6 to 10 inches, closer in rows for cut flowers and when grown in containers
Containers: Yes
Light Requirements: Full sun
Soil Type: Average, well-drained garden soil
Special Conditions: Liquid feeding up to the time the flower stem emerges is an advantage
Comments: Lovely flowers of easy culture, well worth growing, and even in cold climates these plants should be part of the summer color program. Modern cultivars are very showy, so do not forget the quiet, unassuming charm of the species.

The selections of *Gloriosa superba* grown in gardens and used by florists are more brightly colored than the species, seen here in the wild, in Kruger Park, where the wild animals leave this poisonous plant alone.

GLORIOSA
Liliaceae

The name *Gloriosa* derives from the Latin "gloriosa" (full of glory), which is very appropriate for these exotic-looking flowers at home in South Africa and India. At one time there were thought to be as many as 30 species, but today many authorities regard all as being variants of *Gloriosa superba*. They are fleshy tuberous plants, and they multiply quickly. These plants are rightly favorites of florists, and the lovely flowers with their much recurved and twisting petals, in shades of red bordered with gold, are sold singly in individual boxes—they are that glorious. Unfortunately, they are not hardy, though perfect for a cool greenhouse and for frost-free climates. Marvelous container plants, they can be enjoyed in cooler climates, but have to be given protection against all frost.

The tubers should be planted 2 inches deep and 24 inches apart, and as they are prostrate growing they should be given some support over which to scramble. They like a rich soil with plenty of organic matter and good drainage. When they start into growth, fertilize with liquid organic fertilizer, and feed them through the summer. Never allow them to become dry. They require less moisture and no feeding through the winter months. They appreciate sun, but in greenhouses bright, indirect light seems to suit them well, so some shading should be applied to the glass. About the only problem you will experience is aphids, and this only under glass.

Gloriosa superba: Other species, *G. rothschildiana* and *G. carsonii,* are now regarded as forms of *G. superba.* Native to South Africa, the flowers have petals that are much recurved. Their tips often meet above the flowers, with the stamens and stigma at right angles to the main axis of the flowers. The color is shades of red, and the edges of the petals are often golden. The flower stalks carry the flowers 4 inches or more from the stems, and when the plants are well grown, many flowers are produced. There is a yellow form, but I have not seen it listed in any catalogs.

Such striking flowers will add an accent to any garden, but do not rely on the plants to overwhelm you with color. They are not suitable for all gardens, but if you see them in flower you will probably long to grow them. I regard them as I do orchids—aristocrats, if you will. While a pure delight, they are not for the casual gardener, but rather for the very keen grower, whose diligence will be well rewarded.

Botanical Name: Gloriosa
Family: Liliaceae
Common Name: Climbing lily
Flower Colors: Shades of red, petals often edged with gold

Flowering Time: Midsummer into fall

Height: Will scramble for many feet in one season

Spread: Will form sizeable clumps in warm climates

Native Habitat: South Africa, north to Kenya, India

Hardiness: Not hardy

Depth of Planting: 2 inches

Distance Apart: 24 inches

Containers: Yes

Light Requirements: Bright light in green houses, sun outdoors

Soil Type: Rich, well-drained soil

Special Conditions: The plants must have something over which to scramble, such as a wire cage; fertilizer is needed when in active growth.

Comments: Not a plant for everyone but if you can grow these plants well, they will thrill you. These great cut flowers add a lot of character to a garden, but not much volume of color.

In the last few years, wonderful new cultivars of daylilies have been introduced. This one, *Hemerocallis* 'Golden Tycoon', would be a welcome addition to any garden. (Photo by Chester Allen, courtesy of Klehms of Champaign.)

HEMEROCALLIS
Liliaceae

The name is derived from the Greek *hemera,* meaning a day, and *kallos,* meaning beauty. The flowers last but for a day, hence their common name daylily. There are some 15 species and many beautiful cultivars. The plants have roots that are inclined to be tuberous rhizomes and for this reason are, in my opinion, correctly included in any book about bulbs.

Over the years these plants have received a lot of attention from various breeders, and today the hybrids are the desired plants and few species are listed in catalogs. They grow wild in China and Japan, and one is at home in Siberia, obviously quite hardy. *Hemerocallis fulva* is sometimes listed as being native to Europe, but this is questionable. What is certain is that it has been in cultivation for a long time, and being a vigorous plant, it has escaped from American gardens to become established in parts of the country. Where it is happy it soon forms bold colonies, spreading by rhizomes and smothering any competition.

The flowers are trumpet shaped, and a narrow tube at their base flares to give flowers a diameter of 4 or 5, or as much as 8 to 10 inches. The colors are mainly in the yellow, orange and pink tones, but newer hybrids are lavender, purple, white (or nearly so), and black (or nearly so), and many have a yellow throat and white stripes through the center of the petals. In many hybrids there is a third color between the throat and the petals, thus a tricolor flower. The width of the petals varies, too. It must be said that few plants can rival the daylily in ease of culture, adaptability to so many different soils, and such varied and attractive colors. The foliage is basal and quite grasslike. Some plants are evergreen,

Hemerocallis 'Red Razzle Dazzle' is another fine introduction from the famed Klehm Nursery, with good color, strong growth and good health. (Photo by Chester Allen, courtesy of Klehms of Champaign.)

others not. You will be hard put to find any prone to pests or disease.

Plant so the base of the foliage is at soil level, and space 18 to 24 inches apart, but this distance should vary, as taller cultivars ought to be spaced a little wider, dwarf selections closer together. Left alone, they will form large clumps in a short period of time. They will need to be lifted and divided when, and only when, you see that they are becoming very crowded, flower production is dropping, and other signs of discomfort appear, such as much browning of the foliage. Such easy-to-grow plants deserve to be grown more frequently than they are. These are plants landscape architects, for example, should use more often. They like the sun and almost any soil; they appreciate moisture, but when estab-

lished are quite drought resistant (but are better performers if moisture is given). They will accept fertilizers, but do not demand feeding. Perhaps the only flaw that can be attributed to these plants is that the flowers last for such a short time. Even so, many are produced, so that is not a great problem. They are not good cut flowers. I have seen these plants neglected and in poor soil, exposed to reflected heat and receiving the attention of many dogs, getting only moisture that nature provides (and that has not been much in California in the last few years), and yet these plants put on an outstanding display of color. I am of the opinion that these plants thrive on neglect, and we gardeners cause problems when we take too good care of them.

Many daylilies have a lovely fragrance, a feature often overlooked, and certain cultivars have specific times when they are at their best. While daylilies are seldom out of flower completely, there are early, midseason and late-flowering types. Select plants so that there is always one at its peak. Daylilies grow well in containers.

When selecting colors, the following list may be of help:

Cultivars

Golds and oranges

'Alaska Gold': lovely gold color, large flowers, 30 inches tall

'Apricot Surprise': soft apricot color, ruffled petals, 24 inches tall

'Evergold': large ruffled flowers, vigorous, 40 inches tall

'Golden Dewdrop': deep yellow, fragrant, flowers all summer long, 20 inches tall

'Golden Tycoon': golden orange with ruffled petals, green throat, 20 inches tall

'Helaman': one of the largest flowers, up to 12 inches in diameter, bronze-rust edging, fragrant, 30 inches tall

'Prairie Sunset': a blend of apricot and yellow with a hint of pink, 36 inches tall

'Sombrero Gold': large flowers, robust grower, a good golden yellow, 20 inches tall

'Stella de Oro': almost everblooming, golden yellow, 20 to 24 inches tall

Pinks and Peaches

'Bowl of Roses': fragrant, dusty salmon, 30 inches tall

'Cinnamon Pleasure': fragrant, petals have golden edges, 36 inches tall

'Country Uncle': peach-pink, good texture, 20 inches tall

'Gentle Country Breeze': soft pink with golden throat, 24 inches tall

'Jolly Dimples': peach with rose-lavender blush, 18 inches tall

'Joyful Fancy-Free': peach and cream with gold throat, 30 inches tall

'Pink Lavender Appeal': Pink-lavender, green throat, 24 inches tall

'Sirocco': fragrant, salmon pink, very wide petals, great texture, 26 inches tall

'Theresa Hall': pink with hint of gold, large flowered, 36 inches tall

'Upper Class Peach': golden yellow edges to the petals, 40 inches tall

Bicolors

'Lamanite Rainbow': rose-pink and buff chartreuse throat, 24 inches tall

'Prize Picotee Elite': creamy white with purple, 24 inches tall

'Shady Lady': ruffled, yellow with wine-red eye, green throat, 34 inches tall

Red

'Red Razzle Dazzle': wide petals, good, non-fading color, 30 inches tall

'Red Reggatta': faint white edge to petals, 26 inches tall

Botanical Name: Hemerocallis
Family: Liliaceae
Common Name: Daylily
Flower Colors: Cream, rose, yellow, red, pink and purple, with bicolors and virtual tricolors
Flowering Time: Early summer onward
Height: Varies by species and cultivar; from 18 inches to more than 5 feet
Spread: Will soon form large clumps
Native Habitat: China, Japan, Siberia
Hardiness: Very hardy
Depth of Planting: Base of foliage at soil level
Distance Apart: 18 to 24 inches; tall types to 36 inches
Containers: Yes
Light Requirements: Sun; will take some shade but number of flowers produced often reduced in shade.
Soil Type: Will tolerate all types, but prefers average garden soil.
Special Conditions: Appreciates moisture during spring and summer; when established will withstand drought.

Comments: Lovely plants that prefer a warm, summer climate, or flower production drops off as it does in shade. Select with care so you have some always in flower in a wide range of colors. I prefer quantity to fewer but larger flowers—a mass of flowers is a joy to behold. While some gardeners suggest lifting every 3 to 4 years, it is best to wait until you notice a decline in flower production before you do this work.

HERMODACTYLUS
Iridaceae

If you like unusual bulbs, this one should please you! The name comes from the Greek *Hermes*, meaning Mercury, and *dactylos*, meaning finger. *Hermodactylus* used to be classed as an iris, but having only a one-celled ovary instead of a three-celled ovary, it was put into its own genus, where it is the only species. The rootstock is tuberous, producing foliage in fall. In spring the flower spike emerges from among the leaves on top of a hollow stem, to a height of around 12 inches. The flowers are solitary, greenish with very dark purplish marking at the tip of the falls; the claw (which would be the crest in an iris—see illustration, page 8) and standards are light yellowish green. Quite a combination, and somehow it is rather surprising that there is a lovely rose fragrance. In the meantime the underground tuber is creeping away, forming another plant inches from the parent. After the flower fades, the foliage continues to grow. In a few years you have a colony of these plants.

It is unusual and gratifying to see this native of the Mediterranean region, from southern France to Greece, listed in various catalogs. It withstands temperatures down to around 0°F, and it prefers a well-drained soil, and sun. Some organic matter is appreciated, and as soon as the

An unusual plant, *Hermodactylus tuberosus* will creep around and form interesting colonies. The unusual color coupled with a pleasing fragrance make this an interesting and unusual plant that is fun to grow. (Photo courtesy of International Bloembollen Centrum.)

leaves are seen to be growing, a couple of feedings with a liquid organic fertilizer is appropriate. It should have adequate moisture through early summer, and then can be allowed to dry out a little. It will flower in late spring, early summer. Not surprisingly, this plant has the common name "snake's head iris." While it hails from the south of France, it has become widespread in Europe and has been recorded in Great Britain.

A great plant for the rock garden, it is of easy culture and will most certainly be a conversation piece. It will become naturalized in areas where grass is sparse and little else grows. Once it is growing well, leave it alone. Given its habit of creeping around, it does not perform well in containers. I would be tempted to lift a few plants and bring them indoors, however, as the unusual markings and the fragrance should be enjoyed to the fullest.

Hermodactylus tuberosus: Native to the Mediterranean region, but now found in other parts of Europe. Irislike flowers of yellow-green with brownish purple, reaching 12 inches tall. May-flowering, with foliage surrounding the flower spike having four sides. Attractive seedpods are pendant when ripe.

Botanical Name: Hermodactylus
Family: Iridaceae
Common Names: Snake's head iris
Flower Colors: Yellow-green with brownish purple
Flowering Time: Late spring, early summer
Height: 12 inches
Spread: Will form colonies
Native Habitat: South of France and Greece; now found in many parts of Europe
Hardiness: To about 0°F
Depth of Planting: 3 inches
Distance Apart: 6 to 8 inches
Containers: No
Light Requirements: Sun
Soil Type: Average, well-drained garden soil
Special Conditions: Provide moisture from fall through midsummer. Does not like compacted soil.
Comments: A most unusual plant, one that will not put on a startling display of color. Grow it where you can get close to it and appreciate its form and fragrance. This plant is much easier to grow than its appearance would seem to indicate.

HIPPEASTRUM
Amaryllidaceae

The Greek for a knight is *hippeus,* and for a star it is *astron,* but just how these apply to this genus is a mystery. There is frequently a star in the center of the flowers, created by the green base of the petals. The foliage grows to either side of the large bulb, curving up and then swooping down, the flower stem rising from between the leaves (perhaps suggestive of a knight sitting on a horse, the leaves being the haunches?).

While there are some 70 species, all native to South America, it is rare to find any species in cultivation. The popular, commonly grown plants are hybrids, with many bloodlines running through them. They are commonly called amaryllis, and as indoor plants are often purchased potted to bring into flower around the Christmas season. The trumpet-shaped flowers, often 8 to 10 inches in diameter, are carried on leafless stalks. Often two, sometimes as many as five flowers, will be produced on one plant. The largest bulbs often send up two flower spikes that appear before the leaves. The flowers may be white, varying hues of pink and red, or orange. Certain selections have green or reddish veining, and the markings and shadings in the flowers are most attractive. After the flowers have passed, the foliage continues to grow, often to a length of 24 inches. It is strap-shaped, 2 or more inches wide, and fleshy. These bulbs are not hardy. They can be grown outdoors in frost-free areas, where they will flower early in the year, in April or May.

When prepotted, the bulbs are often in a lightweight soil mix that is moisture retentive, but provides little sustenance for them. Despite all efforts of the leaves to produce food, often not sufficient food is produced to allow the bulb to flower the following year. In my experience homeowners will enjoy more success with

There are many cultivars of Hippeastrum, this one named 'Apple Blossom' being superb with long-lasting flowers.

these bulbs if they purchase them in the nursery and treat them in the following way. Select a firm bulb with a good number of root initials (swellings) visible at the base. Plant in a 6- to 10-inch pot, using a regular potting soil. Make certain that only one half to two thirds of the bulb is in the soil, and that the neck is well above it. Water the pot well. From this point until the flower buds begin to emerge, keep the pot moist but not wet, and keep in temperatures in the 65° to 70°F range—comfortable room temperature. As soon as there is a sign of the emerging buds, make sure the plant enjoys good—but preferably not strong, indirect—light. Start to apply a liquid organic fertilizer with every other watering. Continue to keep the pot moist.

When the flower stalk reaches 18 to 20 inches, you may notice signs of emerging leaves. When the flowers start to open, move the plant into lower light and cooler temperatures to prolong the flowering period. As soon as the flowers have passed, remove them. Bring the plants back to better light and warmer temperatures. Keep feeding until the leaves start to die back, and then slowly reduce the amount of water given and stop feeding. If you wish, the plant can be grown outdoors as soon as the night temperatures reach around 55°F. When the foliage has died back, place the pot on its side where it will receive some direct sun. This will allow the bulb to ripen; by now it should be late July or early August. Keep the pots dry. In early September, remove the bulb from the pot, remove the soil carefully so as not to damage the fleshy roots, and carefully repot. Start the entire growing cycle over again.

These are lovely plants. I have seen superb, large plantings of them in various public parks in subtropical areas. If you attend such flower shows as Chelsea in London, you will see masses of these flowers, a grand sight. Even a single, dignified plant is a great joy. There are many hybrids listed in catalogs. Two, *Hippeastrum* 'Papilio' and 'Apple Blossom', deserve particular note.

'Papilio': This is beautifully grown in a large bed at the Huntington Botanic Garden in San Marino, California. Here hundreds of flowers appear at the same time, 6 or more inches in diameter, three petals each edged in green, a central portion of deep crimson, and the three remaining petals green streaked with the crimson. This plant is listed in catalogs, its origins shrouded in mystery.

'Apple Blossom': Enjoyed by thousands over the years, it is an older selection, but superb, white with a lovely pink flush. The shadings in the petals are always attractive, and this is one of my favorites.

Other selections available:

'Blushing Bride': rose, large flowers

'Cocktail': white with red center

'Dazzler': pure white

'Minerva': red with white stripe

'Orange Sovereign': lovely, bright orange

'Springtime': light rose with a white center and white tips to the petals

These selections can be grown outdoors in warm areas. Select a location that is warm and protected, with some sunlight but mostly dappled shade in the heat of the day. Set the bulbs with their necks out of the soil, spacing them 12 inches apart. It is best to plant them in bold clumps, for example, of 15 bulbs, so they will most certainly be noticed and admired. Fertilize as soon as the days get longer and flower buds start to appear; use an organic liquid fertilizer every other week. In late summer allow the bulbs to become dry so they can ripen, cutting away dead foliage in order for the sun to reach them. Perhaps above all else, make certain that the bed is well drained, and keep the flowers dry. Don't allow overhead irrigation to hit them; misting is fine, but large drops will damage them.

Botanical Name: Hippeastrum
Family: Amaryllidaceae
Common Name: Amaryllis
Flower Colors: White, shades of rose, pink, red and orange
Flowering Time: Usually forced indoors for the holiday season(s); outdoors late spring, early summer.
Height: 18 to 24 inches; dwarf selections 8 to 10 inches

Spread: Leaves extend 12 to 18 inches
Native Habitat: Hybrids are cultivated; parentage all South American
Hardiness: Will not tolerate frost
Depth of Planting: Neck and shoulders above soil
Distance Apart: 1 bulb to 6- to 10-inch pot; outdoors, 12 inches
Containers: Yes
Light Requirements: Outdoors, light shade is best; indoors, bright light is preferred
Soil Type: Potting soil in containers, well-drained soil outdoors
Special Conditions: Must enjoy a ripening period after leaves die back, to obtain repeat blooming, see text above.
Comments: The bulbs are not inexpensive, but well worth growing in pots for holidays. If the budget allows, fantastic displays can be had in gardens in warm areas, where the plants should be massed. It is best to purchase bulbs locally and pot them using a soil mix that will feed them; this offers a far better chance of repeat bloom.

HYACINTHOIDES
Liliaceae

These plants were for many years known as *Scilla,* and are often still listed so in catalogs. But the change of name was not a simple one, as *Endymion* and *Agraphis* genera were also involved. The two species of great interest to gardeners are *Hyacinthoides hispanica,* the Spanish bluebell, and *H. non-scriptus,* the English bluebell. The difference between them, both lovely plants, is that in the Spanish bluebell, the flowering stem is upright; the flowerheads are more dense, the flowers held in an upright position, and they open to give quite a wide mouth. The English bluebell's

Certain combinations of plants are eye-stoppers. Here the Spanish bluebell (*Hyacinthoides hispanica*) and the azalea make a very pretty picture. Keep your eyes open for such partnerships and do not hesitate to experiment.

interesting shades of color and intermediate flower forms are found. Both species inhabit woodland areas, liking a humus-rich soil, light shade and moisture in winter and spring. Deeper shade in summer suits them, with the deciduous trees, under which they like to grow, using the available moisture while they take a rest. You should try to duplicate these conditions. Note that these bulbs do not like to grow under evergreens, preferring deciduous shrubs and trees. They can be planted to add color to a rhododendron border, but not under such shrubs.

As might be expected from their common names, these bulbs are at home in the Iberian Peninsula, and Great Britain and much of Europe. One of the grand sights in spring is to see vast areas of these in full flower, with the dappled light making interesting patterns. They soon form bold clumps and spread rapidly; they can even become almost invasive and a nuisance. But I would still plant them, setting them 3 inches deep and 6 to 10 inches apart.

One of the interesting things about these bulbs is that, rather than be consumed by gophers, the animals seem to help spread them! In their burrowing, they split up the clumps. Never plant just a few, but 25 or more at a time, placing them in an informal manner as though nature had done the work; nature never seems to put things in straight lines. Once they are planted, leave them alone. In average soil with humus, there is no need to fertilize or give them any special care. Enjoy them in the garden, as they do not make good cut flowers. *H. hispanica* can be grown in containers, but the foliage becomes untidy.

Hyacinthoides hispanica: Native to the Iberian Peninsula. Often listed as *Scilla hispanica*, and known as the Spanish bluebell. Upright flowering stems to 20 inches, as many as 15 flowers per stem. The flowers, ¾-inch long with

flowering stems are more lax, tending to bend over at the top; the flowers are held closer to the stem and do not open nearly as wide. The foliage of the Spanish bluebell is wider than that of the English bluebell. Both are spring flowering.

The Spanish bluebell has greater color variation, with white, pink, violet and light and dark blue forms known. While some color variation is also found in the English bluebell, few such forms are offered in catalogs. In the wild the two species often hybridize with each other, and very flaring mouths, appear in April or May. The plant is very hardy. Other names that are still used for this species are *H. campanulata* and *Scilla campanulata*. There are a number of selections, including: 'Alba', with white flowers; 'Arnold Prinsen', a fine pink; 'Blue Queen', light blue; 'City of Haarlem', a soft violet; 'Excelsior', violet-blue with marine blue edge; 'Rose Queen', a lovely, pure pink; and 'White Triumphator', strong grower, pure white. In all of these the anthers are blue, another point of distinction from the English bluebell, in which the anthers are cream-colored.

H. non-scripta (syn. *Endymion non-scriptus* and *Scilla non-scripta*): This species is native to much of Europe. The top of the flowering stem bends over and the flowers are carried on one side of the spike. It reaches a height of 18 to 24 inches. While color can vary from blue to white to rose, more often than not the blue form is the one seen. The flowers are pretty, but seem to lack strength, drooping and becoming narrow at the mouth. Anthers are cream-colored. Leaves are quite narrow but often 24 inches in length, and lie on the ground. It flowers in April or May.

Botanical Name: Hyacinthoides
Family: Liliaceae
Common Names: Spanish bluebell, English bluebell
Flower Colors: Blue, white and pink
Flowering Time: Spring; April or May in warm areas
Height: 18 to 24 inches
Spread: Will spread quickly; can become invasive
Native Habitat: Europe, Great Britain
Hardiness: Very hardy
Depth of Planting: 3 inches
Distance Apart: 6 to 10 inches
Containers: H. hispanica only, but rather untidy
Light Requirements: High shade; under deciduous trees or shrubs, never under evergreen

Soil Type: Woodland soil, garden soil with humus
Special Conditions: Provide moisture in winter and spring, a dryer period in late summer
Comments: It is difficult to think of a better plant for naturalizing in woodland. Lovely, easy-to-grow plants to add blue to the garden when the rhododendrons are flowering. If you have even the smallest of gardens, try to find a spot for these plants. Plant lots of them.

HYACINTHUS
Liliaceae

According to legend, Apollo accidentally killed Hyakinthos, and from the ground where his blood was spilled arose the hyacinth. The name was given to this flower by numerous ancient writers, including Homer. There used to be 30 species in this genus, but no longer; now there remain but three. The only bulbs to be considered for the garden are the selections listed in many catalogs, and these fragrant beauties are among the most popular spring-flowering bulbs. A little more expensive than many others, they are well worth the money.

Dense spikes of color in shades of white, blue, pink, yellow and red are carried on stout stems that rise from between firm, almost stiff, leaves. The flowers are tubular and bell shaped, and while in warm climates they last a fair length of time, in colder climates they last longer. Their fragrance alone makes these plants wonderful.

Plant the bulbs outdoors in early October in areas where frost is experienced; wait until early or mid-November in warmer areas where little or no frost occurs. Set the bulbs 5 inches deep (8 inches in warm areas) and 6 to 10 inches apart. If planted alone, space them closer than if mixing them with annuals. In the coldest areas, beware of unexpected late frosts that may dam-

Hyacinthus 'Gypsy Queen' have flowers held clear of the foliage, strong stems and superb fragrance. They bring springtime indoors in a hurry!

age the flowers; a little protection such as sheets of newspaper placed over them will often preserve the blooms. They are great plants in the garden with spring-flowering annuals or massed by themselves. Although I usually prefer to see solid colors planted together, hyacinths seem to look good when colors are mixed. I do not know why this is.

Grow in ordinary garden soil, in sun; provide shade in the hottest areas of the country. These superb container plants can be grown without soil (as described on page 49). Plant three to five bulbs to a 6-inch pot, and keep outdoors in a cool, shady area. When the noses of the bulbs break the soil surface and the plants reach about 1 inch in height, give them increased light. Do not bring them indoors until you can see some color on the buds. If you rush the process, you will end up with short stems. Be patient.

You will find 'Multiflora Hyacinths' listed, mostly by color. Rather than thick, solid flower heads, they produce several stems with the flowers more loosely arranged on the stems. These too have a place in gardens, and while they also can be grown indoors, I do not think they are as attractive when so grown. If growing in containers or without soil, select cultivars that have received special treatment that makes them better suited for this. These are known as "prepared" bulbs. Certain cultivars adapt more readily to this treatment, among them: 'Ann Mary', soft pink; 'Delft Blue', a soft blue; 'Jan Bos', deep red; 'L'Innocence', white; 'Ostara', deep blue; and 'Pink Pearl', deep pink. Among the hyacinths great for outdoor cultivation are:

Cultivars

Blue

'Blue Jacket': dark blue with a small purple stripe in the petals

'Marie': with the largest flower spikes

'Perle Brillante': exterior of the petals is darker than the interior, a lovely combination of blue shades

White

'Carnegie': a creamier white than 'L'Innocence'

'L'Innocence': pure white

'White Pearl': pure white and a strong grower

Yellow

'City of Haarlem': a compact grower, good deep color

'Yellow Hammer': soft yellow, inclined to fade in bright light, but a good plant

Orange

'Gypsy Queen': orange, or is it apricot? Anyway, great color

'Nankeen': orange with a yellow tint

Red and Pink

'Eros': a very deep pink, best in bright shade

'La Victoire': one of, if not the best, reds

'Marconi': an older cultivar, a good, deep pink

Purple and Violet

'Distinction': maroon-purple

'Lord Balfour': rose-purple, spikes not as tightly held as some

'Queen of the Violets': true violet

Doubles

'General Kohler': a lovely blue

'Hollyhock': carmine red

I should mention that these doubles are not ideal garden plants for areas that get a lot of rain. The combined weight of the full flowers and the rain can bend them over. If you are determined to grow them in such areas, then do take the time to give the flowers some support.

You may have wondered, when gazing at photographs of display gardens in Holland, how all of the flower heads are held perfectly upright. There is a simple answer. It may seem cruel, but a thin, strong wire is inserted into the stem to give it strength. The top of the wire cannot be seen. Some 10 inches long, the wire is inserted as the flower spike begins to expand and the uppermost buds are well formed. For your plants, cut 10-inch lengths of coat-hanger wire and insert them into the stems down into the bulbs; your friends will wonder how you grow such perfectly upright flowers.

Should hyacinths be lifted or left in the ground? I have yet to see these bulbs perform as well in their second year as they did in their first. I think it best to lift them when the foliage starts to die down, allow them to dry, then store them in a frost-free area at around 50°F or so. Plant them again in fall. If they perform, I feel lucky; if they do not, then I am not upset. For this reason I prefer to plant them thickly together the second season and hope I am pleasantly surprised! You can leave them in the ground, but they must then have a dry period for 6 to 8 weeks in late summer.

Botanical Name: Hyacinthus
Family: Liliaceae
Common Names: Hyacinth
Flower Colors: Blues, violets, red, pink, yellow, orange, white
Flowering Time: Spring
Height: 12 inches (sometimes a little more)
Spread: Will not spread much, if any
Native Habitat: The Mediterranean and Turkey; most grown today are hybrids
Hardiness: Hardy
Depth of Planting: 5 to 6 inches in cold areas where frosts persist during the day, 8 inches in warm areas with little or no frost
Distance Apart: 6 to 10 inches
Containers: Yes
Light Requirements: Best in bright shade, with some sunlight
Soil Type: Average, well-drained garden soil
Special Conditions: None
Comments: When I smell the fragrance of these

bulbs, I feel spring has indeed arrived. Find a place for a few, and try some in pots to enjoy indoors. I never count on bulbs performing well the second year, and so am sometimes pleasantly surprised when they do put on a show.

IPHEION
Amaryllidaceae

Few bulbs are easier to grow than *Ipheion*. Hardy, not fussy as to soil, and happy in sun or light shade. They multiply rapidly by means of offsets. The plants are hardy, requiring moisture in spring and early summer, but are able to do quite nicely without too much water. The flowers are fragrant, but the foliage has an onion smell when crushed. These are simple little plants.

The name is a mystery; the common name is spring starflower. The plant comes from temperate areas of eastern South America. There are several species, but you will find only *Ipheion uniflorum* listed in catalogs. The plants can become untidy, especially after a few years and when left undisturbed. The flowers are produced singly, on stems that reach 6 inches tall. While there is only one flower per stem, the bulbs send up many stems in late spring. The 1-inch flowers vary in color from white to deep blue, selected and offered as 'Violaceum', and 'Wisley Blue', a deep blue with slightly larger flowers than those of other *Ipheion*.

Plant the bulbs 2 inches deep and 5 to 6 inches apart; they will soon fill in any gaps. In the very coldest areas, mulch them during the winter months. Lift only to divide to increase the stock and plant elsewhere; otherwise leave them alone and they will perform well. I suppose they would grow in containers, but I have not seen them grown this way. No need to worry about any pests or diseases—these plants seem impervious to such problems.

Grow *Ipheion uniflorum* where they have room to spread and will not get in your way. These are excellent plants for the edge of any border.

Botanical Name: Ipheion
Family: Amaryllidaceae
Common Names: Spring starflower
Flower Colors: White to deep blue-violet
Flowering Time: Late spring
Height: 6 inches
Spread: Will spread quite quickly
Native Habitat: Eastern parts of temperate South America
Hardiness: Hardy; mulch in coldest area
Depth of Planting: 2 inches
Distance Apart: 5 to 6 inches
Containers: Yes
Light Requirements: Sun or light shade
Soil Type: Not fussy
Special Conditions: None
Comments: They can become untidy, but they are tough little plants and give great dividends for the time needed to look after them (which, after planting, amounts to practically no time at all).

Plant them in the front of the border or in the rock garden and let them spread. Because these bulbs are very easy to grow, they make wonderful gifts for young children.

IRIS
Iridaceae

If you have hours but not days to spare, don't set out to study this genus. *Iris* is complicated by many divisions, classifications and reclassifications. Papers have been written on the subjects of *Iris* morphology, biology, evolution and taxonomy, and *The Chromosomes of the Spuria Iris* and *Evolution of the Garden Forms*. Fortunately, familiarity with all such learned works isn't necessary to enjoy the beauty of this great genus, named by Theophrastus "a rainbow." The colors are surprisingly varied, all of them lovely. Obviously all irises have the same basic flower form, but the size, height, time of flowering and habit of growth can vary greatly. All irises are at home in the northern hemisphere; *Dietes* and *Moraea* are their counterparts in the southern hemisphere.

Iris versicolor grows between the rocks of New England's shores, happy in very little soil, reflected heat and salt sea spray. The yellow *I. pseudacorus* puts on a grand display in marshy areas and heavy, peaty soils of Ireland. Visiting the botanic garden in Oxford, I have enjoyed beds of old cultivars of Bearded Iris, commonly referred to as *I. × germanica* although many other species were involved in their creation. In the same garden *I. sibirica* put on a lovely display with its feet standing in water. I have seen the Louisiana irises in the botanic garden in Durban, South Africa, and small bulbous irises in the rock garden at the Geneva botanic garden. There is an iris for every type of location, yet all have one basic need: sun.

I took this photograph in Spain, where *Iris xiphium* were growing alongside the road, proving they can do well with little care. Note how the plants have formed an attractive, tightly knit clump.

There are well over 200 species, and 10 times that number of cultivars, if not more. The flowers have six parts; the three upright petals form the standards, and the three lower petals, drooping or horizontal, are the falls.

There are three types of rootstocks: corms, bulbs and rhizomes. But, as there is only one species with a cormous rootstock, *Iris sisyrinchium* some authorities have elevated it to its own genus, *Gynandriris sisyrinchium*. You will not be able to find it listed in any catalog, so we can forget it, as far as this book is concerned. There

I came across a colony of *Iris pseudacorus* in Ireland, all over 5 feet in height, their color striking against a green background.

are several bulbous species worthy of attention. As they require similar culture, become dormant after flowering and can be lifted and stored over the winter and planted again in spring (if not left in the ground), I feel we should look at their needs and the cultivars available. Any good garden soil suits these plants. They prefer good drainage and need sun. Plant 4 inches deep, 3 to 6 inches apart. They grow well in containers and in ordinary potting soil.

The use of irises in arrangements is becoming popular. There are a couple of ways to prolong the life of the flowers. Spray them with a fine mist of water as often as is practical. In addition, immerse only a couple of inches of the stems in the water. Precisely why this should be better for them than being in deep water I do not know, but you will find that it is so. Put a couple of copper pennies into the water, and add a couple of ounces of a soft drink such as 7-Up, and this will work wonders. Some people swear vodka helps; I think it best to drink it, and then the flowers do seem better!

Iris danfordiae: Native to eastern Turkey. While this little iris seldom grows taller than 4 inches with 2-inch flowers, the bright yellow color with green and orange markings is a delight. It is fragrant, flowers very early in spring while the foliage is short, and has the one disadvantage that it seems to divide after flowering and the offsets take a season or two before they reach flowering size.

I. reticulata: Native to the Caucasus and Russia, and parts of Iran, this 6- to 8-inch-high iris is ideal for the rock garden and the front of a border. The leaves are short at flowering time, later growing to some 12 inches in length. The flowers are fragrant and appear in March or April. This is an excellent plant for growing in containers, as are selections of this species. The flowers are deep blue-mauve, and the falls have an orange rib bordered with white. The flower color varies, hence the following selections: 'Cantab', pale blue with an orange blotch on the blade of the falls; 'Harmony', an old and established cultivar, sky blue with a yellow central ridge on the blade of the falls; 'Purple Gem', a good, deep purple; and 'Spring Time', with blue standards and darker falls with a conspicuous orange crest. These are but a few of the number you will find listed.

I. xiphioides: Native to the Pyrenees and northwestern Spain, yet it is known as the English Iris. It grows in damp meadows high in the mountains, flowering in early summer, June or early July. The flowers are quite large, 5 inches in diameter, and the stems are 24 inches tall, with two or three flowers per stem. There is a large golden blotch on the deep blue fall. Several selections are offered, including 'King of the Blues', and 'Mont Blanc', a lovely white faintly shaded violet. This species is a parent of the Dutch Iris, and of selections sometimes listed as English Iris, which will contain variations on the colors of the species. This species, and selections, are good cut flowers.

I. xiphium: The Spanish Iris is native to Spain, Portugal and southern France. It reaches 24 inches in height, and carries one or two large flowers with a deep yellow band along each purple fall, almost to the tip. The standards are erect, wide, and generally of a deeper color than the falls. The flowers arrive in May. Another parent of the Dutch Iris, the other species involved being *I. tingitana*, a blue from Morocco, and *I. xiphioides*. I have often admired this species in the wild in Spain and Portugal.

The Dutch Iris: One of the most popular irises for cut flower production, Dutch Iris are grown in great numbers, and by varying the planting time, they can provide bloom for many months of the year. These great plants do not make much of an impression if not planted *en masse* in a border. If you plant just one here, one there, they will go almost unnoticed. In very cold areas where temperatures remain below 0°F for long periods of time, it is best to plant in spring when the weather starts to warm and there is no chance of severe frosts. For a succession of flowers, plant every four weeks, gradually reducing the time to every 10 days or so by early summer.

I doubt if you will find a more intense blue than the flowers of this grand hybrid, *Iris sibirica* 'Wizardry'. A good grower and very free flowering, it is an outstanding introduction. (Photo courtesy of Roy Klehm.)

Cultivars

'Bronze Perfection': standards are lilac with bronze markings, the falls bronzy yellow

'Convent Garden': a great all-yellow flower

'Golden Harvest': large flowers gold shaded with orange

'H. C. van Vliet': standards are deep violet, the falls bright blue with an orange blotch

'National Velvet': bright purple with an orange blotch on the falls

'Princess Irene': standards are pure white, falls a deep orange

'Professor Blaauw': lovely gentian blue flowers with a narrow yellow line on the falls, a great cultivar for greenhouse forcing and for the garden

'Wedgewood': standards are a lobelia blue, the falls darker with a yellow blotch. This cultivar has been around for many years and is still one of the best. I grew this back in the late forties.

There would not be many iris left in our gardens if we removed the Bearded Iris, which flower in May and June. They are "bearded" because the flowers have a tuft of hairs on the falls. Most people picture Bearded Irises when asked to think about irises. They are easy to grow, but there are one or two things that you should know regarding their culture. Bearded Irises are best planted in summer or very early fall. No harm will come to the plants if you plant later in the year, but you might not enjoy the flowers the following season if you plant late. If your irises do not put on much of a show the first season after planting, the reason more than likely is because they were planted too late.

Irises like the sun; even in the hottest climates they will not object to full sun, but they will appreciate some shade during the hottest times of day. They like a well-drained soil, and if your soil is of average fertility, they will be quite happy. If soil is on the acid side, incorporate some lime at least four or five days before planting. Cultivate the area; when planting, the bed should be firm, not compacted. Set the rhizomes with the tops just at soil level. Spread the roots and firm the rhizomes in the soil, then water them in well. The rhizomes have a blunt end and a growing end, easily distinguished as the shoots and leaves are at the growing end. Point this in the direction you wish the plants to grow. If planting on a slope, point the shoots uphill. How far apart to set the rhizomes depends on the height of the cultivar. Tall plants should be set 24 inches apart, low-growing ones 12 inches apart. If your soil is poor, some fertilizer

can be given in fall, and another dressing applied in spring before the plants bloom. Be careful not to overfeed, or you will find much vegetative growth at the expense of flowers.

With Bearded Iris, after three or four seasons the plants will have reached a good size, and you will notice that there are sections of the rhizomes far removed from the growing tips. It will be time to lift, divide and replant. The closer you can do this to the Fourth of July, the better. Certainly a few weeks later won't present problems, but if you are too late, flower production will be reduced the following season. Remove all of the clump from the ground with a fork, and shake loose as much of the soil as possible. You will see the clump consists of old roots, dark in color, and portions that are lighter in color, the younger roots. At the ends of the lightest-colored rhizomes are the shoots. You may have planted only one rhizome, but now with laterals and the main growing tip, you might well have 10 times the number of growing points. Using a sharp knife, cut the rhizomes so that each growing point is at the end of 4 to 6 inches of root. Discard the dark portions without growing points and shoots. Plant back the younger portions as you did the original plants.

A word of warning: Certain cultivars are more vigorous than others. This can mean that you may need to lift and divide after three years. It also means you should make certain that, when you plant back, you plant a good selection of the cultivars in your collection. Don't let a lovely, less vigorous plant be pushed out by more aggressive plants. The moisture requirements of the Bearded Iris are not complicated: When in growth, they require moisture. After they have finished flowering they do not require as much; they'll appreciate a drink from time to time, but if they become dry between drinks, no problem.

The selection of colors available today boggles the mind. There are so many, and the photographs never show a poor head of flowers. There are a few points to keep in mind when selecting irises. Remember the height of the plants. You can think of irises as falling into three groups: tall (30 to 40 inches), intermediate (15 to 30 inches) and dwarf (5 to 15 inches). The tall types are what you want in the back of the perennial border, the dwarf for the front of the border. If you are creating a bed uniquely with irises you will want to purchase some of each type.

Remember the colors. You might love a particular color, but having all the irises the same color doesn't look as good as having a contrasting color to highlight the color you prefer. Take a moment to list the colors you want, and put these in order of preference. Keep track of the numbers of each color you are going to order, and before you purchase, check to make sure it is balanced the way you want it. Cost is related to the length of time a cultivar has been on the market. New introductions are more expensive, and though they will delight the iris fancier, it may be better to select moderately priced plants until you have grown irises for a few seasons and are certain they will perform well for you. Older, less expensive cultivars are generally available in a wide color range. Here are just a few great plants:

Cultivars

Tall Bearded Iris (30 to 40 inches)

'Beverly Sills': pink

'City of David': deep yellow

'Dazzling Gold': yellow and red

'Full Tide': medium blue

'Glazed Orange': orange

'Grand Waltz': lavender-orchid

'Interpol': purple-black

'Joyce Terry': yellow and white

'Kentucky Derby': cream

'Laced Cotton': white

'Mystique': blue

'Sailor's Dance': medium blue

'West Coast': deep yellow

Intermediate Bearded Iris (15 to 30 inches)

'Appleblossom': pink

'Brown Doll': reddish brown

'Oklahoma Bandit': tannish gold

'Rare Edition': violet and white

'Snow Maiden': white

'Tumwater': blue

Dwarf Bearded Iris (5 to 15 inches)

'Beechfield': bright yellow

'Elfin Queen': white with a touch of yellow

'Grandma's Hat': lilac with a hint of purple

'Irish Seas': greenish

'Little Villain': purple

'Play Misty': white and lavender

'Truly': sky blue

While the major groups of irises have now been discussed, there are others that shouldn't be neglected. One such group is the Siberian Iris.

These are hybrids that involved *I. sibirica,* native to much of Europe and Russia, with blue-purple flowers with a brownish base to the petals and reaching 24 to 48 inches tall, flowering in June or July. Other species were involved, and today there are several hybrids on the market, listed under Siberian Iris. Some of them are superb, among them:

Cultivars

'Heliotrope Bouquet': wide petals, free flowering, heliotrope blue

'High Standards': standards are wide, purplish blue with some white

'Jewelled Crown': good blue with white and gold on the falls

'Pas-de-Deux': a lovely white and soft yellow

'Windwood Spring': light purplish blue with white on the falls

'Wizardry': intense blue with lighter standards

Louisiana Iris: There are several species that are at home in the Mississippi Delta. Combined in various hybrids, they have given rise to the group known as Louisiana Iris. These lovely plants like to have their feet in or near water, and perform well in warm climates. They seem to exude the charm of the Old South, having a grace not found in other groups (but this could be because they like being near water and this softens their appearance a little). The colors range from yellows and oranges to violets, blues and whites, in magnificent combinations. They are quite tall, often over 48 inches, and individual flowers will often be as much as 5 inches in diameter. The species involved are *I. brevicaulis* and

I. fulva from Mississippi, and *I. ochroleuca,* from Greece.

I. ochroleuca had a hand in the creation of the Spuria Irises. It is creamy white with a golden blotch, and when combined with the *I. spuria* from Romania (a pale yellow), resulted in a wide color range. I am always amazed at the many colors found in the progeny of plants which themselves are not multicolored. The spuria are tall (up to 6 feet) and stiff, and flower in early summer.

Japanese Irises: Are selections from *I. ensata* (syn. *I. kaempferi*). These require slightly different culture than others (see below).

Iris bucharica: Native to central Asia, this delightful species reaches 18 inches tall. It has an unusual foliage arrangement, the leaves arranged one above the other, folded and clasping the flower stem. This species is fragrant, golden yellow or creamy white, and flowers in early spring, in March or April. Free flowering, with as many as seven flowers on each stalk, opening in turn. It is good to see that several nurseries are listing this species, but the plant is still comparatively rare. It is quite hardy, but in the very coldest areas give it some mulch in winter, then remove the mulch in early spring, as the rootstock appreciates being warmed by the sun.

I. cristata: Native to the eastern United States. The colors are splendid, pale lilac with a throat and crest of deep yellow. A number of selections have been made of this 6-inch-tall species, including 'Abbey's Violet', a deep violet with white and yellow crest, 'Alba', a pure white form, and 'Dark Blue', all May flowering.

I. douglasiana: A native of California from Santa Barbara north to Oregon. If you walk in the foothills of the coastal mountains, you may see this species flowering in April or May. The colors vary from white to cream, from light blue to dark purple. The falls have a slight ridge in the middle and four parallel, darker veins. When in flower it is quite pleasing, often in shady areas, and thriving in quite poor ground and very dry locations. Out of flower it looks untidy, as the foliage is tufted and often the tips are brown. Give this plant moderate moisture and the change in appearance is quite dramatic—tidier looking—and the flowers easily reach up to 24 inches. The flowering stem is frequently branched.

I. ensata (syn. *I. kaempferi*): This is the Japanese Iris, one of the largest-flowered species, often having flowers 10 inches in diameter. On mature plants there are many branched stems, each bearing two flowers. They like a rich soil, unlike most other species, and appreciate moisture throughout the year. Flowers are produced in July, later than most other species. The foliage is stiff and held erect. These are perhaps the most showy of all iris flowers, and while the species is deep red-purple in color, there is much variation. Some fine selections are listed, including:

Cultivars

'Eleanor Parry': reddish purple, vigorous and free flowering, but the flowers are not as large as many, being 6 inches in diameter

'Great White Heron': pure white, very large flowers

'Maroon Giant': ruffled petals on maroon-red flowers

'Pink Frost': light pink flowers of medium size, ruffled

I. foetidissima: Native to England and much of western Europe. Easy to grow, flowering in June, 24 inches in height with flowers of a pleasing bluish lilac. However, the flowers are not as attractive as the seeds, which in late summer and early fall are bright red. As there are many flowers, there are many seedpods that display these brilliantly colored seeds.

I. pallida: This species is found along the Dalmatian coast in the former Yugoslavia. I remember seeing it on the slopes above Dubrovnik, in combination with the yellow of *Spartium junceum,* Spanish broom. The flowers are carried on strong stems 24 to 36 inches in height. They are a pale mauve-blue, with prominent beards, and are carried well above the foliage. Flowers in April or May. There is a form with variegated foliage, 'Variegata' which is planted to beautiful effect with *I. ensata* 'Variegata' at Wisley gardens. All of these forms are well worth growing.

I. pseudacorus: Native to the British Isles and much of Europe. It likes wet conditions, and the yellow flowers are carried to heights of 6 feet. Flowering is any time between May and August, the main period being in May and June. Graceful and elegant, but while the "yellow flag," as it is commonly called, looks great in natural settings, I feel that the rather shy flowering habit makes it questionable for many gardens. A double form 'Flore-Plena' is listed, but this is not as attractive as the single form.

I. tectorum: A native of China and Japan. Not as hardy as some species, preferring milder winters and hot, moist summers. Given these conditions, this blue-violet species, reaching only 12 inches, will perform well. It flowers in late spring. A form 'Alba' is listed, but do not expect this to be pure white; there is an overlying glaze of light blue.

Botanical Name: Iris

Family: Iridaceae

Common Names: Iris, yellow flag, blue flag, and so on

Flower Colors: Many, often bicolors

Flowering Time: Depending on species and type, early spring to late summer. Successive plantings of such types as Dutch Iris will prolong the season.

Height: Varies by species and type: 4 inches to more than 6 feet

Spread: Will form bold clumps, some more quickly than others

Native Habitat: Native to northern hemisphere

Hardiness: The majority of species are hardy, but not every one; see listings

Depth of Planting: Bulbous types 4 inches deep, rhizomes just break the surface of the soil

Distance Apart: Varies by species and type: dwarf types 6 inches, tall types to 24 inches

Contianers: Bulbous types only.

Light Requirements: With few exceptions, full sun

Soil Type: Majority like average garden soil. Some prefer boggy and very moist conditions, others thrive on stony ground.

Special Conditions: Can vary by species, but no species is very demanding.

Comments: Irises are rightly popular, deserving of consideration by all gardeners. With such varied colors and different times of flowering there is no reason why these plants can't be enjoyed during many months. Many species not commonly grown deserve greater recognition, and many should be considered for planting along our highways where they would be enjoyed by all.

If gardeners knew how easy to grow *Ixia* are, more of these fine plants would be grown. An attractive feature is that their stems move in the slightest breeze.

IXIA
Iridaceae

Theophrastus used the Greek word *ixos* for these plants, the meaning of which is birdlime, referring to the clammy sap of these plants. The common names for these plants are wand flower, given because the wiry stems make the flowers wave around like wands, and corn lily, because this genus has numerous species that grow in grassy areas. All species are native to South Africa. They love to be planted in full sun in well-drained soil, with moisture in winter and spring. The erect, sturdy-looking foliage is sword-shaped, 3 to 5 leaves produced from each corm. The number of flat, saucer-shaped flowers per stalk is often 20 or more, the petals recurving a little at the tips. The stamens arise from the perianth tube and are quite prominent in the middle of the flower. As the tube is often darker in color, and another color is often present at the base of the petals where they join into the tube, the flowers often give the impression of being tricolored. They are not hardy, but withstand temperatures down to about 20°F. In cold areas (where frost occurs), lift at the end of summer, store over winter and replant in spring; in warm areas they are left in the ground. They flower in spring or early summer.

The corms should be planted 2 inches deep and 3 to 4 inches apart. Planted in bold masses, they add an interesting dimension to a mixed border. Ixias do well in containers. Plant 6 to a 6-inch-pot, 20 to a 12-inch pot. Use ordinary potting soil and then keep moist while growth is active. When the foliage starts to die back, reduce the water given and allow the plants to become dry. In their native habitat, *Ixia* have much rain in winter and spring, and little in summer. In the wild, where I have had the good fortune of seeing them many times, they inhabit grassland. As soon as fire has passed through an area, *Ixia* seem to jump out of the soil. Few bulbs are easier to grow or as trouble free. The color range is wide, but today it is hybrids that tend to be grown in our gardens. The exception to this is *Ixia viridiflora*, with flowers of a unique greenish blue. I have not been able to find this in the wild, unfortunately, but many nurseries list it in their catalogs.

This is a plant gardeners in warm climates should grow more often. Give it some room, leave it alone and it will multiply quickly. Strangely, this presents a problem in commercial production fields. No matter how carefully the corms are harvested, some cormels are left in the ground, only to pop up the following spring and flower. Lifting them so they do not become

mixed with the following crop means quite a lot of hand pulling. This just shows how easy they are to grow. These plants are ideal for the rock garden, sunny corner and grown among grasses on slopes in warmer areas. The hybrids are charming in a mixed border.

Strangely, I have not seen these flowers used as cut flowers. They would seem to be ideal for this. Cut and stuck in water, they last for several days. I think their potential is great for such work, with thin but strong stems, an interesting shape to the flowers and many colors. Named selections appear occasionally in catalogs, but this is rare. You will more commonly find them listed by color. The species *viridiflora* is sometimes listed.

Ixia viridiflora: A native of Cape Province in South Africa, now rare in the wild. A lovely color, blue-green, which I have yet to see accurately depicted in photographs. The flowers grow up to 2 inches in diameter, with centers of deep crimson or maroon, and reach 18 inches. The foliage is basal, held in a fan shape. Flowers in early summer, May or June.

Botanical Name: Ixia
Family: Iridaceae
Common Names: Wand flower, corn lily
Flower Colors: Red, white, yellow, pink, white and green-blue
Flowering Time: Late spring, early summer
Height: 18 inches
Spread: In warmer (frost-free) climates, will spread quickly if left in the ground
Native Habitat: South Africa
Hardness: To 20°F; in cold climates lift, overwinter and replant
Depth of Planting: 2 inches
Distance Apart: 3 to 4 inches
Containers: Yes

Light Requirements: Sun

Soil Type: Average garden soil, potting soil in containers

Special Conditions: Ixia appreciate a dry period when the foliage has died back.

Comments: These lovely flowers deserve more attention, especially in warmer climates where they should be left to spread and will soon fill a large area. Crowd them together in a container. Even in colder areas they can be planted in spring for summer flowers.

IXIOLIRION
Amaryllidaceae

Lirion in Greek means lily. *Ixos*, as explained on page 178, was used by Theophrastus in describing the sap of *Ixia.* These flowers are like miniature lilies, only a little over an inch across when fully open. *Ixiolirion* are native to Turkey and western and central Asia. It was thought that there were three or four species, but in recent times *I. ledebourii, I. montanum* and *I. pallasii* have been all grouped under *I. tataricum,* which is sometimes listed in catalogs. While deserving of greater recognition, *Ixiolirion* needs hot (in excess of 80°F), dry summers to do well. The bulbs are quite hardy, but where temperatures fall around 20°F it will need protection in the winter. They can either be lifted and stored over the winter for planting in spring, or grown in pots to be brought indoors.

The blue flowers appear in short umbels of up to 15 flowers. The stamens are short, and the bright yellow pollen contrasts well with the petals. Eighteen inches in height, the plants flower in late spring or early summer. Plant the bulbs 4 inches deep, 6 to 10 inches apart. The leaves are grasslike, sheathing the lower part of the flowering stems. Average garden soil with good drainage and full sun are needed, and the bulbs

Dainty plants, these *Ixiolirion tataricum.* The flowers come in many shades of blue, all most pleasing. This is perhaps one of the finest blue-flowering bulbs.

must remain dry into fall and early winter. It is this last cultural requirement that presents a problem, making it easier to lift, store and then replant. The plants don't multiply quickly, so if you wish to increase the size of your planting, lift in fall and divide, then either plant back at once (in warmer climates), or hold the bulbs for spring planting.

Botanical name: Ixiolirion

Family: Amaryllidaceae

Common Name: None known

Flower Color: Blue

Flowering Time: Late spring, early summer

Height: 18 inches

Spread: Very slowly

Native Habitat: Turkey and western and central Asia

Hardiness: To 0°F with protection of a mulch

Depth of Planting: 4 inches

Distance Apart: 6 to 10 inches

Containers: Yes

Light Requirements: Sun

Soil Type: Average garden soil

Special Conditions: Must have a dry resting period through fall and into winter

Comments: I am always pleased to see these plants. Those fortunate enough to live in areas where the necessary dry conditions can be given should grow them, but I do not think it is worth the effort of constructing a shelter just for this plant alone. If you do have a frame where it can be kept dry, grow it.

LACHENALIA
Liliaceae

Werner de la Chenal (1736–1800) was a professor of botany in Basel, Switzerland, and this genus was named in his honor. There are some 50 species, and thanks to my friend Graham Duncan of the Kirstenbosch Botanic Garden in Cape Town, the confounding nomenclature of these great plants is being unraveled. All species are native to South Africa. One common name is wild hyacinth. There is a bit of similarity between these plants and hyacinths, but *Lachenalia* have fewer flowers on a stem, and they are fleshier in appearance, the foliage more succulent. Other common names are Cape cowslip (*Lachen-*

Lachenalia aloides were favorites in the Victorian era, and I am pleased to see them making a come-back as pot plants. They remain in flower for many weeks.

alia looks a little like the European cowslip) and leopard lily (some species have spots on the foliage and flowering stem).

This is one of those plants that seems to slip in and out of popularity. When I was a boy, these were very popular pot plants, long-lasting, easy to grow and care for, unusual in appearance, yet most attractive. Today one rarely, if ever, sees these plants in florists' shops. Fortunately there are several species listed in catalogs, and while not at all hardy, they can be easily grown in a cool greenhouse, and they grow well outdoors in frost-free climates.

Two thick leaves envelope the base of the flowering stem. The petals form a tube, and the individual flowers are 1 inch long. There are many flowers in a spike that will grow 20 inches tall. The flowers are held closely together on the upper part of the flower stem, and quite frequently the lower part of the stem is mottled. They remain in flower for many weeks, and it is not unusual for them to last for two months. The majority flower in spring. The bulbs are small and fleshy. Plant them 4 inches deep in a sandy soil with good drainage. Space 6 inches apart. In containers, use potting soil mixed with some sharp sand. The shallower fern pots can be used. Space the bulbs much closer together than when planting outdoors; having only two leaves is an advantage, as this allows for such tight planting. When the bulbs have made about 2 inches of growth, give them an occasional watering with an organic liquid fertilizer, and continue feeding until the flower spike has reached several inches in height. Each bulb may send up more than one flower spike, which accounts for the long flowering period. As these bulbs are tender, treat them with care. They enjoy sun, and in the wild they live in sandy soils. For this reason I suggest you cover the top of the soil, in both containers and borders, with about ½ inch of sharp sand. This helps prevent attacks of *Fusarium*, a fungus that causes bulbs to turn pinkish. Infected bulbs will rot and should be discarded.

The colors available are orange, coral-red with green, white and bluish. With all these colors found in the species, why has more work not been done on producing hybrids? I have a feeling that an even greater color range is possible, that flower size can be increased and, if these "improvements" came to pass, that *Lachenalia* would once again become much sought after.

Lachenalia aloides: Native to the eastern Cape. Commonly listed in catalogs as *L. tricolor*, the correct name is *aloides*, there being several varieties of this species. Two broad leaves with purple markings arise from each bulb. The flower spike reaches 10 to 12 inches in height, and the flowers are somewhat pendulous, with green inner segments tipped with burgundy and deep rose, or crimson outer segments that grow yellow at the tips. The colors are magnificent. In var. *quadricolor*,

the base of the petals turns from a light to a dark crimson. Var. *aurea* has almost solid golden colors, and var. *pearsonii* has bright orange flowers edged with claret red. All flower in spring.

L. bulbifera: Native to the southwestern Cape Province, this species is regarded by many as the most striking. Up to 15 inches in height, it has fewer flowers on a spike, but they are larger, coral red edged with green or purple. It has been used as a cut flower, flowering in February or March.

L. contaminata: This is another native of the southwestern Cape Province. It is unusual for its grasslike foliage and pure white flowers, more open than tubular. Late April or early May flowering.

L. mutabilis: This species, native to Namaqualand, is unusual in that the flowers at the top of the 10-inch stem are sterile and have a bluish color. The lower flowers are copper green. Early spring flowering.

Botanical Name: Lachenalia
Family: Liliaceae
Common Names: Wild hyacinth, Cape cowslip, leopard lily
Flower Colors: White, red, green, blue, purple and yellow, in all sorts of combinations
Flowering Time: Mostly spring and early summer
Height: To 18 inches
Spread: Will form colonies if grown in borders in warm climates
Native Habitat: South Africa
Hardiness: Will not tolerate frost
Depth of Planting: 3 inches
Distance Apart: 6 inches
Containers: Yes
Light Requirements: Sun and bright, indirect light
Soil Type: Requires well-drained, sandy soil. It is

an advantage to add sharp sand to both border soils and potting soil.

Special Conditions: Water in well and keep moist while growing; when they die back they should be kept dry.

Comments: Few plants are as beautiful, and few bulbs remain in flower as long as these. Of comparatively easy culture, they require above all else good drainage. If you have a greenhouse where you can keep temperatures above freezing, grow these plants. If you live in a warm climate, grow these plants in the border. *Lachenalia* are underplanted and underappreciated—they deserve more recognition.

LEUCOJUM
Amaryllidaceae

The derivation of the name is disputed. Some maintain it comes from *leuoeion*, the Greek word meaning white eye, and this name was used by Hippocrates. Others feel the name comes from the Greek *leukos*, meaning white, and *ion*, meaning a violet, because *Leucojum vernum* has the fragrance of a violet. The bulbs of the nine species in this genus come from Europe and the western Mediterranean. Almost all the flowers are white and enjoy the common name snowflake. The bell-shaped flowers are sometimes solitary, sometimes several in a loose umbel. The petals have a touch of green at the tip, and are of equal length, or nearly so, which distinguishes them from the snowdrops (*Galanthus* species), with shorter inner segments. The species flower at different times, some in spring, others in summer and fall. They are hardy to −10°F and will withstand colder temperatures with some protection, provided by a mulch or heavy snowfall.

Plant the bulbs 3 inches deep, 6 inches apart. Average garden soil is fine. They require

A lovely plant, *Leucojum aestivum* 'Gravetye Giant' is always dependable and delightful. One clump will produce many flowering stems over a long period of time.

moisture during their growing season; this means these late-summer–flowering bulbs need some summer moisture. They are best planted in sun, but will tolerate some high shade. In a few seasons they will develop quite large clumps and spread readily. They grow well in containers, and *L. roseum* is best grown this way so the delicate and elusive pink flowers can be enjoyed. Use ordinary potting soil, and crowd the bulbs a little.

Leucojum aestivum: This species grows wild in Great Britain and central Europe. It is perhaps the hardiest of the genus. Flowers appear in late spring or early summer. The stems are 12 inches in height, and the number of flowers will vary from one or two per stem to seven or eight, and one bulb can produce more than one stem. A more robust plant is 'Gravetye Giant', a chance seedling found in William Robinson's garden, Gravetye Manor, in Sussex. So superior is this that I wonder why some nurseries still list the species.

L. autumnale: This is native to southern Europe, including Spain and Portugal. The flowers are white, one to four to an umbel, and there is a hint of pink at the base of the petals. It can be distinguished from *L. roseum,* another fall-flowering species with pinkish flowers, by its height (*L. roseum* is 4 inches, *L. autumnale* up to 8 inches) and by its longer pedicels.

L. roseum: Native to Corsica and Sardinia, this species is shorter than *L. autumnale.* The solitary flowers have a pinkish hue and appear in fall.

L. vernum: Native to most of southern Europe, usually in moist places. This early-spring–flowering species is known as the spring snowflake. The flowers are white, delicately fragrant and solitary (rarely are there two). The plants are 6 to 12 inches in height, more often on the shorter side. The foliage is grasslike. A vigorous plant, it spreads quite rapidly. The color on the petal tips varies from green to yellow. Some people give the yellow form the name var. *carpathicum.*

Once planted, these bulbs should be left undisturbed and allowed to spread. With such different flowering times, it is a good idea to plant some bulbs of each species, so the little white flowers can be enjoyed for many months.

Botanical Name: Leucojum
Family: Amaryllidaceae
Common Names: Snowflake
Flower Colors: White, light pink (one species)
Flowering Time: Spring, early fall
Height: To 12 inches
Spread: Will naturalize quite quickly
Native Habitat: Europe
Hardiness: To about −10°F
Depth of Planting: 3 inches
Distance Apart: 6 inches; closer in containers
Containers: Yes
Light Requirements: Sun
Soil Type: Average garden soil; *L. vernum* likes moist soils
Special Conditions: Moisture during growing season.
Comments: Leucojum never look untidy, and they can form large clumps and smother out weeds. If you have some room between shrubs where you can pop in a few snowflakes, do so, but do not expect them to do well if you do not give them sun.

LILIUM
Liliaceae

The Greek word for lily is *leirion,* and it was used by Theophrastus for the Madonna lily, *Lilium candidum.* The genus is confined to the northern hemisphere, and found in many of the temperate zones from Europe, to Asia to America. There are many species, subspecies and varieties. And, thanks to the pioneer work accomplished by Jan de Graaff at the Oregon Bulb Farms, there are now many hundreds of cultivars available. Today breeding programs in Holland, the United States and Japan exploit the openings made by Jan de Graaff and his team of hybridizers.

Lilies are superb garden plants, great cut flowers and ideal container plants. They can be held in cold storage, and by planting at specific times, flower growers can have these bulbs in flower throughout the year. In our gardens, we can have lilies in flower from early summer right through to fall. Many lilies have a lovely fragrance, and one such plant in flower will perfume an entire home. There are lilies for sun and for shade, and there are tall-growing and dwarf selections.

In my book *Bulbs,* a two-volume work pub-

This particular clump of an old but good hybrid, *Lilium* 'Bellingham Hybrids', has been left undisturbed for more than 25 years. Each year it seems bigger and better, and it loves its location: shady, occasional sun, good moisture during the summer. It is as simple as that!

lished by Timber Press, I wrote a description of *Lilium* I do not think I can improve upon: "The flowers often are large and some are fragrant. They can be erect, held horizontally, or pendulous. Generally, more than one is produced per stem and they then are joined in a raceme. The perianth segments are produced in many forms: free; joined to form a tube; much reflexed; or presenting a flat face. All six perianth segments have a nectary at their bases. The six stamens generally have slender filaments tapering from the base, and the style is usually quite long, often protruding from the mouth of trumpet flowers and above the anthers. The ovary is three-celled and contains many seeds."

As a student I knew of Jan de Graaff's work, and at Wisley Gardens had seen many of his hybrids in flower and admired them. In Holland I heard more about them while visiting various shows. While in France working with the great landscape architect Russell Page, I learned more about these plants and grew some of them myself. I did not dream that I would one day leave Europe for the United States, and work for de Graaff in Oregon. I had no idea I would spend many pleasant working hours in his company, but such was my good fortune. The reader will understand that it is not possible for me to say anything about these plants without feeling that they are a part of me. The years I spent working with lilies were some of the happiest of my life. It is still a thrill for me to see them, and they are my favorite flowers.

From the beginning of the Christian era, one lily was closely associated with the Church, the Madonna lily (*Lilium candidum*), which became the symbol of purity. But this was not the first time this lily had been highly regarded. It was depicted on a Minoan vase dated to 1300 B.C. Lilies were also depicted on monuments of the great Egyptian and Assyrian civilizations. *Candidum* means dazzling white, so it is no wonder it has been closely associated with subjects of importance.

When the Renaissance brought with it the freedom of travel, it was not long before the lilies of America found their way to Europe. In 1629 John Parkinson described *L. canadense* in his *paradisus terrestris*. As the fame of lilies grew, one lily, *L. auratum*, took the world by storm. It was exhibited in London by the famous nursery Veitch. By the end of the twentieth century, millions of bulbs of this species were being exported from Japan and sent to Europe and the United States. The stock in the wild became sadly depleted. Transportation was not speedy, refrigeration not used for the shipping of bulbs, and as

Breeding for Quality

The nucleus of a plant cell usually has two sets of chromosomes, and so is called diploid. During the reproductive cycle, the nucleus splits into two generally equal halves; these cells are then said to be haploid. When a haploid male cell joins with a haploid female cell, the "normal," diploid count is restored.

It is possible to cultivate plants that are haploid by cultivating a pollen cell under certain conditions. It is also possible to combine diploid cells, resulting in cells, and consequently plants, called tetraploid. As tetraploid plant cells have so many "extra" chromosomes, they show many more characteristics expressed by those chromosomes, and this allows for greater variation in the physical properties of a plant. If the right combination of traits is manipulated and expressed, tetraploid plants can exhibit exceptional vigor, larger and greater flower production, and other desirable characteristics.

Such is not always the case, however. For example, in some tetraploid plants the amount of foliage produced might be far greater, but the flower size and number might remain the same as obtained from diploid plants. Such plants are not always desirable, except of course if they are grown for their foliage. Breeders sometimes are fortunate in obtaining advantageous combinations of chromosomes, and sometimes they are not. The possible advantages of breeding to produce plants with more chromosomes are worth exploring. Should the reader wish to investigate in greater depth the question of haploid, diploid and tetraploid plants, then a textbook of botany should be consulted.

the shippers knew little about the bulbs' needs, it was the custom to remove most of the roots, and pack the bulbs in dry material such as wood shavings in large, wooden crates. The bulbs arrived at their destination in poor condition, dried out and much weakened.

Combine weakened bulbs with the incidence of virus, and it was no wonder that the reputation of the lily suffered. Lilies came to be regarded as rather difficult bulbs to grow. *L. auratum* is a beautiful lily, and it was readily accepted that such a beautiful bulb was difficult to grow; how could such a treasure be easy to cultivate? But just as these unfortunate circumstances were taking place, one of the most important plant discoveries was being made, the finding of *L. regale* by E. H. Wilson. Soon after the turn of the century he introduced not only the Regal lily, but also *L. davidii* and *L. sargentiae*. *L. regale* was easy to grow; while having great beauty and a fragrant trumpet, it lacked the exotic look of *L. auratum*. Interest in lilies started to climb nonetheless. Even today, some people feel lilies are difficult plants, but this is not the case.

In the 1930s Jan de Graaff, whose family had for centuries been connected with the bulb industry in Holland, settled in Oregon. In fact, he was sent to collect monies owed to his family's firm by a nursery. De Graaff saw the nursery, liked it and Oregon, and decided to stay. Quickly establishing himself as a bulb grower, he introduced many *Narcissus* cultivars onto the market. (Two of those introductions are grown today, 'February Gold' and 'Mount Hood', and it speaks highly of the improvements made that these bulbs are in commerce after more than 60 years.) Before long, de Graaff began raising lilies. Soon such cultivars as 'Enchantment', 'Golden Splendor', 'Pink Perfection' and 'Imperial Crimson' were introduced. Today no lily is more widely grown than 'Enchantment', and while the strains of 'Golden Splendor' and 'Pink Perfection' have been improved with deeper colors and flowers of better texture, de Graaff must be called the father of the hybrid lily.

The introduction of so many cultivars made the need for a horticultural classification essential. Fortunately, the classification worked out and was adopted by the Royal Horticultural Society and the North American Lily Society. There are 10 divisions, each with subdivisions to accommodate the forms of the flowers of the cultivars.

Classification

Division I, Asiatic Hybrids

Hybrids derived from these species or hybrid groups such as: *L. amabile*, *L. bulbiferum*, *L. cernuum*, *L. concolor*, *L. davidii*, *L × hollandicum*, *L. lancifolium* (formerly *L. tigrinum*), *L. × maculatum*, *L. maximowiczii*, *L. pumilum*.

> **Subdivision a.** Early flowering, upright, single or in an umbel, such as 'Enchantment'
>
> **Subdivision b.** Those with outward-facing flowers, such as 'Prosperity'
>
> **Subdivision c.** Those with pendant flowers, such as 'Citronella'

Division II, Martagon Hybrids

In which one parent has been a form of *L. martagon* or *L. hansonii*, such as the Backhouse Hybrids.

Division III, Candidum Hybrids

From *L. candidum*, *L. chalcedonicum* and other related European species such as *L. × testaceum*, but excluding *L. martagon*.

Division IV, American Hybrids

Of American species, such as 'Bellingham Hybrids' and 'Shuksan'.

Division V, Longiflorum Hybrids

Derived from *L. longiflorum* and *L. formosanum*, such as *L. × formolongi*, but excluding forms and polyploids of either species.

Division VI, Trumpet Hybrids

Hybrid trumpet *Lilium* and Aurelian hybrids derived from Asiatic species, but excluding those derived from *L. auratum*, *L. japonicum*, *L. rubellum*, *L. speciosum*.

> **Subdivision a.** Trumpet type: all hybrids having flowers of strictly trumpet type, such as 'Black Dragon Strain', 'Golden Clarion', 'Limelight'
>
> **Subdivision b.** Bowl-shaped flowers; all hybrids having clearly bowl-shaped flowers, outward facing such as 'Heart's Desire' Hybrids.
>
> **Subdivision c.** Pendant type; all *Lilium* with flowers that are distinctly pendant-type, such as 'Golden Showers'
>
> **Subdivision d.** Sunburst type; all *Lilium* having flowers that open flat and are star shaped, such as 'Sunburst Hybrids' and 'Thunderbolt'

Division VII, Oriental Hybrids

Of Far Eastern species such as *L. auratum*, *L. japonicum*, *L. rubellum*, *L. speciosum*, including their crosses with *L. henryii*.

> **Subdivision a.** Trumpet type. (At time of writing, no such hybrids are offered for sale, but some will be released in the near future.)

Trumpet lilies such as *Lilium* 'Golden Temple' add a lot of sparkle to summer borders, and will do so for many years without any effort on the part of the gardener. (Photo courtesy of Edward McRae, Van der Salm Bulbfarm Inc.)

Subdivision b. Bowl-shaped flowers such as 'Empress of India'

Subdivision c. Flat-faced flowers such as 'Jillian Wallace'

Subdivision d. Recurved flowers such as 'Potomac Hybrids'

Division VIII
Contains all hybrids not provided for in any previous division.

Division IX
Contains all true species and their forms.

Subdivision a. *L. martagon* form with reflexed flowers, such as *L. cernuum, L. chalce-*

donicum, L. davidii, L. duchartrei, L. hansonii, L. martagon, L. monadelphum and *L. wardii,* but excluding those of American origin

Subdivision b. Upright flowers such as *L. bulbiferum, L. dauricum, L. tsingtauense*

Subdivision c. Bulbs of American origin

Subdivision d. Forms and polyploids of *L. formosanum, L. longiflorum, L. philippinense*

Subdivision e. Bowl-shaped or trumpet flowers, such as *L. candidum, L. regale, L. sargentiae* and *L. sulphureum,* but excluding those mentioned in I d

Subdivision f. Asiatic *Lilium,* short trumpet or slightly recurved pendulous flowers, such as *L. bakeranum, L. nepalense, L. primulinum*

Subdivision g. Forms and varieties of *L. auratum* and *L. speciosum*

Subdivision h. Asiatic *Lilium.* Unusually dwarf with affinities toward *nomocharis,* such as *L. henrici, L. mackliniae, L. nanum, L. sheriffiae*

Division X
Contains species and forms of *Cardiocrinum.*

This may seem cumbersome. It follows the flowering sequence, as the Asiatics flower before the trumpets, which flower before the Oriental Hybrids. Attend a lily show and you will see cultivars exhibited in most of these divisions, and the differences become quite obvious.

The basic requirements of lilies can be summed up briefly: They like their feet in the shade, their heads in the sun, and they do not like wet feet. To enjoy the rather subtle colors of some hybrids, light shade during the heat of the day is an advantage as the flowers fade less. Good drainage is essential, and good garden soil with a high content of organic matter slightly on the acid side is ideal. Woodland conditions are great for many species, but Asiatic Hybrids should be grown in full sun. Most, if not all, lilies listed in catalogs will be hardy anywhere in the United States. In the coldest climates a mulch is advised, not so much to prevent the bulbs being frozen, but to prevent repeated freezing and thawing that can "lift" the bulbs and break established roots.

Plant lily bulbs as soon as you receive them. Make certain the soil is well prepared to a depth of at least 12 inches. Lilies should be planted with 8 inches of soil over them. The tall, trumpet types should be spaced 24 inches apart, the shorter types such as the Asiatic Hybrids, 12 inches apart. If growing in rows for cut flowers, space 4 to 6 inches apart, with the rows 36 inches apart. After planting, water the bulbs in to settle the soil around them. As soon as the shoots appear above ground in spring, apply a feeding of balanced fertilizer. Repeat the feedings according to the product label until you see the buds form, then stop. Keep moist throughout the growing season.

Lilies have strong stems, but some of the trumpet hybrids will become so tall (I have seen them well over 6 feet) they need support. Place the stake as close as possible to the stem, but make every effort not to spear the bulb. When the flowers have finished blooming, remove them so that seed is not produced. Leave the stems until the foliage has become brown, at which time they can be cut down. It pays to mark the location of your lilies as, should you break the stem when it appears in spring, you will not have any flowers that year. So take care. When cutting flowers for use indoors, leave as much of the stem as you can. The foliage of lilies is on the flowering stem, and this produces food for the bulb. Leave it and let it do its work.

Bulbs should be left undisturbed for years. Lift, divide and replant only when the bulbs be-

The lovely Madonna lily (*Lilium candicum* 'Cascade Strain') has been enjoyed for centuries, and its grace and form are still superb. (Photo courtesy of Edward McRae, Van der Salm Bulbfarm Inc.)

come very overcrowded and flower production has declined. If all is going well, do not disturb. I have seen some bulbs growing happily for more than 15 years in the same location.

Lilies are superb container plants. Use regular potting soil and deep containers. There will be production of roots on the stems above the bulb, so containers must accommodate deep planting. Set the bulbs 6 or more inches deep. As soon as the tips of the shoots appear above the soil, start a fertilizer program using liquid organic fertilizer. Keep this program going until the flower buds are evident, then stop feeding, but continue to keep the containers moist. Asiatic

Lilium 'Casa Rosa' is one of the lovely new range of hybrids, which are really colored Easter lilies. They are at home in the garden or in containers. (Photo courtesy of Edward McRae, Van der Salm Bulbfarm Inc.)

Hybrids and the shorter selections of the other types are best for containers. I have grown lilies in the same pots for several years, but each fall I remove the top few inches of soil and replace them with soil rich in organic matter. What I am doing is providing new soil each year for the stem roots. I repot when I see the bulbs are asking for it. Ordinary potting soil is fine, but if you add some organic matter, the lilies will love it.

Few pests or diseases will bother your lilies. If you select carefully, you can have lilies in flower for many months. I have yet to see a hybrid I do not like, but must admit that some of the species give many hybrids a good run for their money. Some species have colors and forms not found in hybrids. Having given all this information, I must mention one exception to all of the above, *L. candidum*. This species produces a rosette of leaves in June, held close to the soil. They are evergreen and remain over the winter. Plant these bulbs only just deep enough to cover

them, about ½ inch. These plants appreciate a little shade. Many say this species is attacked by botritis and that the foliage is seldom unmarked by the ravages of this fungus. I have not seen this, and feel that with ordinary hygiene, keeping the plants healthy and in good form by feeding them in early spring, this lily is no harder to grow than any other.

One of the popular lilies is the tiger lily (at least, so one would understand, since many people call all Asiatic Lilies "tiger lilies"). The true tiger lily, *L. lancifolium* (formerly *L. tigrinum*), has the habit of producing a lot of little bulbils in the axils of the leaves. In some cases these miniature bulbs can be seen putting out roots. You can remove these bulbils and sow them in shallow drills. Grown on in this way, they will reach flowering size in about three seasons. This characteristic has been passed on to many of the hybrids with *L. lancifolium* blood in them. Another lily with this habit is *L. speciosum*, and here the bulbil production is exploited commercially, and sometimes encouraged, by laying the stem in a trench and covering it with several inches of soil; bulbil production is increased by this.

Propagation is best accomplished, though, by lifting the parent bulbs in fall, and removing the stem bulblets and small bulbs produced around the older bulbs. Plant back as soon as possible. Bulbs with a circumference of 3 inches or more will probably flower the following season; some Asiatics will flower from even smaller bulbs. Small bulbs and bulblets can be grown on to flowering size in nursery rows. The number of species of lilies listed in catalogs is declining, in my opinion a great pity.

Lilium auratum: Native to Japan, it may be the loveliest lily of all. Flowers appear in late summer, bowl shaped, outward facing and up to 10 inches in diameter. When well established the plants can reach over 6 feet in height, with as many as 25 flowers per stalk. The tepals are white, and in the center there is a golden band, sometimes more visible than others, but it is this band that gives this lily its common name, gold band lily. At the base of the tepals are papilae, protuberances thought to provide landing places for butterflies that come to sample the nectar and thus help in pollination. The tepals are spotted with crimson-brown and the tips curl back a little. There are several forms, the most vigorous of which is var. *platyphyllum*, with broad leaves often more than 8 inches in length. Var. *virginale* is pure white without spots, but the yellow band may be present. The var. *rubrovitatum* happens to be my favorite; it has a deep crimson band down the center of the tepals, and the throat is an apple green—quite a startling flower. A number of named selections of this species are often listed. It flowers in late summer.

L. canadense: This species is native to the eastern seaboard of North America from Nova Scotia southward to Virginia, and as far west as Alabama. It is a graceful plant, reaching up to 6 feet tall, with leaves in whorls. The flowers on long pedicels are lemon yellow spotted with crimson dots, and they face downward. It is happy on the edge of woodlands, and prefers some shade. The var. *flavum* is a plant with clear yellow flowers, and the selection 'Melted Spots' has flowers so thickly spotted they seem to melt together. Flowers in early to midsummer.

L. candidum: This is the Madonna lily, also known as the Annunciation lily and the Bourbon lily. This species comes from the eastern Mediterranean; its exact habitat is not known, but is thought to be in the Balkans. It is unusual in that it should be planted so the top of the bulb is at soil level; it produces rosettes of leaves that lie on the soil surface. The stems reach a height of 48 or more inches, each with as many as 20 flowers of pure white with prominent golden stamens. Flowers can be 5 inches in diameter and have a grand fragrance; they appear in June. The 'Cascade Strain' has great vigor and is American grown; for far too many years the only stock available came from Europe, and it was not of the best quality.

L. catesbaei (syn. *L. carolinianum*)*:* This lily is at home in Florida, Louisiana and South Carolina. It is, with *L. philadelphicum*, special among lilies in that it grows in swampy ground. It reaches 12 to 24 inches, with upright yellow-and-scarlet flowers 4 to 6 inches in diameter, and narrow tepals. The principle interest is that it grows in swampy ground; the plant is of no great beauty.

L. henryi: This native of China is often called the orange speciosum, as the tepals are much recurved, giving the "speciosum" look. A strong grower, often over 6 feet tall, producing 20 or more flowers in late summer. This lily was once very popular, but while still listed in catalogs, it is becoming rare in cultivation. Because of its height it needs support.

L. lancifolium (syn. *L. tigrinum*)*:* The tiger lily is native to Japan. Because of its vigor and ease of growing, this lily has been in cultivation for a long time. The bright orange flowers and recurved tepals are themselves striking, but so are the black stems endowed with white hairs, giving the impression the plant is covered with cobwebs. Many bulbils are produced in the leaf axils, as many as three in each axil not being unusual. In a well-formed flower head you will find as many as 20 flowers, each 4 inches in diameter and at their best in July or August. Once planted, these lilies should be left undisturbed; you will soon have a colony to enjoy.

L. martagon: This lily is native to much of Europe, and north into Russia and Mongolia. Known as the Turk's cap lily, it features thick tepals that are much recurved and long lasting, light purple with many dark spots. Up to 6 feet in height and flowering in early summer, it is at its best in woodland settings. However, I have seen beds in full sun in Oregon thrive with little summer moisture. There are several varieties, var. *album* being pure white, var. *dalmaticum* a deep burgundy. While not as popular as they were when fewer lilies were available, this species deserves to be planted, and I hope it will not disappear from our gardens.

L. monadelphum: Native to the Caucasus, with yellow flowers that are fragrant, pendulous and that appear in early summer. Looks its best in a woodland setting. It reaches 48 inches, and loves a soil rich in humus. This species hates being transplanted and will make little if any growth in the first season. When established, it puts on a great show every year.

L. regale: This lovely trumpet lily, with its vigor and free-flowering habit, rekindled the gardening public's interest in lilies, and this had a dramatic impact on our gardens. It is native to western China. Fragrant white trumpet-shaped flowers sit atop 4- to 6-foot stems. It exhibits an unusual form of flower head, as the stalks of the flowers all seem to arise from the same point of the stem, forming a "crown" that adds to its regal appearance. This summer-flowering species loves the sun and does well in ordinary garden soil, but needs good drainage. Leave it alone and it will multiply.

L. speciosum: Native to Japan. There are several forms of this lovely species, and it has been used in creating many hybrids, imparting the lovely red color and margins of silver to its offspring. The tepals are much recurved, the stamens thrust forward and quite striking. (Often the stamens are clipped off, which to my mind spoils the flower.) Late summer–flowering, the plant is often over 5 feet tall. It produces bulbils in the leaf axils, and is one of the most vigorous of lilies. It loves the sun and will grow in a great many soils, but must have good drainage. One of the finest cut flowers, this lily has a wonderful fragrance. Individual flowers range from 4 to 5 inches across. The plants are very floriferous. *L. speciosum* var. *rubrum* has a darker color, and var. *album* is the white form. Well worth growing in any garden or in large, deep containers.

L. superbum: Native to the eastern part of the United States, from Massachusetts south to Florida. The flower head is well arranged, and when well grown the plants will carry as many as 40 orange flowers, but even so I do not think it is a "superb" lily. It will tolerate more moisture than most lilies, and flowers in late summer. This plant can grow tall, and 5 feet or more isn't unusual. The orange flowers turn crimson at the tips of the tepals as the flower ages; the center is spotted with deep maroon.

L. × testaceum: Possibly the oldest lily hybrid, a cross between *L. candidum* and *L. chalcedonicum*. The flowers are yellow with a hint of orange, and spotted with red. The tepals recurve. This lily reaches a height of 48 inches and flowers in July. It is sad to think that a lily that has been around for many years is no longer grown much. Newer hybrids have taken over, but I doubt whether any will last as long in our gardens as this old hybrid. If for no other reason than its historical position in lily culture, *L. × testaceum* should be considered.

The world of hybrid lilies is quickly changing. Today's hybrids are vigorous. Many of them are tetraploids, and the breakthrough that made colored forms of the Easter lily possible signals but one more step in the development of these grand flowers. Just how fast is the progress? A look at some of the production figures gives an idea. In 1991 there were approximately 5,000 acres of lilies cultivated in the Netherlands. In 1992 this had increased to approximately 5,500 acres—percentage-wise, an incredible jump. The acreage of trumpet lilies declined. The acreage of hybrids between the Easter lily and Asiatic Hybrids went from zero to well over an acre, and these types were unknown just a few years ago. Asiatic and Oriental lilies are increasing in popularity, but it must be remembered that most of the increase is due to the increasing popularity of these plants as greenhouse crops for flower markets around the world. The most popular lily is 'Star Gazer', cultivated on more than 1,000 acres, almost one-fifth of all lilies grown. The mind boggles at the thought of the number of bulbs this means; even at 10¢ a bulb, it would knock a large hole in the national debt!

Classification

Division 1, Asiatic Hybrids

Subdivision a. Upright flowering
'Antarctica': white, lightly spotted with pink, 24 inches

'Chinook': salmon, large flowers, 48 inches

'Connecticut King': Bright yellow, unspotted, 48 inches

'Enchantment': nasturtium orange, 36 to 48 inches

'Golden Pixie'; pure yellow, superb in containers, 18 inches

'Montreux': deep pink, 36 inches

'Pixie Flame': orange-red with golden blotch, 18 inches

'Pollyana': bright yellow with deep golden blotch, 60 inches

'Roma': a soft cream to white with few spots, 36 inches

'Rosefire': a tricolor—the tips are red, center of tepals yellow, center of the flower bright orange-red, 36 inches

Subdivision b. Outward-facing flowers
'Ming Yellow': bright yellow, 36 inches

'Orange Glow': Clear orange, unspotted. 36 inches

Subdivision c. Pendant flowers
'Apricot Supreme': great color, dark foliage and stems, 48 inches

'Elf': bright pink, 36 inches

Division III, Candidum Hybrids

'Cascade Strain': vigorous, 48 inches

Division IV: American Hybrids

'Bellingham Hybrids': over 6 feet tall, vigorous, shades of red, orange and yellow; an older introduction but still very good

Division V. Longiflorum Hybrids

'Casa Rosa': rose with deeper blush in the center, 30 inches

'Summer Breeze': a lovely, clear pink of great texture, almost with a sheen, 30 inches

Division VI, Trumpet Hybrids

Subdivision a. Trumpet types
'Amethyst Temple': pink, fragrant, later

flowering than others in this section, coming into flower late July; 5 or more feet

'Black Dragon': Fragrant white with reverse of tepals very dark, 5 feet tall.

'Golden Temple': Golden yellow with dark bronze reverse to the tepals, 48 inches

Subdivision b. Bowl-shaped flowers
'Golden Sunburst': flowers open wide, free flowering, 6 feet tall

'Thunderbolt': color of cantaloupe, 6 feet tall; give a little high shade to preserve the color

Division VII, Oriental Hybrids

Subdivision a. Trumpet flowers:
None as yet on the market

Subdivision b. Bowl-shaped flowers
'Casa Blanca': large flowers, pure white, fragrant, 48 inches

'Elegance Series': There are a number of these: 'Crimson Elegance', a crimson; 'Gold Elegance', 'Silver Elegance', the colors evident from the name. Superb flowers, 48 or more inches tall, fragrant

'Star Gazer': flowers held erect, very large, red with silver edges to tepals, 36 inches tall, a stocky plant superb in pots and for cutting

Botanical Name: Lilium
Family: Liliaceae
Common Names: Lily, tiger lily, speciosum lily
Flower Colors: All except blue
Flowering Time: Varies from early summer into fall.
Height: 18 inches to more than 6 feet
Spread: Will form clumps in a few seasons

Native Habitat: Temperate zones of the northern hemisphere
Hardiness: Hardy; in very cold areas need some protection
Depth of Planting: 8 inches, except *L. candidum*
Distance Apart: 12 inches
Containers: Yes
Light Requirements: Most require full sun; some are better suited to woodlands and appreciate high shade
Soil Type: Average garden soil; good drainage is essential. Some prefer wet conditions; see individual species.
Special Conditions: Lilies appreciate some fertilizer upon emerging from their winter sleep.
Comments: There must be room in every garden for some of these great plants, truly the aristocrats of the garden. Exciting breakthroughs in breeding are bringing new forms and colors onto the market. Great in containers. Plant a selection so that you can enjoy them all summer long.

LYCORIS
Amaryllidaceae

In some books you will read that this genus is named after a lady who figures in Roman history; they are being polite, as it as named after the mistress of Marc Antony. There are some 14 or so species, all native to China or Japan. They are not far removed from *Nerine* and look similar to them, but *Lycoris* have petals that are often twisted and recurved, and they are not held closely together to form a trumpet. Their common name of spider lily was inspired by the long "spider legs," the prominent stamens of each flower. The flowers appear in late summer on the top of strong stems that vary in height by species, but all in the 18- to 24-inch range. The strap-shaped leaves appear after the flowers have passed.

These plants appreciate a sunny border where, for the period from midsummer until they make their move to flower, they like to be fairly dry and warm. Moisture should be given as the growth starts to emerge, and a feeding at that time is appreciated. They will grow in average garden soil with good drainage. Excellent pot plants, they are happy with ordinary potting soil. Plant the bulbs 4 inches deep and 8 to 10 inches apart. Plant as soon as you get the bulbs, ideally planting in midsummer. In pots it is good to crowd them a little, say, 3 bulbs to a 12-inch pot. Keep the pot barely moist, and increase the amount of water when the leaves appear. *Lycoris albiflora*, *L. aurea*, *L. radiata* and *L. sanguinea* are hardy to around 10°F with a good mulch and in a protected border. *L. squamigera* is much hardier, withstanding temperatures down to −20°F. In colder areas, grow *Lycoris* in containers or in a cool greenhouse.

Once planted, *Lycoris* should be left undisturbed. Lift only when you wish to increase your stock. This is best done after the foliage has died back in late spring. Do not be impatient with these plants; they may not flower at all the first year, but will the second. It is just that they resent having been moved.

Lycoris albiflora: Native to Japan, the white spider lily has creamy flowers and very prominent stamens. This untidy but attractive flower appears in late summer or early fall, with up to five quite long-lasting flowers per plant.

L. aurea: The golden spider lily is native to China, Taiwan and Upper Burma. Lovely flowers of golden yellow on stems 24 inches tall. This fall-flowering species is one of the most popular of the genus.

L. radiata: The spider lily comes to us from

A border that can hardly be claimed to be interesting is transformed in late summer by an eruption of color—*Lycoris aurea*—and almost overnight these spider lilies take over.

China and Japan. The flower color can vary from pink to deep red or scarlet; most forms offered seem to be crimson/scarlet. Earlier flowering than the other species, it is often in flower in late August. The plants are 18 inches in height, with more flowers in a head than the other species.

L. squamigera: The magic lily is from Japan and it is the hardiest of the species. With fragrant rose-pink flowers with a bluish cast, this is a great cut flower at 24 inches tall. It is often a while before the leaves appear, and do not be surprised if they take a month or more to emerge.

They can persist until summer. The plants flower in late summer, early fall. If you cannot give these plants the dry period they like in mid- to late summer, you might grow them in pots. Then, as they start into growth, plunge the pots into the border. *Lycoris* must have this dry period to perform well.

Botanical Name: Lycoris
Family: Amaryllidaceae
Common Names: Spider lily, magic lily
Flower Colors: White, yellow, shades of scarlet-crimson
Flowering Time: Late summer into fall
Height: 18 to 24 inches
Spread: Will spread in time
Native Habitat: China, Japan, Taiwan and parts of Burma
Hardiness: Varies by species; the hardiest, *L. squamigera*, to −10°F
Depth of Planting: 3 inches
Distance Apart: 8 to 10 inches
Containers: Yes
Light Requirements: Sun
Soil Type: Average garden soil
Special Conditions: Must have a dry period before coming into bloom.
Comments: Lycoris add unique charm to the warm, sunny border. Perhaps they are not for gardens where space is limited, due to their need for a dry period in midsummer—difficult to provide when growing different plants together. *Lycoris* are attractive in containers, and I am surprised that more are not grown commercially, for their flower form is quite unusual.

MONTBRETIA. See *Crocosmia.*

MORAEA. See *Dietes iridioides.*

MUSCARI
Liliaceae

These plants have a musklike fragrance, and as the Latin word for this is *muscus*, the name of the genus acknowledges this. There is much discussion concerning this genus; several species that were once assigned to *Muscari* are now in *Bellevalia*, others have been placed in *Muscarimia*, those that have tufts of sterile flowers at the top of the flower spikes are now in *Leopoldia*, and species with flowers that are more bell shaped are in *Pseudomuscari*. No doubt before long all of this will again be changed. The grape hyacinths, as these plants are called, have provided much work for botanists. However, this does not make them any less beautiful, or more difficult to grow!

These are among the easiest bulbs to grow. I have planted a good number, and upon returning to the garden a couple of seasons later, have been surprised to see how much they have spread. I would not say they had become invasive, but close to it. Some species spawn numerous bulblets, so you had best make certain they have room to spread when you plant them in your garden. But being so easy to grow is, to me anyway, an advantage. They will not multiply in subtropical climes.

Muscari will frequently send up their grasslike foliage in fall, then the lovely spikes of blue flower in spring, and the foliage will just keep on growing. It will eventually die down, the bulbs enter their dormant state, and then start their cycle all over again—except that there will be more of them. They thrive in a wide range of soils, and they like the sun. They are hardy and will survive very cold weather. Plant 2 to 3 inches deep and space them 3 to 4 inches apart. *Muscari* are great plants to grow in shallow containers. Crowd the bulbs together in ordinary potting soil, and place them outdoors in a cold area to get the roots started.

When the shoots appear, you can bring them indoors and enjoy them. They will grow at a good rate and soon be in flower, and last that way for quite a while.

The uses for *Muscari* in the garden are numerous. I like to pop some in the borders of rose beds, and along the front of shrub borders. They do not mind moisture throughout the year, so you do not have to select any special spot for them. Try planting them to represent a little stream, with tulips and narcissus along the sides of the planting; the blue *Muscari* add a lovely contrast. Let them appear in drifts on a bank; they are stunning viewed from afar, and only get better each year. Great in a rock garden, and around the base of trees or shrubs planted in lawns, these plants are versatile. Perhaps best of all is that they are inexpensive. And surprisingly for their height, they make quite good cut flowers, especially *M. armeniacum.*

Muscari armeniacum: This species, native to Turkey, is widely distributed from the Balkans to the Caucasus. It grows 6 to 8 inches in height, with leaves that are quite long. The deep purple-blue flowers, each with a white rim at the mouth, appear in April to May. A great number of flowers are carried in each flower head. Selections are often offered by nurseries. 'Blue Spike' has double flowers of a softer blue, and 'Cantab' has flowers of an even lighter blue.

M. azureum: This species comes from the Caucasus and eastern Turkey. Of all the species, this is perhaps the easiest to grow—it is

For much of the year this corner of the garden is not very interesting, but in the spring, these grape hyacinths (*Muscari armeniacum* 'Early Giant') put on a display that lasts for weeks.

almost impossible not to grow it well! Bright blue flowers, in compact flower heads 4 to 6 inches in height, appear in March or early April. A white form is listed as 'Album'. 'Amphibolis' has flowers that are just a little lighter than the species, and the flowers are a little larger.

M. botryoides: Native to France and Italy. The height is from 6 to 10 inches, the color sky blue, with a white rim at the mouth. The flowering time is late spring to early summer. This is regarded as the true grape hyacinth, and a number of forms are regarded by some authorities as being worthy of species rank. Several forms have also been selected because of their color and will be listed in catalogs as 'Album', with pure white flowers, 'Carneum', with rosy flowers, and 'Pallidum', with flowers of a paler rose. Quite possibly all these are but variations caused by their growing in different locations.

M. comosum: The tassel hyacinth is native to the Mediterranean region, mostly southeastern Europe. Taller than most other species, the top of the spike has sterile flowers of blue, with the lower, fertile flowers a greenish brown. Flowers in April.

M. latifolium: This is a native of Turkey. Like *M. comosum* it has two tiers of flowers, the fertile ones above being violet, the sterile ones a good blue. The height of this species is 10 to 12 inches. An unusual feature is that it generally produces only one, wide leaf, hence the name, which means "broad leaf." The flowers appear in late spring or very early summer.

Botanical Name: Muscari
Family: Liliaceae
Common Names: Grape hyacinth, tassel hyacinth
Flower Colors: Blue, some white forms and rose, the latter color rare
Flowering Time: Spring to early summer
Height: Depends on species, 4 to 12 inches
Spread: Can become almost invasive
Native Habitat: Mediterranean region, Turkey, Balkans and Caucasus
Hardiness: Very hardy
Depth of Planting: 2 to 3 inches
Distance Apart: 3 to 4 inches
Containers: Yes
Light Requirements: Full sun; tolerates high shade
Soil Type: Ordinary garden soil
Special Conditions: None; this is one of the easiest bulbs to grow
Comments: Find room for *Muscari;* they are easy and so rewarding that if you cannot grow them there must be something wrong! Versatile plants, great in shallow containers, in the front of borders, drifting among shrubs, and in bold plantings that imitate flowing water. These bulbs are a great value, as they are not expensive and multiply quickly.

This Triandrus hybrid (*Narcissus* 'Hawera') is at least 60 years old and still going strong! Seemingly impervious to inclement weather, it is a very fine plant for any garden.

NARCISSUS
Amaryllidaceae

The genus is so named because of the narcotic properties of these plants, the Latin *narcoum* meaning to make numb. The common name for these plants is daffodil, which causes some confusion as it is generally applied only to those yellow, trumpet daffodils such as the well-known 'King Alfred'. When a plant has more than one flower, definite fragrance and is predominantly white, the common name given is narcissus. In fact, all daffodils are *Narcissus*. I doubt if there is a spring-flowering bulb as popular as the *Narcissus*. They are so closely identified with spring that, while they can be brought into flower during many months of the year, they remain uniquely springtime flowers—there is apparently resistance to using them in arrangements at any other time. No doubt this will gradually be overcome, as it has somewhat with tulips, lilies, for example, are found in florists' shops year 'round, and gladiolus are another popular year-'round cut flower.

The number of species varies, depending on which authority is consulted. Some say there are more than 70, some far fewer, and others advocate breaking the genus into several genera. Studies of the genetic makeup of these plants has led to a better understanding of the species. While such discussions will certainly continue for years, we have (thanks to the Royal Horticultural Society) a good Horticultural Classification. I thank the R.H.S. for permission to print it here, verbatim. I am of the opinion that it is as clear and as concise as it can be.

Classification

Division 1, Trumpet daffodils of garden origin. One flower to a stem; corona ("trumpet") as long as, or longer than the perianth segments ("petals").

Division 2, Large-cupped daffodils of garden origin. One flower to a stem; corona ("cup") more than one-third, but less than equal to the length of the perianth segments ("petals").

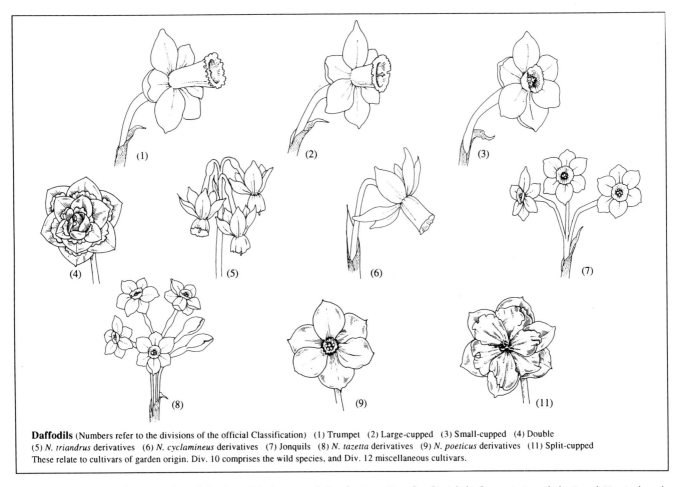

Daffodils (Numbers refer to the divisions of the official Classification) (1) Trumpet (2) Large-cupped (3) Small-cupped (4) Double
(5) *N. triandrus* derivatives (6) *N. cyclamineus* derivatives (7) Jonquils (8) *N. tazetta* derivatives (9) *N. poeticus* derivatives (11) Split-cupped
These relate to cultivars of garden origin. Div. 10 comprises the wild species, and Div. 12 miscellaneous cultivars.

From The New Royal Horticultural Society Dictionary of Gardening. *Reproduced with kind permission of the Royal Horticultural Society and The Macmillan Press Ltd. and Stockton Press, New York. Illustration by Christine Grey-Wilson.*

Division 3, Small-cupped daffodils of garden origin. One flower to a stem; corona ("cup") not more than one-third the length of the perianth segments ("petals").

Division 4, Double daffodils of garden origin. One or more flowers to a stem, with doubling of the perianth segments or the corona or both.

Division 5, Triandrus daffodils of garden origin. Characteristics of *N. triandrus* predominant: usually two or more pendant flowers to a stem; perianth segments reflexed.

Division 6, Cyclamineus daffodils of garden origin. Characteristics of *N. cyclamineus* predominant: usually one flower to a stem; perianth segments reflexed; flower at an acute angle to the stem, with a very short pedicel ("neck").

Division 7, Jonquilla daffodils of garden origin. Characteristics of the *N. jonquilla* group predominant: usually one to three flowers to a rounded stem; leaves narrow, dark green; perianth segments spreading not reflexed; flowers fragrant.

Division 8, Tazetta daffodils of garden origin. Characteristics of the *N. tazetta* group predominant: usually three to twenty flowers to a stout stem; leaves broad; perianth segments spreading not reflexed; flowers fragrant.

Division 9, Poeticus daffodils of garden origin. Characteristics of the *N. poeticus* group predominant: usually one flower to a stem; perianth seg-

Notes—The characteristics for Divisions 5 to 9 are given for guidance only; they are not all necessarily expected to be present in every cultivar assigned thereto.

—Divisions 10 and 12 are not illustrated owing to the wide variation in shape and size between the flowers involved

ments pure white; corona usually disc-shaped, with a green or yellow center and a red rim; flowers fragrant.

Division 10, Species, wild variants and wild hybrids. All species and wild or reputedly wild variants and hybrids, including those with double flowers.

Division 11, Split-corona daffodils of garden origin. Corona split rather than lobed and usually for more than half its length.

Division 12, Miscellaneous daffodils. All daffodils not falling into any one of the foregoing divisions.

Those readers interested in studying the classification of species of this lovely genus I respectfully refer to my two-volume work *Bulbs*, published by Timber Press. Classification is important, but as it requires some knowledge of botany, I feel it goes beyond the scope of this book. (I don't mean to imply that readers have no knowledge of botany, though.)

Narcissus are hardy. While they tolerate a wide range of soils, they prefer a soil that remains moist from the time they are planted until their foliage has died down in late spring or early summer. They ask for well-drained soil and a sunny location. They are found in the wild in the Mediterranean regions, North Africa, China and Japan.

There is conflicting advice on when to plant *Narcissus*. The planting time varies with climate. In the very coldest areas, the bulbs should be planted as soon as they are available, in very early fall. In climates that experience considerable cold weather, they should be planted in early October. In climates that experience frost but not for prolonged periods, they should be planted in late October or early November, and in frost-free areas they should be planted in late November or early December. Having said that, I can assure you that I have seen them planted in late December and early January in California, and they have flowered well. However, they are better off in the ground by early December in even the warmest areas of the country. Narcissus make great cut flowers and are good plants for containers. Certain species are ideal rock garden plants. They can be naturalized in grass (allow at least 6 weeks after the flowers have passed before cutting the grass), and make glorious garden plants in almost any setting except perhaps the truly formal garden, as narcissus foliage tends to become untidy.

As a rule of thumb, and I give this as the size of *Narcissus* bulbs varies greatly, they should be buried with about twice their height of soil above them. Thus a bulb standing an inch in height should be buried with 2 inches of soil over it. Most narcissus hybrids, the most popular bulbs, should be buried some 8 inches deep. They can be spaced 4 to 6 inches apart. Once planted they should be left undisturbed for years. A dry resting period of several weeks in late summer is wanted. If this isn't possible, then after the foliage has started to die back, lift and store the bulbs, planting them again at the correct planting time for the area in which they are to be grown.

When lifting bulbs, take care not to damage them. Bruising will often lead to rot setting in. Discard any damaged bulbs. Offsets can be used to propagate the stock. Line them out at planting time and grow them on, removing any flowers so the bulb attains full flowering size quickly. The smallest bulbs will take two years, and in my opinion it is better to purchase bulbs each year.

When *Narcissus* are grown in containers, deep planting doesn't have the same importance,

but the bulbs must be nonetheless well covered. Place the container in a cool area so roots can develop before the bulbs are given warmer temperatures. Once forced (that is, brought into flower earlier than their normal flowering time by exposure to warm temperatures), the bulbs are best discarded. It is too much effort for most home gardeners to coax these bulbs back to normalcy, and their flowering can't be assured once they have been forced. Many of the smaller species can be grown in pots and, while not forced, used effectively indoors. Simply bring them indoors when the first buds start to open. They can, and should, be grown on and enjoyed the following season. Keeping them in the pots and giving them a ripening period in late summer is much easier to accomplish than when they are grown in the open border.

With healthy stock, the home gardener will seldom run into any problems with these bulbs. Rot can set in, and any soft bulbs should be discarded. A healthy bulb will be firm and have a good sheen to the tunic that surrounds it. In the case of home-grown bulbs, however, the tunic may not always be of good color.

You will notice that new bulb introductions are quite expensive to purchase. The home gardener should purchase bulbs that are less expensive, buying novelties or recent introductions only when the budget allows. I would rather grow a dozen of a tried-and-true cultivar than one bulb of a novelty. By far the greater number of *Narcissus* listed in catalogs today follow the divisions agreed upon by the Royal Horticultural Society and those in the bulb industry. For this reason, the following list of suggested cultivars follows the order of the classification. Note that the heights given here are average for areas with some frost and moderate snowfall, except as noted; soil, temperature and light conditions all play their part, and affect heights and time of flowering.

Cultivars and species

Division 1, Trumpet daffodils of garden origin, 12 to 18 inches

'Dutch Master': Considered by many superior to 'King Alfred', long the favorite of gardeners; great texture, soft yellow, a noble flower

'Golden Harvest': very large flowers, often more than 6 inches in diameter; a good yellow, a little earlier in flower than some

'King Alfred': rich golden yellow, the classic most people imagine, an old timer, 'Dutch Master' giving it good competition

'Mount Hood': a classic, pure white, long-lasting flower

'Unsurpassable': deep yellow, good-sized flowers and an excellent selection for naturalizing

Division 2, Large-cupped daffodils of garden origin, 12 to 18 inches

'Carlton': the corona is attractively frilled, soft yellow, good in pots

'Duke of Windsor': the perianth is pure white, wavy edges to the soft orange cup, a great bulb for naturalizing

'Flower Record': pure white perianth, deep red corona

'Fortune': rich golden yellow perianth, the corona a coppery orange-red

'Ice Follies': perianth pure white, the corona is flat and turns from a yellow hue to white; flowers last a long time

'Professor Einstein': white perianth, the orange corona serrated at the edge

Division 3, Small-cupped daffodils of garden origin, 12 to 18 inches

'Barrett Browning': pure white perianth, large, flat orange corona; an older cultivar and still one of the best

'Homefire': perianth is a good golden yellow, fine red cup

'Polar Ice': perianth pure white, cup is shaded green in the center

'Quirinus': soft lemon perianth, the cup is golden yellow with an orange-red edge; most attractive, long-lasting cut flower

Division 4, Double daffodils of garden origin, 12 to 18 inches

'Cheerfulness': lovely double flowers, very fragrant, yellow center

'Dick Walden': a good yellow, the center of the flowers a deeper yellow

'Erlicheer': a center of yellow surrounded by white

'Petit Four': the outer color is pale cream, the center pink-apricot; stunning

'Texas': yellow with brilliant orange, the heads so large that if they get wet, the flower stems have a hard time supporting them, but well worth growing, and super in containers

Division 5, Triandrus daffodils of garden origin, approximately 12 inches

'Hawera': only 8 inches in height, clear lemon yellow, perianth segments quite reflexed; bad weather does not bother this cultivar

'Petrel': each bulb will produce several stems, white form of 'Hawera'

'Thalia': snow white flowers, old but very good

Division 6, Cyclamineus daffodils of garden origin, 8 to 10 inches

'February Gold': long in cultivation, long in flower, great yellow and comes into flower in February

'February Silver': Much as previous cultivar, but with milk white flowers

'Jenny': the perianth segments are white and reflexed, the corona a soft white with a hint of yellow, one of the finest in this group

'Jetfire': the perianth segments are golden yellow, the corona a good orange; an unusual combination of colors, a very popular cultivar for pot culture

'Peeping Tom': a deep yellow, the corona is long and narrow.

'Tête à Tête': perianth segments are lemon yellow, the corona of a deeper color.

Division 7, Jonquilla daffodils of garden origin, 10 to 12 inches

'Baby Moon': fragrant, free-flowering, soft yellow

'Lintie': the perianth segments are rounded and yellow, fragrant, flat and edged bright orange

'Suzy': perianth yellow, corona a marvelous, intense orange

'Trevithian': yellow, very fragrant and a good cut flower. I have grown this in my garden for several years, and despite not having a good resting period, it comes back year after year.

Division 8, Tazetta daffodils of garden origin, 10 to 12 inches

'Cragford': perianth pure white, the cup a deep orange

'Geranium': fragrant, pure white with an orange corona (cup); one of the best in this group, always does well in containers and the garden

'Grand Soleil d'Or': good golden perianth with an orange cup, fragrant; this cultivar has been a favorite for many years

'Silver Chimes': perianth white, as is the corona (cup), but with a hint of yellow at the base

Division 9, Poeticus daffodils of garden origin, 10 to 12 inches

'Actaea': large snow-white perianth with a small yellow corona edged with red; flowers often more than 4 inches in diameter

'Sinopel': perianth white, the corona is distinctive with a deep yellow edge and noticeably green center

Division 10, Species, wild variants and wild hybrids.

Narcissus asturiensis: Native to northern Portugal and northwestern Spain, this plant grows on the higher slopes of mountains in well-drained soils. It is a perfect miniature of the large-trumpet types, deep golden yellow but only 4 inches in height, flowering in early spring. Flowers are borne singly and tend to look at the ground. Good in the rock garden.

This trumpet *Narcissus* ('Mount Hood'), with pure white flowers, is very reliable and a superb cut flower.

N. bulbocodium: The hoop petticoat narcissus is at home in Spain, Portugal and southwestern France. In this delightful species the outer perianth segments are nearly absent; the corona, narrow at the base, quickly flares into a wide-open flower. The flowers, yellow with a hint of orange, appear in March or April. This little species grows 8 to 10 inches in height and spreads quite rapidly.

N. canaliculatus: This native of southern Europe, including Sicily, is fragrant and reaches 8 inches. The perianth segments are white, the corona a rich yellow with a hint of orange. Flowers appear in April.

N. jonquilla: The common name is jonquil. Native to southern Spain and eastern Portugal, this species has long been cultivated for its fragrance. It has become naturalized in many places in southern Europe. Umbels of six golden yellow flowers appear on strong stems that reach a height of 12 inches. Flowers in March or April. The foliage is dark green and rushlike.

N. obvallaris: The Tenby daffodil was given this name because it escaped from gardens in southern Wales and now grows wild in that area. Precisely where it comes from is unknown. The flowers are bright yellow and reach 10 to 12 inches in height. A tough plant and a good choice for naturalizing.

N. tazetta: This native of the Mediterranean region, especially southern Portugal, is found growing in meadows, pastures and cultivated fields, determined to survive! It reaches 16 to 18 inches in height and produces as many as 15 fragrant flowers in a head. The flowers are yellow with a shallow yellow or orange corona. Cultivated for hundreds of years, there are numerous variants.

N. triandrus: Angel's tears is native to Spain, Portugal and northwestern France. The color varies from white to yellow, and the height from 6 to 12 inches. The number of flowers per stem can vary, too; there are generally 2 or 3, but they may be solitary. Perianth segments quite separated and narrow, cup small and very narrow at the base.

Division 11, Split-corona daffodils of garden origin
Sometimes these are listed as butterfly or orchid flowering.

'Marie Jose': perianth is creamy white, the corona split into 6 with an orange stripe in the center of each split portion, surrounded by white; 12 inches tall

'Orangery': perianth segments white, almost covered by the orange, split corona, which lies almost flat on top of the perianth segments; 18 inches tall

'Printal': perianth segments white, the split corona pale yellow. In addition to being split, the corona also is curled, giving a very full look. Earlier flowering than the others mentioned.

Division 12, Miscellaneous daffodils.

Few, if any, are offered in catalogs.

Botanical Name: Narcissus
Family: Amaryllidaceae
Common Names: Daffodil, jonquil
Flower Colors: Yellow, white, orange and pink
Flowering Time: From early in the year through spring
Height: 4 to 24 inches
Spread: Many will naturalize
Native Habitat: Europe, North Africa and western Asia
Hardiness: Hardy; in the coldest areas they may need protection. Tazetta types hardy to 10°F.

Depth of Planting: Twice the height of the bulb (most cultivars 8 inches)
Distance Apart: 4 to 6 inches
Containers: Yes
Light Requirements: Sun
Soil Type: Average, well-drained garden soil; potting soil in containers
Special Conditions: Naturalized plantings should be fed in spring as soon as their noses poke through the soil. Use a balanced formula.
Comments: No flower symbolizes spring quite as much as the daffodil. There should be space in every garden for them; if space is tight, grow some in pots. From the many different types there will no doubt be those that catch your fancy, so buy them! If space allows, naturalize them. It is best to lift and store the bulbs if you cannot give them a resting period in mid- to late summer. *Narcissus* are not for formal beds, but they are splendid in most other plantings.

A noble successor to the famed 'King Alfred', *Narcissus* 'Dutch Master' is as reliable and as strong a grower. The flowers seem to look right up at you, an admirable trait.

NECTAROSCORDUM
Amaryllidaceae

The drink of the Gods was *nektar* in Greek, and *scordion* means smelling of garlic. The foliage of *Nectaroscordum* smells of garlic when crushed. This is a small genus, closely related to *Allium*; indeed, the three species now in the genus were at one time in *Allium*. Native to the eastern Mediterranean, these easy-to-grow plants can be invasive, thriving in almost any soil. They like the sun, yet are very hardy. Usually only one species is listed, *Nectaroscordum siculum* (syn. *Allium siculum*). The flowers are green with purple and white markings on the petals (some a little more reddish than others), bell shaped and summer flowering. The leaves, if crushed, give forth a garlic smell.

Crush the foliage and you will understand why *Nectaroscordum siculum* was regarded as an *Allium* for many years. Inclined to be invasive, it will fill an area quickly.

The bulbs should be planted 2 inches deep and 18 inches apart. They will soon fill any space allowed to them, and appreciate moisture through winter up to flowering time. The seedpods are attractive and can be used in dried flower arrangements. The plants reach heights of up to 24 inches. I'm glad some nurseries offer these plants, but have a feeling *Nectaroscordum* won't win any popularity polls. Still, if you have a large area that you wish to see covered, this may be the species for you.

Botanical Name: Nectaroscordum
Family: Amaryllidaceae
Common Names: None known
Flower Colors: Green with purple and white margins
Flowering Time: June
Height: 24 inches
Spread: Can be invasive
Native Habitat: Southern France, Mediterranean region

Hardiness: Very hardy
Depth of Planting: 2 inches
Distance Apart: 18 inches
Containers: Yes
Light Requirements: Sun
Soil Type: Any soil
Special Conditions: None
Comments: As this has never has been a very popular plant, I am quite surprised to find the genus listed. If you are a keen plant person, then you should grow it, otherwise, only if you like invasive plants and have space for it.

NERINE
Amaryllidaceae

The name is from the Greek *Nereis*, the name of a mythological sea nymph. There are perhaps 20 species, and though few are listed, a number of hybrids are to be found in catalogs. A firm in Britain has available a good number of them, and while they are very attractive, I think it is going to be an uphill battle to make these plants popular. The bulbs are not hardy below around 20°F, demanding the protection of a cold greenhouse or frame, not within everyone's means. As they are good container plants, there is no reason any person wishing to grow them cannot do so.

The bulbs are native to South Africa. One species, *Nerine sarniensis* (which, with *N. bowdenii*, is a parent of many hybrids), has an interesting history. In 1659, a ship of the Dutch East India Company was on its way home to Holland. It ran into stormy weather and was wrecked. Among its cargo were crates of bulbs of *N. sarniensis*. Spilled into the sea, they washed up on the isle of Guernsey. I suppose they were happy to be saved, and took root in the sand—quite surprising, considering the salt content of beach sand. Once established, they worked their way inland

and prospered. They had earned their name of Guernsey lily.

There is considerable discussion over the recommended depth of planting. I like to plant them at or just a little below the surface of the soil. In cold climates they can be set a little deeper to give some added protection, but I think a 2-inch mulch would be preferable. Space the bulbs 12 inches apart, and give them sun and a well-drained spot. For containers, add some sharp sand to regular potting soil. As these bulbs flower in late summer or early fall, they should be planted in early summer, in June. The soil should be moist, but not at all wet. The flower spike will emerge in late summer, and then additional moisture will be needed. When the leaves emerge, the plants can be given a light feeding of balanced fertilizer. Keep moist until the foliage dies back in late spring. Then, allow the bulbs to become dry. Start to give a little moisture in June or early July, and the cycle begins all over again. In pots, plant so the neck of the bulb is at soil level. Follow the same procedures regarding moisture, but in colder areas bring indoors to protect from frost, or place in a frost-free greenhouse or frame. There is no need to repot. Just remove some of the soil and replace it with fresh mixture.

Nerine bowdenii: Native to the southwestern Cape. Perhaps the hardiest, this is the species I would suggest be the first grown. It is a lovely plant, 24 inches tall, with 10 to 15 flowers, each 6 inches or more in diameter. The blooms are carmine-pink, the petals have wavy edges, and the tip curls back a little. While there will be some leaf growth when the flowers appear in late summer, most of the growth is made after the flowers have passed. The flowers can be compared with those of *Hippeastrum,* except the petals are not as wide. With a good bud count, these flowers remain attractive over a long period of

Nerine bowdenii has it all: great color, superb lasting power as a cut flower, free flowering and easy to grow. An added attraction is its late-summer flowering time and the ability to grow superbly in containers.

time. This species is a good cut flower and grows well in containers.

N. sarniensis: The Guernsey lily grows on the slopes of Table Mountain above Cape Town, and during winter and spring will often be in fog. The flower color varies from white to deep carmine. It appears iridescent under electric light, one reason it is so admired by florists. As many as 10 rather large flowers appear atop a 24-inch stem, with stamens that thrust forward. It requires the same cultural treatment as *N. bowdenii*. A number of selections or hybrids are listed, among them: 'Cherry Ripe', rose-red; 'Early Snow', a pure white; 'Radiant Queen', a rose-pink; and 'Salmon Supreme', a good, salmon pink.

It is perhaps not surprising that crosses have been made between *Nerine* and *Amaryllis*, as the flowers are quite similar in appearance. To my knowledge none of these intergeneric hybrids is grown today, but given the beauty of these flowers I can well understand the enthusiasm of those raising hybrids. Perhaps we will soon enjoy new and exciting hybrids from the late-summer—flowering genera—certainly the potential is there.

Botanical Name: Nerine
Family: Amaryllidaceae
Common Name: Guernsey lily
Flower Colors: White, rose, deep carmine
Flowering Time: Late summer, early fall
Height: 24 inches
Spread: Will spread in time if left undisturbed
Native Habitat: South Africa
Hardiness: Not hardy; grow outdoors in relatively frost-free areas
Depth of Planting: 3 inches
Distance Apart: 12 inches
Containers: Yes
Light Requirements: Sun
Soil Type: Average, well-drained garden soil
Special Conditions: The plants need a dry period after the foliage has died down; moisture needed during the growing period.
Comments: One of the grandest sights is *Nerine* in full glory. While I have seen them grown outdoors in warmer climate zones, I feel these plants look far better in containers. It is easier to appreciate their beauty and flower form in pots, as they never quite seem to stand out with authority in the garden. The flowers last a long time and merit attention.

While inclined to be a little untidy, *Ornithogalum nutans* 'Silver Bells' is tough, easy to grow and quite showy for many weeks.

ORNITHOGALUM
Liliaceae

The name comes from the Greek *ornis*, meaning a bird, and *gala*, meaning milk, used by Dioscorides. These plants have quite a wide distribution; they are found in the temperate climates of Africa, Europe and Asia. Certain species are quite hardy. *Ornithogalum umbellatum*, for example, the star of Bethlehem, is found in Great Britain and much of Europe. In the United States the same common name refers to *O. thyrsoides*, perhaps because the British common name of this species, chincherinchee (an onomatopoeic expression of the sound made when stems of this species are rubbed together) is difficult to pronounce. Many times I have stood in fields of this species covering well over 10 acres, watching the stems being cut for shipment to all parts of the world. *Ornithogalum* is an easy flower to ship, and highly valued for cutting, especially, for some reason, in Japan.

The hardiness of these bulbs depends on the species, so I have described their hardiness (or lack of it) under the species headings. Plant the bulbs 3 inches deep and space them 12 inches apart. If growing for cut flowers, plant them 4 inches apart in rows; in borders, clump them. A sandy, well-drained soil suits them all. They need moisture when the foliage is growing, then can be allowed to dry out a little. They all appreciate sun. Almost without exception, they produce numerous offsets and will form sizeable clumps in a few seasons. They grow well in containers, the dwarf species being particularly appropriate. Container plantings are a good way to enjoy them in colder areas, or lift and store them over the winter just as you would *Gladiolus*. It is only a question of time before these plants are more commonly grown as cut flowers, as they are practically trouble free.

With the exception of some species from South Africa, the flowers are white with a green stripe in the petals, and held in a spike. Some South African species are in the orange-red-yellow range. I have seen some lovely colors in new hybrid selections not yet on the market. Species cross readily. Seed can be sown for flower in just three seasons, a comparatively short period of time.

Interestingly, the Greeks eat the shoots of *O. pyrenaicum* as we would eat asparagus. I understand the bulbs are quite palatable when boiled, though I have not tried them.

Ornithogalum arabicum: Native to the Mediterranean area, this species flowers in May. The white flowers have a conspicuous black ovary visible in the center. Many flowers are held in a spike, the lower ones on long pedicels and the upper ones on shorter pedicels, a well-formed head. The plants often grow more than 20 inches tall, but never much more than 30. It is said that if the cut stems are waxed, this flower will last several months in arrangements, but I question this. This species is not hardy, so do not expose to frost. It is a great plant for containers or the cool greenhouse; or, plant in spring, lift in fall and protect over winter.

O. balansae: This dwarf species from Turkey reaches only 6 inches. The flowers, white with a green reverse to the petals, appear from March to May. This species can withstand some frost, but not temperatures of 25°F and colder.

O. narbonense: From Turkey and Iran, it grows 12 to 18 inches, with white or creamy flowers with a wide green stripe on the outside of the petals. The plants produce a good number of flowers per stem, but they are not very large. Flowers in early June. This species is not very hardy, but will withstand some frost.

O. nutans: Silver bells are native to many parts of southern Europe, and the plants have spread over much of Europe. Hardy to +10°F with the protection of a good mulch. There are as many as 12 flowers on each spike, reaching to 18 inches, and as the flowers are held close to the stem, the effect is quite striking. The green midrib to the back of the petals is more pronounced here than in other species. This is a good border plant, and I would suggest it might be the first species to grow. Flowers in late spring. Pop 5 bulbs in a clump and try them in different parts of the garden. Where they do best, increase the planting.

O. saundersiae: The giant chincherinchee comes from Natal and Swaziland. Rather rare, it is listed in a few catalogs. This species should be grown only in warm climates, or in a greenhouse where temperatures never fall below freezing. Reaching up to 36 inches in height, it is a strong grower. The flowers are ivory with green-black centers, and are held almost flat. This plant can be treated as a gladiolus; planted in spring, it will flower some 5 months later.

O. thyrsoides: Chincherinchee is native to the southwestern Cape. By far the majority grown are white, but in the wild yellow forms are known. The cup-shaped flowers are crowded together on 24-inch spikes. Not hardy, but can be planted in spring, lifted in fall and overwintered. The plants need free drainage but appreciate summer moisture. Early summer flowering, obviously much later when planted in spring after the frosts have passed.

O. umbellatum: The star of Bethlehem is native to Europe, including Great Britain. This is the hardiest species, able to withstand temperatures down to 10°F. The white flowers sport a green stripe on the reverse, but this becomes almost hidden when the flowers are wide open. The plants reach 6 to 8 inches, flowering in April or May. One of the unusual features is that the flowers open in the afternoon and close again at night. Despite this activity, the flowers last a long time. This little bulb is a good one for the front of the border or the rock garden, and also rather fun in containers. It will self-sow and can become invasive, but only if it is very happy. While not a tall plant, it often will produce as many as 20 flowers, so it is of interest for quite a long period of time.

Botanical Name: Ornithogalum
Family: Liliaceae
Common Names: Chincherinchee, great chincherinchee, silver bells, star of Bethlehem

Flower Colors: Most plants listed in catalogs are white with green stripes
Flowering Time: Spring, early summer; later in summer from spring planting, as when grown in colder areas
Height: Varies by species; 8 to 24 inches
Spread: Some can be quite invasive
Native Habitat: South Africa, Mediterranean area, Europe
Hardiness: Varies by species; many not hardy, some quite hardy
Depth of Planting: 3 inches
Distance Apart: 12 inches; smaller species can be closer
Containers: Yes
Light Requirements: Sun
Soil Type: Average, well-drained soil
Special Conditions: None
Comments: The hardier species are well worth growing, and I would like to see *O. thyrsoides* more widely grown as a cut flower. The potential of colored hybrids is great. I think these plants can rival *Alstroemeria* as cut flowers, as they are certainly as attractive and as long lasting. Perhaps a sleeper as far as potential as a commercial crop is concerned.

OXALIS
Oxalidaceae

The Greek name for sharp (as regards taste) is *oxys*, and for salt, *als*. The genus name refers to the flavor of the sap of these plants. One of the common names is sorrel (not to be confused with the sorrel from which an excellent soup is made; this is a species of *Rumex*, and not a bulb). This very large genus comes mainly from the warmer parts of the world, from South Africa, and tropical and subtropical America. Many species are not bulbous, and many species are very invasive. *Oxalis cernua* has become an invasive weed in parts of California, where the bright yellow flowers can be seen in waste areas and thriving in very harsh conditions. Were it not so invasive, it would be much sought after! These plants make great groundcovers, but make sure you can keep them under control.

When confined to cracks between pavings or planted in hanging baskets, these are great little plants. They are not fussy as to soil, and will grow in sun and shade, but flower best when they enjoy sun. They do not like heavy clays. Plant 1 inch deep and space 3 to 4 inches apart. In containers, use regular potting soil. Color ranges from white and yellow to pink and crimson, but the flowers open only in the sunshine. The kernel of the bulb, though small, is fleshy and rich in a fine-grained starch that animals like to eat and native people in South Africa grind and give to children to control tapeworm. While the leaves are eaten in salads by some, I understand that if too many are eaten they can be harmful.

Some species and selections may reach 12 inches in height, but most plants carry their flowers at ground level. Certain species are very free-flowering, quite attractive when grown in small pots.

Oxalis adenophylla: This species is at home in Argentina and Chile. It is found growing above the tree line in the Andes, and is a very hardy plant. Dwarf, only 2 to 4 inches in height, it produces tight rosettes of leaves, and flowers in early to midsummer. The color is attractive, white with touches of pink and with a distinct, purple center to the singly borne flowers. It loves the sun and is ideal for a crack in a wall, rock garden or pot. If you can plant it where it can be seen at eye level, so much the better. When I was younger I would stoop over to see such plants; now I prefer to plant them where less effort is needed to admire them!

Oxalis adenophylla forms a neat and compact mound, low growing and extremely hardy. It is a joy to see covered with quite large flowers with various shades of pink. Wonderful in small pots. (Photo courtesy of International Bloembollen Centrum.)

O. cernua: I list this only so that when you have the chance to visit California in February or March, you will know what the yellow flower is that grows all over the place. It is called the Bermuda buttercup, yet it comes from South Africa. With bright green leaves, and very free-flowering, each little bulb will take off and give an outstanding performance.

O. deppei: The good luck plant, or four-leaved clover, comes from Mexico. The rose-colored flowers appear in an umbel. This species reaches 12 inches in height and flowers in June or July. The leaves often have a prominent marking in and form the shape of an Iron Cross, and sometimes the plant is listed as the Iron Cross plant. This plant does well in containers, and for several years I used to have fun judging plants grown as a competition by Kelly Girls (temporary help). Some plants that were produced were lush and most attractive, and so were the competitors!

O. purpurea: This is another native of South Africa, with reddish purple flowers, with a good yellow eye. The plants grow 1 to 2 inches in height, and flower in late summer and into fall, and can continue for several months. This is a plant for only the warmest climates. Pink and white forms are known, but seldom listed. These plants are often grown indoors, and are most attractive.

O. regnellii: From South Africa, this is an unusual species as the rootstock is a rhizome, not a bulb. It can become quite a problem as it is inclined to be invasive in the garden. It makes a great houseplant, where it is confined and cannot ramble. The white star-shaped flowers are carried above lush foliage to a height of 10 inches. The species is white, but you will find pink forms sometimes listed. Summer flowering.

O. versicolor: Another species from the Cape Province of South Africa. This is an unusual plant: The flowers are white and somewhat trumpet-shaped; in bud they exhibit red-and-white striping, marking found on the backs of the petals when the flowers open. The plants grow to 4 inches in height, flowering in late summer into fall. They will stand some frost, but not below 15°F. In colder climates grow this as a container plant. The foliage is attractive, and because of the striping these plants are often known as "candy cane."

Botanical Name: Oxalis
Family: Oxalidaceae
Common Names: Sorrel, candy cane
Flower Colors: White, yellow, pink, crimson
Flowering Time: Varies by species: some spring, others summer and into fall
Height: Seldom over 12 inches
Spread: Some species can become invasive
Native Habitat: South America, South Africa
Hardiness: Varies by species
Depth of Planting: 1 inch
Distance Apart: 3 to 4 inches
Containers: Yes
Light Requirements: Sun
Soil Type: Average garden soil; some thrive in poor soils
Special Conditions: None
Comments: In the right place, certain species are great plants. Many are good container plants and provide a great deal of interest for many weeks. Not at all difficult to grow, and as they grow quickly they are good fun for children.

PANCRATIUM
Amaryllidaceae

Dioscorides gave this plant the name *pankration*, derived from the Greek *pan*, meaning all, and *kratos*, meaning strength. Of this small genus, only one species is ever listed in catalogs, *Pancratium maritimum*. This is found growing in many areas around the Mediterranean, the Black Sea and in Portugal. The common names are sea lily and sea daffodil. It is found in sandy soil along the coastlines. The flowers have a wonderful fragrance. They resemble daffodils. The outer segments curl back and the stamens broaden at the base and form the cup, which is quite deep and large. Twelve pointed tips arise from the lip of the cup. The color is pure white, and the plants are evergreen in warm (frost-free, or nearly so) areas.

Pancratium bulbs, not fully hardy and resentful of being lifted, should be grown in containers in areas where frost is experienced. In frost-free areas they are great garden plants, flowering in midsummer. Well-drained soil, not particularly rich, is ideal. When growing in containers, add sharp sand to regular potting soil. Once planted in containers or in the garden, leave them alone for several years.

The bulbs are large. Plant them with just an inch or two of soil over the bulbs, and space them 12 inches apart in the garden. Plant one bulb per 12-inch pot, this may sound like rather a large pot (even though the bulbs are large), but allowances have to be made for the numerous offsets produced, and these plants hate disturbance, which can mean loss of flower production. The stems grow up to 24 inches tall. This plant must have warmth or it will not produce flowers. Make certain it has a warm spot in the garden, and do not place containers in the shade. Some catalogs advise that the plants be lifted and stored over winter in temperatures in the 60°F range. I feel this is a mistake, because when the leaves are growing on, lifting the plant gives it a nasty shock. It is far better to grow them in pots and, if necessary, plunge the pots into the ground in the border—much less stressful to the plant.

While not demanding of a great deal of moisture, these evergreen plants should never be allowed to be completely dry. When growth is active, moisture is needed.

Botanical Name: Pancratium
Family: Amaryllidaceae
Common Names: Sea lily, sea daffodil
Flower Colors: White
Flowering Time: Late summer into early fall
Height: 24 inches

Professor Arne Strid of the University of Copenhagen notes that *Pancratium maritimum*, which can be found on many sandy beaches in Greece, is becoming endangered due to excessive development. I hope that in other areas where it grows wild it is given the respect it deserves. (Photo courtesy of Dr. Maurice Boussard.)

Spread: Will increase in time, but slowly.
Native Habitat: Around the Mediterranean, the Black Sea and Portugal
Hardiness: Not hardy, but will take a little and occasional frost
Depth of Planting: 1 to 2 inches of soil over top of bulb
Distance Apart: 12 inches
Containers: Yes
Light Requirements: Sun
Soil Type: Average, well-drained garden soil
Special Conditions: Hates disturbance
Comments: I am in a quandary about this plant. Grown well, it is a superb addition to any garden, mainly for its fragrance. While the flowers are not unattractive, a daffodillike flower in late summer does not fit in the garden. As a container plant, it is superb and well worth growing.

Few flowers have as much fragrance as the tuberose *Polianthes tuberosa*. It must have warmth and be on the dry side to do well, not unusual perhaps for a plant native to Mexico. (Photo courtesy of Dr. Alfred Byrd Graf.)

POLIANTHES
Agavaceae

The name is logically derived from the Greek *polios*, meaning white, and *anthos*, meaning flower. One of the few species in this genus, *Polianthes tuberosa* has been a very popular cut flower since the sixteenth century. While, given the delightful fragrance of the flowers and their long-lasting qualities, this should not be surprising, it is a surprise because these bulbs are native to Mex-ico. This speaks a lot for the toughness of these bulbs, that they could survive rather primitive transportation and what must have been a considerable shock to their systems. It is interesting to think how skilled the gardeners were, and obviously these bulbs were propagated and sold way back then. A point that often goes unappreciated is the debt we owe to earlier growers. The common name of this plant is tuberose.

This genus was for many years in Amaryllidaceae, but now is in Agavaceae, and I think this is about the only bulb listed in catalogs in this family. The white, tubular flowers grow on a spike, carried in pairs in the axils of the bracts. When open, the flowers reach 2 inches or more in diameter. Their bases form a tube, and they have a waxy appearance. The leaves are basal.

The bulbs should be planted 3 inches deep and spaced 8 to 10 inches apart. They must have sun and a warm location. Plant only when the ground is warm. I have had difficulty getting these bulbs off to a good start. I planted them too early in the year, not thinking of their native habitat and planting them as soon as they became available. By all means, purchase the bulbs as soon as you can in spring, but start them off under protection, in a greenhouse or a frame. Keep them barely moist. When growth has started, plant them out in beds. They are not hardy, and should not be grown where more than occasional frost is experienced. In warm areas they are great garden plants, and just a few spikes will give lovely fragrance to an entire home. *Polianthes* will grow in average garden soil; in containers, use regular potting soil. They are good container plants, and this is the way to grow them in colder areas. Otherwise, lift them at the end of summer, store them over winter and plant again in spring. Take care; as the bulbs seem always to split after flowering, they may not flower year after year. For this reason I suggest that you plant some each year.

If they are happy in their location, these flowers can be carried on stems that reach 36 inches, but most will be 24 inches tall. One of the great features of these flower spikes is that all the flowers will open, even if in very tight bud when cut. Obviously this is a great advantage when used in arrangements.

The most commonly grown selection is the cultivar 'The Pearl', a double-flowered selection long in cultivation. 'Double Excelsior' is another. Sometimes there are listings for the straight species, which might be described as 'Single Tuberose' or 'Single Mexican Everlasting'.

Botanical Name: Polianthes
Family: Agavaceae
Common Names: Tuberose
Flower Colors: White
Flowering Time: Midsummer
Height: 24 to 36 inches
Spread: Will multiply in time
Native Habitat: Mexico
Hardiness: Not hardy; will take some frost, but not for outdoor growing in areas where long, hard frosts are experienced
Depth of Planting: 3 inches
Distance Apart: 8 to 10 inches
Containers: Yes
Light Requirements: Sun
Soil Type: Average, well-drained garden soil
Special Conditions: Soil must be warm at planting time; do not plant too early, or the bulbs will not perform.
Comments: When in full flower these plants are among the most fragrant imaginable, and they are worth growing for that feature. Great container plants, they can be lifted and stored over winter in a frost-free area, but quite honestly, I question the practicality of this, given their propensity to split after flowering. Either plant some each year and leave in the ground, or purchase new stock each year. Savings when compared with work involved and the bulbs' habit of splitting makes such work of dubious value.

PUSCHKINIA
Liliaceae

A glance at the name is enough to reveal its Russian origins. The genus was named after Count Apollos Apollosvich Mussin-Puskin, a botanist who collected plants in the Caucasus. Despite the count's long name, this is a small genus, and only one species, *Puschkinia scilloides*, is listed in catalogs. This species is widely found, in Turkey, Iran, Syria, Iraq and Lebanon, as well as the aforementioned Caucasus. These bulbs often grow at altitudes over 10,000 feet, so perhaps it is not necessary to state that they are hardy.

Well-drained, moisture-retentive soil with organic matter is required, and sun is essential. Plant the bulbs 2 inches deep and 6 inches apart. Ensure that they have moisture from fall right up until the foliage dies back, which will be quite

Puschkinia scilloides is a tough plant, for all that its color is such a delicate, light blue. *Puschkinia* are good container plants and perfect for filling odd corners of the garden. (Photo courtesy of International Bloembollen Centrum.)

late in spring, into early summer. The flowers appear in April or May, depending on local climates, and the foliage continues to grow long after the flowers have passed. Planted in small pots, these bulbs perform well; it is an advantage that the species commonly grown produces only two leaves, and thus the bulbs, planted quite close together, put on quite a display with their lovely blue flowers. After the flowers have finished blooming, the pots can be set outdoors long before the foliage reaches the point of being untidy.

As many as six flowers are carried on each flowering stem. Every flower grows on a short pedicel, but as the stems reach only 6 to 8 inches in height, these plants should be placed at the front of the border where they can be appreciated. In the center of each flower is what appears to be a little dome, formed by the filaments of the stamens; this is quite prominent. The flowers are one inch in diameter.

The bulbs can remain in containers for at least two seasons before they need to be repotted. In the ground, let them alone as long as they are happy; in time they will give you pleasing little colonies. If you wish to propagate, lift, remove the offsets and replant in early summer before the foliage has dried completely. Although you should never let the plants dry out completely, they can be on the dry side after the foliage has died back. One of the rather unusual things about these plants is that they will frequently seed themselves. For that reason, take care when weeding around these plants—you do not want to pull up the little puschkinias!

Botanical Name: Puschkinia
Family: Liliaceae
Common Names: Sometimes called squill
Flower Color: Blue
Flowering Time: Spring
Height: To 8 inches

Spread: Will form little colonies in a few seasons
Native Habitat: Turkey, Caucasus, Syria, Iran, Iraq and Lebanon
Hardiness: Very hardy
Depth of Planting: 2 inches
Distance Apart: 6 inches
Containers: Yes
Light Requirements: Sun
Soil Type: Average garden soil
Special Conditions: Allow the foliage to continue growing after the flowers are finished.
Comments: I love these little plants—so easy to grow, so dainty and tidy with just two leaves. Their frail look is deceiving. Do give them sun; they try hard when in shade, but obviously need and miss the sun. I am always sad to see plants putting on a brave show in locations that are not ideal for them, and then hear gardeners say that the plants are not much to look at!

RANUNCULUS
Ranunculaceae

Pliny used the name, deriving it from the Latin *rana*, meaning frog, because many of the species in this genus like damp places. There are not many species that are bulbous. In the case of the popular hybrids derived from *Ranunculus asiaticus*, the rootstock is a tuber, but unlike many other tubers, they have no objection to being dried. This species is native to Asia Minor. I must mention the lovely species that grows on Mt. Cook in the south island of New Zealand. Although *R. lyallii* has a rhizomatous rootstock, for some reason this plant is very difficult to grow in cultivation. The pure white flowers are more than 4 inches in diameter, and in the wild the plants spread themselves over a wide area, growing almost without competition from any other plants, in shallow, peaty soil at quite high elevations. If this species has not been used in hybridizing, it should be.

Although there is a simple classification that distinguishes between the French, peony-flowered, Persian and turban types, based on the form and size of the flowers, most ranunculus listed in catalogs are offered by color. The colors are rich tones of gold, pink, red, rose, orange, white, yellow and mixed. Two strains are head and shoulders above all others, the Hadeco and Tecolote strains, with a high percentage of double flowers. The mixture of colors in the "mixed" offerings is nicely varied.

I have had the privilege of seeing many acres of these plants in full flower. The most knowledgeable growers do not let them remain in flower for long, but send a deheading machine up and down the rows as soon as they have been able to check the mixture of colors This stops the plants from producing seed, and the root-stocks are better nourished and larger. In my garden, I like to set ranunculus tubers randomly among other spring-flowering annuals. But I live in an area that is usually frost free. In areas where the temperature falls below 15°F in winter, spring planting for summer color is the way to go. To plant a bed uniquely with ranunculus, I recommend you plant them in a formal manner: Space them 6 inches apart in rows 8 inches, but stagger the rows. Set the tubers 3 inches deep. The plants themselves are rather informal in appearance, and while the rows can be made out, the plants will grow up into a pretty mass of flowers. When the plants have finished flowering, they will lie down. They can quickly become untidy. Some gardeners say tubers should be lifted, dried and planted again, but I question this. The cost of purchasing new tubers is not great (for the price of a good meal, you can purchase all you will need). There is always work to be done in the garden, and saving ranunculus tubers is low on my list of priorities! In warm (frost-free

The best way to grow *Ranunculus* 'Hadeco Strain' is to crowd them together; the effect is spectacular. It takes years of careful selection to obtain such a high quality strain as this.

or nearly so) areas you can leave them in the ground. They will grow again the following year, but as they sprawl or flop when old, I think it best to lift and discard.

The plants reach 18 to 24 inches in height. The good strains are in flower for a long time. Do not expect the flowers to be exactly the same shades. Some will be lighter, some darker. I do not recall seeing these plants put on a good show in small containers, but in large ones (more than 24 inches across) they look fine. Ordinary potting soil should be used. These plants should not be allowed to become dry. A further word of warning is in order. As mentioned above, once these plants start to fade, they soon become quite untidy. You should have another batch of plants ready to plant, especially if the bed is in a prominent location. It is for this reason I prefer to plant ranunculus with other flowers. This is of greater importance in warm climates, where these plants are not at their best for as long as they are in cooler climes.

Botanical Name: Ranunculus

Family: Ranunculaceae

Common Names: Colored buttercups, ranunculus

Flower Colors: Red, rose, pink, orange, gold, yellow, white and mixed

Flowering Time: Depends on planting time; spring from fall planting, summer from spring planting

Height: 18 to 24 inches

Spread: Will not spread much

Native Habitat: Modern hybrids derived from many species

Hardiness: Not very hardy; plant in fall in frost-free (or nearly so) areas, in spring in colder climates.

Depth of Planting: 3 inches

Distance Apart: 6 inches

Containers: In large containers only

Light Requirements: Sun

Soil Type: Average garden soil

Special Conditions: Do not let them dry out

Comments: These flowers put on quite a display, but the most you can expect from them is about six weeks of good color, so select the areas where you are going to grow them with care, and either plant them among other plants or have another crop ready to pop in as soon as these become untidy. These are good cut flowers, a point often overlooked. I would not attempt to make these plants the main attraction of a garden, but they are great plants nevertheless.

It is pleasing to see low-growing *Rhodohypoxis baurii* being used as container plants, but they are great garden plants as well (unappreciative, however, of frost).

RHODOHYPOXIS
Hypoxidaceae

The name is from the Greek *rhodon*, meaning rose, and *hypo*, meaning under, no doubt because these charming little plants grow under most other plants. Reference is made in literature to "flower relationship," but I don't know what is meant by this. The rootstock is like a corm and, as with everything else about these plants, very small. Though small, these plants stand head and shoulders above many other bulbous plants. They are easy to grow, with lots of pleasing flowers that remain a joy for many weeks. In recent years nurseries have been growing these plants in very small pots and selling them in full flower. *Rhodohypoxis* are deserving of a place in many gardens, and in every home. They are great value for the money, flowering from spring through summer.

There is disagreement concerning the number of species in the genus. Some authorities feel that there is only one, *Rhodohypoxis baurii*. This is the only species you will find listed in catalogs, along with the selection 'Appleblossom', an apt description of the lovely soft pink flowers.

Rhodohypoxis is native to South Africa, where it grows high in the Drakensberg Mountains. Although there the plants will, from time to time, be covered with snow, I would not try to grow them in regions where temperatures drop below 10°F in winter. As they are superb container plants, the task of moving them indoors to a warm place should not present much difficulty.

The plants reach only 3 inches in height. The little, hairy leaves clothe the stem, on top of which sits a lovely flower in shades ranging from white to deep pink. The individual flowers may be more than an inch in diameter, opening to be quite flat. Each plant will produce a number of flowering stems. Plant an inch deep, 3 to 5 inches apart in the border, closer together in a container. They like well-drained soil and sun. If possible, keep them on the dry side during winter, and give moisture during the spring and summer months. Never allow the soil to become waterlogged, or you will kill them. Plant in bold clumps and leave the plants undisturbed.

Botanical Name: Rhodohypoxis
Family: Hypoxidaceae
Common Names: None to my knowledge
Flower Colors: White to pink to crimson
Flowering Time: Spring through summer
Height: 3 inches
Spread: Will spread to form quite large colonies
Native Habitat: Drakensberg Mountains, South Africa
Hardiness: To about 10°F
Depth of Planting: 1 inch
Distance Apart: 3 to 4 inches
Containers: Yes
Light Requirements: Full sun
Soil Type: Average, well-drained garden soil; appreciates peaty soil

Special Conditions: Keep the plants on the dry side during winter
Comments: One of the loveliest of the low-growing bulbs, these plants rival creeping phlox in effect. I suggest that, as well as growing them in containers, rock gardens, and the front of borders, you try slipping some into cracks in stone walls, and any other such niches.

SCADOXUS
Amaryllidaceae

This genus was formed when plants in the genus *Haemanthus* were examined, and it was decided to separate those that carry their foliage on an elongated stem (rather than emerging directly from the bulb). There are several species, all coming from Africa, both tropical and Mediterranean climates. Only one species, *Scadoxus multiflorus*, will be found listed in catalogs. This is the most attractive species. Strangely, it is not the flowers that are beautiful, but the multitude of stamens and their filaments forming a veritable pincushion of red tipped with gold, and as the flower heads mature they become globe shaped. The bulbs are large and fleshy. They do not like to be disturbed, and require a resting period (though not a dry period). I have seen these bulbs in full glory at Victoria Falls, in the rainforest, where in most years they will scarcely see a day without rain. They enjoy very warm temperatures in summer, and I doubt whether they ever experience temperatures below 50°F. Perhaps it is stating the obvious to say these plants are not hardy!

I have grown *Scadoxus* in my garden in San Francisco. They gave a good account of themselves the first year, flowering well and remaining in flower for quite a long time. It is interesting that after skipping a year, these bulbs flowered in 1993. It would appear that in the first season

Scadoxus multiflorus ssp. *katharinae* is not as commonly grown as it should be. In my garden in San Francisco it is a joy to behold for two months. It makes an excellent container plant for cold climates.

root growth and accommodate the offsets that are produced. Do not repot completely; instead, remove the top few inches of soil, down to where the roots are, and replace it with good potting soil.

Scadoxus multiflorus ssp. katherinae: Native to South Africa, Swaziland and Zimbabwe, it reaches 24 inches in height, with a flower head 10 inches in diameter. Bloom is long lasting, usually starting in early summer, but can be later. The foliage persists for much of the summer. Ssp. *multiflorus* has a somewhat smaller flower head of a deeper crimson.

Only in the warmest climates would I try *Scadoxus* in the border, and then only where moisture is available during their growing season. Keep the area as humid as possible when growing in containers. You can place the pot on gravel in a saucer filled with water, for example, or tuck moist, green sphagnum moss around the top of the pot. Misting with fine spray is also a good idea. These flowers are exotic looking, and if you like unusual and fun plants, I think you will enjoy having a shot at growing them.

of growth here in this country, they tried to flower during the same time of the year as they would in their native habitat, September to early October through to November, which is early summer in their home. Then they skipped a year, making good growth and producing foliage, but no flower. Finally, they flowered at the right season, early summer, coming into flower in June. I would expect that from now on, having adapted themselves, they will flower each year at this time. Plant the bulbs with their necks at soil level or slightly below, spacing them 12 inches apart, in sun or light shade. Soil must be free-draining. These plants can be grown in containers, but the pots should be of sufficient size to allow for good

Botanical Name: Scadoxus
Family: Amaryllidaceae
Common Names: Pincushion flower, shaving brush flower
Flower Colors: Shades of crimson
Flowering Time: Early summer, can be later
Height: 24 inches
Spread: Will increase, but slowly
Native Habitat: South Africa, Swaziland and Zimbabwe
Hardiness: Not hardy; will not withstand frost
Depth of Planting: Neck at soil level
Distance Apart: 12 inches
Containers: Large containers only
Light Requirements: Sun or very high shade

Soil Type: Rich, well-drained soil

Special Conditions: Prefers to be warm at all times; the range of 40° to 95°F is ideal.

Comments: In their native habitat the flowers are fantastic, and with Victoria Falls as a backdrop they make a breathtaking sight. I have not yet worked out why these plants are bulbs, as they do not seem to have any harsh conditions to contend with. Their needs are for much moisture and warmth, and in the rainforest they colonize by the hundreds; in dryer areas they are more scattered, seldom more than 3 or 4 in a clump.

SCILLA
Liliaceae

The word *scilla*, which means to wound or harm, was used by Hippocrates to describe the plants in this genus, a reference to the poison contained in their roots. *Scilla* is a large genus found in Africa and many parts of Europe. Recent studies have resulted in the genus being broken into several genera. The English bluebell, for example, has been moved to *Hyacinthoides*. Still remaining in *Scilla* are several important species that are great garden plants. All of them are quite easy to grow, thriving in well-drained garden soil with a good humus content. For the most part the species appreciate some shade, especially during the warmest parts of the day.

The bulbs of *Scilla natalensis* and *S. peruviana* are very large. These should be planted with the top of the bulbs at or just above soil level. The other species should be planted 3 to 4 inches deep. Space them 6 or 12 inches apart (according to the bulb size). All species enjoy moisture while in active growth, with a dryer resting period afterward. Once *Scilla* are established, leave them undisturbed for years. The South African species are not hardy, but fortunately they are great container plants, the best way to grow these bulbs

Delightful and charming, little *Scilla tubergeniana* are best grown in large plantings, as individually grown they are too small, albeit beautiful. (Photo courtesy of International Bloembollen Centrum.)

in colder areas. I wish more gardeners would grow *S. natalensis*, as even a single plant puts on quite a show. In its native habitat, I have seen these growing between cracks in rocks, and thriving!

Scilla bifolia: This species is found in Europe and Asia Minor. In its native habitat it frequently comes into flower right when the snows melt. Regarded as one of the finest spring-flowering bulbs, this species is often listed in catalogs. As the name suggests, it produces two leaves. The flower spike is 6 to 8 inches tall, and despite this rather low height will carry as many as eight flowers, each 1 inch in diameter, of a lovely blue. Forms with lighter colors are known, and a rose-colored form is sometimes listed. The best situation for these plants is a woodland area or among shrubs that can give it some, but not too much, shade. It flowers in very early spring, February or March.

S. natalensis: Native to South Africa, this is one of the most exciting species in the genus. I have seen spikes reach well over 48 inches tall, but in the garden 36 inches is more likely. Unfortunately, it is not hardy, but is nonetheless worthy of being grown in a container in colder areas so it can be brought inside for protection from winter frosts. The bulbs are very large. The light blue flowers begin to appear in early summer. When the first flowers open, the flower head is quite compressed; it elongates as the flowers develop. The foliage is short at flowering time, but becomes quite long and strap-shaped. The flowering period spans 3 to 4 weeks, so the total yield of flowers must number in the hundreds.

S. peruviana: You might think that this bulb comes from Peru, but it comes from Spain and Portugal. Apparently someone told Linnaeus that the bulbs were on a ship that came from Peru, so the plant was given the name *peruviana*; what was not said was that the ship had stopped in Spain on its way, and the bulbs were put on board then—an interesting point.

Not fully hardy, this scilla has been grown at Sissinghurst, England, so clearly it can take some frost. I doubt it can survive temperatures lower than 15°F. It might be worth trying in colder areas with a hefty mulch over it in winter months, but I suggest you do this only when you have a few bulbs to spare. It is an excellent container plant. The lovely blue spike of flowers appears in early summer. The head of the spike grows as the flowers develop, being quite compact when the first flowers open. It will reach 18 to 24 inches. There is a lovely white form, and I remember seeing both the blue and white forms side by side in a Spanish garden right on the

Mediterranean coast, a glorious planting that had extended to cover a considerable area, but the blue was the stronger grower. The foliage is quite fleshy in appearance and consists of many strap-shaped leaves.

S. pratensis (syn. *S. litardierei,* sometimes listed under this name): Native to Yugoslavia, these flowers are blue with a hint of lilac, May flowering. A compact-looking plant at 8 to 12 inches tall, it features erect foliage and solid, strong flower stems. The flowers are freely produced, often with several stems per bulb. The species can withstand frost if given a sheltered location and a good covering of mulch in winter.

S. siberica: The Siberian squill is native to Iran, Turkey and the Caucasus. A popular spring-flowering bulb, especially the form 'Spring Beauty' with vivid blue flowers, the squill blooms in March. The flowers are pendant, and as the spikes reach only 4 to 5 inches, one is always looking down at this plant. Because it is so small, it must be planted in bold clumps. It likes cool growing conditions, such as areas shaded by shrubs. These little plants are wonderful when crowded together and grown in containers. The flowers appear before the foliage has made much growth, so they only become untidy after the flowers have finished putting on their show. There is a white form, often listed as 'Alba', not nearly as attractive as the regular blue types.

S. tubergeniana: This has recently been given the name *S. mischtschenkoana* (which I seem to recall was the name of a Russian general—the old name is easier to pronounce!) Native to Iran and the Caucasus, it is a hardy species. Again, as with other dwarf species, plant a good number in a clump for these bulbs to make a show. Each bulb sends up 3 or 4 spikes, which reach 4 to 5 inches in height, flowering in February or

March. The color is light blue, with a darker stripe in each petal. The foliage is more in evidence at flowering time but does not hide the flowers.

Botanical Name: Scilla
Family: Liliaceae
Common Names: Squill, Siberian squill
Flower Colors: Blue, white
Flowering Time: Spring, summer
Height: Varies by species: from 4 to 48 inches
Spread: Can form large colonies.
Native Habitat: Europe, South Africa, Caucasus, Iran and Turkey
Hardiness: Some very hardy, others not at all hardy
Depth of Planting: Large bulbs right at the surface, others 3 to 4 inches
Distance Apart: Small bulbs 6 inches, large bulbs 12 inches
Containers: Yes
Light Requirements: Varies by species: most prefer sun, some light shade.
Soil Type: Average garden soil
Special Conditions: Attention should be given to the individual requirements regarding when moisture is needed.
Comments: I would count *Scilla natalensis* among my favorite bulbs—long-lasting, tough plants, but unfortunately not hardy. *Scilla peruviana*, which grows in my garden, is pleasing and a good performer. While not essential garden plants, the considerable charm of squills almost demands they be considered.

A veritable rainbow of colors is found in the species *Sparaxis tricolor*, and these plants are trouble free and tough. Loving the sun, they are ideal for any dry, sunny corner of the garden.

SPARAXIS
Iridaceae

The name is given because of the lacerated spathes that surround the flowers, as in Greek *sparaso* means to tear. Sparaxis are known in their native land, South Africa, as harlequin flowers because of their bright colors. The rootstock is a corm. While not hardy, the plants grow well planted in spring, then lifted for winter and replanted again the next spring. In warm areas they can be left in the ground, and will multiply very quickly. While certain catalogs will list "mixed colors" under the species *Sparaxis tricolor*, I think that little or no breeding has been done, as the species itself is quite varied. The flowers have indeed three colors, as the yellow centers are outlined in black, having red, yellow, crimson, orange or yellow petals.

I must say that these bulbs are tough. I once saw an area where they grew, rototilled. The gardener thought this would get rid of them. On the contrary, they came back the following year thicker than ever. Where there had been only a few patches of *Sparaxis* before, there now were many, flowering their heads off. (Makes one wonder why we bother paying attention to planting depths and distances apart!) These corms should be planted 2 inches deep and 4 inches apart. Any well-drained spot in full sun will suit them. Be bold and plant at least 25 bulbs in a clump. Keep them moist until flowering has finished and the rather coarse leaves have died down; then, try to keep them dry so the corms can ripen. The basal foliage, held in a fan shape, may take quite a while to start to die back. If you want to lift the corms, wait at least six weeks after flowering has finished before lifting them, or better yet, eight weeks.

Botanical Name: Sparaxis
Family: Iridaceae
Common Name: Harlequin flower
Flower Colors: Red, yellow, orange and white, all with yellow and black centers
Flowering Time: Early summer; later from spring planting
Height: 10 to 12 inches
Spread: Will multiply quite quickly
Native Habitat: South Africa
Hardiness: Not very hardy; will take some frost
Depth of Planting: 2 inches
Distance Apart: 4 inches
Containers: Yes; use ordinary potting soil
Light Requirements: Sun
Soil Type: Average, well-drained garden soil
Special Conditions: None
Comments: Tough, colorful and quite long lasting, these plants look good in containers. If you live in a warm climate and have a bank that you would like to see in living color, plant these! When you see them *en masse* they will take your breath away.

Perhaps the flowers of *Sprekelia formosissima* are the most unusual of any produced by bulbs, and this is why they command a lot of attention. Native to Mexico, they need warmth to perform well. (Photo courtesy of International Bloembollen Centrum.)

SPREKELIA
Amaryllidaceae

J. H. von Sprekelsen of Hamburg, Germany, sent a plant to Linnaeus in 1658, and as the specimen was then unknown, Linnaeus named the plant in his honor. There is but one species, *Sprekelia formosissima*, a most unusual flower. The uppermost petal is very wide, two lateral petals are strap shaped, the lowest petal is two-lipped, while the remaining two petals curl toward the base and form a tube. It is deep crimson, rises to a height of some 18 inches on a sturdy stem, and is native to Mexico. Earlier in this century *Sprekelia* was called *Amaryllis formosissima*, and for such an unusual plant it has a surprising number of common names: Jacobean lily, St. James lily and Aztec lily. Upon closer examination, it was found to merit its own genus. It is not hardy, but a great plant for the cool greenhouse, and in warmer climates it can be grown in the border where it will command a lot of attention when in flower.

The bulbs are large and should be planted with the top of the neck right at the soil surface. If growing them in the border, set them 12 inches apart. The flowering stem is sent up before the leaves are grown, but when they do grow, the leaves will reach more than 24 inches in length. Planted in fall, *Sprekelia* will flower in early summer; planted in spring, it will flower in late summer. After flowering, keep moist as long as the foliage is growing, then give it a dry period. During this dry period the pot can be left in full sun. Shield plants in the border from rains by erecting a shelter. I quite understand if you think this is too much work, and I happen to agree with you, but you might be tempted by the pictures of this unusual flower in catalogs, and so you should know just what is involved in growing it. They aren't fussy as to soil—ordinary potting soil is fine for containers—but make certain drainage is good.

Botanical Name: Sprekelia
Family: Amaryllidaceae
Common Names: Jacobean lily, St. James lily, Aztec lily
Flower Colors: Crimson
Flowering Time: Early summer; late summer from spring planting
Height: 12 inches
Spread: Very slow
Native Habitat: Mexico
Hardiness: Not hardy
Depth of Planting: Neck at or just above soil level
Distance Apart: 12 inches
Containers: Yes
Light Requirements: Sun
Soil Type: Average, well-drained soil

Special Conditions: Must have a dry period after foliage has died down.
Comments: I do not like to damn a plant with faint praise, but I can't work up much enthusiasm for this plant. (Now I will receive letters from *Sprekelia* lovers all over the world!) There are so many bulbs worthy of culture that are not grown, why promote this species, perhaps at their expense?

STERNBERGIA
Amaryllidaceae

Count Kaspar Moritz van Sternberg of Prague, a botanist, was honored when this genus was named after him. He wrote, "Revisio Saxifragarum," the revision of the Saxifragerias in 1810. *Sternbergia* is a small genus of five species, all native to the Mediterranean region and the Middle East. On seeing this plant, one would think it was either a colchicum or a crocus. It differs from these genera because it has six stamens; crocus has three. *Sternbergia* has an inferior ovary, *Colchicum* a superior one. Only one species is listed in catalogs, and beyond any doubt it is the most attractive. This is *Sternbergia lutea*, a lovely, low-growing plant with brilliant, golden yellow flowers appearing in fall. The flowers are egg shaped and carried on 10-inch stems, well above the developing foliage, which continues to grow after the flowers are past.

Plant the bulbs as soon as they are received, in full sun in average garden soil, setting them at least 6 inches deep and 4 to 6 inches apart. They require moisture in fall, winter and spring, but it is essential that they have a dry period in mid- to late summer. Some organic liquid fertilizer can be given after the flowers are open, but do not overfertilize; while one or two feedings will strengthen the bulb, too much will make it soft and less capable of withstanding cold tem-

Rightly regarded as the finest yellow fall-flowering bulbs *Sternbergia lutea* should be planted and then left undisturbed, and enjoyed year after year. (Photo courtesy of International Bloembollen Centrum.)

peratures. It can be quite hardy, but in areas where temperatures drop below 0°F, make sure you give it a heavy mulch.

Once planted, these bulbs should be left undisturbed. They can be grown in containers; if doing so, place five or six bulbs in a pot in April or May, and place them outdoors in a cool area, keeping them barely moist. As soon as they poke their noses above the soil put them into full sun. Keep them moist and bring them indoors as soon as you see signs of the buds appearing. After the flowers have finished, place them in a cool area so the foliage keeps growing. Then, when the foliage dies down, gradually reduce the amount of moisture so that by early summer they can enjoy the rest they require. While *Sternbergia* will perform well in pots, I am never happy when they are grown this way. Somehow, to me they belong in a sunny border. Some plants look great in containers, but not these noble plants.

There are a number of spring-flowering *Sternbergias*, but there is too much competition

from other spring-flowering species for them to stand out. For a deep, golden yellow color in the border in fall, however, it is hard, if not impossible, to beat *Sternbergia lutea*.

Botanical Name: Sternbergia
Family: Amaryllidaceae
Common Names: None known
Flower Colors: Yellow, some white species
Flowering Time: Fall
Height: 10 inches
Spread: Will spread, but this takes time
Native Habitat: Mediterranean region
Hardiness: Quite hardy; may have problems in areas where temperatures fall below 0°F, and then they are best in a cool greenhouse or in pots.
Depth of Planting: 6 inches
Distance Apart: 4 to 6 inches
Containers: Yes
Light Requirements: Sun
Soil Type: Ordinary soil
Special Conditions: Must have a dry period in mid- to late summer
Comments: You will not find a more attractive or more brilliant color than that of the rich, golden flowers of *Sternbergia*, perfect in borders. I have doubts about it being grown in containers—it does not seem quite right to me (But I suppose it is better than not enjoying them at all.) Give them a very protected area and much mulch in colder climates, rather than growing them in pots.

TIGRIDIA
Iridaceae

The large cup in the centers of the flowers is very heavily spotted and hence was given the name *tigris*, which means tiger in Latin. This is a large genus of plants that come from Mexico and South America, but many species are not in cultivation. One species, *Tigridia pavonia* from Mexico, has long been cultivated and is listed in many catalogs. The common name is Mexican shell flower. It is a summer flower, in bloom from July to September.

The foliage is sparse what there is of it is sword shaped and reaches only 10 to 12 inches, about half the height of the flowers. The flowers are quite unusual—very colorful, lasting for only a day, but the plants are extremely free-flowering. Reaching several inches in diameter, the blossoms are made up of three broad, rounded petals that bend at a 90-degree angle, and the lower parts of these petals, together with three shorter petals, form the distinct cup. Frequently there is a dart of color from the cup extending up into the broad petals. In the species *Tigridia pavonia* can be found yellow, white, red and orange flowers, most with purplish spots. By selection, the bulbs sold by nurseries have a very wide color range, and they are also sometimes listed by color. All are great plants for the summer border, best seen against a background of dark color, so their bright colors stand out.

These plants thrive in any well-drained soil, in full sun. Plant them 4 inches deep and 6 to 10 inches apart. In cold climates, plant after all danger of frost is passed; in warmer climates they can be planted in fall. In containers, where they grow well, use ordinary potting soil and crowd them. The little corms are not very large, so place them, in pots, about 2 inches apart. Make certain the drainage is good.

After the flowers have passed, allow the plants to die down, then lift. Keep the corms dry, then brush them off and store them clean and dry at temperatures of around 50°F over the winter. Then, plant them again in spring. The length of time they are in flower is about 8 to 10 weeks, so while they can't be counted on to give you color all summer long, they will add much inter-

You must plant a lot of *Tigridia pavonia* in order to enjoy them because individual flowers last but a day. They must have sun and good drainage, but are easy to grow and do multiply. (Photo courtesy of International Bloembollen Centrum.)

est to the mixed border. You must plant in bold clumps for best effect. These bulbs deliver good value for their cost, and with care you will have a good stock for planting year after year. You might find that certain colors become more prevalent than others, so purchase some of the missing colors and mix the corms together.

Botanical Name: Tigridia
Family: Iridaceae
Common Names: Mexican shell flower, tiger flower
Flower Colors: Varied, white to yellow to red to orange, all with spots.
Flowering Time: Summer
Height: 18 to 20 inches
Spread: Will not spread until established, which will occur only in warm climates
Native Habitat: Mexico, Guatemala and South America
Hardiness: To around 10°F with mulch, but best lifted and stored
Depth of Planting: 4 inches

Distance Apart: 4 to 6 inches, closer in pots
Containers: Yes
Light Requirements: Full sun
Soil Type: Average, well-drained garden soil
Special Conditions: None.
Comments: These plants should be grown more often, as they are unusual in color and in form. Great for added interest and color in mixed borders, but do not try them with shrubs. The plants need to ripen after the foliage dies back.

TRILLIUM
Liliaceae

If you look at these plants, you will see that the parts are in multiples of three, hence *tri*, meaning three in Latin. The common names are wake robin, birth-root and lamb's quarters. I have yet to understand how these common names have been earned.

Three leaves are carried in a whorl on each stem, and the flowers emerge from the center of the whorl. Some flowers are sessile, others grow on stems of varying lengths, and some become pendant as they age. Oftimes the leaves are mottled, an added attraction. There are some 20 or more species. They come from different parts of the world, from the Himalayas to Japan, yet the species most commonly cultivated in our gardens, and gardens all over the world, are from North America. The North American species are hardy. These plants are at home in the woods, and they look best in woodland settings. In a properly shady spot they should be able to persist for years, gathering strength, the clumps increasing in size in a comparatively short span of time. Plant 4 inches deep and 8 to 12 inches apart. They appreciate a moisture-retentive soil rich in organic matter. These plants should never be allowed to become dry. In the warmest climates it

is essential that moisture be provided in quite liberal quantities, and while you may get away with growing them in some sun in cooler climates, in warmer areas the hot sun will kill them.

I have mentioned that certain bulbs should be placed so that the plants grow at eye level. Trilliums, however, should be viewed from above. They are best placed close to a path as they are not tall plants, generally from 12 to 24 inches tall, and can't be appreciated at a distance. Some species are much shorter.

Trillium cernuum: This species is native to the eastern United States. The common name is nodding wood lily. It can grow 24 inches tall, but is often shorter. The leaves are 6 inches in length, and two or three stems are produced by each rootstock. In the center on a rather weak stem (hence it nods) grows the flower, which is white, sometimes (but rarely) pinkish. The petals are about an inch in length, and when fully open the flower is about 1 inch in diameter. This species flowers in late spring.

T. erectum: Commonly called birth-root, or lamb's quarters, this species is native to much of the eastern United States and Canada. It reaches 12 inches, and the flower color can vary from white to yellow; there are some green forms as well, often with a reddish hue. In catalogs the plants most commonly listed are the white 'Album' and pale yellow 'Luteum'. This species flowers in April on into June, somewhat depending on where it is growing. The flowers face out and are tilted a little upward.

T. grandiflorum: Often regarded as the finest of the genus, these plants occur in much the same areas as *T. erectum.* The flowers are large, often 3 inches in diameter when fully open, and face sideways. There are a number of forms, including fine doubles. While the most common color is white, some forms are quite pink, and are often marketed as var. *roseum*. The flowers appear in April to June, depending on where they are growing; the colder the area, the later the flowering.

T. ovatum: This species is from the western United States and is also found in British Columbia. It is often found growing with redwoods and with such evergreens as Douglas firs in the northern regions of its habitat. A lovely species, it grows 8 to 12 inches in height. The white flowers turn a lovely rose as they age. In the southern parts of its habitat it flowers in February; the season is later farther north, and it is not until April that it flowers in British Columbia.

T. rivale: This California native, also found in southern Oregon, is generally seen at elevations above 1,000 feet. This species is unusual in that the leaves, rather than being sessile, have leaf stalks some 2 inches long. Despite the fact that it is a dwarf plant, often less than 4 inches tall, the flowers are more than 1 inch across. While this species is listed, I do not feel it has the charm of the taller species. Flowers appear in April.

T. sessile: This species is found throughout the United States, from the East to the West Coasts. Reaching 10 to 12 inches in height, it bears flowers that are sessile, hence the name. The flowers are dark crimson. There is a yellow form, called var. *luteum*, and var. *californicum*, that has greenish or greenish yellow flowers that often turn purplish with age. This species is quite variable, but in my opinion it is one of the best. When well grown in a situation that pleases it, it will be a little taller than 10 to 12 inches. The leaves are very large with interesting mottlings, but this coloration is another variable characteristic. Flowers appear in April to June.

A truly American species, and a great plant for any shady area, *Trillium sessile* should be planted where you can get close to them.

A garden with any shady areas should have a selection of trilliums, especially if that garden is located in the cooler areas of the country.

Botanical Name: Trillium
Family: Liliaceae
Common Names: Wake robin, birth-root, lamb's quarters
Flower Colors: White to yellow, pink to crimson
Flowering Time: Spring to early summer
Height: From 4 inches to 24 inches (most plants are 12 to 24 inches)
Spread: Will form good-sized colonies in time
Native Habitat: Most cultivated species from North America
Hardiness: Hardy
Depth of Planting: 4 inches
Distance Apart: 8 to 12 inches
Containers: Not recommended
Light Requirements: Shade
Soil Type: Garden soil with good organic content
Special Conditions: Must have moisture throughout the year
Comments: These plants deserve a place in any and every woodland garden, in fact, in any gar-

den with a woodsy feeling. If given moisture and organic matter, they will perform well. The foliage is attractive.

TULBAGHIA
Amaryllidaceae

In my opinion, *Tulbaghia violacea* is a bulb that deserves much more attention than it receives. It is a glorious addition to any garden.

The genus was named in honor of Ryk Tulbagh, one of the Dutch governors of the Cape Province. There are several species, but only two are ever listed in catalogs, *Tulbaghia simmleri* and *T. violacea*. Often *T. violacea* is sold in gallon cans, and not in a dormant state. I am pleased to say these plants are becoming more popular, and I see them quite frequently in gardens in California. They are not very hardy, but will withstand temperatures from 15 to 20°F with a good mulch and in a protected area. In colder areas they should be grown in cool greenhouses or planted in spring, then lifted in fall. They are in flower for much of the summer, and consequently I think they merit this extra work. Most certainly they are great plants for warm areas of the country.

The common names are wild or society garlic, sweet garlic and pink agapanthus. This last name is easily understood, as *Tulbaghia* is frequently found in the wild with *Agapanthus*. The smell of garlic from the flowers and crushed foliage is very mild. The flowers form an umbel, pink or sometimes a little lighter in color, tubular, with the tips recurving. Plant in the sun. Put the bulbs 2 inches deep and 6 to 12 inches apart. They need good drainage. The rootstocks of *Tulbaghia* can vary by species, from rhizomatous to tuberous or cormous. The plants are much used in medicine in their native South Africa, the rootstocks in preparing baths to relieve the pain of rheumatism, the leaves for tea and also rubbed on the head to give relief from headaches. (I have tried the latter, and it works! Or was this mind over matter?) The plants need moisture during winter and spring, but are quite drought-resistant when established. During the many recent years of drought in California these plants thrived; they loved the sun-baked soils, but had a good soaking in winter and spring. I hope that more of these trouble-free plants will be grown, and that parks departments will appreciate their value.

Tulbaghia simmleri: Native to the eastern Transvaal of South Africa, this is a lovely plant. Local authorities there have used it extensively to adorn the roadsides, and it looks splendid. I feel the head is a bit tidier than that of *T. violacea*. It reaches 18 inches in height. Spring to early summer is the main period of flowering, but odd flowers are produced throughout the summer. The color can vary from mauve to bright lilac, and a white form is also known.

T. violacea: Perhaps the prettiest species for the garden, this is a more robust plant of easy culture and very tidy appearance. The leaves are bright green and shiny. The tuberous roots will produce several flowering stems. The flowers appear in umbels, each containing as many as 20 flowers, each of which is pink with a yellow eye (you have to look closely to see the eye). This plant will form colonies of considerable size in the wild. I first saw it in the Tsitskamma forest on the eastern seaboard along the Garden Route of South Africa. It rarely grows more than 24 inches in height. I feel this species should be more popular.

Botanical Name: Tulbaghia
Family: Amaryllidaceae
Common Names: Society garlic, wild garlic, pink agapanthus, sweet garlic
Flower Colors: Shades of pink; white forms are known
Flowering Time: Spring into summer; sporadically through summer
Height: 12 to 24 inches
Spread: Will form large colonies
Native Habitat: South Africa
Hardiness: Not fully hardy; will take some frost, but not much, so lift and replant in spring in colder climates.
Depth of Planting: 2 inches
Distance Apart: 6 to 12 inches
Containers: Yes, but use a large container
Light Requirements: Sun
Soil Type: Average, well-drained garden soil
Special Conditions: These plants like a dry summer, but good moisture in winter and spring.
Comments: These plants deserve more consideration for summer bedding. The foliage is clean and bright. They are easy to grow, and the flowers are attractive.

Tulips are available in many shapes, sizes and colors, but fringed tulips are among, if not the, most unusual.

TULIPA
Liliaceae

The name is derived from the Turkish *tuliban*, meaning turban. Presumably this is because the colors and general shape of a turban are mimicked by tulips. There are some 100 species, and well over 2,000 registered names of hybrids. It is through the good offices of Ogier Ghiselin de Busbecq, Ambassador to Suleiman the Magnificent (c.1529), that we enjoy the tulip. He sent the bulbs and seed back to Vienna, where Carolus Clusius grew them and, when appointed professor of botany at Leiden in the Netherlands, took his bulbs with him. Thus they came to Holland, though not for the first time; records indicate they were already known, and much prized, prior to the arrival of Clusius. Reportedly the bulbs were stolen from Clusius, and gave the bulb industry of Holland its start.

The tulip had been grown in Turkey for a long time. Even at the time of Busbecq, numerous cultivars were known, and as far back as the eighteenth century, records indicate some 1,300 kinds were named. Such complex breeding lines make continued breeding difficult. It is said that no wild species known today can be identified with certainty as the species from which our modern hybrids are descended.

With so many hybrids, both ancient and modern, there have evolved tulips with distinctive shapes and characteristics. These distinctions, together with flowering time, are the basis of a horticultural classification. Only a few years ago there were divisions known as Darwin and Mendel; lines of breeding have since blurred the boundaries between these and other tulips.

Because the classifications are based on hybrids, as the hybrids change, so must the classifications. As such divisions as the Darwin tulips (given division standing in 1899) pass from prominence, they are reassigned and included with other types.

The Lily-flowered tulips, with their pointed petals, were separated from the Cottage tulips in 1958. In 1981, the Fringed and the Viridiflora tulips were given separate divisions. As the form of the tulip flower evolves, so does the classification. Note it is form more than color that determines whether a cultivar is placed in one division or another, the one exception being the Viridiflora tulips, because they have green in their petals.

The cultivation requirements of all tulips is basically the same. I must point out that gardeners in warmer climates, where soil temperatures don't fall below 40°F, are somewhat at a disadvantage. Early flowering tulips do not seem to appreciate warm weather. They like the cold. In-

areas where winter temperatures do not fall below 20°F, I recommend that none of the cultivars that fall in the following divisions be planted, unless they are container grown and stored at low temperatures: Single Early, Double Early, Kaufmanniana, Fosteriana and Greigii. Still, this leaves a great number of lovely hybrids for gardeners living in warm climates to grow and enjoy. It might be worth noting why this is so. The answer is quite logical and, in a way, fascinating. How does a bulb know when it is time to start into growth? What are the factors that trigger growth? In the case of early flowering tulips (and later flowering ones, for that matter), temperature appears to be the trigger. At a given temperature, a tulip bulb will start to send out roots; this is when temperatures descend. We plant in fall, roots are produced and then, in spring, the shoots appear. As the temperature levels off and starts to climb, the bulbs send up their shoots, the flowering stems. They flower and seed, and the species is continued. Descending temperatures stimulate root growth, this in time to allow for good root development to be accomplished before rising temperatures dictate shoots should be produced. The time frame between these two growth stimuli must be of a given length.

With later-flowering tulips, growth is triggered by warmer temperatures, and there is sufficient time for good root development before that growth is triggered. In warmer climates good root growth can be made by later-flowering bulbs before they start shoot growth. If you plant early-flowering hybrids in warm climates, the bulbs are not well-rooted enough to produce sufficient supplies for such growth. The result is that they flower poorly—some plants are okay, some are not. The display of color is disappointing. These bulbs must use food stored in the bulbs without the backup of food supplied by the roots.

This is the same basic principle we use when

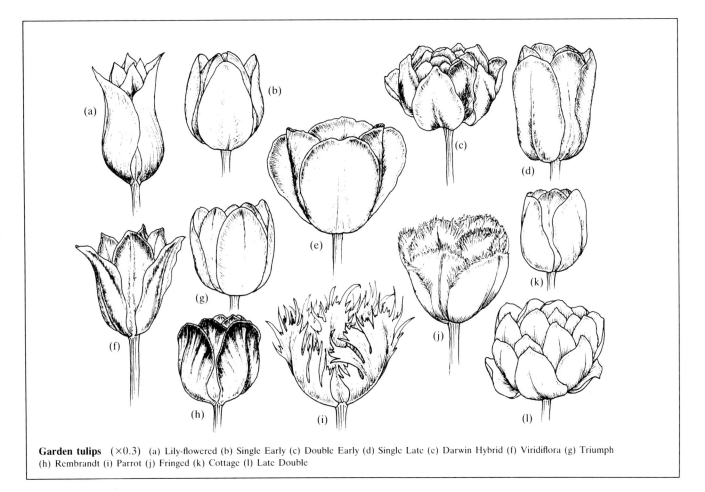

Garden tulips (×0.3) (a) Lily-flowered (b) Single Early (c) Double Early (d) Single Late (e) Darwin Hybrid (f) Viridiflora (g) Triumph (h) Rembrandt (i) Parrot (j) Fringed (k) Cottage (l) Late Double

From The New Royal Horticultural Society Dictionary of Gardening. *Reproduced with kind permission of the Royal Horticultural Society and The Macmillan Press Ltd. and Stockton Press, New York. Illustration by Christine Grey-Wilson.*

forcing bulbs into flower out of season. They must be given adequate time and those temperatures that enable them to produce good roots before warmer temperatures are given to induce flowering. Hence growers have cold rooms, and the home gardener places the bulbs in the coolest part of the garden.

What conditions do tulips need to grow in our gardens? They seem to dislike competition, and should be planted in soil well prepared to a good depth. They require good drainage, and sun or high shade. They should be planted to a depth of 8 inches in very sandy soils, at least 6 inches deep in average soils, and spaced 4 to 6 inches apart. While they like well-drained soil, moisture should be available at all times during the growing cycle.

While bone meal is a good fertilizer to apply just before planting, or mixed into the bottom of the hole if bulbs are planted individually with a trowel, such fertilizer should not come in contact with the bulb. A fertilizer with a high percentage of nitrogen should not be used, and the soil should not contain too high a content of fresh manure or compost. Fast growth should not be encouraged, as it can result in a soft bulb susceptible to rot, and lush foliage will be encouraged at the expense of good flowering.

Planting should be done in October in the colder climates, and in late November or even early December in the warmest areas. As soon as the bulbs appear above the ground in spring, a balanced fertilizer can be applied. In colder climates, tulips can be left in the ground, but they must have a dry period in mid- to late summer so they can ripen. However, I am of the opinion that all tulips, in warm and cold areas alike, are best lifted, cleaned and kept dry over summer, then given 6 to 8 weeks of precooling prior to planting again in fall. The tulips that are replanted should not be expected to produce as good a crop of flowers as they did the first season, but they are perfectly good enough to be planted in rows for cut flowers. In colder areas, some of the Kaufmanniana, Greigii and Fosteriana hybrids can be left in the ground and will perform quite well, even for more than two seasons, but I feel this is as much a question of luck as good culture. I would still lift and replant. With tulips it is essential that rotation be practiced. Do not plant them in the same bed year after year; their performance will fall off as the soil is depleted of necessary trace elements, and when pieces of bulbs or roots are left in the soil, they can rot. After three or four years, give a particular location a one- or two-year rest.

Having said this, I must admit that many of the true species can remain in place year after year and give a great account of themselves. Why the difference between the cultivars and the species? I would hazard a guess that, being more basic, less highly bred, their vigor is far greater. Inbreeding means weakness in all of nature's kingdom. I suppose this is due, in short, to a lack of genetic toughness.

Many of the leading suppliers of bulbs offer them according to the horticultural classification. Here are the various divisions and cultivar suggestions for each.

This Triumph tulip ('Dreaming Maid') has the classic form of the class. It is understandable that these tall-growing types are popular.

Classification

Division 1, Early Tulips, Single Early

These are quite short, between 6 and 16 inches tall. The flowers have contrasting edges to the petals, flecks of color or a central flame of color on the exterior. They flower in late March to early April. Cultivars include:

'Apricot Beauty': a soft salmon with apricot edges

'Beauty Queen': pink with a salmon flush, ruffled edges

'Beauty of Volendam': pure white with flares and brushings of deep crimson-red

'General de Wet': combination of gold and orange

'Princess Irene': orange flamed with purple

Division 2, Double Early

Between 12 and 18 inches tall, these plants flower in early to mid-April. The flowers are fully double, bowl shaped and 3 or more inches in diameter. The colors range from white through yellow to red, with contrasting edges or flecks. Cultivars include:

'Carlton': scarlet, tips of petals flecked with gold

'Electra': cherry red, lighter edge to petals

'Monte Carlo': a lovely, clear yellow

'Peach Blossom': a rosy pink, creamy flare on the outer petals, a lovely cultivar

'Schoonoord': pure white, forces well

Division 3, Mid-season, Triumph

The height varies between 18 and 20 inches. These tulips come into flower in late April, exhibiting a wide color range from white through yellow, orange, pink, red to deep purple, with contrasting edges or flecks. Cultivars include:

'Abu Hassan': purplish mahogany, edges of petals a good yellow

'African Queen': burgundy with white petal edges

'Dreaming Maid': raspberry pink with white edges, color deepening as the flowers age

'Merry Widow': deep red edged with white

'New Design': cream tinted with pink and apricot, white petal edges

'Peerless Pink': large flower, satiny pink

Division 4, Darwin Hybrid Tulips

These lovely flowers resulted from crossing Darwin Hybrids with *Tulipa fosteriana*. They are 24 to 30 inches in height, with very bright colors of yellow, orange and bright red, often with contrasting edges. They come into flower in May. Cultivars include:

'Apeldoorn': scarlet edged with yellow

'Beauty of Apeldoorn': orange-yellow brushed with red

'Daydream': very unusual and lovely hybrid, opens yellow and then turns apricot with hints of orange

'General Eisenhower': red edged with yellow

'Gudoshnik': one of my favorites, and no two flowers seem alike—creamy yellow flecked or otherwise marked with red

'Holland's Glory': very large flowers, this in a division distinguished by large flowers; scarlet with hint of orange

Division 5, Late Tulips

This division contains tulips that were once classed as Darwin and Cottage tulips. They grow 24 to 30 inches tall. The flower head has a definite rectangular shape. The colors range from ivory through yellow, salmon and pink to nearly black, often with contrasting edges or feathering. They come into flower in mid- to late May. Cultivars include:

'Anne Frank': pure white, very large flower

'Aristocrat', an older cultivar (but very good), pink with just a hint of lavender, petals edged with white

'Blushing Beauty': yellow brushed with rose

'Clara Butt': I grew this tulip back in the forties, and it is still listed today; salmon with a hint of lilac

'Halcro': flowers are oval and carmine-red; stands up to the rain well

'Mrs. John Scheepers': another old cultivar, an excellent pure yellow (perhaps the best yellow available)

'Queen of the Night': You do not have to like Mozart to appreciate the song this flower sings; black, or almost

'Shirley': white edged with lavender-rose

Division 6, Lily-flowered

The distinguishing feature of this group is the pointed petals. These tulips are 18 to 24 inches in height, the colors ranging from white to yellow to deep violet. They flower in April or May. Cultivars include:

'Ballade': pink, base white tinged with pink

'China Pink': soft pink, white base, tips recurve a little

'Queen of Sheba': deep red with golden edge

'West Point': getting on in years now—first introduced in the forties but still the finest yellow

'White Triumphator': pure white

Division 7, Fringed

The petals are fringed with hairs that are translucent or of a contrasting color. These May-flowering tulips have become very popular. The height is generally in the 18- to 24-inch range. The colors include white to peach and apricot, yellows and bronze. Cultivars include:

'Aleppo': peach and apricot

'Burgundy Lace': a lovely wine red

'Fringed Elegance': yellow with pink flecks

'Maja': pale yellow with a bronze-yellow base

Division 8, Viridiflora

These tulips grow to a height of about 18 inches. Horticultural classifications are constantly updated to accommodate new forms of cultivars. This is one of the new divisions. These May-flowering hybrids have caught the imagination of the gardening public and are very popular. The petals contain varying degrees of green. Cultivars include:

'Golden Artist': gold with red and green flushes

'Greenland': pink, with a large green flare surrounded by cream that heightens the effect. I like this plant, and found it lasted a long time on my deck in San Francisco.

'Spring Green': ivory-white with a green flare

Division 9, Rembrandt

In this division are found those tulips with striped or feathered markings. Such marking is caused by a virus that can be transmitted from one bulb to another by aphids. The consensus of authorities is that before too long this division will be dropped. I cannot look at these flowers without thinking of the paintings by the Old Masters, in which they were so often featured. There are not many to be found listed in catalogs. One, 'Beauty of Volendam', I have listed under 'Single Early' tulips, as so often these are not classified as 'Rembrandt' cultivars in catalogs. Strictly speaking, this cultivar should be placed in this division. If you are not acquainted with these tulips, try some before they disappear from the scene.

Division 10, Parrot

For the most part the tulips in this division were not hybridized for inclusion here, but were "breaks" or mutations from other tulips. They have large flowers with petals often deeply cut and twisted. The name "parrot" was given because the petals curl around each other in a way reminiscent of a parrot's beak. The height varies from 20 to 24 inches, with the flowers often opening to be as much as 8 inches in diameter.

They are often bicolored, with the edges of the petals fringed or wavy, an attractive combination of characteristics. Before you go out and purchase a lot of these bulbs, I must caution that if you experience rains in May, remember that these large flowers are not immune to damage; they can become very heavy and be torn by spring rains. Plant them where they do get a little protection. They are spectacular cut flowers. Cultivars include:

'Apricot Parrot': pale apricot with white, rose pink and green

'Black Parrot': very dark purple, possibly the darkest tulip of all

'Estella Rijnveldt': white flushed with yellow and crimson

'Fantasy': salmon pink and green, and flushed with rose

'Orange Parrot': a lovely combination of gold and mahogany

'White Parrot': pure white with red tips and flushes of green

It would be difficult to select only one cultivar. I seldom like to see mixed colors in plantings. However, I do feel that a mixed bed of Parrot tulips can be more attractive than just one cultivar planted *en masse*.

Division 11, Double Late or Peony-flowered
These tulips have very large flowers, and like the Parrots they can be damaged by inclement weather. For this reason they are more commonly raised under glass in pots. They flower in May, with heights that vary from 18 to 24 inches. Cultivars include:

'Angelique': pale pink with a darker flush, the edges of the petals are ruffled

'Carnival de Nice': white feathered with deep red. This is an interesting cultivar because the leaves are green with cream edges.

'Eros': deep pink with a hint of blue

'Gold Medal': a good, deep yellow

'Mount Tacoma': a pure white

Division 12, Kaufmanniana
Often called the waterlily tulips, they flower very early in spring. The petals are strap shaped, and when the flowers are fully open they are almost flat, hence their common name. The height varies from 6 to 9 inches. The leaves can be plain, but are often marked with dark green–brown. The flowers are white to red, with edges of a contrasting color. Cultivars include:

'Fritz Kreisler': the throat is cream to deep pink, the exterior of the petals salmon edged with yellow

'Heart's Delight': the leaves are mottled, the exterior of the petals carmine-red edged with milky pink, the interior pale rose, the throat yellow

'Shakespeare': salmon streaked with yellow and red

'Stressa': the leaves are mottled, the exterior of the petals yellow marked with red. This cultivar is an old one, but I think one of the finest still.

Division 13, Fosteriana
The height can vary greatly, from 8 to over 24 inches. The leaves are sometimes variegated. The flowers range from white through yellow to pink or dark red. These are early-flowering tulips. Cultivars include:

'Madame Lefeber': also commonly listed as 'Red Emperor' and a lovely cultivar, with large, bright red flowers

'Orange Emperor': vivid orange, the shade of the exterior and interior varying a little

'Pink Emperor': sometimes listed as 'Spring Pearl', a pink-red with a definite sheen, and yellow center

'Purissima': large, long-lasting flowers, white with a yellow center

These cultivars are tried and true. Other introductions come and go, but the Emperors seem to just keep on going.

Division 14, Greigii

The height varies between 8 and 12 inches. The leaves are always mottled with brown-purple, and are indeed an added attraction. The flowers range from yellow through apricot to red. As to flowering sequence, they come a little later into flower than the Kaufmanniana. The foliage is often very close to or lies on the ground. Cultivars include:

'Corsage': rose with a yellow edge, the interior feathered with gold.

'Golden Tango': yellow with red and green

'Plaisir': Cream with a broad vermillion flame

'Red Riding Hood': scarlet, the exterior a little darker

The Greigii Hybrids, as we used to call them, are wonderful garden plants in cooler climates. 'Plaisir' is, to me, one of the finest of these.

Division 15, Other species, including selections and hybrids

There are many species, but the following are the most commonly listed, for the good reason that they do well in most gardens.

Tulipa acuminata: Named the horned tulip because the petals stick up like horns, this tulip comes from Turkey. It features long, twisted, red-and-yellow petals, and reaches 18 inches in height. It flowers in April and May. Certainly it offers a different effect!

T. altaica: Native to central Asia. This is said to be the species from the northernmost geographic limits of the genus. Very hardy, it stands 6 inches in height. The yellow flowers appear in April.

T. aucheriana: Native to Iran and Syria. The bulb is unusually small, only ½ inch thick, yet it will send up as many as three flowers, pink with a yellow-brown blotch at the base of the petals, only 4 inches tall. With prominent brown veining and a hint of green in the flower, this little species is quite a nice one to have in the garden.

T. bakeri: Native to Crete, it grows 4 to 6 inches tall and offers a rich purple with yellow at the base in March. It is inclined to be rather shy of flowering in colder climates, but does well in warmer areas if it has a dry resting period in late summer. The form 'Lilac Wonder' has circular flowers, with light purple exteriors, pastel mauve interiors.

T. batalinii: Native to Bokhara, these tulips reach only 4 to 5 inches in height. They bloom buff yellow with a yellow-gray blotch at the base of the petals. Several selections are listed in catalogs, including a yellow form, 'Bright Gem', and

'Bronze Charm', which has a bronzy hue—an interesting little species.

T. biflora: This plant is native to the Caucasus and Caspian regions. While dwarf—seldom over 4 inches tall—each bulb will produce several flowers of white with yellow centers. The exterior of the petals are stained green and crimson. The flowers open flat and put on quite a show. With flowers in early spring, this can be the first of the tulips to bloom.

T. celsiana: Though it comes from Spain it is, surprisingly, also found in Morocco, perhaps the only species from Africa. The flowers are fragrant, star shaped when open in May, and reach 6 inches.

T. chrysantha: This has rather strange species that has not been found in the wild; just where it comes from, no one knows. It grows 6 to 8 inches in height, producing small yellow flowers with red petals on the exterior. It's a striking little species and fun to see.

T. clusiana: Commonly called Hardy Tulip or Candy Tulip, the species is named after Clusius, often regarded as the father of the bulb industry in Holland. These flowers have a white interior and red exterior with a blue base. Most grow to about 12 inches tall, but I have often seen taller plants. It flowers in April or early May. This species can persist year after year in the garden. The clumps never seem to increase in size, but just keep on going.

T. eichleri: Native to Transcaucasus, these April flowers are a lovely, bright scarlet with a yellow margin. The plants reach 10 inches. Very long lasting in flower, they can be used in bedding plantings.

Grown well and planted in bold groupings, few tulips put on as grand a display as the Cottage Tulips (here, 'Twinkle') with their wide-opening flowers.

T. hageri: This charming little species with unusual coloring comes from Greece and Asia Minor, and flowers in April. It reaches 8 inches and has a branched stem, each carrying 2 to 4 flowers of scarlet with buff and green exteriors. The inner segments are often margined with yellow. The form *splendens* has coppery bronze flowers. This charming species is well worth growing.

T. humilis: This species is very variable, and possibly there are geographic variations, as this tulip has a wide distribution, found in Iran, Asia Minor and the Caucasus. The colors vary from bright pink to deep purple. Inside are blotches at the base of the petals, and these blotches may be pink, purple, yellow and even shades of blue. All the plants are dwarf, 4 inches in height, and early flowering. What were once several species are now combined under *T. humilis.* You might find listings for *T. pulchella alba,* a white form, and *T. pulchella humilis,* with violet-pink flowers touched with yellow at the base.

T. kolpakowskiana: From Turkestan, this species reaches 6 to 8 inches. Often there are two flowers per stem, bright yellow, the interior of the petals being olive with a red flush. The flowers appear in April, and as is the case with many of the species, they open flat.

T. linifolia: This little species (only 4 to 6 inches tall) comes from Bokhara and the Pamir mountain range in Asia. The petals are pointed. The red flowers are produced quite late in the season, in May.

T. praestans: This species from central Asia is quite tall, reaching 16 inches, with as many as four cup-shaped flowers on each stem. Dark red in color, this popular species has inspired selections. 'Tubergen's Variety' has scarlet-orange flowers, and for some unexplained reason it is sometimes called the "hosta tulip." It flowers in April.

T. saxatilis: This species from Crete is best suited to warmer areas. The flowers are pale lilac with a yellow blotch, 6 to 8 inches tall, and appear in April. Do not think of growing this plant if you cannot give it sun, good drainage and a dry resting period in late summer.

From time to time, you may find other species of *Tulipa* listed. While some may sound exciting, do remember that while many species are quite easy to grow and can remain in the ground, their performance often depends on their receiving the correct growing conditions. Although I have outlined some of these in the descriptions of the species, do take time to find out the exact conditions required before you purchase. Many firms have sales staff available to answer questions, so make certain that you speak to a knowledgeable person. It is your money; do not waste it on a plant you know nothing about.

Botanical Name: Tulipa
Family: Liliaceae
Common Name: Tulip
Flower Colors: Yellows, bronze, red, orange, purples, pinks—but no true blue; many bicolors and different flower forms
Flowering Time: Spring
Height: Dwarf types 3 to 4 inches; taller types 24 or more inches.
Spread: Not much increase in clumps; species sometimes do, but rarely
Native Habitat: Mediterranean region, Greece, Asia Minor, Turkey, Syria, Morocco; it is mostly cultivars that are grown in gardens.

Hardiness: Hardy; some species prefer warmer climates

Depth of Planting: 6 to 8 inches

Distance Apart: 4 to 6 inches

Containers: Yes; use potting soil

Light Requirements: Sun

Soil Type: Average, well-drained garden soil not—repeat, *not*—rich with fresh organic matter

Special Conditions: Do not replant in the same area, but give the soil a rest for two or more years.

Comments: Obviously tulips are lovely spring flowers and great for cutting. They also do very well in containers. I wish gardeners would have more fun with these bulbs, planting them with different combinations of annuals, in different configurations and so on. They are essential to most gardens.

VELTHEIMIA
Liliaceae

The genus was named in honor of a patron of botany, August Ferdinand Graf von Veltheim, a German who lived from 1741 to 1801. The plants are native to South Africa. At one time there was a great number of species, but many have since been grouped together. Only one species is to be found in catalogs, *Veltheimia bracteata*. This has a common name of red-hot poker, which correctly describes its form. Held in a dense raceme, the flowers are tubular. The leaves are up to 18 inches long and up to 4 inches wide.

For many years *Veltheimia* were widely grown as pot plants. They cannot be grown where temperatures fall below 40°F, and thus are best for the cool greenhouse, being suitable outdoors in only the very warmest areas. I suggest that keen gardeners try them in containers in

Only a few years ago *Velthemia bracteata* were popular pot plants. They have not changed, but tastes have. They have lovely waxy-looking flowers, which last for months.

colder locations. They are lovely plants when in flower. They need bright light, but not direct sunlight. Well-drained soil and moisture during their growing season are essential. They flower anytime from December through March, lasting several weeks in flower. The flowers are a pale rose.

The flower stalk and foliage are mottled, so the plants are not unattractive when not in flower. Bulbs should be set with about 1 inch of soil over them, 6 to 10 inches apart outdoors, 3 to 5 inches apart in pots. Both in pots and in the border, leave them undisturbed once planted. Feed them two or three times in spring with liquid organic fertilizer. If planting in pots, make sure the containers are of a good size so you do not have to repot for several seasons. The plants have a fleshy appearance that is almost exotic. They grow up to 20 inches tall, many inches of which are covered with flowers.

In Victorian times, and indeed even when I was a boy, there were any number of cultivars and selections of these plants. All my aunts and uncles seemed to have some of them in their conservatories, a rather grand word for what were really little greenhouses attached to the houses, upon which one looked from the living room. These charming rooms were filled with all sorts of flowers, and many of them were from places with, it seemed to me, exotic-sounding names. While our standard of living is no doubt higher now, there were certain facets of life, such as this keen interest in plants from foreign lands, that were enriching. It seems a shame that such interests have in large part fallen by the wayside.

Botanical Name: Veltheimia
Family: Liliaceae
Common Name: Red-hot poker
Flower Colors: Pale rose flecked with green
Flowering Time: December to March
Height: 20 inches
Spread: Not very fast, but will form colonies outdoors
Native Habitat: South Africa
Hardiness: Not at all hardy
Depth of Planting: 1 inch
Distance Apart: 6 to 10 inches
Containers: Yes
Light Requirements: Bright, indirect light
Soil Type: Average, well-drained garden soil; potting soil in containers
Special Conditions: Moisture when growing, and a few (but not many) feedings
Comments: I wish more people would grow these plants and that once again commercial nurseries would try them. It is a shame that many lovely cultivars have been lost to cultivation.

WATSONIA
Iridaceae

The genus was named in honor of an Englishman, Sir William Watson, who was a physician and a naturalist, and well known for his research on electricity. The genus is unique to South Africa. In appearance they are not unlike *Gladiolus*, and not being hardy, they must be grown in the same way these plants are in colder climates. The difference between the two genera is that, in *Watsonia*, the stigmas divide twice, forming six branches; in *Gladiolus* they divide only once, into three branches. The tubular flowers are carried on strong stems and face in two directions. The color range is quite wide, and the form of the flowers can vary from a narrow tube to an open flower of considerable diameter.

Fortunately, hybridizers have worked on the genus and quite a wide color range is available, mostly in pastel shades. The height can be as much as 48 or more inches, but nearly always over 36 inches; *Watsonia humilis* is an exception at 18 inches tall.

While there are deciduous and evergreen species, to my knowledge only the deciduous are available in this country. The corms should be planted in a protected border where they can enjoy reflected heat, set at a depth of 3 inches and spaced 6 to 9 inches apart. While in growth they should receive good moisture, but after the fo-

Another genus that is waiting to be discovered and should be more widely grown is *Watsonia*. If hybridizers start working with this genus, I think the colors that will become available will prove even more startling than the ones we know now.

liage has died down they can be allowed to dry. In colder climates lifting and storing the corms over winter should be done only after the foliage dies. Flowering will be in mid- to late spring in warmer climates, where they are left in the ground, and mid- to late summer when planted in spring. *Watsonia* are good container plants. Use containers of good size and ordinary potting soil, and ensure good drainage.

Watsonia aletroides: Native to the Cape of Good Hope, this species can often be seen growing along roadsides, as they love the good drainage the gravel gives them, and the reflected heat from the blacktop. They seem impervious to pollution from oil and fumes from cars. The flowers are tubular, and the colors salmon to a deep red to white. The plants may reach 36 inches tall. The foliage is stiff and held close to the flowering stem. Flowering will be in March to May from fall plantings, later from spring plantings.

W. ardernei: Although listed under this name in catalogs, this species is more correctly divided into *W. obrienii* (syn. *W. alba*, *W. iridifolia*, *W. pyrimidata* and *W. rosea ardernei*). These plants are native to the Cape Province. The flowering stem reaches to 36 inches and is often much branched. The flowers, large, white and flaring, appear in May or June. A lovely species now apparently extinct in the wild, but fortunately a great number of these plants are grown in parks and gardens.

W. galpinii: Native to the Indian Ocean side of South Africa, this is one of the few species found growing in some shade and moist areas. The flower color varies from terra-cotta to pink. It remains a long time in flower, and grows shorter than most other species, only 18 inches tall. It is later to flower than others, from June-August from fall planting, and I doubt it would be in flower from spring planting before the first frosts are experienced in fall. Perhaps it is not for colder climates, but a great plant for warmer areas of the country.

W. 'Califlora': These are a strain, various species being involved, and they will be found listed in catalogs. Ideal for spring planting in colder areas. A number of named selections have been introduced, and these include:

'Bright Eyes', pink
'Dazzler', orange with a purple throat
'Malvern', large flowers, orchid-purple
'Mrs. Bullard's White', the finest white
'Pink Opal', bright, soft pink
'Rubra', pinkish to fuchsia red

I hope that readers will be tempted to grow some of these bulbs. It is a delight to see them planted in large plantings in the Kirstenbosch Botanic Garden in Cape Town.

Botanical Name: Watsonia
Family: Iridaceae
Common Name: Bugle lily
Flower Colors: White, pink, red, terra-cotta
Flowering Time: Spring and summer
Height: Varies by species: 18 to 36 inches.
Spread: Will spread in warm climates when left in the ground.
Native Habitat: South Africa
Hardiness: Not hardy
Depth of Planting: 3 inches
Distance Apart: 6 to 9 inches
Containers: Yes, but the container must be large
Light Requirements: Full sun; one species, *W. galpinii*, appreciates shade
Soil Type: Average, well-drained garden soil; *W. galpinii* likes more moisture.
Special Conditions: None
Comments: Well worth growing. As a rule, *Watsonia* flower over a longer period than *Gladiolus*, and for that reason, I think they deserve wider recognition as good garden plants for warmer areas.

ZANTEDESCHIA
Araceae

This genus was named in honor of Giovanni Zantedeschi, an Italian botanist. Way back in the seventeenth century, Linnaeus placed *Zantedeschia aethiopica* in the genus *Calla*. Later, Kunth moved it to *Richardia*, and thus two common names of the plants in the genus, Calla and Richardia, came into being. Other common names are arum lily and spotted or pink calla; I am sure there are others as well.

All species are native to South Africa. The flowers are on a crowded spadix, male on top, female below, without any sterile flowers between. The spathe is the attractive part of these plants, colored white, yellow and shades of rose and purple. Much hybridization has been done in New Zealand, and many lovely shades are now listed in catalogs.

Zantedeschia aethiopica, the common calla, is a very handsome plant. It is grown for commercial flower production and used in bouquets and flower arrangements. It has escaped from cultivation, and I have seen this plant occupying large areas in Malta and elsewhere around the Mediterranean. In its native habitat, on the edges of wooded areas in South Africa, in wetland, it will grow to over 6 feet tall. The flower size is far larger in the wild than I have ever seen obtained in cultivation. In England we used to grow these plants in containers, moving them indoors over winter, as they are not very hardy. (I remember top dressing the pots with well-rotted chicken manure, which they seem to love!)

Bright light and rich soil with plenty of moisture are what these plants enjoy. Plant the rhizomes 4 inches deep and 12 inches apart. Keep moist and feed as often as you like. If the temperature is right, you will have a hard time getting rid of established plants. I have seen them virtually poking their way through blacktop, thriving on neglect in abandoned gardens, and I am sorry to say many people regard these plants as weeds in certain parts of California.

Zantedeschia aethiopica: This is the most commonly grown species, native to South Africa. In most gardens it reaches 3 to 4 feet in height and will form bold clumps if given half a chance. The problem is that it is too easy to grow, and thus not looked upon with favor by some gardeners. The spathe can reach up to 10 inches in length, and is white or creamy in color. The plants have arrowhead-shaped leaves; the spadix is a bright yellow. The form 'Crowborough' is reportedly hardier than the species type, which is hardy down to around 10°F. At such temperatures the top growth will be killed, but the rootstock will send up fresh shoots in spring. The form 'Green Goddess' has flecks and markings of green in the flower; it is beloved by some, particularly flower arrangers, while others find it not at all appealing. These plants flower in spring and through the summer.

Z. albomaculata: Native to Natal in South Africa, this smaller version of the above species has whitish translucent spots all over the foliage. It reaches 30 inches and flowers in May or June. The foliage has a habit of dying back after flowering has finished.

Z. elliottiana: Native to the Transvaal, the startling yellow color of the spathe sets these plants apart; they are stunning when in flower. The foliage is covered with silver blotches. The flowers are produced from early through late summer, and the plants reach heights of 24 inches, sometimes a little more.

Z. pentlandii: This species comes from South Africa, and is much like *Z. elliottiana* except that the leaves are smaller and unspotted. I

Attractive foliage and most attractive flowers of a pleasing color make *Zantedeschia elliottiana* a good garden plant.

see no reason for anyone to grow this, as the flowers (spathes) are smaller, and it is not as free-flowering to begin with.

Z. rehmannii: This may be the prettiest of all the species, native to the Transvaal in South Africa. The foliage is unusual in that the base of the leaf blades taper into the leaf stalk and are not lobed. The flowers (spathes) vary, from white through rose and pink to deep shades of maroon, tones that contrast with the yellow spadix, a most pleasing combination. Several selections are often listed in catalogs. The plants flower over a long period, generally starting in midsummer. They reach a height of about 24 inches. I suspect that various listings in catalogs of named selections, often called "hybrids," are in fact the species. 'Flame' is a reddish purple, 'Gem' a rosy lavender, and 'Lavender Gem' a deeper tone than 'Gem'. All are great plants.

These plants are becoming more popular, and they deserve to be more widely grown. The hardiness is often in question. If planted in colder climates and given a good winter mulch, the survival rate would be quite high, I think. Catalogs that recommend certain species as indoor plants for flowering in December, without giving instructions, give the home gardener little to go on. Before purchasing, obtain precise instructions.

Botanical Name: Zantedeschia
Family: Araceae
Common Names: Calla lily, arum lily, pink or yellow calla, spotted calla
Flower Colors: White, yellow, white with green, rose, deep pink
Flowering Time: Early to midsummer, some quite early in spring; it greatly depends on when planted and the climate enjoyed.
Height: 18 inches to over 6 feet
Spread: Will form large colonies
Native Habitat: South Africa
Hardiness: They are probably hardier than often thought, worth trying in cooler climates (where temperatures remain below 32°F all day), but not in very cold areas. In cool climates, give protection of a mulch and favored location.
Depth of Planting: 4 inches
Distance Apart: 12 inches
Containers: Yes
Light Requirements: Sun; light shade in hottest areas
Soil Type: Average garden soil is fine if enough moisture is provided for the plants to flourish

Special Conditions: The more you feed them, the better they grow.
Comments: Deserving of a place in gardens in warm areas, especially where not much else seems to do well. The foliage, and flowers of some of the colored selections are quite attractive. Maligned by some gardeners, incorrectly, in my opinion.

ZEPHYRANTHES
Amaryllidaceae

The Greek word *zephyros* means the west wind, and *anthos* means flower. Native to the southeastern United States, Mexico, Colombia and Guatemala, these plants seldom grow taller than 8 to 12 inches. The flowers are tubular at the base, the petals flaring to give an open flower. The flowers are white, sometimes flushed with pink. These are not hardy, but interesting plants for warmer climates. While they will perform well in containers in colder climates, I think there are far more exciting plants that should be grown before one grows these. The common names are zephyr lily, fairy lily and Atamasco lily.

Bright, indirect light, average garden soil with good organic content, and moisture during the growing period and warmth are what these plants appreciate. Set the bulbs 2 inches deep, 3 to 4 inches apart. In those areas where little or no frost is experienced, and where it does not linger during the day, these plants can and should remain in the ground. The evergreen species do not need a resting period after growth stops, but decidous types appreciate a rest and somewhat dryer conditions.

Zephyranthes atamasco: The swamp lily ranges from Virginia to Florida. Flowers of white tinged with pink appear in April, May or June, carried to a height of about 12 inches. The flowers are quite large, more than 3 inches in diameter. The foliage is produced with the flowers.

Z. candida: This evergreen species from South America has white flowers flushed with pink, and is not unlike a crocus in shape. Flowers appear in early fall. The foliage is quite rushlike. The plants grow 4 to 8 inches tall. Var. *major* has larger flowers.

Z. citrina: This species from Trinidad is not hardy. The flowers have a greenish tube, and the petals turn yellow as they flare. Ten inches tall, it flowers in late summer to early fall.

Z. grandiflora: Travel in Guatemala and you will see this flower growing in damp woodlands. The blossoms are pink and quite large. The plants reach 8 inches, flowering in August or September. This plant has become naturalized in parts of South Africa, one of the few South American plants to do so.

Z. rosea: From the West Indies and Guatemala, this species has rose-pink flowers and reaches some 7 inches in height, flowering late in the summer. Despite its native habitat, it will stand some (but little) frost, and is best grown in a cool greenhouse.

I do not quite know what I think of this genus. I am not very enthusiastic; the flowers are quite pretty, reminding me of some lilies, much smaller and not as tall growing, I must admit that I hardly think they are fabulous. As they are listed in catalogs, people must purchase them. I do not think I shall—a mistake perhaps?

Zephyranthes rosea are listed in most bulb catalogs, and while they are not among my favorites, they are quite attractive, reminding me of miniature lilies. (Photo courtesy of International Bloembollen Centrum.)

Botanical Name: Zephyranthes
Family. Amaryllidaceae
Common Names: Zephyr lily, fairy lily, Atamasco lily
Flower Colors: White, pink
Flowering Time: Late summer into fall
Height: To 12 inches
Spread: In warm climates will become quite invasive
Native Habitat: Parts of southeastern United States, Mexico, Guatemala, Colombia
Hardiness: Not really hardy, perhaps down to 25°F with mulch and a favored location
Depth of Planting: 2 inches
Distance Apart: 3 to 4 inches
Containers: Yes
Light Requirements: Bright, indirect light
Soil Type: Average garden soil high in organic matter with good moisture
Special Conditions: Moisture is needed. These plants can be planted in spring and lifted in fall, overwintered and then replanted.
Comments: I may be doing these plants an injustice, but I don't find them exciting.

Hand-colored prints were used to illustrate books prior to the advent of photography. This print, published by Wm. Curtis, Botanic Garden Lambeth Marsh in the eighteenth century, accurately depicts *Narcissus hispanicus*. The beauty of this flower is obvious from this print, but *N. hispanicus* is not widely grown today. Collectors' items today, such botanical prints are becoming increasingly rare.

R & U indicates rare and unusual plants. I indicates iris, D indicates daylilies. If no specialty is indicated, the source offers a general listing.

B & D Lilies
330 P Street
Port Townsend, WA 98368
(206) 385–1738

BioQuest International
P. O. Box 5752
Santa Barbara, CA 93150–5752
(805) 969–4072
R & U

Breck's
6523 North Galena Road
P. O. Box 1757
Peoria, IL 61656–1757
(309) 691–4616

W. Atlee Burpee & Co.
300 Park Avenue
Warminster, PA 18991–0001
(800) 999–1447

Caladium World
P. O. Drawer 629
Sebring, FL 33871–0629
(813) 385–7661

Cooley's Gardens
P. O. Box 126
Silverton, OR 97381–0126
(800) 225–5391
I

The Daffodil Mart
Route 3, Box 794
Gloucester, VA 23061
(804) 693–3966

Dutch Gardens
P. O. Box 200
Adelphia, NJ 07710–0200
(908) 780–2713

French's
Box 565

Pittsfield, VT 05762–0562
(802) 746–8148

Russell Graham
4030 Eagle Crest Road N.W.
Salem, Oregon 97304
(503) 362–1135
R & U

Heronswood Nursery
7530 288th N.E.
Kingston, WA 98346
(206) 297–4172
R & U

Hoog & Dix Export
Heemsteedse Dreef 175
2101 KD HEEMSTEDE
The Netherlands
(Surcharge on order under
$250.00)

Jackson & Perkins
P. O. Box 1028
Medford, OR 97501
(800) 292–4769

Klehm Nursery
Route #5, Box 197 Penny Road
South Barrington, IL 60010–9390
(800) 533–8715
D

McClure & Zimmerman
108 W. Winnebago
P. O. Box 368
Friesland, WI 53935
(414) 326–4220
R & U

Mellinger's Inc.
2310 South Range Road
North Lima, OH 44452–9731
(800) 321–7444

Oregon Trail Daffodils
3207 S.E. Mannthey
Corbett, OR 97019
(503) 695–5513

George W. Park Seed Co.
Cokesbury Road
P. O. Box 46
Greenwood, SC 29647–0001
(803) 223–7333

John Scheepers, Inc.
P. O. Box 700
Bantam, CT 06750
(203) 567–0838

Swan Island Dahlias
P. O. Box 800
Canby, OR 97013
(503) 266–7711

K. Van Bourgondien & Sons, Inc.
245 Farmingdale Road
P. O. Box 1000
Babylon, N.Y. 11702–0598
(800) 622–9997

Van Tubergen
Bressingham
Diss
Norfolk IP22 2AB
England
(011) 44–379–88–8282

Wayside Gardens
One Garden Lane
Hodges, SC 29695–0001
(800) 845–1124

White Flower Farm
Litchfield, CT 06759
(203) 496–9600

THE USDA PLANT HARDINESS MAP OF NORTH AMERICA

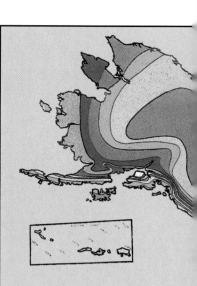

Average Annual Minimum Temperature

Temperature (°C)	Zone	Temperature (°F)
-45.6 and Below	1	Below -50
-45.8 to -45.5	2a	-45 to -50
-40.0 to -42.7	2b	-40 to -45
-37.3 to -40.0	3a	-35 to -40
-34.5 to -37.2	3b	-30 to -35
-31.7 to -34.4	4a	-25 to -30
-28.9 to -31.6	4b	-20 to -25
-26.2 to 28.8	5a	-15 to -20
-23.4 to -26.1	5b	-10 to -15
-20.6 to -23.3	6a	-5 to -10
-17.8 to -20.5	6b	0 to -5
-15.0 to -17.7	7a	5 to 0
-12.3 to -15.0	7b	10 to 5
-9.5 to -12.2	8a	15 to 10
-6.7 to -9.4	8b	20 to 15
-3.9 to -6.6	9a	25 to 20
-1.2 to -3.8	9b	30 to 25
1.6 to -1.1	10a	35 to 30
4.4 to 1.7	10b	40 to 35
4.5 and Above	11	40 and Above

This zone map provides a broad outline of various temperature zones in North America. However, every garden has its own microclimate.

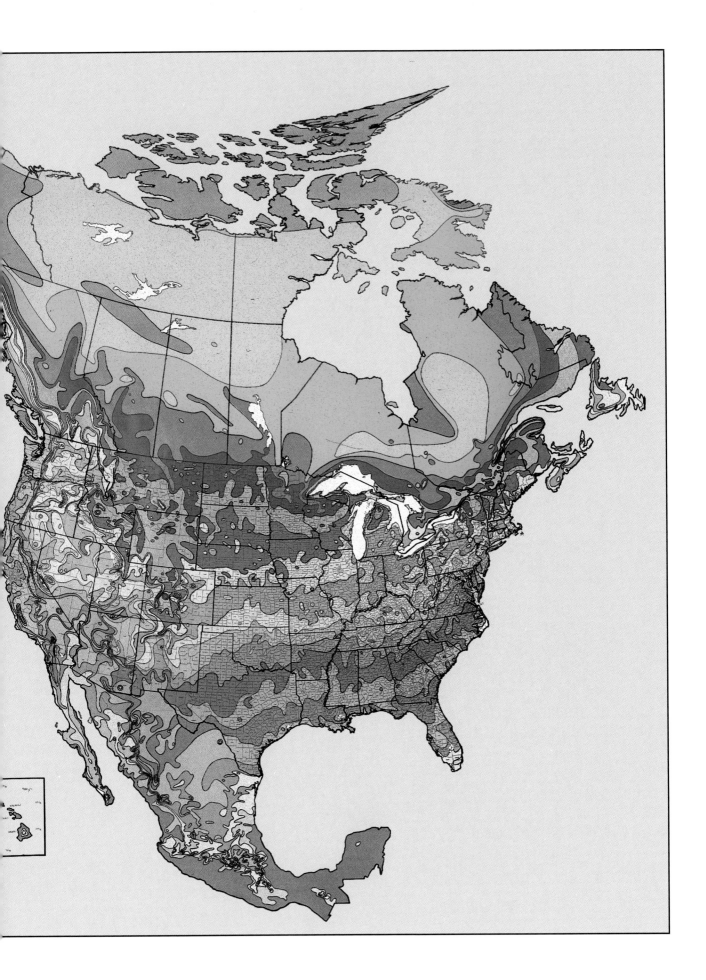

INDEX

Number in parentheses refer to illustrations.